A Breath of Life

FEMINISM IN THE AMERICAN JEWISH COMMUNITY

Sylvia Barack Fishman

THE FREE PRESS
A Division of Macmillan, Inc.
NEW YORK

Maxwell Macmillan, Canada
TORONTO

Maxwell Macmillan International
NEW YORK   OXFORD   SINGAPORE   SYDNEY

The Free Press
A Division of Macmillan, Inc.
866 Third Avenue, New York, N.Y. 10022

Maxwell Macmillan Canada, Inc.
1200 Eglinton Avenue East
Suite 200
Don Mills, Ontario M3C 3N1

Macmillan, Inc. is part of the Maxwell Communication Group of Companies.

Printed in the United States of America

printing number
1   2   3   4   5   6   7   8   9   10

Library of Congress Cataloging-in-Publication Data

Fishman, Sylvia Barack.
    A breath of life : feminism in the American Jewish community /
Sylvia Barack Fishman.
        p.   cm.
    ISBN 0-02-910342-8
    1. Women, Jewish—United States.   2. Feminism—United States.
    3. Women in Judaism—United States.   I. Title.
HQ1172.F57   1993
305.48'8924073—dc20   92-47003
                                                                CIP

FOR PHILIP

CONTENTS

PREFACE

It is the first beautiful weekend in May and my neighbor and I are catching up. We have scarcely talked to each other all during the dismal, cold gray months of the New England winter and early spring.

Her daughter is dancing with a ballet company in the Midwest. My daughter, married one year, is entering a graduate program in clinical psychology. We talk about how focused our daughters are, how clearly and how early they have known what they want from their careers. Unspoken are our questions about how they will arrange the other pieces of their lives. She tells me about her progress in the graphic arts; I tell her I have almost finished a draft of this book.

"This has been a hard book to write," I say.

We stand together in the street, two Jewish women, each approaching fifty, she in shorts, her handsome face sweaty from her usual Saturday-morning lawn work, I in a suit and straw hat, just back from walking my parents home after our usual Saturday morning prayers in the synagogue. She looks directly into my eyes and the flash of identification is immediate.

"This has been a hard book to *live*." She laughs.

And, as if perhaps I do not understand what she means, she explains, "We are transitional women."

In the United States these years have been stirring ones for transitional Jewish women and their daughters. Feminism in general and Jewish feminism in particular have influenced demographic, educational, occupational, sexual, social, and religious trends. This extraordinary development in Jewish history has given women unprecedented choices and control over their own destiny. For the past two decades the Jewish community has been galvanized by debate over feminist agendas and the role of women within Jewish life. Today almost every major area of Jewish life is affected by feminist perspectives in some way. From dramatic changes in secular and Jewish education for women, to shifts in the formation of Jewish families, to the widespread entry of women and women's issues into Jewish public life, to a new awareness of women's issues in the synagogue and in scholarly forums, to utopian initiatives for a less polluted planet and peace in the Middle East—Jewish feminism has had and continues to have a profound impact on the social, intellectual, and religious fabric of the American Jewish community.

This is a picture of our changing lives, of the lives of Jewish women in the last decade of the twentieth century, and of the lives of our friends, families, colleagues and communities as well. Interviews that I conducted from January 1990 through September 1992, with 120 American Jewish women, ages eighteen to eighty, who have varying personal and professional histories and live in communities across the United States, provide anecdotal materials and illustrate transitions and transformations in American Jewish life today. Narratives and direct quotations that appear without citation are drawn from this series of conversations with scores of women. Their stories, articulated in their own words, reflect a diverse range of experiences and attitudes.[1]

The overall parameters of change are indicated by the most recent quantitative research drawn from demographic data gathered from national and local studies of more than two dozen Jewish communities across the country. New national data on Jewish women from the 1990 National Jewish Population Study,[2] in addition to data on Jewish women in individual cities, provide a sweeping picture of transformations in the Jewish community. Scholarly works, popular literature, and vivid "evidence" drawn from contemporary American literature—fiction, poetry, essays, and memoirs—supplement the nonfiction materials.

During our lifetimes assumptions about women's roles that have held true for most of recorded history have undergone the process of change. We have responded with all the individuality that marks our very different talents, personalities, values systems, and previous life experiences. We have unprecedented choices and options today, abounding with conflicts, many of them painful. The conflicts are not, however, between selfishness and morality but between different types of moral obligations. Women struggle to balance obligations to innate talents and energies with obligations as members of small and larger societies—of families, of Jewish and civic communities, of a precarious world.

ACKNOWLEDGMENTS

My FIRST ACKNOWLEDGMENTS go to the women who generously shared their experiences, insights, and observations with me. Their honesty was inspiring, their friendship an unexpected bonus. I hope that they will find accurately represented here the history they are simultaneously living through and shaping.

I have been lucky to have editors who have helped me envision the shape of the entire manuscript. I am delighted to thank Joyce Seltzer at The Free Press for her perceptiveness, energy, and friendly rigor; her ability to envision the shape of the entire manuscript from the beginning onward is awesome. I would also like to thank the editors of the *American Jewish Year Book,* David Singer and Ruth Seldin, who suggested and edited my earlier article, "The Impact of Feminism on American Jewish Life," and encouraged me to write this book.

A great debt of gratitude, as always, goes to my colleagues at Brandeis University. I warmly acknowledge the wise guidance of my late colleague and mentor, Marshall Sklare, for bringing me into the scientific study of American Jews—a field he virtually invented—and for sharing with me his gentle but incisive humanistic approach to it. I am pleased to thank Marc Brettler, Sylvia Fuks Fried, Archbishop

Krister Stendahl, and Gabriel Berger for reading the entire manuscript and making numerous useful suggestions; Jonathan Sarna for reading the chapters on Jewish religious developments; and Joyce Antler for reading those on American feminism. My colleagues Gary Tobin, director, and Lawrence Sternberg, associate director, of the Cohen Center for Modern Jewish Studies, supported my work by not only releasing time for research and writing but also providing me with a series of able graduate student assistants: It is my great pleasure to thank Elizabeth Brandwein and Raquel Kosovske for the diligence, intelligence, and pleasantness with which they handled a variety of research and clerical tasks; and Miriam Hertz and Gila Diamond Shusterman for their yeomen's tasks wrestling with the quantitative data sets. Earlier research was assisted by Paula Rhodes and Francine Green. Sylvia Riese facilitated the progress of this manuscript with her usual efficiency and aplomb. My thanks to Shulamith Reinharz and the Brandeis Women's Studies Program for their ongoing encouragement. Friends from outside Brandeis were kind enough to help as well: I am grateful to Louis and Felice Dickstein and Leah Shakdiel, who read sections on the impact of feminism on American Orthodox Jews in an earlier incarnation of this manuscript.

Each of these friends and colleagues has made invaluable contributions to this study; for any flaws I alone am responsible.

For my family, who lives with me in these transitional times, I am thankful. My father, Rabbi Nathan Barack, has devoted his life to Jewish scholarship and to the Jewish people; it was he who gave me the unshakable belief that when people grow up they write books. To our mutual delight, my mother, Lillian Astrachan Barack, my childhood companion, has become in my middle age one of my best friends. I learn every day from my children, who forge the future— Lisi, with her husband, Joshua; Eliot; and Joseph. In their blessings I am blessed. And to my husband, Philip, for twenty-five years of living and loving and growing, this book is dedicated.

Chapter One

Discovering Jewish Feminism

In many feminist circles my Judaism has been dismissed as patriarchal, and in some Jewish circles my feminist politics . . . has been
seen as ridiculous or fundamentally opposed and threatening to
Jewish life. Plagued by the question, am I a Jew or a woman first, I
awoke one night with an enlightening thought: had I been born a
boy I would still have been a Jew, therefore I am fundamentally
Jewish. I have a vision of a place where I am not "split at the root."

—Raquel Kosovske[1]

"I FEEL TORN IN TWO," is a common complaint among American Jewish women. As members of the most numerous Jewish community in
the post-Holocaust world, many feel that they bear a special responsibility for Jewish communal survival. They worry that the vitality of
the Jewish community may be threatened by a spectrum of interre-
lated demographic factors, such as increased rates of intermarriage
and lower levels of Jewish identification. Desiring their own individual fulfillment along with the well-being of their families, friends,
and community, contemporary Jewish women feel besieged. In the
workplace they are pressured to produce to their fullest potential.
Within the Jewish community they are pressured to marry early, to
have larger families, and to volunteer their time to further Jewish
causes. They wonder how they can accommodate both a personal
and a communal agenda. It sometimes seems as though any decision

1

in one direction constitutes a betrayal of loyalties in another. They feel, as Adrienne Rich writes, "split at the root."[2]

The divided loyalties experienced by Jewish women today appear, in retrospect, to have been embryonic almost from the inception of contemporary American feminism. This feminism was born in an environment that nurtured ethnic pride and assertiveness, fostered scorn for the perceived hypocrisies of a conformist consumer culture, and encouraged social activism on behalf of civil rights and other movements. It emerged from the antiwar and civil rights protest movements in the late 1960s as dynamic, idealistic women faced the shocking realization that they were being treated as auxiliaries to a male struggle. Although women were no longer forced to emulate the perfect homemaker image, dominant countercultural movements provided different—but equally reductive and demeaning—stereotypes of women.[3]

Feminists explored and asserted the importance and potential of women in all areas of life. They worked for new legislation that would protect and promote the rights of women in the workplace. In growing numbers they began to enter training programs in lucrative, prestigious, and/or physically demanding professions previously dominated by males. In time, feminist criticism emerged in every discipline in the humanistic arts and the social sciences. Feminists rejected what they saw as subjective, patriarchal male determinations of legitimacy and excellence and asked questions that had never before been systematically pursued in the academy. Where were the women in texts on ancient or contemporary history and literature? Why had there been so few "major" female artists? Who determined the canon and why? Religious life also came under feminist scrutiny. Why did so many Western religions seem to be spiritual systems by and for men? How had the voices of women been suppressed in religious texts and traditions? And, more important, how could they attain equal participation in and access to their own religious birthrights?

In the beginning many of the most active contemporary American feminists of Jewish birth devoted little attention to themselves as Jews (except occasionally to deride traditional Judaism as one more egregious example of patriarchal power.) Betty Friedan's *The Feminine Mystique* (1963) became an early bible of the movement,[4] read by many Jewish women, although it did not focus on the Jewish nature of either its author or its readership. Friedan's book faulted the American dream, which posited that every woman's ideal fulfillment came in the form of a nuclear family in the suburbs: working father, homemaker mother, several children, perhaps a pet or two, in a single-family house (complete with appliances), in a green, residential area, with a station wagon in the driveway. Such a life-style, charged Friedan, trapped women in a gilded but deadly cage: They became unpaid household workers and chauffeurs, cut off from meaningful work, intellectual stimulation, and personal development.

Friedan said that the "feminine mystique" was based on the assumption that women were emotionally and intellectually unsuited for the brutal environment of labor-force participation and independent life. Even when they studied in universities, women were geared toward personal refinements rather than career preparation. Deprived of occupational skills and confidence in their ability to live independently, Friedan suggested, women evaluated themselves primarily in terms of their physical beauty and their housekeeping and hostessing skills. Removed from the graduated evaluations of the marketplace, homemakers measured themselves against a standard of absolute perfection and always came up lacking. Thus, rather than assuring women a life of fulfillment and serenity, the "feminine mystique" guaranteed them one of emptiness and frustration.

While younger, academically oriented women were often the first proponents of feminism, each year brought feminist ideas to a wider and wider circle of grass-roots America. Many middle-aged Jewish women assert that feminism changed their lives. Esther Feier, president of the San Diego chapter of Brandeis University National Women's Committee, remembers vividly her "conversion" to feminism in the early 1970s. "I was a housewife," she recalls:

> *Ms.* magazine had just come out. Then I read *The Feminine Mystique.* I realized I had "the disease that has no name." I started a consciousness-raising group in which I was the only Jew. After we had met for a while, we began to work for the Equal Rights Amendment. We had a "truthmobile" and went from shopping center to shopping center telling the truth about the ERA. I went back to school and got my master's degree at the Harvard Graduate School of Education. Then I got real paying jobs—starting with a job as coordinator in Northern Essex Community College. I have been very active all my life promoting so-called women's issues such as child care, parental leave, education of the underclass, teenage pregnancy, and Head Start as basic human issues that would benefit all of society.

"I could never have done any of this without feminism," adds
Feier. "Without feminism, we waste 50 percent of our human potential."

Furthermore, feminist critics charged, the seemingly idyllic, normative American family unit could be disrupted without warning, by
death or divorce, leaving the bereaved wife without necessary occupational skills and without the confidence to face the world as an
independent adult. For many feminists the family—long women's
raison d'être—became the enemy, a repressive patriarchal institution
that restricted women to the domestic domain. Gloria Steinem ex-
plained the origin and purpose of marriage as means "to restrict the
freedom of the mother—at least long enough to determine pater-
nity." Men promoted religious and societal restrictions of female
sexuality so that they might control "the most basic means of production—the means of reproduction."[5] Shulamit Firestone found
even gestation and childbirth barbarous processes that served no
useful purpose except to enslave women.[6]

A wide variety of organizational subgroups formed, with the purpose of translating feminist insights into social change. Initially perceived as a wild group of radical "women's libbers," the National
Organization of Women (NOW) evolved into the largest and most
centrist feminist group. NOW, and other groups that attracted large
numbers of mainstream American women, concentrated on economic issues, such as promoting legislation to prevent discrimination against women in the marketplace through the Equal Rights
Amendment (ERA). They worked to guarantee reproductive rights
for women, so that decisions that affected a woman's body and life
could not be controlled by outside forces. Other groups, such as
Women Against Pornography, worked against pornographic literature and films, which they characterized as a species of hostility
against women, as well as against overt violence, sponsoring marches
to "Take Back the Night." Smaller, leftist groups, such as the Society
for Cutting Up Men (SCUM) and No More Nice Girls, were openly
anti-male, recommending either independent or lesbian life-styles.
Together these feminist groups made up a movement devoted to the
radical transformation of the interpersonal, educational, occupational, communal, and political positions of women in the United
States.

People who sought to discredit the goals of feminism often employed the tactic of deliberately confusing the goals of the larger,
centrist groups with those of the smaller, radical groups. NOW, even

in the 1970s and 1980s, when its ranks included thousands of middle-class wives and mothers, was sometimes characterized by detractors as a hotbed of "bra-burners" and militant lesbians who were using the ERA to promote the goal of unisex bathrooms. Right-wing propagandists portrayed the feminist movement as a force for anarchy rather than for social reform.

In the first flush of commonality, feminists were loath to admit to differences between women. Womanhood was perceived to be an overriding identity, stronger than any other social or economic grouping. Women around the world and through the ages were seen to be united in a sisterhood of victimization, through their oppression by patriarchal religious, political, and socioeconomic systems. Because the admission of diversity might disrupt the unity necessary to accomplish their goals, feminists in the 1960s often lumped together very diverse forms of oppression of women. In their attempt to show that all women were indeed sisters under the skin, the differences between cultural manifestations of misogyny were minimized or ignored, and parallels were drawn between suttee, the Hindu ritual practice of the immolation of widows on their husbands' funeral pyres, and the exclusion of women from the Catholic priesthood.

Many of the most articulate young feminists who proclaimed that "sisterhood is powerful" in the late 1960s had grown up in middle-class homes and were the products of a secure and comfortable existence.[7] They assumed the normative female experience to be that of the white, middle-class American woman of secular humanist persuasion.

Little attention was paid to the fact that women who derive from oppressed racial or ethnic groups often suffer more severely as a result of their color or religion than of their gender. Or, to be more precise: Their sufferings are increased as a result of their gender, but the baseline oppressive conditions of their lives are created by the fact that they belong to a specific group.

It was almost a decade before feminists acknowledged that women of African American, Hispanic, and Third World heritages were seldom trapped in the gilded cage of domesticity. Indeed, the cages that trapped the majority of these women were of another order entirely. Not only were they "allowed" to work, they almost always *had* to. The protections that so stultified and crippled middle-class white American women had seldom been extended to them—instead, they were oppressed by poverty and racism.[8]

Ironically, the struggle for economic and political equality that absorbed feminists would have been virtually impossible without the presence of an impoverished underclass of women—who were available to care for children and clean houses while middle-class women struggled for "equality" with men of their own socioeconomic level. While the struggles of middle-class American women benefited all women, their occupational, intellectual, and social interests were often far more firmly aligned with their male colleagues than with their female household help—or, often, even their female secretarial help. Women of color often felt that they and their concerns were "shunted to the side within the predominantly white movement whose universalist claims about the nature of women's oppression denied the realities of racism." As Sara Evans notes, "Black women had remained deeply suspicious of the new women's movement, perceiving it as 'basically a family quarrel between White women and White men.' "[9]

The tendency of the women's movement to homogenize female experience extended to areas of religious, ethnic, and cultural heritage as well. Although a substantial proportion of early feminist writers were Jewish, the milieu they identified with and wrote about was melting-pot America—that amorphous amalgam of ethnicities and religions blended into a secularized white Anglo-Saxon Protestant culture. They barely acknowledged the historically unique suffering and concerns of the Jews and the distinctiveness of the American Jewish experience.

Feminism with a specifically Jewish focus became distinct from the generalized movement rather early in the evolution of contemporary American feminism. The exploration of Judaism as a culture and as a religion from a feminist perspective was encouraged by the protest movements and youth culture of the 1960s, which advocated "doing your own thing," including the celebration of ethnic differences. This was reinforced by American Jewish feelings of pride immediately after the 1967 war in the Middle East, during which Israel defended itself brilliantly against the massed armies of the Arab states. In a parallel development, American Jewish intellectuals and artists had become extremely influential and often not only acknowledged but emphasized their Jewishness, further increasing ethnic and cultural self-esteem.

Since Jewish consciousness and self-esteem were at a high, it was perhaps inevitable that Jewish feminists turned their attention inward. Trude Weiss-Rosmarin and Rachel Adler examined traditional Jewish life and values. Weiss-Rosmarin's "The Unfreedom of Jewish Women" focused on the "unfairness of Jewish marriage laws to divorced and abandoned women,"[10] and Adler's "The Jew Who Wasn't There"[11] contrasted male and female models of traditional Jewish piety. These articles set the stage for a feminist focus on women's experience of Judaism.

By late 1971 Jewish women's prayer and study groups were being formed. Women from the New York Havurah (one of the new egalitarian worship and study groups that developed on college campuses and spread into Jewish communal settings) joined with likeminded friends to explore the status of women in Jewish law. This group evolved into Ezrat Nashim (a double entendre that refers to the area in the synagogue traditionally reserved for women but that also means, literally, "the help of women"), a particularly influential, albeit small, organization. Committed to equality for women within Judaism, Ezrat Nashim comprised primarily women who identified as Conservative Jews and were thus in the center of the spectrum of American Judaism.[12] Many of them had relatively high levels of formal Jewish education, had attended the Hebrew-speaking Ramah camps sponsored by the Conservative movement, and had some facility in Hebrew and liturgy.

Susan Shevitz, who teaches Jewish education and organizational theory at Brandeis University, remembers the early days of Ezrat Nashim as being "a time of great excitement and great frustration. We had taken our Jewish education seriously. We served as cantors and congregational leaders at camp and at teen services. But in the adult congregational world there was no room for the woman skilled in liturgy or sermonizing or Jewish studies. We knew that the going was very hard, but we also felt tremendously empowered and hopeful about the future." Their appearance at the convention of the Conservative Rabbinical Assembly in 1972—the same year that the Reform movement voted to admit women to its rabbinical program—was an important first step in the process of influencing leaders to consider admitting women to the Conservative rabbinical program.[13]

In 1973 Jewish feminism went from a small, localized effort to a broader, more diverse operation at the first national Jewish women's conference, organized by the North American Jewish Students' Network. Drawing more than five hundred women of varying educational levels and wings of Judaism from throughout North America, the conference spawned new groups, regional and local conferences, and a National Women's Speaker's Bureau. A second national Conference on Jewish Women and Men, in 1974, also drew hundreds of participants and gave birth to the Jewish Feminist Organization (JFO), committed to promoting the equality of Jewish women in all areas of Jewish life. The JFO survived only a short time, however, and was succeeded by the more limited New York Jewish Women's Center, which was active from approximately 1975 to 1977.

The development and growth of Jewish feminism have been documented in a variety of publications. The ideas and issues percolating within the formative Jewish feminist movement were published and widely circulated in a special issue of *Response* magazine, called *The Jewish Woman: An Anthology*. Edited by Elizabeth Koltun, the 192-page issue included thirty articles and a bibliography. Many of the authors represented in this issue and in a later revision became key figures in Jewish feminism.[14]

One striking piece of evidence of the legitimation of Jewish feminism by the Jewish intellectual and religious establishments was the appearance in the 1977 *American Jewish Year Book* of a special article, "Who Hast Not Made Me a Man: The Movement for Equal Rights for Women in American Jewry." In this piece Anne Lapidus Lerner captured the atmosphere of hopeful ferment that pervaded many Jewish religious and communal arenas. A unique literary product of Jewish feminism is the glossy magazine *Lilith*, which was created to explore religious, political, communal, and personal aspects of Jewish life through the eyes of Jewish feminism. The premier issue, published in 1976, featured a photograph of a woman wearing *tefillin* (phylacteries) and an interview with Betty Friedan. In the same year the comprehensive and highly readable *The Jewish Woman in America* utilized historical, sociological, and literary sources to trace the odyssey of women in American Jewish life.[15] In these and other publications it was possible to follow the progress of Jewish feminism in the United States on many fronts, including the gradual entry of women into Jewish studies, the rabbinate, and leadership positions in Jewish communal life.

It is ironic that at a time when most American Jewish men seemed to be drawing away from Jewish ritual, and few men worshiped regularly with prayer shawls and phylacteries, some Jewish women began to explore these and other traditionally male modes of religious expression. Similarly, while Jewish men were less attracted to the rabbinate, partially because restrictive codes barring them from other professions had almost disappeared, increasing numbers of

Jewish women were entering it, first in Reform (1972) and Reconstructionist (1974) and later in Conservative (1985) Jewish seminaries. Among the masses of American Jewish boys and girls, the percentage of females receiving Jewish education began to draw close to that of males in households among all the wings of Judaism, and the great majority of boys and girls celebrated the climax of their Jewish education with the gala American bar/bat mitzvah. Even the Orthodox Jewish world, although the most resistant to change, was being transformed by feminism in many acknowledged and unacknowledged ways.

At the same time many Jewish feminists were propelled into a feminist exploration of Judaism not only because of their own personal interests but also because of the overt expressions of antisemitism that had emerged within feminist ranks. American Jewish women quickly embraced feminism, but they often found, as historian Ellen Umansky remembers, "that they were embraced as women but scorned as Jews."[16] This rejection of their Jewish ethnic, cultural, and religious identity struck at their deepest core of being.[17] Jewish feminists responded to overt or subtle expressions of feminist hostility to their Jewishness by discovering and developing a new—in many ways unique—variety of feminism.

The first intimations were political, and they came as a tidal wave of anti-Israel sentiment. The repeated condemnation of "Zionist oppression" was recalled with horror by Jewish participants at a series of international women's conferences. Letty Cottin Pogrebin, cofounder of *Ms.* magazine, dates her reentry into Jewish life partially to the shock she and her sister Jewish feminists experienced at such conferences. Many women from Third World countries attacked Israeli and other Jewish women as being responsible for "the worst moral outrages of the twentieth century."[18]

Women from countries that still routinely practice clitoridectomies on infant girls, countries where women are compelled to shroud themselves in concealing clothing, and countries that sanction corporal punishment for rebellious wives repeatedly singled out Israel as a monster. Jewish feminists at these conferences were incredulous that even among women they were perceived as the "other." "In Copenhagen, I heard people say that Gloria Steinem, Betty Friedan, and Bella Abzug all being Jewish gives the American Women's Movement a bad name. I heard, the only way to rid the world of Zionism is to kill all the Jews. The antisemitism was overt, wild, and irrational," Sonia Johnson, an ERA activist, recalls. Health activist Paula

Doress remembers, "I heard a Danish woman tell an American, 'I was handing out PLO leaflets and my Jewish friends saw me. I was so embarrassed.' The American answered, 'My Jewish friends saw me too, and I don't give a shit.' "[19]

Perhaps most shocking, Jewish feminists heard Jews once again being described in ways that relegated them to subhuman status. "A U.N. staff person said to me, 'Denmark is wonderful, but the Germans take it over in the summer, and I hate them. They only did one thing right—they killed the Jews,' " says novelist E. M. Broner. "I made choking sounds. 'Oh, did I hurt your feelings,' she asked, 'are you German?' "[20] With sickening certitude, Jewish feminists—who had thought that their true community resided in the community of women—acknowledged that sisterhood was not powerful enough to conquer an age-old hatred of the Jews.[21] Bella Abzug concludes grimly, "I don't believe there's a difference between anti-Zionism and antisemitism. I believe that the statement that 'Zionism equals racism' is an antisemitic slur."[22]

Christian and Muslim feminists revitalized the ancient charge of deicide, castigating Judaism for "killing" the fertility goddesses—and the matriarchy—and introducing patriarchal monotheism and religious repression of women into the world. Some Christian feminist theologians asserted that Christianity was ruined by Judaism, for Jewish patriarchalism sullied what would otherwise have been purely egalitarian, humanistic Christianity. Just as Protestant thinkers once blamed the Old Testament for infusing values of vengeance and carnality into Christianity, feminist theologians ascribed the strikingly misogynist and antisexual attitudes of some of the New Testament to "a concession to Judaism" or "an unavoidable contamination" by "the sexism of first century Palestinian Judaism," charges Susannah Heschel, a Jewish feminist theologian. Consequently Jewish feminist scholars have sometimes felt constrained in their approach to classical Jewish texts, apprehensive that their critiques might "be misunderstood or even misappropriated as providing further proof to Christian feminists for their negation of Judaism."[23]

Feminist attacks on Judaism proliferated in the context of feminist spirituality. However, the specific content of these slurs was often as ancient as antisemitism itself. Reviewing ten books that explore feminist spirituality, written during the 1970s, Annette Daum pointed out, "The old Christian charge that the Jews murdered God incarnate in the ultimate masculine body form of Jesus Christ—rejected in recent times by many denominations—is now being resurrected by some revolutionary feminists in different form: the accusation that the Hebrew people were responsible for the destruction of the ultimate feminist deity, the Goddess."[24]

This version of history, favored by some feminists, leaves out the fact that the goal of monotheism was to replace all pagan, idolatrous worship of both male and female pagan deities. For example, Merlin Stone charges in her book, *When God Was a Woman,* that the ancient Hebrews "ruthlessly" rooted out goddess worship and substituted "the montheistic *male* Hebrew deity: *Into the laws of the Levites was written the destruction of the worship of the Divine Ancestress, and with it the final destruction of the matrilineal system.*"[25] Such formulations ignore the fact that it was polytheism and orgiastic, often homicidal pagan rites that were frequently the objects of monotheistic reformist fervor, not the gender of the deity.

Large numbers of the most influential Christian feminist thinkers promulgated the notion that the ancestors of contemporary Jews invented patriarchy. According to their revisionist histories, before the rise of the ancient Hebrews, people worshiped a benign goddess, and after the decline of the Jews Jesus tried to re-create a more egalitarian approach but was "foiled by the persistence of Jewish attitudes within the Christian tradition."[26] With such charges feminism became one more Christian weapon against Judaism. It was similarly assumed that rabbinical texts written centuries after the death of Jesus were contemporaneous with him. Moreover, they selected only the dicta of the most misogynous rabbis and ignored those who showed considerable compassion and respect for women. By making Jews into the "witches" who ruined Christianity, Christian feminists conducted a "witch-hunt" to "exorcise" these alien elements rather than face up to the misogyny in their own tradition.[27]

Another form of antisemitism relegated Jewish feminists to virtual invisibility. Some feminists insisted that the American Jewish experience was nondistinctive and unworthy of any study, indulging in *ad feminem* attacks on Jewish feminists for being spoiled, aggressive "princesses." Joyce Antler, a professor of American history and founder of the Women's Studies Program at Brandeis University, recalls that at a conference on women's issues that included talks on the black, Hispanic, and Irish Catholic female experiences, the conference organizer insisted, "Jewish women are just white middleclass

women. There is nothing that differentiates them from the ruling
majority. There is no reason to treat them as a specialized minority
or to devote any of our time to their particular experience." A professor who specializes in Calvinist American literature and also
teaches courses in Judaic studies reports, "There is much more antisemitism on campus than sexism—and antisemitism is tolerated in a
way that sexism would never be. I've been told that if I teach Jewish
literature it will cause people to lose respect for me."

Many departments sent mixed messages to their Jewish feminist
employees. They seemed to tell them simultaneously to explore—
and not to explore—Jewish subjects. Poet and translator of Yiddish
poetry Kathryn Hellerstein found resistance to her commitment to
Yiddish literature at Wellesley College, despite the fact that she got
the job over five hundred candidates—presumably because of her
expertise in Judaica. "When I started interjecting American Jewish
literature into the American literary canon, I got a lot of flack," says
Hellerstein. "Various of my female colleagues told me explicitly,
loud and clear, that work in Yiddish wasn't valuable." Not just Yiddish literature, but even prizewinning American Jewish authors were
suspect. "Someone looked at one of my syllabi, which included Bel-
low, Ozick, and Malamud—three Jews out of ten American writers.
They said that the course should concentrate instead on early mod-
ernism, that I should eliminate those three and add James and How-
ell. This was a good, liberal, humanitarian person—he would never
have accused me of having too many Black novelists!"

The fracture lines within the women's movement continue today.
At the 1992 fifteenth annual meeting of the National Women's Studies Association—whose theme was "Enlarging the Circle" and
whose stated purpose was to heal and unify—the choice of keynote
speaker, Annette Kolodny, dean of the University of Arizona's Faculty of Humanities, was denounced because she was a "white
woman" and a "heterosexist." Minority women complained that
they had been insufficiently highlighted, and ecofeminists complained that every meal served at the conference included meat. Jewish women were offended and received an apology from conference
organizers because a Friday-night session had been scheduled, dis-
rupting Sabbath observances.[28]

In reaction to the pressure that they either repudiate or at least
keep silent about their Judaism, even secular Jewish feminists have
frequently discovered, explored, and begun to take pride in their
Jewishness. Jewish feminism has initiated the Jewish commitments

of some women and intensified the Jewish involvements of others. It has worked as a catalyst to revitalize Jewish awareness and interest among women. In Ellen Umansky's words, Jewish feminism has "emerged as a means of asserting both Jewish visibility within the feminist movement and feminist consciousness within the U.S. Jewish community."[29]

Feminism and Jewish feminism together have had an enormous positive impact on women's lives. They have worked to expand choices and opportunities for women in both secular and Jewish spheres. Some Jewish women today pursue both vocational and avocational interests, some marry and have children, some lead independent lives. Many explore their own spirituality and religious depths. Recent polls show that more than any other ethnic group, Jewish women have absorbed and responded to the emphasis on individual freedom that is explicit in feminist ideology as well as inherent in the broader secular humanistic American culture.[30]

Jewish organizations have taken strongly feminist stances on women's issues. The American Jewish Committee, the American Jewish Congress, Hadassah, the Jewish Labor Committee, Na'amat, the National Council of Jewish Women, Women's American ORT, the National Jewish Community Relations Council, the Union of American Hebrew Congregations, and the Women's League for Conservative Judaism have worked together to lobby for reproductive rights. Some women's divisions of national organizations, such as B'nai B'rith Women, have created enormous institutional unrest by pushing for more egalitarian treatment within the organizational structure. Women have actively pursued both professional and volunteer leadership positions in Jewish organizations.

Some have wondered whether Jewish feminism is truly a distinctive social movement or whether it might more correctly be typified as a response by Jewish individuals to feminism per se. Some have gone so far as to condemn Jewish feminism as a species of "ideological *sh'atnez*," a prohibited mixture of fundamentally irreconcilable substances. Jewish historian Lucy Dawidowicz rejected the "new Amazons" of women's liberation, claiming they were more feminists than Jews. Unlike "Jewish women of achievement" in the past, who were "animated as much by passionate Jewish commitment as by personal ambition," she argued, most contemporary Jewish feminists "are merely an adjunct of the worldwide feminist movement." Indeed, according to Dawidowicz, "only the most Jewishly committed feminists seem even to be aware of the incompatibilities between some objectives of the feminist movement and the Jewish communal need for stability, security, and survival."[31]

In contrast, many passionately committed Jewish feminists have asserted that only Jewish feminism can save American Judaism from the quantitative and qualitative decline that has afflicted it for decades, a decline most recently demonstrated by data from the 1990 National Jewish Population Study (NJPS). Susannah Heschel suggested: "The issue is not that feminism poses insoluble problems to Jewish law, but that Judaism has long ago died in the way it had existed for nearly two thousand years. The crisis has not been brought on by feminism, but feminism clearly discloses the morbid condition of Judaism that has continued, untreated, throughout the modern period."[32] Indeed, some observers within the Jewish community, ignoring an increasing alienation of American Jews from their Judaism, which clearly antedated the development of Jewish feminism, have conveniently "blamed" feminism for all the ills of modern Jewish society.

Some see Jewish feminism as a potentially destructive collision between two very different worldviews; some see it as a yoking together of two ideological systems that can only cooperate for limited amounts of time before pulling apart; and some see Jewish feminism as a complex but potentially fertile union that has and will continue to breathe new life into American Judaism. Feminism is not the first political movement to place Jews in a position of ambivalence or conflict between ostensibly universalistic and Jewishly particularistic goals. The Jews who committed themselves to national and social movements in the nineteenth and twentieth centuries, for example, often found themselves embraced as nationalists or socialists but scorned as Jews. Out of these conflicts emerged such distinctively Jewish movements as Zionism, the Bund, Labor Zionism, and the kibbutz system.[33] Jewish feminism, in its diverse manifestations, is a similar creative response to positive and negative stimuli in the political environment. And, like Jewish nationalism and Jewish socialism, Jewish feminism has merged two commitments to produce a vigorous hybrid that has already done much to revitalize modern Jewish life.

Despite many fundamental divisions between the international feminist movement and committed Jewish feminist activities, Jewish feminism continues to share much with American feminism. Numerous conflicts experienced by Jewish feminists are culturewide and are experienced by other middle- and upper-middle-class women. However, even shared phenomena have particular ramifications and a particular flavor in Jewish life. As Jewish women confront issues of family formation, higher education, career paths, sexuality, religious and spiritual expression, and political and civic activism, both Judaism and feminism influence their dialogue and their ultimate decisions. Not least among many challenges facing contemporary American Jewish women is the challenge of balancing Jewish and feminist goals.

Chapter Two

Contemplating Marriage

If we treat singles or divorcees or gays or intermarrieds with respect—even with love, perhaps as images of God—[we fear that]
we run the risk of losing the next generation of Jews. After all, how
can we affirm those who fail at or flaunt the Jewish family which we
know has been responsible for the survival of the Jewish people.

—Rabbi Sheila Pelz Weinberg[1]

CONTEMPORARY AMERICAN JEWS are caught in a dilemma: In the past
Jewish societies have used a carrot-and-stick approach to ensure that
men and women marry early, stay married, and remarry in the case
of divorce or widowhood. Jewish law and culture have promoted
marriage as the one productive state for adult life; nonmarriage has
been stigmatized. Today, in the wake of feminism and other social
movements that emphasize individual autonomy and realization,
many Americans view nonmarriage as a genuine option for part or
all of their lives.

Many Jewish women experience tension and conflict over the proliferation of choices in their personal lives. From the communal
standpoint, some observers fear that if they are concerned, supportive, and welcoming to those who do not live in conventional married
households they will be weakening the traditional Jewish family.
Anxiety about legitimizing nontraditional households frequently focuses on women and often "blames" feminism for undermining Jew-

17

ish families. For centuries women were extolled as the cornerstone of the family. To the extent that the traditional Jewish family appears threatened today, women and the women's movement are often held responsible.

The model of the woman as the pivotal force of Jewish family life has had a long and powerful impact. In traditional Jewish communities, prior to the mass emigrations of Jews to the United States (1880–1924), the marital unit was seen as the basic building block of Jewish society, for when two Jews married they created a *bayit ne'eman b'yisrael,* "a faithful household among the people of Israel." During many periods of Jewish history women were active in business and the marketplace as merchants and artisans. However, regardless of a woman's other activities, the state of marriage was considered normal, exemplary—and sanctified.[2]

In memoirs, fiction, and historiography of the nineteenth and early twentieth centuries, unmarried Jewish men or women were depicted as enduring a marginal existence. Lifelong celibacy was considered an aberration, both within rabbinic discussions and within the cultural norms of European and Sephardi Jewish communities. Most scholars agree that with a few notable exceptions, "Asceticism has been foreign to Judaism of every period; the Jewish religion has never in all of its 2500-year history had eunuch priests or virgin priestesses, never had a celibate clergy, never had monastic orders of either sex, never had any ideal for its spiritual elite other than marriage and fatherhood."[3]

In European Jewish societies both men and women were pushed toward the monogamous marital family unit from the cradle to the grave. The first blessing both infant Jewish boys (at their circumcision) and girls (at their naming in the synagogue) received is that they should mature to get married, to perform good deeds, and (for boys) to study the Torah. Talmudic prescriptions (Avot 5:21) suggest that men should be married by the age of eighteen and that adults should strive to marry and to remarry when bereavement or divorce occurs. Jewish law was basically accepting of the occasional necessity for divorce. Talmudic discussion suggests that infidelity should not be the only reason for divorce, because if it were, men who had grown to despise their wives would be tempted to accuse them of extramarital sexuality in order to exit from the union. Instead, even feelings of revulsion toward the spouse were admitted as grounds for divorce, so that divorce would not carry any moral stigma.

Once a man or woman became single again, Jewish society made every effort to remarry him or her to an appropriate partner. Age was no impediment to remarriage, because reproduction was not seen as the only reason for marriage. Jewish law assumed that marriage was the most normal, productive state for adults of all ages, and that the goals of marriage were companionship, an orderly physical environment, affection, and sexual activity. Jewish law directed husbands to provide their wives with material goods to the best of their ability, with affection, and at appropriate intervals with sexual satisfaction. Wives were directed to create an orderly home life and to be affectionate; the wife who withheld sexual activity on a regular basis specifically to torment her husband was considered to be a rebellious wife and a candidate for divorce—however, she was never to be forced into sexual compliance. Rabbinic literature prohibits husbands from raping their wives and urges them to acquire the arts of matrimonial seduction, such as flattery and tender words.

Jewish law viewed marriage not as a necessary compromise with human frailties but as a positive good, and traditional Jewish societies frowned upon postponed marriage or deliberate nonmarriage. Children were regarded as the glory and the reward of a successful marriage; however, childhood was seen as a training ground for adulthood, and the wisdom of the elders—rather than the energy of youth—was emulated. Both children and adults were exhorted to attend to their familial and communal responsibilities, rather than to their rights and individual opportunities. The extended family— aunts, uncles, cousins, and in-laws—also had social and moral claims on the nuclear family unit. As a result the husband and wife in their middle years were responsive to other family members and units as well as each other.

Within Jewish families, men were accorded greater autonomy, authority, and public status, but the family unit nonetheless depended heavily on the physical energy and skills of its women—especially those of the mother. Although gender differences were emphasized through a division of ritual tasks and by strict separation of such external markers as clothing, little is seen of images of the "macho" male and the weak, incompetent female. Jewish fathers were expected to be involved parents, and the scholarly and sensitive man was accorded high status in society. Conversely, women were expected to be strong, capable, organized, and good in business affairs.

The emotional equilibrium of the family unit was a crucial goal in Jewish law and custom. *Shalom bayit,* the psychological serenity and goodwill of the home, was to be a primary consideration of all members of the family, but most especially the wife, who was regarded as the moral and emotional center of the household. Both within and outside the Jewish community it was widely believed that the Jewish family had escaped the most violent forms of dysfunctionalism. While there is ample evidence that Jewish families may have had lower rates of such dysfunctions than did their non-Jewish neighbors, there is also ample evidence that abuses existed in every Jewish society. Eastern European Jewish writers portray a world in which corporal punishment was an accepted fact for children, although it almost always took the form of spontaneous slaps in the context of anger and seldom assumed a methodical sadism. Although some rabbinical commentators, including Maimonides, say it is permissible for a husband to beat his wife in order to reestablish the orderly serenity of the household, indications are that extreme physical abuse was infrequent—although by no means nonexistent—in Jewish families. So strong was this cultural ideal that where problems existed—alcoholism or wife or child abuse, for example—they were often swept under the rug because of the shame attendant on them. When abuses did occur, even until quite recently, the wife who complained was often assured that the problem wasn't as severe as she believed it to be and urged to work around it for the sake of *shalom bayit*.[4]

Certainly Jewish families did not always function according to the ideal, and in dysfunctional ones the strengths of the Jewish family were sometimes distorted and became weaknesses. The Jewish disposition for verbal expression could become a weapon in the mouth of an overworked mother or a harassed husband. Yiddish writers in the late nineteenth and early twentieth centuries often depicted scholarly men who neglected the material needs of their households because they devoted themselves to full-time study, sometimes at the side of a distant religious leader. As described in the stories of I. L. Peretz, Sholem Asch, and Chaim Grade, the wives and children of such men sometimes endured bitter physical privations, such as malnutrition and inadequate clothing and medical care. Wives who protested such difficulties might be verbally bullied into submission by threats of eternal damnation for disturbing the sacred male task of study. Prohibited from any firsthand knowledge of rabbinical sources, such women could be convinced that their very complaints cut them off from any joy either in this world or the one to come, as in Peretz's story "A Woman of Wrath."[5]

Some Jewish fathers were absent from the household for long periods of time, either on business travels, studying in the yeshiva, or, for Hasidim, on extended visits to the court of the *rebbe* (charismatic religious leader). In such households, immortalized by writers such as Asch (*Salvation*) and Sholom Aleichem (*The Adventures of Menachem Mendel*), the mother often became a single parent and sometimes also the breadwinner, aided by an extended family when she was lucky. Together with women who were officially single mothers, such as widows, divorcées, and *agunot* (women whose husbands had abandoned them or disappeared without granting them a religious divorce, or a *get*), Jewish mothers struggled to raise their children in a society that, as the novels and memoirs of Grade and the poems of Hayyim Nahman Bialik document, expected hard work from them but often granted them little status as a reward.

In addition the stories of Yiddish writers sometimes portray impoverished young women married off to grossly inappropriate—but wealthy—men in order to save their entire families from the miseries of hunger, cold, and poor health. That women often went willingly into such arrangements out of a sense of altruism and family loyalty did not ameliorate the bleak lives some of them led. Nevertheless, abject poverty was usually the overriding factor in such cases, and one reads little of economically motivated matches made out of a father's sheer greed. Moreover, not only young women sometimes used marriage as an escape from physical privation: The literature also describes poor but scholarly twelve-year-old boys married and miserably dispatched to their in-laws and impoverished young men matched up with wealthy widows of "a certain age."

The ideal goal, however, was to match like with like, and marriage brokers did attempt to create unions in which similarities of age and background would be most likely to grow into an affectionate and harmonious union. As David Biale suggests, "Rather than assuming that arranged marriages were devoid of sentiment and built on cold calculation, we should imagine a society that expected the arranged marriage to be accompanied by love. Those who rebelled against parental authority did not espouse different values from their parents, but rejected the specific choices offered to them."[6] When Sholom Aleichem's notoriously inept character, Menachem Mendel, tries his hand at matchmaking, he arranges a match between two young people who share educational level, family reputation, and economic status—only to discover that the two spouses-to-be are women![7]

*   *   *

With emigration to the United States, patterns of family behavior changed and gradually became less distinct from those of American society. For the children of immigrants, peer groups and school and work settings became as important as the family in establishing cultural norms. Authors of the immigration period, such as Anzia Yezierska, Norman Fruchter, and Jo Sinclair, describe the chasm that often developed between mothers and daughters, as first-generation mothers struggled against seemingly insurmountable odds to hold their families together physically and emotionally and to maintain traditional life-styles, while their daughters struggled to become "real" Americans. During the first half of the twentieth century, though second-generation Jewish women looked more and more like their gentile counterparts, there were still differences. On average Jewish women completed more years of secular education, got married a little later, were more likely to use birth control and have somewhat fewer children, were less likely to consume alcohol on a regular basis, and were more likely to assume a protective and highly involved stance vis-à-vis their children.[8] Like other American women, they grew to expect their husbands to provide the exclusive financial support for the family unit.[9] This pattern was interrupted by the years of World War II, which often threw them back onto their own resources. When the war ended, however, Americans married and bore children far earlier than they had in the difficult years of the depression and World War II and had larger families than they had had in decades. A longing for peace, stability, and normalcy created strong cultural pressures for large, loyal, harmonious family units among the American middle class, which in some ways echoed the Jewish emphasis on the normative family.

But the overt similarities between the American family ideal and the Jewish family ideal obscured profound differences. If, in traditional Jewish society, the father had been expected to be a moral force and an exemplar of lifelong learning and dedication to Judaism, in twentieth-century American life the father had often dedicated himself to the American ideal of material accomplishments instead. Those fathers who succeeded in business endeavors were often physically and emotionally removed from their families for long periods of time and often had little moral or religious input into their children's spiritual development. Those fathers who did not care to compete or did not succeed in materialistic strivings were sometimes held in contempt by their wives and children. Jewish writers describe fathers who clung to Eastern European traditions and never really adjusted to American life. Some such fathers tried to retain their patriarchal privilege; others were, as Sylvia Rothchild describes them, "broken men."

The daughters of many such families had already had a taste of independence, working and going to school in environments that differed quite drastically from the neighborhoods in which they had been raised. Often their work changed centuries-old patterns of traditional family behavior. Rothchild, for example, studied science at Brooklyn College at night and went to work during the day for a quartz crystal company during World War II. She was the first woman hired—and the company executives wanted to see if women could grasp the complexities of the business and work under "hideous conditions." She did so well that she was put in charge of training women twice her age, who called her the "boss lady." Like many American Jewish men and women, Rothchild found that her job made it necessary for her to work and travel on the Sabbath—and put an end to the until-then perfectly maintained Sabbath traditions of her parental household. "The first time I got on a train to cross the Williamsburg Bridge on a Saturday, I thought the bridge would fall down," says Rothchild. "But it didn't."

Despite the exhilaration Rothchild experienced at work, she left her scientific work and married at twenty-one when her husband-to-be came back from the Pacific. Her early experiences mirror those of many American women for almost two decades following World War II. With women basically ejected from the marketplace by the homecoming servicemen, gender divisions were clarified and underscored by fashions in clothing and behavior that glorified the strictly "female female." Portrayed in song, story, and film as pretty, soft, sweet creatures, best protected from the "jungle" outside the home, American women, and among them Jewish women, were urged to devote their full physical and emotional energies to the task of homemaking.

While substantial numbers of women in fact continued to work outside the home for pay, they often felt guilty for doing so and kept quiet about their work lives. Women who aspired to other roles than that of homemaker were scolded by mental health professionals and by the media for not fully accepting their femininity. Women's magazines featured articles and advice columns that placed responsibility for the entire family's happiness squarely at the feet of the "normal" mother, cheerfully and efficiently cooking, cleaning, chauffeuring, listening, encouraging; like her Victorian prototype, the white, middle-class American woman in the 1950s was exhorted to be an "angel of the hearth."

Jewish women, many of whom were extensively Americanized by the middle of the twentieth century, often adopted both the external and the internal prescriptions of this domestic image. In 1946 more than half of American Jewish women were married by age twenty-two, and more than four out of five were married by age twenty-five. In 1953 almost two-thirds of Jewish women were married by age twenty-two, and more than three-quarters were married by age twenty-five. More than any other ethnic group, Jewish women planned their families carefully, having their children a little later, providing space between siblings, and concluding their childbearing a little earlier than other women—with the result that their families were somewhat smaller. Jewish women were impeccably reliable in the matter of expected family size: If they expressed the hope that they would have a given number of children, they almost always did. In the 1960s non-Jewish women had an average of 3.5 children per household, while Jewish women averaged 2.8 children.[10]

Forty years later, in the last decade of the twentieth century, statistics reflect a dramatically different contemporary profile of Jewish women in the United States. Only a small fraction of them have married in their late teens or early twenties. In 1990 fewer than two-thirds of Jewish women (62 percent) lived in married households—compared to four out of five in 1970. More than three times as many Jewish women over age eighteen had never been married—18 percent—compared to 5 percent in 1970. Another 9 percent were currently divorced—more than double the 1970 rate—and 11 percent were widowed. Until recently Jews were the most universally married of all American populations—with more than 95 percent of adults ages thirty-five to forty-four living in married households in 1970—but in the 1980s more than one-third of Jewish women in the United States did not live in married households. The numerous men and women who lived together either before marriage or in lieu of marriage are not computed; they appear as single adults.

When 1990 data on Jewish women are broken down by age and decade, only 12 percent in the eighteen-to-twenty-four age group are currently married (see Table 2). In the twenty-five-to-thirty-four age group, 62 percent are married, as are more than 75 percent of women aged thirty-five to sixty-four. Thus, a perhaps startling 25 percent of

Jewish women aged thirty-five to sixty-four are not currently married. During these decades, as might be expected, the percentage of divorces has grown as well. For decades Jewish women married somewhat later than other white American women but were married by the time they reached their thirties. Today Jewish women still marry slightly later than other white women—and all Americans marry later now than they did forty years ago. However, Jewish rates of marriage and divorce today much more closely match those of the general population than they have in the past.

Feminism has influenced this trend toward later marriage in several ways. Most contemporary American Jewish women do not have the same economic impetus to marry as women did in many previous Jewish societies; the vast majority today consciously pursue higher education and acquire skills that enable them to be economically independent on some level, though certainly not necessarily affluent. The very acquisition of these skills often delays thoughts of marriage until education and vocational training are completed.

The fact that one-third of American Jewish women are currently unmarried makes the nonmarried state seem less threatening than it once did, and encourages women to "float" socially, with less pressure to marry than they might once have experienced. Indeed, the appearance at regular intervals of studies that show that unmarried women are more serene emotionally than are married women strengthens single women's impression that a bad husband is considerably worse than no husband at all.[11] Such studies are reported first in scientific journals but are typically appropriated—often in vivid prose—by popular newspapers and magazines. A cultural emphasis on examining the quality of relationships has spurred women to hold prospective and current marital partners up to close scrutiny. Professionally many women have themselves attained high levels of education and career achievement and don't want to marry "down." In addition, they are more savvy about personal qualities: They want responsive, caring husbands who seem capable of sharing many of the burdens of parenting and maintaining familial relationships. Women today are leery of being trapped in an unsatisfactory relationship; the quality of desperation that once made women accept a suitor's flaws and failings seems to have diminished with women's greater independence.

Delayed marriage has caused distress among Jewish communal leaders, families, and sometimes among single women as well. Commu-

nal leaders are concerned about delayed marriage because single
Jews are much less likely to join synagogues, work for Jewish organizations, and be involved in Jewish ritual and cultural activities.
Jewish parents are anxious to see their daughters married, settled in
"good Jewish" families and normative life-styles. Jewish women
themselves almost always say that they want to marry and have
children but are often unclear about how to enhance their chances
of accomplishing these goals. Often young women who want to get
married, have families, and live Jewish lives postpone the pursuit of
this aspect of existence for ten or fifteen years.

A forty-year-old physician supervising eight other physicians in a
Boston clinic has found herself caught short by her own conflicting
goals. She is thinking of leaving the East Coast if she can find "another city where there are more Jewish men my age—who don't
mind the fact that I'm successful" and thinks that her success has
made both her and prospective suitors more critical of each other.
"Guys have enough trouble dealing with a female physician," she
says, "but a lady doctor who's in charge of eight male doctors just
blows their minds." She admits that the other side of the coin is that
she has been "turned off" in the past by men who weren't "as ambitious" as she is. "I could never marry a man who didn't have as
much energy as I have. So with every promotion I received there were
a whole class of men I wasn't interested in anymore."

Now, she laments, appropriate single and divorced men in their
forties are "put off not only by the fact that I'm a doctor and an
executive but also by the fact that I'm probably beyond the age where
I can easily have children. Single Jewish doctors in their forties don't
marry single Jewish women their own age—they marry women in
their late twenties who'll stay home and have and raise their kids.
And if they can't find Jewish women who'll fit the Stepford wives[12]
stereotype, there's always an obliging gentile nurse around who'd be
thrilled to marry a Jewish doctor."

A thirty-eight-year-old psychologist working in a large East Coast
city, who says of herself that she "never had any problem attracting
men," recalls that she "put all relationships on hold until I got my
Ph.D." because she "had a magical idea that there was a God and the
right man would arrive when I finished it." She let the men she dated
while she did her graduate work know that she would not be interested in permanent commitments until she finished her degree. Moreover, she gravitated toward men who would be unlikely to press her

to rearrange her priorities. She was shocked and hurt when she finished her degree and did not find appropriate potential life partners waiting in the wings.[13]

The end result of such postponements is sometimes unplanned intermarriage. One woman said there was "no question" in her mind that she was looking for a Jewish man, because "I have always had a strong Jewish identity and an urge to keep Judaism alive. More than anything, I want a Jewish home for my children." She did eventually meet Jewish men and start dating but found that all of them had some inadequacy: "The Jewish men I dated," she said, "lacked a sincere spiritual identity. I have a sense of awe and the miracle of life that they just didn't share. Nor did I sense that they had achieved any real individuation from their families. Somehow, they were not men yet." Eventually, she reported, she met her "soul mate" at a church dance.[14] A forty-year-old professor of English, who has had a number of affairs with Jewish men ranging in age from the twenties to the fifties, says, "When I look back on it, I see that I was with men who were ultimately rejecting or devouring—almost all of them Jewish."

Many Jewish women today have high standards for potential husbands. If they cannot find Jewish men who fit the bill, they are ready to marry non-Jewish men or to stay single. Given their other standards for appropriateness—levels of education and career achievement; personal qualities such as sensitivity, responsiveness, or fairness—religious background often takes a back seat in an assimilated, open society, especially as they see the years pass. Moreover, some women indicated that they thought Jewish men as a group possessed undesirable attributes, such as self-centeredness, pushiness, excessive attachment to their mothers, and, as one woman put it, "egos the size of Montana." Single Jewish men, conversely, often harbor negative attitudes toward Jewish women and avoid dating them.

Such stereotypes contribute significantly to attenuated singlehood. Some Jews remain single for a long time because they have deep-seated hostilities toward Jews of the opposite sex, yet they are uncomfortable about the idea of intermarriage. Unable to resolve their conflicts, they continue to date non-Jews almost exclusively, but do not marry them. Jewish feminist therapists suggest that communal intervention in the form of workshops and public awareness of destructive stereotypes, such as the "Jewish American princess," the "Jewish mother," and the "Jewish mama's boy," may work to counter this.[15]

As a result of diverse factors, Jewish women and Jewish men marry non-Jewish spouses at rates that continue to rise. For decades Jewish men were much more likely than Jewish women to marry out. Today that gap has disappeared nationwide. Nationally rates of intermarriage among Jewish men and women over the last decade have been about even.[16] Jewish women who marry non-Jewish men marry them almost three years later, on average, than those who marry men who were born Jewish; in a study of eight American cities of diverse sizes and geographical locations, women who inmarried had a mean marriage age of 23.2, while women involved in a mixed marriage had a mean marriage age of 26. This dramatic discrepancy is no doubt caused in part by feelings of conflict and ambivalence about Jewish and non-Jewish men as appropriate marriage partners, as in the cases cited above.[17]

Another factor in the rising rate of outmarriage among American Jewish women is the continually increasing rate of outmarriage among American Jewish men. Outmarriage among Jewish men, combined with their propensity to marry women younger than themselves, decreases the pool of available and appropriate Jewish mates for women over thirty, further exacerbating the spiral of outmarriage among women. Many Jewish women who marry non-Jewish men say they would have preferred, all other things being equal, to marry Jewish men. Some of them may deliberately have deferred marriage for educational and occupational reasons; others may simply not have met men who appealed to them when they were younger.

The net result—as many single women in their thirties and forties report—is that single Jewish men in their own age group do not seriously consider them as potential marital mates. Single Jewish men in their thirties and forties are far more likely to marry considerably younger Jewish women if they are interested in establishing a Jewish family. In addition many Jewish bachelors are single precisely because they are primarily attracted to non-Jewish women and haven't yet decided to marry out.

Many Jewish women who did not marry in the years immediately after college report that they are "squeezed out" of the "prime" Jewish marriage market. "It's not polite to admit this," says a thirty-eight-year-old computer programmer, "but the Jewish men I meet are all leftovers. They are seriously flawed people—bitter, self-hating, self-centered, or just plain strange. And each one thinks he's God's gift to women because he's Jewish. Like he's this prize and you're nothing." "It gets to the point," says a thirty-three-year-old nurse, "when you say to yourself—look, what good is it if the man is Jewish if he's not a *mensch*. You just make a list of the things you really want in a man, and his being Jewish gets less and less important. Last year I met a Protestant doctor who really makes me feel terrific about myself. Can you imagine—my mother is having a fit! 'A doctor and he's not Jewish,' she says. But I'm not going to wait around any more for a Jewish prince charming. This may be my only chance for happiness, and I'm going to take it."

Increasing rates of outmarriage among Jewish women and increasing rates of mixed marriage seem to threaten directly the qualitative future of the American Jewish community. Some Jewish women succeed splendidly in maintaining Jewish households and raising Jewishly identified children with the cooperation of a non-Jewish spouse. Women who are Jews by choice and have converted into Judaism often make a wholehearted commitment to their new religion and raise their children as Jews. However, within most mixed marriages the Jewish identity of the household is ambiguous. Children are raised in such a way that they feel themselves to be partly Jewish and partly Christian. The larger society, being predominantly Christian, tends to reinforce the child's Christian identity. Two-thirds of mixed married couples have Christmas trees in their home—compared to fewer than 5 percent of inmarried couples. Only 41 percent of them provide their children with any formal Jewish education—compared to 95 percent of inmarried couples and almost as many conversionary families. Most Jewish women who enter a mixed marriage do so intending that their household will be Jewish and their children raised as Jews. However, the success of mixed-marriage households in transmitting Jewish tradition to the next generation is extremely unclear at best.[18]

Differences in social expectations between women and men persist. Within outmarriages gentile men married to Jewish women are far less likely than are gentile women married to Jewish men to convert to Judaism. Women still seem more willing to change and adapt in order to please their men. The vast majority of conversionary marriages involve Jewish men married to women who were not born Jewish but now consider themselves to be Jews. Non-Jewish men who are married to Jewish women, on the other hand, often express the feeling that conversion will alter their essential being, an idea they find unpalatable.[19]

For millennia Jewish women were socialized to be loyal to their families and to the Jewish community, sometimes sacrificing their own personal happiness in the bargain. Partially because of this, for most of the twentieth century American Jewish men were far more likely to marry non-Jews than were Jewish women. Today, however, women take pride in being their "own person." Feminist insistence that each woman has a moral obligation to place her own personal fulfillment and emotional health and happiness high on her list of priorities has eroded the impact of more traditional concerns. For perhaps the first time in Jewish history, Jewish women in large numbers are marrying late and marrying out.

In addition to staying single longer, American Jewish women are now divorcing more often than in the past. In Jewish law divorce is as old as the institution of marriage. Rates of divorce among Jews today, however, are unprecedented, and they have risen for many of the same reasons that they have risen among the general American population. During the late sixties, seventies, and eighties, cultural imperatives for individual fulfillment added further strain to the usual marital conflicts. Men who were attracted to women outside the home were sometimes more willing to leave their families because of the much-publicized glamour of freedom. Women who felt constrained by traditional roles were emboldened to leave them, both because they now had viable job skills and because the ideology of women's liberation encouraged independence rather than compromise.

Sometimes a feminist emphasis on women's emotional and financial independence has unexpected negative—and ironic—consequences on women's lives, by taking philandering husbands off the hook. "If my father had a mistress, he would have felt guilty about leaving his wife and children in the lurch," insists the ex-wife of a man prominent in Jewish communal life, who left his wife after twenty-one years of marriage. "He would have felt he should stay with them for emotional as well as financial support. But men like my husband today assume that all women should be out working anyway. They don't value women like me who have devoted their lives to their families. All I wanted from life was to love my husband and raise nice Jewish children. They leave us for reasons as old as mankind—but they have a brand-new modern reason for not feeling guilty. My husband murdered my whole adult life, and I have the feminists to thank for his guilt-free departure."

When women have rejected feminism, behaved in very traditional ways, and been left with a sidetracked career path and young children, feelings of anger are especially intense. A woman whose husband recently announced to her and their two daughters, aged five and ten, that he was leaving home to pursue a relationship with another woman, set aside early plans to attend law school at her husband's urging. "When we met I was a paralegal and he was new to the firm. I had already filled out my law school application," she recalls. "But he pleaded with me not to go to school, not to work. He asked 'Why do you want to have other people raising our children? So I didn't go to law school. I had the girls. I took care of them. I worked for our temple and for Hadassah. Now I'm left without any direction to my life. I feel duped."

The experiences of such women suggest that much in contemporary American culture contributes to the prevalence of divorce, not least the persistence of the youth culture and the pervasive pleasure principle in American society. "This year my husband turned forty-five and this year his mother died," she says. "I guess his behavior is classic male midlife crisis. But it's all so sordid!"

One Jewish historian suggests that in many such instances, "the divorce is a reassertion in middle age of youthful goals and dreams which have not been fulfilled in real life. Breaking the bonds of marriage is a last-ditch effort to 'begin again,' with presumably a more congenial and exciting partner, one more likely to gratify the fantasies still persisting from the past. In other cases, couples who married when they were young find that they have grown away from one another. One partner may have matured more than the other, developed new interests, or achieved a higher level of success. It cannot be denied that biological urges and socioeconomic promptings such as these play a decisive role in the upsurge of middle-aged divorce in our times."[20]

In divorces that take place after decades of marriage, wives are often deeply shocked. Women in their fifties and sixties frequently have no professional life to turn to, and their social circles are being narrowed by illness and death. Most of them have shaped their entire lives and self-images around their husbands and view divorce, unlike widowhood, as a devastating shame. "Whatever he wanted I did it," said one sixty-four-year-old woman. "He wanted blintzes, I made blintzes. He wanted help in the store, I helped in the store. You name it, I did it. How does he say 'Thank you'? He lies; he cheats; and for an encore, he defects."[21] Sometimes women in their fifties and sixties feel abandoned by the Jewish community as well as their husbands. While their husbands maintain ties in patriarchal synagogue and communal institutions, divorced women have difficulty finding a niche and drift away. Many eventually intermarry.[22]

Such legal innovations as no-fault divorce laws had the unpredictable consequence of making it easier for men to initiate divorce—often leaving the very women it aimed to help in extremely difficult circumstances. Debra Kaufman argues: "No-fault divorce laws . . . have liberated many men from the obligation to support their wives and children."[23] However, no-fault divorce laws have also eased the way out of unhappy marriages for women. The net result is increased rates of divorce.

While attraction to younger or more "interesting" women continues to play an important role in the breakup of marriages, the sudden onset of career ambitions by a wife is also reported by divorced couples as a significant factor. "Suddenly my wife got bitten by the feminist career bug," says a prominent Judaica college professor. "First she started making all kinds of demands on me to take care of the children and the house. Then she wanted to leave the marriage altogether." Like many other ex-husbands, he harbors a bitter resentment over the fact that his wife received custody of the children under these circumstances. Not surprisingly, perhaps, female colleagues report that his bitterness toward Jewish feminism has spilled over into his professional life, where, they feel, he treats Jewish female colleagues with contempt, and he has repeatedly publicly denounced as "profoundly sexist" lectures focusing on Jewish women.

Some contemporary divorces may indeed be linked to the greater ambition of women today. Career goals may lead to stress within marriage, and thus to divorce. About one-third of divorced Jewish women have master's degrees, compared to half as many married women with children at home.[24] (In fact, a surprisingly high proportion of divorced women in the general population have master's degrees. Women who obtained them before marriage are not more likely than average to be divorced, whereas women who obtained them after marriage are far more likely to be divorced. Marriages in which the wife entered as a professional may be psychologically far better adjusted to weather career pressures than those that began with more conventionally divided gender roles.[25]

*   *   *

Married women have been affected by feminist insistence that marriage be a partnership of true minds rather than an economic convenience. A Chicago real estate agent divorced her husband of twenty-five years when he "became unable to really be a husband to me in all the ways I need." After her husband's younger sister died, her mother-in-law made incessant phone calls from Milwaukee, about two hours away; her husband, she recalls, began shuttling to his mother's house to "help" her with bills and household chores several times a week. "Look," she says, "my husband owns a good business and he makes a lot more money than I do, and I have two teenage daughters, which is no day at the beach, but the days are over when a woman has to stay chained to a man who has ceased to function in a relationship. I'm only fifty years old. I have my whole life left to live."

Both men and women today are often less committed to marriage as a permanent state and more interested in beginning a new life rather than making do with an imperfect situation. Self-described Jewish Orthodox feminist and mother of five Blu Greenberg insists: "It goes without saying that feminism has had a powerful impact on the rising divorce rate in the Jewish community. As a young, divorced rabbi recently put it when asked why he divorced: 'My ex-wife got into this women's liberation thing, and I was too immature to know how to cope with it.' (He was being kind in not saying that his wife also did not know how to cope with it.) I am convinced that three-fourths of the marriages that succeed could have come apart at ten different points along the way," Greenberg adds, "and some three-fourths of the marriages that fail could have been put back together again at twenty points along the way. A great deal has to do with how one negotiates the inevitable impasses in an intimate relationship."[26]

Certainly in the popular imagination, the changing role of women is tied into rising divorce rates—albeit in sometimes paradoxical ways. In Linda Bayer's novel, *The Blessing and the Curse,* a Jewish father-in-law makes the darkly humorous claim that there was no reason to divorce when women were blandly interchangeable. Today, when women are free to develop their own distinctive personalities and talents—and to make money—another woman may seem much more attractive than one's own wife. He laments the fact that his son has left his college-professor Jewish wife to take up residence with a very wealthy non-Jewish lawyer:

If you really want to know what I think, it's all the fault of Women's Lib. . . . In my day, no one got divorced the way they do today. I

mean, if somebody was crazy or something was *really* wrong, but . . .
it would be like divorcing your mother, you know what I mean? The
point is that she was *yours*. Women then were pretty much all the
same—one a little nicer looking, maybe, one a little fatter, one complained more, but basically, you wouldn't have a reason to change
one for another. . . . But now, you have women who make a hundred
thousand, it's a temptation. It isn't right.[27]

One study of divorced individuals shows that most of the women
who initiated divorce did so prior to forming a romantic liaison,
while all the men who asked for a divorce were already involved with
another woman before they initiated proceedings. Judith Wallerstein
recalls Margaret Mead's troubled reflections on the rising rate of
divorce: "There is no society in the world where people have stayed
married without enormous community pressure to do so."[28]

On the most basic level, such divorces often make life very difficult
for women because of financial privations. The devastating economic effect of divorce on women, as compared to men, is revealed
in data from Jewish population studies. In Boston (1985), for example, twice as many divorced women as divorced men reported annual
incomes of under $15,000 a year. All but 15 percent of Boston's
divorced Jewish women made under $50,000 a year; in comparison,
almost one-third of the divorced men made over $50,000 a year. In
Rochester (1987), similarly, well over half of divorced Jewish
women made less than $20,000 per year—while virtually none of the
divorced Jewish men made less than $30,000 a year. Indeed, about
half of divorced Jewish men made between $30,000 to $40,000 a
year, compared to 11 percent of divorced women. Forty-four percent of the divorced men made between $40,000 to $74,000 a year,
compared to about one-quarter of the women.[29]

Regardless of who initiates divorce proceedings and why, Jewish
women and men who emerge from marriages join a singles culture
that is often very different from the one they had experienced before
marriage. Judith Lang describes women caught in a "cruel squeeze
play": "Women's liberation offers vistas of growth, 'creative divorce,' and personal happiness, when the reality is often a long period of loss and mourning, and societal rejection of the middle-aged
woman in favor of youth and good looks."[30] Single mothers have
been described as experiencing overwhelming feelings of isolation
and loneliness, sexual frustration, hopelessness, anxiety, fear, inadequacy, guilt, failure and anger.

One Orthodox single mother speaks of special problems that women in her position—and their children—suffer through. "When we go to the synagogue on Saturday morning and my little boys go to the other side of the *mekhitzah* [partition dividing men from women in the synagogue], no one takes an interest in them. They run around wild, and everyone says, 'Tsk, tsk, how come she doesn't discipline her children better?'—but no man calls them over and says, 'Here, sit down near me, I'll show you what we're doing now.' I think that providing the male children of divorced women with male role models is something the whole community should be concerned with, rather than leaving us on our own this way."

All denominations of Jewry have been influenced by the American propensity to divorce, but religious observance still has an inverse relationship to the number of divorces, with unaffiliated Jews experiencing the greatest number of divorces. Brodbar-Nemzer found that Jews with a low rate of ritual observances are eight times as likely to be divorced at some time in their lives than Jews who have a greater commitment to traditional Jewish observance.[31] It may be that a shared value system and more extensive communal social support systems in the Orthodox community contribute to more stable marriages. Social stigmas attached to divorce may also play a role.

Nevertheless, the Orthodox Rabbinical Court (*beth din*) of New York reports that divorce rates are rising among Orthodox Jews and even among members of Hasidic sects. By 1975 Rabbi Nahum Josephy, executive vice president of the Rabbinical Alliance of America and secretary of its rabbinical court, reports that numbers of Jewish divorces (*gittin*) to be granted by his court were almost double the number granted the previous year. He commented that the majority of these couples were between nineteen and twenty-eight years old, that all had children, but that most of them were clearly not ready for the responsibilities of marriage. Parents, who arrange many of these marriages, he continued, also exacerbate marital conflicts by siding with their own child instead of encouraging conciliation.[32]

It is the most traditional Jewish women who are the most affected by one mushrooming problem in Jewish life around the world: the dramatically increasing number of *agunot*. According to Jewish law a woman who remarries without a *get* is officially an adulteress, and any children who are born of that relationship are *mamzerim,* "bastards." (In contrast, the children of unwed mothers are legitimate Jewish children with the same rights as other Jewish children.) Unscrupulous husbands have used the fact that their ex-wives need the

Jewish divorce as a bargaining tool that often verges on blackmail, demanding that the women forgo alimony, houses, and often custody of the children.

The problems of *agunot* have often been neglected or at least underemphasized by male rabbinic coteries, and have consequently become an important cause for Jewish feminist solidarity, especially in the United States and Israel. As Chicago attorney Barbara Fox, who has done extensive work in such cases, explains:

> The Jewish communal consequences of *mamzerut* (illegitimacy) are irrevocable.[33] Unequal bargaining power yields lots of opportunities for exploitation. There are no statistics on the number of women who end up giving in to blackmail. The community has to deal with this on a case by case basis—no policy decisions have been made. Lots of rabbis encourage women to "pay off" their husbands—They say, "It's only $50,000, your father is rich—pay him off!"

Fox, who is herself Orthodox, comments wryly on the indignities sometimes visited upon women working for a fairer, more consistent response on the part of the *beth din* in the context of an Orthodox environment. "As a feminist, I try to be goal oriented and I try not to get distracted by disturbing details," she says. "If they ask me to sit at a separate table, I sit there, but I won't let anyone dislodge me from my ultimate goal of getting them to deal responsibly with the fate of these women."

Scores of new *agunot* appear in the United States each year, according to rabbinic figures, and the Israeli rabbinate reports the existence of ten thousand *agunot* in Israel, where the ranks of women in marital limbo are swollen by the disappearance of Israeli soldiers in the line of duty, leaving their wives still legally married but with no actual husbands. Until such husbands are either found or proved dead, their wives cannot remarry, reports Orthodox feminist Rifka Haut, perhaps the person most consistently involved with advocacy on behalf of *agunot*. Haut discusses the basic inequality between husband and wife that is clearly exposed by the proliferation of *agunot*. She notes that many prenuptial agreements have been suggested, including the "Lieberman" clause in Conservative *ketubot* (wedding contracts) and some formulations that have been authorized as acceptable even in the most right-wing circles. However, these clauses, which provide for a divorce for the wife in the event of a husband's disappearance, abandonment, or recalcitrance, are not utilized on a regular basis—often because of resistance on the part of the newlyweds, who insist that they will be in love forever.

Words of condemnation for the obliviousness to the larger needs of Jewish women—rather than the narrow needs of a particular movement—can be shared equally by both ends of the religious spectrum. Of the right wing, Haut asserts, "It is only when it comes to women's issues that the Orthodox world is unable to resolve halakic issues." She documents instances of corrupt Jewish courts that work in collusion with the husband because of his financial clout or communal status, and she points out that in the religious court system there is no system of higher and lower courts, thus no possibility of redress or appeal.

However, the Reform movement also plays a pernicious role in the plight of *agunot*—by giving the nod to men who pursue a divorce through civil courts but deliberately and maliciously refuse to give their ex-wives a *get*. Essentially, says Haut, the Reform movement is more interested in its ideology—that a Jewish writ of divorce is not necessary—than it is in the plight of the women who are trapped. Although the marriage has been entered into through a religious contract, they insist that a civil contract is adequate to disband it. "The Reform movement should not allow itself to be used as a haven for men who won't give their wives a *get*—but want a religious ceremony when they themselves get remarried," she declares. "Many men would come around if their Reform rabbis would only insist that they give a previous wife a *get* before they can have a *ketubah* for their new wife."

Thus, in the cases of both Orthodox and Reform rabbis, male solidarity often preempts concern for women. Regardless of whether they identify as traditional or liberal, rabbinic hierarchies still often resist putting the needs of women on an equal basis with those of men.

Feminists and Jewish feminists also urge concern for widows, a group primarily older than the never-marrieds and the divorced. Although the options and problems of widows are significantly different from those of the younger group of "singles," they, too, are deeply affected by the changing expectations brought about by feminism. For many of them widowhood means being plunged into an unrecognizable world.

Today more than ever, the daughters of elderly Jews are part of a "sandwich" generation. Because American Jewish women are now, by and large, getting married and having their children later and working throughout their lives, they are frequently in the position of trying to meet the needs of school-age children, pay household expenses, and deal with aging parents at the same time. The dual-pronged nature of these responsibilities ranges from emotional pressures to simple physical demands for time: "Should I attend my son's Little League game or go with my mother for her doctor's appointment?" Women caught in this bind often report that the first commitment to be obliterated is time for themselves. Many of these women report fantasies of escaping, of getting "out from under."

When the woman caring for children and aging parents is herself a divorcée or widow, the emotional and physical demands are exacerbated, often leaving her feeling almost unbearably "stressed out." As Jewish women continue to postpone marriage and childbirth, and as the American Jewish population as a whole continues to "gray," the prevalence of Jewish women caught in the middle will continue to increase.

However, from a statistical standpoint the life situation of sandwiched women is often invisible. It differs from Jewish societies in the past, in which relatively young grandparents frequently helped to raise grandchildren, and older grandchildren helped to meet the needs of their aging grandparents, often living in physical proximity to each other. While such intergenerational support systems were never universal—as some Jews nostalgically imagine them to have been—they were fairly common and still are in non-Western cultures. Among contemporary American Jews, however, an intergenerational shared domicile is uncommon enough (fewer than 5 percent of households) to be considered almost an "alternative lifestyle," especially when juxtaposed with the typical small American nuclear family.

The traditional Jewish emphasis on the family stands in the way of communal response to the needs of women who do not fit the mold, because some fear that by supporting those who live in alternative households, "we are validating them," suggests Reform Rabbi Sheila Pelz Weinberg.[34] It is important to place challenges to the Jewish family in the context of wider societal change. American society as a whole currently struggles with the challenges of supporting "family values" and family units and yet not delegitimizing people who live in nonnormative households or choose alternative life-styles. The

Jewish community faces the same challenges to the normative family unit—and, because of a shrinking proportion of Jews in the American population, sometimes experiences them as a crisis. While it has always been tempting for communal leaders to employ the tactic of blaming women—*cherchez la femme*—feminism is but one important element in a wide spectrum of recent social transformations.

Not only is it important to have a clear understanding of the role that feminism does—and does not—play in these changes, but it is perhaps even more crucial to realize that delegitimizing Jewish feminism will not save the American Jewish family. Jewish women and men seem unlikely to abandon their very American pursuit of happiness, a mind-set that feminism did not create but merely attempted to extend to women.

Ironically, a primary tool in working to strengthen the contemporary Jewish family is *not* making the normative family the condition for Jewish life-styles. Single Jews have always tended not to affiliate with Jewish communal institutions,[35] tending to wait until they are married to "do Jewish things." This postponement of Jewish activity had a much more benign effect when singleness was only a short way station between childhood and adulthood. However, with current levels of postponed marriage and lengthy single years, numerous single Jewish women and men have reported walking away from Judaism because they couldn't reproduce idyllic family scenes on Friday night. Quite simply they thought that Judaism didn't belong to them because they weren't married. The belief that Judaism was exclusively a family-based religion disenfranchised Jews during their single years. Later, when they decided to get married, they were already estranged from the Jewish community and Jewish behaviors.

Divorced women have also complained that they are made to feel unwanted in Jewish communal settings. In addition to the pain that may be intrinsic to their life situation, many divorced women complain about what they perceive as a hostile or punitive Jewish communal reaction to their circumstances. Sheila Pelz Weinberg, for example, notes that it is particularly difficult for single mothers to find a social niche in the Jewish communal world. "The divorced woman does not quite fit in with the couples or the child-free singles," she writes of her divorce at thirty with two small children. "My agendas are different from the first (I am somewhat of a threat, even here), and my energy does not mesh with the others. I fall into self-pity and spiral downward."[36]

In group contexts divorced Jewish women require more sensitivity
and attention, as well as a broad spectrum of services, from the Jewish community. An Oakland, California, group suggested that mothers emerging from divorce "should get help in finding affordable
housing and day care—the same help immigrant families get. Single
mothers are the new poor in the society." Weinberg describes some
of the difficulties: "The needs of a single mother—the pressure for
money, the lack of time, the need for help with housework, home
and car repairs, child care, the need for some respite from the lonely
burden, are the needs writ large of most families. . . . They are often
exacerbated by vengeful exhusbands, and money- and energy-
soaking legal embroilments."[37]

Rabbi Lyn Gottlieb, spiritual leader of Congregation Nahalat Shalom in Albuquerque, New Mexico, believes that her congregation
has made a start toward meeting the needs of the new Jewish family.
She suggests that rather than trying to convince young Jews that they
need a family to have a Jewish household, giving each single Jew the
ability to create his or her own Jewish household enhances their
ability to remain tied to the Jewish community and to Jewish life
throughout their single years. Like many innovative Jewish feminist
leaders today, Gottlieb also urges that synagogues and other Jewish
communal institutions work "to strengthen family life by producing
a new generation of Jewish women and men who see in each other
spiritual, intellectual, and physical individuals worthy of love and
respect, rather than as a means to an end."

Because of the realities of the open society in the United States,
attempts to influence contemporary Jewish women—or men—to behave in certain ways because it is "good for the community" or "necessary for Jewish survival" are likely to be ineffective. Like many
traditional communities, Jewish societies in the past have used communal sanctions to encourage marriage and remarriage. Today,
however, hostility to existing nonnormative Jewish households can
only be destructive and alienating. Singles, divorcées, single mothers,
and widows say that they need Jewish communal support; demographic trends make it virtually inescapable that their numbers will
be more significant, not less so, in coming years. American Jewish
feminists believe that supporting alternative Jewish households will
not diminish the community's commitment to normative families,
and that it will enhance the chances for the creation of traditional
Jewish families in the future. They suggest that Jewish women and
men who find Judaism and the Jewish community a source of spiri-

tual and emotional strength in their single years may ultimately form the strongest Jewish homes.

The Jewish community therefore faces the dilemma of reinforcing the normative family while welcoming and nurturing Jews who do not live in typical family units. Fortunately the contemporary environment not only provides American Jews with challenges but with clues to the answers as well. Those Jews whose life-styles blend a search for personal fulfillment and an active involvement with Judaism and Jewish family life say that Judaism and Jewish family life are an important part of their happiness. In other words, while Jewish women will not build Jewish families for altruistic reasons, just because doing so will make someone else happy, they will do so if they believe that building and living in a Jewish family will make them happy.

Such attitudes seem to grow best, many women feel, when Jewish children are provided with a meaningful understanding of Jewish history, culture, texts, and moral, social, and ethical precepts. When Jewish women and men see Judaism as their birthright, when they are deeply committed to Judaism and the Jewish people, the chances that the creation and maintaining of a Jewish home will be a part of the package of fulfillment they choose for themselves are strengthened.

The powerfully motivating effect of deep attachments to Jewish family life has been described by women at every point in the denominational spectrum. Thus Orthodox feminist Blu Greenberg muses: "When I think of our Shabbat table, and I think of the rituals—which we do in a very traditional, gender-divided way—and I think of our children all talking about their week and sharing their lives with us, and the singing and the warmth and the joy—well, I wouldn't trade those hours for anything in the world."

Reform businesswoman Phyllis Brotman, who speaks warmly of her family's weekly candlelit Friday-night meals, when her grown children come to visit, says that her life choices were confirmed for her by a midlife illness. Her reflections illustrate the way some women successfully blend their love for their families, their work, and their Judaism:

> I had a special opportunity. When I was thirty-nine I was diagnosed with breast cancer. I spent days thinking deeply about the way I had lived my life, what I had done, and what I wanted to do. And I realized that I would not have wanted to change one minute of my life. When

my husband and I were young, we knew we had to help each other. When my children were very small, I spent a lot of time volunteering for Jewish organizations. My career grew from a one-person public relations firm in 1966 to a national agency employing twenty-eight people [Image Dynamics in Baltimore], with international accounts. As my children were growing up, they were always involved with my work and I was always involved with them. They used to help me collate and staple reports on the dining room table, and I used to rush home from work to get them from one activity to another. They all got a good Jewish education, although Baltimore Hebrew College didn't offer bat mitzvahs at the time. They're all grown now, and they all have remained tied to the Jewish community, and they all say those growing-up years were wonderful years.

Looking at the open—and often confusing—spectrum of options available today as Jewish women contemplate forming their own households, many American Jewish feminists urge that each individual woman confront the question of what she wants most in life. Women who find alternative households comfortable and fulfilling now have the option of living in them, and many feel that Jewish communities should welcome all Jews as cherished members of the community, regardless of the households in which they choose to live. One of the greatest goals of feminism is to provide women with choices and the tools to accomplish them. More than one woman noted that the aphorism, "Be careful what you wish for—it might come true," is perhaps truer today for women than ever before in history, and it may be truer in terms of personal fulfillment than in any other area of life.

For contemporary Jewish women, an honest and realistic appraisal of personal goals will become increasingly important. Now that they have moved beyond a closed, structured society, today's women are less likely merely to drift passively into satisfying personal relationships and into the formation of Jewish homes. Jewish women whose personal goals include marriage and family will be best able to realize these personal goals by confronting them proactively and giving them increased priority, evaluating personal options with the same clearminded incisiveness they bring to other areas of life. Such choices involve asking hard questions about romance, marriage, and the birth and raising of children—and the optimum realistic time frame for accomplishing each of these goals. Needless to say, none of this comes with a guarantee. However, just as women have learned to take responsibility for accomplishing aims within the spheres of higher education, careers, and personal development, the new freedom of American Jewish life encourages them to work toward creating the kind of Jewish home in which they would most like to live. If Jewish tradition called the woman "the cornerstone of the household," today's Jewish women have the opportunity to participate in the architecture of their homes as well.

Chapter Three

Choosing Jewish Parenthood

I knew exactly how I wanted to arrange my life. I had a game plan. First I would make partner, then I would have two children. My mother bugged me all the time, "When am I going to be a grandmother? Are you afraid to give me a little *nachas*?" [joy, satisfaction] Her nagging just made me more determined not to get derailed. After I reached my goal, we tried to start a family. Three years of infertility—it was hell! It hurt all the more because I felt so guilty. It got so I hated my fancy office and I hated all pregnant women. When I finally conceived our only child, I didn't call my mother right away. I didn't want her to act as though now I was a "good girl." Also I was terrified that she would rub it in about how I delayed and almost wasn't able to have any children. But she was really supportive. It changed my feelings about her and about a lot of things she had said in the past. I don't think you really understand your mother until you become a mother yourself.

—Washington, D.C., attorney, age forty-two

CHOICES ABOUT WHETHER and in what context to become parents carry great emotional weight. Particularly in the Jewish tradition, which valued families as institutions for producing and educating the next generation of Jews, and valued women most when they were mothers, the idea of deliberate nonparenthood is threatening. Within the Jewish feminist world, lines have been sharply drawn over issues of family and parenthood. At one end of the ideological spectrum, some

45

Jewish feminists dismiss the importance of the traditional, normative family, insisting that the nuclear family is not central to Jewish continuity. They assert that there are other types of relationships and households in which children may be born and initiated into the Jewish community, and that arrangements outside heterosexual unions can offer companionship and intimacy. According to such Jewish feminists, the demise of the nuclear family with children need not necessarily threaten Jewish survival. Perhaps even more important, individuals can contribute to the survival of the Jewish community through many pathways, they maintain, through other means than having children. "Heterosexual nuclear families are not the only contexts in which people can or do covenant, nor are they the only units in or through which people may express love, or long-term care and commitment," prominent feminist Martha Ackelsberg insists.[1]

Other Jewish feminists insist that Jewish vitality is inseparable from traditional normative Jewish family life. Reaching back to Genesis, with its poignant preoccupation with matchmaking, marriage, and procreation, Judaica professor Susan Handelman posits that the Jewish family was the primary and most enduring institution of Judaism. The family not only enculturated the young and supported Jewish institutions, it was the embodiment of Jewish values. To speak of Judaism without the primacy of the traditional Jewish family, she suggests, is to commit an irreparable violence on both the religion and the culture.[2]

In traditional Jewish communities, infertility was regarded as a curse. Children were the highly desired goal of marriages involving women during their fertile years. Problems with infertility—often assumed to be the wife's "fault"—were a valid reason for divorce if a marriage were childless for ten years, should the husband so desire. In practice, however, few divorces took place on this basis. Instead, after the prohibition against polygamy took hold in Ashkenazi communities (during the Synod of Rabbenu Gershom Ben Yehudah, 1000 C.E.), childless couples often frantically pursued all remedies, running from rabbi to rabbi, from doctor to doctor, and sometimes availing themselves of folk remedies from surrounding cultures as well. Children were considered to be a blessing to the individual family and to the Jewish people, and the birth of a child evoked the Hebrew aphorism, *ken yirbu,* "thus we shall increase," from members of the community. Nevertheless, on the rare occasions when a pregnancy seemed to threaten the physical health of the mother, the mother's well-being always took precedence over that of the fetus and the pregnancy was terminated.

Although children were cherished, Jewish culture focused on adults and adult activities and was not, in the contemporary sense, child centered. Jewish parents tended to be affectionate to infants and very young children, but age rather than youth was respected, and childhood was regarded as the training ground for adulthood. Elderly parents were the responsibility of their middle-aged children even more extensively than young children were the responsibility of their parents, according to Jewish law. Grown children were accountable to provide not only for the physical but even more for the emotional and social well-being of their aging parents, ensuring that they maintained their dignity and communal status in social situations.[3]

The tendency of some contemporary Jewish feminists to downplay the importance of childbearing, conversely, has been seen as a harsh threat to Jewish continuity. Children were valued both because they represented physical renewal and perhaps even more because they were the link to the religious and cultural continuity. Some of the most acclaimed of the older Jewish female intellectuals have voiced clear opposition to feminist agendas that they think endanger family values. Marie Syrkin, for example, put the conflict between individual fulfillment and Jewish family values in the most pragmatic terms. She pointed out that the significance of late marriages, smaller families, and mixed marriage in the general population is very different from that in the Jewish population:

> There may be a conflict . . . between feminism and the national survival of the Jewish people. In view of intermarriage and the low Jewish birthrate in the Diaspora, the specter of the vanishing Jew haunts real debates about Jewish survival. Insofar as feminism liberates women from traditional roles and encourages life-styles antithetical to procreation and the fostering of the family, feminist ideology affects the Jewish future. The question of national responsibility is peculiar to Jewish feminism. American women have no worries about the vanishing American when shaping their personal lives.[4]

While such women as Syrkin have indicted feminism as the enemy of Jewish survival, other Jewish feminists have indicted the Jewish family as the enemy of women. Some feminists have portrayed the family as a repressive, patriarchal device enabling men to own and control their women and children. Indeed, feminist discomfort with the Judaic emphasis on family formation reaches back to critiques of the Bible. They have argued that when the matriarchs and other biblical heroines who rebelled against their own infertility prayed, pleaded, and wept for children, they were expressing not their own desires but those of their husbands. They see biblical motherhood as a "patriarchal mechanism" and not the "personal tendency of women." They believe that this patriarchalism is proved by the fact that God intervenes only to facilitate the impregnation of married women, with, presumably, husbands who desire progeny; if women were the true focus, they believe, God would arrange for the impregnation of unmarried women as well.[5]

According to this viewpoint, women have no intrinsic desire to become mothers, either in contemporary society or in the past. Jewish culture is seen as a particularly egregious example of a patriarchal male power structure brainwashing women into wanting something that is actually destructive to their own best interests.

The conflict between feminist and Jewish attitudes toward the family is wrestled with and played out in the lives of American Jewish women daily. On the one hand, Jewish women have absorbed feminist goals more fully than have other ethnic groups: They are more highly educated, work in higher-status professions, are more sweepingly in favor of reproductive rights, and are more desirous of freedom and independence for their daughters than any other group.[6] On the other hand, the vast majority of American Jewish women remain committed to the ideals of marriage and family.

This negative reading of a woman's yearning for children, along with critical attitudes toward the married, heterosexual family unit, seems to have more impact on women whose connections to Judaism are generally weak. Typical of such women is Robin Marantz Henig's reflection: "When we were young and thinking about whether even to have children, Jeff and I dutifully drew up a list of pros and cons. The cons I remember well: kids are expensive, they're demanding, they restrict your freedom. I can't imagine what we wrote down on the pro side, because we couldn't possibly have understood, when we were 25, what it means for a child to give shape to your life."[7]

Choosing parenthood is often correlated with the strength of a woman's Jewish connections and behaviors. Data from the 1990 National Jewish Population Study show that women who identify themselves as "Jewish by religion" are much more likely to have children than women who consider themselves to be secular Jews. Being a Jewish mother is also strongly associated with belonging to a synagogue, belonging to and working for Jewish organizations, making donations to Jewish charitable causes, having mostly Jewish friends, observing Jewish holidays, and seeing Judaism as a "very important" aspect of one's life. Women who call themselves Orthodox are more likely than others in the same age group to be married and have children; as a group Orthodox women alone are currently having children above replacement (2.1 children per family) levels. Conservative women expect to have more children than Reform women, but among thirty-five- to forty-four-year-old Conservative and Reform women few differences in actual family size exist.[8]

Despite differences between particular groups of women, there are sweeping changes in childbearing patterns among large segments of the Jewish population. With the exception that larger proportions of non-Jewish white women have children in their early twenties than do Jewish women, patterns of childbearing among Jewish and non-Jewish women are similar.[9] Changes in marriage patterns have affected both the timing and the size of today's families. In 1990, 93 percent of Jewish women aged eighteen to twenty-four had not yet had children. More than half (55 percent) of those aged twenty-five to thirty-four had no children. Among Jewish women aged thirty-five to forty-four one out of four had no children. While almost all Jewish women aged forty-five or over reported having children, either biological or adopted, it is not clear that all or even most of the 24 percent of childless women in the thirty-five-to-forty-four age group will in fact achieve the status of motherhood. As a result of delayed marriage and childbirth, the societal preference for smaller families, and unwanted infertility, most demographers now estimate the completed size of the contemporary Jewish family to average fewer than two children per married household.[10]

The vast majority of Jewish women still place an enormous value on having children. Jewish women are less likely than any other religious or ethnic group to state that they wish to remain childless.[11] Most American Jewish couples hope to have children "someday." Unlike women of other ethnic groups, in which higher education is associated with lower expectations of childbearing, the more highly educated a Jewish woman, the more children she expects to have. Calvin Goldscheider and Frances Kobrin Goldscheider, relying on data that deal with expected family size, point out that among Jewish populations—unlike among Protestants and Catholics—"educational attainment is directly rather than inversely related to the fertility expectations." Thus "Jews with doctorates expect 2.2 children and only 11 percent expect to be childless; Jews with 'only' college degrees expect only 1.8 children and 21 percent expect to be childless." In contrast the reverse is true of highly educated Protestants and Catholic women.[12]

However, highly educated Jewish women do not actually have as many children as they once expected to. Although Jewish career women are more committed to having families than is any other group of career women, they are at least as likely as other white middle-class women to postpone the onset of childbearing until they have reached what they consider to be an appropriate level of financial or occupational achievement. Expectations do not always give way to reality. Jewish women sixteen to twenty-six years old who were interviewed in a national study in 1969–70 expected to have an average of 2.5 children; that cohort, today thirty-five to forty-four years old, have in fact borne an average of 1.5 children and expect an average completed family size of 1.7 children.[13] Contrary to the expectations of both women and demographers, "as education increases among both Jewish men and women, the proportion with no children increases." Indeed, "Among those with a masters degree . . . Jews have significantly higher levels of childlessness than non-Jews."[14]

Often childlessness is unintentional. When a couple conscientiously uses birth control as part of "family planning," they do not imagine that one day the promotion rather than the prevention of conception will be their focus. Over and over again one hears the same story: "We were married for ten years, and then I was in my thirties, so I decided it was time to have a child, my biological clock was ticking." When Cindy Shapiro* says these words, there is no trace of irony in her voice. In 1984, after a year of trying to conceive, Cindy and Rob were diagnosed as having an infertility problem, a problem shared by approximately 15 percent of American couples. Eight years later they were still struggling with a spectrum of medical techniques designed to help them achieve their goal of a healthy child.

However, women's biological clocks are ticking all along. Fertility is not an even playing field bounded on one side by menarche and on the other side by menopause. For reasons still not clearly understood

* Asterisk indicates pseudonym.

by the medical community, some women who easily conceive and carry pregnancies to term in their twenties have problems with conception and gestation in later years. This has caused many women to rethink their priorities. It is one thing to postpone having children; it is quite another to risk never having one.

Some feminists have questioned such medical reports. For example, Susan Faludi contrasts two medical reports on infertility. Citing the one she views as more politically correct, Faludi declares that of women between ages thirty to thirty-four "*only* 13.6 percent" would suffer from infertility—"a mere 3 percent higher than women in their early twenties."[15] However, a 13.6 percent rate of primary infertility (infertility among women who have never had a child) is not an insignificant figure among a population of married women who are currently trying to have children; what it means is that one out of every seven childless women between the ages of thirty to thirty-four who is trying to have a child will encounter difficulty or be unable to conceive altogether.

In seeking to reassure women that they can take their time before bearing children, Faludi actually distorts the data. Her figure of 13.6 percent infertility includes only women in their early thirties currently trying to have children who have not yet given birth. It does not include women who postpone beginning their families until their late thirties or even their forties, when conception is even more difficult. It also does not include women trying to conceive a second child. Recent studies have shown that the birth of a first child may actually signal an increase in, rather than the cessation of, infertility problems, especially for older mothers. One childless Jewish woman reports: "According to the National Center for Health Statistics, as of 1982 some 4.5 million American women either could not get pregnant or could not carry a baby to term; more than half of them already had at least one child. . . . some risk factors do increase with time. Naturally, a couple is older when they try to have children again, and fertility clearly declines with age."[16]

Women who wait until they are over thirty-five to try to conceive and then have primary or secondary fertility problems are often filled with anger: "Women feel they have been sold a bill of goods that they can wait to get established in a career and then have a family." As if to add insult to injury, "Some secondarily infertile couples turn to adoption. But by then they may have passed the age limits set by adoption agencies. Some agencies won't even consider couples who have a biological child."[17] Many women who find themselves chronologically disadvantaged because they have made choices based on feminist ambivalence toward childbirth and parenting feel, on some level, betrayed.

In addition, the comparison of women in their thirties with women in their early twenties is specious, because they are different groups. The vast majority of middle- and upper-middle-class women are not trying to conceive in their early twenties. Faludi presents a lower-class population of women who become impregnated in their early twenties—with all the health problems attendant on that population—and compares them with a different, healthier middle-class population of women who marry and begin families in their thirties. Neither we nor she knows what the fertility rates would be if this same population of middle- and upper-middle-class women, currently encountering difficulty conceiving, had begun their families earlier.

From a feminist perspective, no doubt it is not fair for it to be easier for women to have children in their twenties than in their thirties and forties. *Reproductive rights* is a term that has important political and legal implications but is nonbinding on the human body. Feminism has been a significant force in convincing women that it is their right to have children only when they wish those children to become part of their lives. Jewish women have taken this message very much to heart—as individuals and as a group. Mainstream Jewish organizations have issued strongly worded public statements defending reproductive rights for all Americans.

Our national cultural preoccupation with a woman's right to defend herself against unwanted pregnancies obfuscates an important fact—we can legislate a woman's right not to have children, but we cannot legislate her right to bear children at will. The medical difficulties that can result from postponed childbearing are little discussed, partially because they conflict with our profound attachment to the idea that each individual *ought to* have control over his or her own destiny. Feminism sharply upped the ante of the notion of the absolute right of the individual woman to shape her own destiny, especially her own reproductive destiny. However, feminism has yet to confront or come to terms with the physical limitations of this doctrine on the one hand and its moral complexities on the other.

Feminists are also concerned that, in their yearning for children, women can become pawns in an expansive, male-dominated technology. The insistence that women shall not be reproductively controlled by men via the production of children creates a deep mistrust of male participation in the childbearing process. Powerfully demonstrating these inconsistencies within feminism, feminist and nurse Margaret Sandelowski charges that some feminist theorists take a harsh view of infertile women, demanding that they should not use high-tech genetic and reproductive techniques, because the research and medicine in these areas is dominated by men. Such feminists concentrate on male technicians rather than on the infertility experience of women. As Sandelowski summarizes:

> Recent feminist writing has emphasized the continuing medicalization of childbearing and motherhood and the male expropriation of reproductive power from women, furthering female subordination. Reproductive technologies are tied to patriarchal concepts of womanhood, parenthood, and family, making their further development and use unjustifiable in terms of the potential consequences for women as a social group, despite the promise they might hold for some individual women. . . . There is little in their discussions about reproductive technology or infertility that suggests real empathy with infertile women.[18]

When feminist theoreticians concentrate on a patriarchal medical establishment rather than on the deep pain engendered by infertility, they are influenced by a fundamental conviction that—were it not for patriarchal control of cultural norms—women wouldn't care so much about having children. Even the perseverance of infertile women who undergo heroic measures in order to give birth to children is seen as a sign of perversity and male domination.[19] In dealing with conflicts between individual and familial goals, some feminists take what is at best an ambivalent attitude toward children. Children are not seen as inherently precious individuals or as the source of essential parental delight and faith in the future; they are seen from conception onward as the constraint and burden of a woman's life. The bearing of children is certainly not seen as a religious or moral imperative. In fact, children become—as they have always been for certain callow men—objects, possessions, something to be purchased at the right time, in the right way, and only on our own terms. In such theories, it is children, and not women, who are objectified. Children are the final "other."

Attention to demographic data should not be misconstrued as "blaming the victim." Although statistically age is a factor in female infertility, infertility can and does strike both men and women at any age. Much statistical and anecdotal evidence is available on the incidence of unwanted childlessness afflicting couples of all ages. Ironically, because of today's social environment, friends and relatives often assume that such infertility is deliberate and make insensitive comments ("You're so lucky not to be tied down with children," in the case of friends, and, "When is she going to stop concentrating on her career and have a family?" in the case of potential grandparents).

Many Jewish feminists urge the Jewish community to get more involved in facilitating adoptions and providing emotional support to infertile women. Some also urge Jewish feminism to confront and come to terms with issues of fertility in order to be fair to Jewish women. They say that Jewish women almost universally hope for children—but they are not given all the information they need to enhance their chances to have those children.

Lucy Steinitz, director of Baltimore's Jewish Family Service, experienced infertility herself and adopted two Hispanic children. Steinitz charges:

> The Jewish community is suffering from an epidemic of infertility which has only been acknowledged and dealt with adequately in some locales. Those of us who are not observant have had multiple sexual partners, without ever realizing that asymptomatic, sexually transmitted diseases might affect our fertility some day. . . . Contemporary infertile Jewish women are not about to take no for an answer. We are driven to get what we want out of life, even when it's very hard. And that works well for us—because persistence is the single most important attribute for those who want to succeed at adoption.

The moral responsibility of Jewish feminism to discuss issues of reproduction and infertility is sharply underscored by the fact that Jewish women may have particularistic feelings about infertility. Historical events of the twentieth century—including the Holocaust, in which one million children among six million Jews were slaughtered, together with a strong cultural and religious bias in favor of normative families with children—intensify the painful widespread psychological implications of infertility. Sherry Blumberg shares her bitter experiences as an infertile Jewish woman:

> I am an *akarah,* a barren woman. After three years of the latest modern tests and drugs, of artificial inseminations (using my husband's sperm), of long hours in doctor's offices, of humiliating tests

and frustrated hopes, and of moments of despair, I am still a barren woman. . . . Soon my husband and I will give up the infertility doctors and begin the next frustrating process of adoption. There are few babies, hardly any Jewish babies, and we are too old to go through the normal channels. We will join the many others who look for children with lawyers, doctors, rabbis, and friends. We may have to go to another country. We will spend what we need to spend.[20]

Jewish history and demographics give contemporary Jewish women a special sense of obligation to choose Jewish parenthood. Linda Bayer's *The Blessing and the Curse*, a fictional exploration of fertility issues among Jewish women, underlines the role of the Holocaust in fertility decisions. Three women sit on a bench outside Yad Vashem, the Holocaust memorial in Jerusalem: the protagonist, Ida, who is a childless thirty-nine-year-old-Jewish woman; a nun; and a red-haired Jewish mother of three. They weep, overcome, after seeing photos of some of the children slaughtered by the Nazis. To emphasize the fact that no niche exists within traditional Judaism for a childless life-style, Bayer deliberately places Ida, whose husband has always refused to have children, between the nun, who, unlike Ida, has chosen her childlessness, and the mother of three, who has purposefully contributed to the continuity of the Jewish people. Indeed, a famous Yiddish aphorism states, *By Yiddn zayn nishto keyn nones*, "Jews don't have nuns."[21]

Some Jewish feminists would clearly be more comfortable if the logistic conflict between career accomplishment and fertility were never raised. Historian Paula Hyman has castigated Jewish community leaders who seem to value women more for their reproductive value than for the contribution they *as individuals* can make to the Jewish community.[22] However, without intending to relegate women exclusively to uterine productivity, one must understand that infertility issues have a resonance for contemporary Jewish women and for the Jewish community at large in terms of recent Jewish history, a shrinking American Jewish population, and meaningful Jewish survival.

New styles in family formation have created the necessity for new services to Jewish women who are wrestling with these issues. The best approach may be to advocate for earlier childbearing, whenever possible. Blu Greenberg points out that even without special infertility problems, "by delaying childbirth from the 20s to the 30s, we lose an entire generation every three decades. Career counseling with the Jewish people's needs in mind," she suggests, "would temper feminist claims with Jewish ones; it would enable couples to consider more seriously the option of having children first and then moving on to dual careers."[23] Such counseling may only have an impact when it is made clear that the couple's interests in having a family are at stake. If the needs of the Jewish community are made the primary thrust of such counseling, probably only the family planning decisions of a very small proportion of couples, who already have a highly developed sense of Jewish responsibility and involvement, would be influenced. Nor would such counseling be particularly useful for those women who, through their own choice or not, do not marry until they are in their thirties.

Women who have struggled with infertility report that national organizations such as RESOLVE have proved very useful to many infertile would-be parents, but they do not deal with the specifically Jewish concerns that often arise: On the most basic level, infertile Jewish couples must learn how to cope not only with their own frustrations but also with those of the potential grandparents. Thus they often struggle not only with personal grief but also with feelings of guilt and disappointment having to do with their lack of participation in Jewish physical and spiritual continuity.

Infertile Jewish women speak powerfully about the pain of confronting the "stigma" of "barrenness," which is often seen as punishment. As Sherry Blumberg puts it, "My rational mind says that my feelings are foolish, based on irrational ideas; the traditional materials (such as biblical and rabbinic texts) and rabbis could not have been so unfeeling. But my feelings are my feelings. I feel the pain of emptiness, the despair of wanting to carry out the *mitzvah* (of having children) and not being able. If these feelings are not enough, there are those who say that any couple who does not have at least three children is guilty of addition to the decline of the Jewish population. . . . When I hear that statement, I freeze. I respond with anger, but what I feel is pain."[24]

Jewish teachers, rabbis, caregivers, and communal workers must be sensitive to the needs of infertile clients and congregants. When rabbis and Jewish communal professionals seem insensitive, infertile women sometimes feel that Judaism as a religion and a culture has no place for them, precipitating a crisis in faith. Such reactions can be minimized through alertness to the connotations of language: Adoptive parents feel far more included in Jewish tradition when references to family life speak of "raising children" rather than "bearing children." In addition, couples who are engaged in extensive fertility testing and experimental procedures are often under onerous financial burdens despite their income levels.[25] More Jewish-sponsored aid to adoption would signal community concern for these couples. The most recent surveys of Jewish populations have only begun to ask questions related to adoption, and the exploration of vigorous, creative programming to meet the needs of would-be adoptive parents within the Jewish community is similarly in its infancy.

Unwed motherhood is still rare among American Jewish women. When it does occur, it has little impact on major demographic trends in the Jewish community, because the numbers of children involved are so small. However, Jewish women who choose unwed motherhood are often highly educated and highly motivated individuals. Many of them have a strong Jewish consciousness and strong ties to the Jewish community. The Jewish unwed mother is likely to be a woman in her late thirties who hears her biological clock ticking and chooses to have one child, rather than a teenager who uses birth control only sporadically if at all and has several children by the time she reaches her twenties. Some such unwed mothers live alone; some live with other family members; and some have lesbian companions. Despite the relatively small numbers of children involved, especially in certain communities the phenomenon of Jewish unwed mothers is significant enough to warrant Jewish communal attention. Like a forty-one-year-old Boston executive and unwed mother—by choice—they hope "that the Jewish community will accept me and my little Tamar for what we are—a Jewish mother and her daughter."

Most of the members of the New York chapter of Single Mothers by Choice are Jewish. Many of these women name their children in the synagogue, send the children to Jewish day schools and supplementary schools, and raise the children with a strong Jewish consciousness. Others, however, fearing censure by the Jewish community, hover at the outskirts instead. "If single mothers' ranks keep swelling and if more of them turn to the Jewish community, synagogues and other institutions will have to begin to examine and come to an understanding of this new type of Jewish family," says Ruth Mason, a New York journalist.[26]

When Ida Morgan-Weiss, a fictional divorced heroine, decides in her late thirties to have a child out of wedlock rather than forgo forever the opportunity to be a mother, her own mother is horrified

at the prospect. Significantly, Mother Weiss is not primarily worried
about the social stigma that may accompany her daughter's unwed
childbirth. She worries that her daughter is provoking a possibly
malevolent and envious fate because she is taking her destiny into her
own hands instead of drifting passively, as she thinks women have
always done. Mrs. Weiss voices the opinion that women deserve
only just so much, that they have no right to control their lives so
completely, to flout the rules of society, and to decide for themselves
exactly what they want.[27]

Changing life-styles may be most striking in such phenomena as
the Jewish "Murphy Brown" syndrome, in which Jewish career
women in their thirties and forties decide to bear and raise children
without husbands. But the expectation that women can take charge
of their own destinies, and can combine motherhood with a multifaceted life plan, is not confined to unmarried women—it is typical
of today's married women as well.

Even women happily ensconced in traditional Jewish families have
different values and behaviors than they did twenty-five years ago.
Traditional Jewish families have been radically transformed, partially by the domestication and ubiquitousness of feminist attitudes
and goals among all segments of the American Jewish community—
including those that claim to reject feminism altogether. Contemporary Jewish women tend to have received much more formal
education, both secular and Jewish, than their mothers did, and they
are often consciously concerned with providing for their own interests, needs, and fulfillment. Even when Jewish women may not articulate these goals for themselves, they project them onto their
daughters.

A survey of Jewish and non-Jewish women in the heartland of
America showed that married Jewish women—unlike non-Jewish
ones in their geographical and socioeconomic groups—aimed more
than anything else that their daughters be independent, educated,
assertive, intelligent, and self-sufficient. In a 1985 study of Jewish
and non-Jewish women, conducted by Sid Groeneman for B'nai
B'rith Women, only 22 percent of Jewish women had family-oriented
goals for their daughters, such as wanting them to "have a good
family, husband, marriage, children" or being "loving, caring, good
parents." In contrast, non-Jewish women ranked personal qualities
such as helpfulness, neighborliness, and devotion to family much
higher on their "wish list" for their daughters than did Jewish
women. Although many Jewish women in Middle America did not

see themselves as "feminists," they had clearly absorbed feminist goals, especially when they thought of their daughters' lives.[28]

Focused careers are the goal of many Jewish mothers for their daughters. More than two-thirds (69 percent) of Jewish women wanted their daughters to have qualities that would help them function successfully in the world, such as being "independent, self-reliant, self-sufficient, self-supportive, determined, ambitious, intelligent, knowledgeable, talented, skillful, and creative." Sixty percent or more of Jewish women disagreed with the following statements: (1) "A marriage without any children will normally be incomplete and less satisfying"; (2) When both parents work, the children are more likely to get into trouble"; and (3) "Most women are happiest when making a home and caring for children."[29]

A generation ago many Jewish mothers might have sounded like Grandmother Berg in Marge Piercy's *Small Changes* (1972), who affectionately (!) comments on her granddaughter's fine mind by saying, "You're not pretty, Miriam mine, so you better be smart. But not too smart."[30] They might have behaved like Renee Feuer's mother in Rebecca Goldstein's novel *The Mind-Body Problem* (1983);[31] when Renee achieves Phi Beta Kappa and magna cum laude status at Barnard, her mother sighs sadly, "Nu, Renee, and will this help you find a husband?" When, however, Renee calls from Princeton, where she is pursuing a graduate degree in philosophy, to report that she has become engaged to a Jewish genius, her mother is moved to a rare moment of happiness: "This is why God gave you such good brains, so that you could make such a man like this love you."

A generation ago Jewish mothers were likely to agree with Faith Darwin Asbury's mother in Grace Paley's stories, who was horrified at the idea that her daughter might become an entrepreneur: "Why should you go into business? You could be a social worker for the city. You're very good-hearted, you always worried about the next fellow. You should be a teacher, you could be off in the summer. You could get a counselor job, the children would go to camp."[32]

Today Jewish mothers and daughters agree that their "good brains" should be used and developed on behalf of themselves as well as others. Contemporary Jewish mothers seem to want most for their daughters the freedom to choose the things in life that make them happy and the skills and strength to be able to follow through on their choices. Almost universally Jewish women want their daughters to be able to depend on themselves and to have the self-

confidence to do so. In an interview, novelist Ruth Knafo Setton
expressed the feelings of many:

> Goals for my daughter? Good question. She's a tough, spunky little
> girl and I'm glad. I want her to continue to have the courage to stand
> for her convictions. I want her to continue to be herself, in all its
> complexity—I want her to be proud and not to be afraid. I hope her
> life will fully integrate all the parts of herself—artist, Jew, female,
> mother—whatever she wants to be. I hope the world allows her to. I
> know it won't be easy.

Women like Setton, who is a deeply committed novelist and also
a deeply committed mother, illustrate a pattern of mothering that is
now the norm rather than an aberration. When writer Sylvia Rothchild remembers her own similar life-style decades ago, as she nursed
her babies, wrote, and painted, while most Jewish women around
her devoted themselves to domesticity and voluntarism, she reports
that she felt both "strong" and "isolated." She and women like her
were pioneers, finding ways to be professionals, women, mothers,
and Jews. Today Jewish women pursue many goals but seem to remain passionately involved in mothering.

Jewish women with children—even those with high-powered careers—often block time and plan ahead in excruciating detail to
make sure that their children feel loved, supported, and nurtured.
When teenage or young adult Jewish women speak about their mothers, the old, familiar complaints about "protective" and "overin-
volved" Jewish mothers still prevail. Constellations within family
groupings, however, have often been deeply affected by feminism.
Many young Jewish women speak admiringly of their mothers' professional activities and regard them as role models. Many also speak
about their fathers as active, highly involved—and, yes, overprotec-
tive—parents. Thus feminism does not seem to have lessened the
complexities of the mother-daughter relationship, but it does seem
to have produced a new generation of highly involved Jewish fathers.[33] Moreover, many women agree with Boston Federation professional Susan Ebert that today's Jewish families are likely to
produce "children who respect their mothers' (and fathers') professional commitments and confidence and self-reliance because they
have learned independence early in their lives."[34]

Feminism has changed the division of labor for many (though by
no means all) couples. Jewish couples today seem to regard parent-

hood as a shared responsibility. Even in families in which fathers do not share equally in cleaning, cooking, and shopping tasks, both fathers and mothers report that fathers are very conscious of and conscientious about parenting. The old American Jewish model of the father who is exclusively devoted to breadwinning and the mother who is exclusively devoted to the home often produced households in which the fathers were emotionally absent. Many of today's young fathers bitterly resented their own fathers' absence. Among Jewish parents in their thirties, fathers change diapers, feed infants and toddlers, help with homework, and in general participate as fully as they can in child care on a regular basis. Primary-grade private- and day-school teachers say that a surprising number of fathers show up for class plays and performances and parent-teacher conferences, even during the day. Rather than giving children less parental involvement, feminism has encouraged parental involvement from both genders, rather than primarily from the mother alone.

Jewish women remain, as they have been in the past, intensely aware of and concerned with medical and psychological prescriptions for raising healthy, happy children. However, feminism often gives women the confidence to resist the waves of parental advice books and articles that appear—often with contradictory advice from year to year.[35] Mothers of different ages can recall being told that formula was superior to breast milk—or that only breast feeding babies could produce healthy adults. Some recall being told that picking up a crying baby would destroy the child's nervous and digestive system if it was done more often than on a four-hour schedule; others remember the absolute tyranny of on-demand feeding. Writer and mother Sonia Taitz eloquently expresses the feelings of many Jewish mothers of young children today who have been strengthened by feminism and grown impatient with the dogmatic approach of many experts.[36] "I am the best expert about my own children," Taitz insists, "and you are the best expert about yours."

Some in the Jewish community have speculated that Jewish communal life and especially Jewish family life could be "cured" of all its ills if only women would return to older life-styles and attitudes. Such attitudes are expressed by people who run the gamut from some rather highly placed Jewish scholars and communal leaders to the rank and file. A modern-day Tevye, a middle-aged man with five daughters, attending a panel on Jewish feminism at a Friday-night Oneg Shabbat in St. Louis in 1975, expressed his bewilderment: "I don't understand what this is all about. What do these women want with working and praying and talking all the time?" He paused for a moment and then added, with perfect seriousness, "If they would only be pregnant every other year like our grandmothers were, and peddling fruit on the side, they wouldn't have the time or energy to worry about all this foolishness!"

No aspect of feminism has aroused as much anxiety and debate in the Jewish community as its possible impact on Jewish parenthood. When they think about parenting options, numerous American Jewish women feel caught between two value systems—between feminist directives that give priority to a woman's talents, strengths, and yearnings when she makes decisions, and Jewish directives that give priority to the needs of the family and community first. Unfortunately the easy gloss, "What's good for the woman is good for the family, because a happy woman makes for a happy family," is not always true. When confronting choices in regard to working, beginning or ending marriages, sexual activity, geographical mobility, and other major life decisions, individual women have found that what is greatly advantageous for an individual may be painful or perplexing for the people around her. Conversely, what is good—or at least more convenient—for the family or community may severely constrict her life.

Obviously factors other than feminism have contributed to new trends in family formation. American society places great emphasis on individual fulfillment. It encourages individuals to take charge of their own lives, to consider all the available options, to analyze each decision and discover which choices would bring the greatest personal happiness, and to repeat these analyses throughout one's lifetime. Feminism partakes of these values and extends them to women. The transformed Jewish family—like the transformed American family—has been influenced not only by feminism but by a cultural ethos that stresses individual achievement and pleasure; by materialistic expectations that elevate the perceived standard of what a middle-class life-style comprises; by a tightening economic market requiring dual incomes to maintain such a life-style; by the widespread availability of easily used contraceptive techniques and the accompanying sexual revolution; and by patterns of chronological separation that split families by sending adolescents to far-off university campuses and grandparents to the Sunbelt.

Jewish feminists face the challenge of confronting honestly some of the conflicts between "pure" feminism and Jewish family life.

Many feminists have been resistant to information that doesn't fit a "politically correct" theoretical mold and thus might putatively interfere with "free choice." As a result Jewish women have seldom been provided with the same levels of information about enhancing their chances for Jewish marriages and families as they have with information about enhancing their careers. In contrast, no one thinks that career counseling interferes with choices—quite the contrary.

Many older single Jewish women believe that "good" Jewish men (defined by the women interviewed as "not terribly neurotic," "nice," "men who aren't absorbed in themselves," "caring and sensitive," "*menschen*,") tend to marry relatively early, so that the undergraduate and graduate years would have been prime time for finding appropriate Jewish mates. Women are instructed on the best time to take exams in pre-law and pre-medicine; they know all the pitfalls of bad marriages, but they are given little information on how to form healthy, permanent relationships.

Similarly, infertile Jewish women in their thirties and forties sometimes speak bitterly of lack of information on the possible greater ease of conception earlier in their reproductive lives. Such reflections suggest that women who want to marry and have families as well as to develop themselves in other areas should be given the information that would allow them to pursue these family-related goals as realistically as they do others.

New challenges to family formation are closely tied to two areas of Jewish women's lives that have been transformed by feminism: sexual/gender issues and labor force participation. Significantly, many women feel that feminism, by offering them choices in these areas, has strengthened family life as well. For example, many women speak warmly of the positive impact of feminism on family relationships, particularly its encouragement of men to participate actively and lovingly in their children's lives from infancy onward. Feminism has surely opened up to both men and women the widespread notion of more permeable—and thereby richer and more fulfilling—gender roles.

As one woman with a very demanding career put it, "I don't think the family has to be defined in the same gender-controlled ways as in the past in order to have richness and intimacy. I watch my husband playing with my son and they have a wonderful tenderness with each other. Even within the family structure feminism teaches us to create new kinds of intensity, richness, and supportiveness."

Feminism, with all the increased opportunities it has opened up, has not lessened the intense desire of Jewish women to have families. Indeed most American Jewish women either have children or report that they hope to. Feminism has, however, changed the timing of childbearing and has sometimes complicated the decision to have children. Intermarriage and divorce also frequently complicate the tasks of Jewish parenthood today. Even in inmarried "intact" families, including nondivorced Jewish parents and children, family lifestyles today often differ significantly from those in the past. Although contemporary Jewish women want to choose parenthood perhaps just as much as Jewish women in the past, the households shared by them and their children are yielding new as well as familiar challenges and joys.

Chapter Four

Working, Volunteering, and Jewish Living

"What can I tell you?" she says to me. "Either you were going to make a hell in the house or you were going to be happy. I wanted to be happy. He didn't want me to work. I stopped working."

We are quiet together for a while. Then I say, "Ma, if it was now and Papa said he didn't want you to work, what would you do?"

She looks at me for a long moment. She is eighty years old. Her eyes are dim, her hair is white, her body is frail. She takes a swallow of her tea, puts down her cup, and says calmly, "I'd tell him to go fuck himself."

—Vivian Gornick[1]

FOR MUCH OF JEWISH HISTORY, Jewish women have had responsibilities outside the home. The particular activities encouraged by Jewish society, however, depended a great deal on cultural factors. Today the majority of Jewish women expect to be employed for pay throughout their lives, including during their children's preschool years. This continuing involvement of women in the workplace has caused several types of communal anxiety. Men and women who matured prior to the 1970s, in an American society that put a strong emphasis on the domestic woman as the cornerstone of a wholesome family, often charge that "Jewish women never worked unless they had to" and that current trends toward lifelong employment among

65

women are detrimental to Jewish life. Leaders of Jewish organizations are sometimes convinced that paid employment has robbed
these organizations of many talented volunteers. And proponents of
the "new familism"[2] have charged that American children may suffer neglect and deprivation of crucial informal, home-based early
education because they have working mothers.[3]

Each of these attacks, however, misrepresents the past and mis-
understands the present. Although some insist that the traditional
Jewish mother anchored her family and preserved home life by eschewing money-making activities and focusing exclusively on her
husband and children, Jewish women have worked at nondomestic
tasks both inside and outside the home at many times. Rather than
being a contemporary innovation, working for pay was an accepted
part of the lives of many Jewish women in the past. Unlike the prototype of the shy and sequestered "little woman," which held sway
in Victorian societies, Eastern European Jewish women often had a
"characteristic aggressiveness and marketplace activism,"[4] which
they saw as an intrinsic part of their commitment to family and to
community. In Europe, middle-class as well as impoverished Jewish
women participated in acquiring the livelihood for the household. In
some communities women in elite families were encouraged to take
on this responsibility exclusively, in order to enable their husbands
to devote their time to the study of sacred texts.[5]

A myriad of cultural and historical factors contributed to the tol-
erance shown toward the marketplace activity of women. Jewish
tradition did not set the woman on a pedestal and limit her to maternal tasks. In fact, religious texts depict active, busy women engaged in productive work. Proverbs 31 praises the "Woman of
Valor" who buys fields and has vineyards planted out of her own
earnings. Talmudic commentaries on the proper role for women exhibit a horror of idleness, which was seen as leading only to mischief.
The rabbis assumed that women were diligent and preferred to be
occupied. If a man is so wealthy that his wife has few tasks, they
advise that it is better that she should knit a specific amount each day
rather than be unoccupied. A man may not prevent his wife from
such work no matter how affluent he is. Women so dislike being
unoccupied, the rabbis assert, that when they have nothing else to
do, they will play checkers rather than sit idle. A woman who is
nursing a baby should be assigned a smaller work load. (For women
raising older children, however, no such reductions were deemed
necessary.[6])

Economic realities were certainly a major factor in pushing Jewish women into marketplace activities. European Jews were frequently limited by antisemitic laws to commercial and middleman activities. Even where legal constraints were less onerous, Jews tended toward business enterprises because such activities gave them independence and autonomy. Women's skills were especially useful in family businesses and were fully utilized.

Glückel of Hameln (1646–1724) was one such woman. A middle-class merchant in an import-export business and pious mother of thirteen, Glückel also wrote Yiddish memoirs that have given historians one of the best pictures of the social, economic, and cultural life of Central European Jews during that time.[7] In the twentieth century, Bella Chagall recalls her middle-class mother keeping store in *Burning Lights*,[8] and Chaim Grade elegizes his impoverished mother, who fed her children out of the proceeds from baskets of withered fruit in *My Mother's Sabbath Days*.[9] Many American Jews can recall immigrant grandmothers and aunts who worked as storekeepers or seamstresses, presided over orderly and hospitable homes, and were often the guiding personalities of the household as well.

Ironically, European and immigrant Jewish writers influenced by the Jewish Enlightenment and the ideas of utopian socialist movements, and sympathetic to the plight of Jewish women, often strived to put an end to the marketplace activities of Jewish women. Stories by such writers as I. L. Peretz depict mothers overwhelmed by the burdens of earning a livelihood and raising a family while their husbands devoted themselves to sacred study, seemingly oblivious to the needs of their wives and children.[10] In the eyes of these writers, women were the proletariat of the proletariat, the most oppressed of all groups. They believed that the division of labor would approach fairness only when Jewish mothers were freed of the demands of working and enabled to devote themselves exclusively to domestic labors.

Industrialization increased employment options for women both in Europe and the United States. Before emigration, with the proliferation of factory workplace settings, many young Jewish women found jobs making cigarettes, garments, and other items. Some sewed items by hand, but those who were able to learn how to operate sewing machines were considered fortunate, the elite of the industry, and generally earned higher wages. It is a mark of how accepted marketplace activity was for women—as scholarship was for men—that seamstresses were regarded with great respect among

Eastern European Jews, while tailors were often regarded with humor or even derision.[11] The head start some European Jewish girls and women got in acquiring skills appropriate to the garment industry served them in good stead after they emigrated to the United States.

In the United States, Jewish women actively sought employment outside the home. They became extremely active and influential in some industries, especially the garment industry, because they possessed useful skills and enthusiastic attitudes. As Susan Glenn points out, "Jewish women brought with them a well-developed craft pride and a sense of competence that stood in sharp contrast to the stereotypic images of female workers as insecure, unambitious, and apathetic toward their jobs."[12]

Single women commonly did factory work, while married Jewish women often did piecework at home, laboring long hours at the sewing machine; some took in boarders; some ran dry goods and grocery stores to help support their families. When married women ran stores or took in boarders, however, they often reported to census takers that they did not work—in the minds of such women and their families, "working" implied employment in a factory or other non-household-connected setting.

Indeed, a curious transformation took place in the minds of American Jewish immigrants as regards the propriety of married women working. Within American society, they saw, unemployed married women were accorded great respect as domestic paragons, following the Victorian model of "the angel of the hearth." In non-Jewish, established American culture, women who worked outside the home were the object of pity, their husbands of scorn. A competent husband, it was felt, should earn enough money so that his wife could devote herself to domestic life and need not supplement the household income. This was the inverse of the ingrained Eastern European Jewish attitude, which gave the domestic woman little societal prestige but valued her marketplace activity, which freed her husband and sons for sacred study.

Underscoring this profound change in attitudes toward employed women was the advice in *Sholem Aleykhem tsu Imigranten,* produced in 1903 by established American Jews of German Origin (the Educational Alliance in New York) for their less-acculturated Eastern European immigrant brethren. The piece warned husbands not to "throw the burden of work and worry" on their wives, not to sit "idle" and expect their wives to earn a living. American courts would insist that men fulfill their "duty" to support their families, according to the brochure, and would go so far as to levy a fine on recalcitrant husbands.[13] Such warnings echoed the castigations of the literary *maskilim* (enlightened intellectuals), who had taken Jewish husbands to task for imposing all the burdens of daily life and livelihood on their wives.

In America, immigrants learned, the man who studied and left his wife to earn a household income was regarded as a wastrel. The fiction and memoirs of Anzia Yezierska and other immigrant writers capture the painful and sometimes violent conflicts that developed in families when wives wished their husbands to take on financial responsibility for the family, in the American mode, and husbands wished to continue with their lifelong study or occupation, which had gained them enormous prestige in their communities of origin. When Yezierska, as a child, asked her mother why she could not have birthday parties like the janitor's daughter, for example, her mother instead advised her daughter to weep because she was born: "Have you a father like other fathers? Does his wife or his children lay in his head?" Mother wiped the sweat from her face with a heavy hand. "Woe is me! Your father works for God and His Torah like other fathers work for their wives and children. You ought to light a black candle on your birthday. You ought to lie on your face and cry and curse the day you were born."[14]

Quick to acculturate, Jewish immigrants soon took on labor force participation patterns in which husbands, sons, and daughters worked outside the home but married women were likely to be limited to a home-based or family business. Thus, in 1911, the United States Immigrant Commission reported that 85 percent of Jewish husbands and 36 percent of their children said they were employed; only 8 percent of married Jewish women reported being employed—although 43 percent of them said they took in income from boarders or lodgers. Not all immigrants adopted American ideology so quickly. Married Italian women, in comparison, were more than twice as likely as Jewish women to report employment.[15]

In 1909–10, about two-thirds of the women employed in the garment industry were Jewish; within that industry Jewish women—described with admiration as *vunderbare farbrente meydlekh* (wonderful, fervent girls)—provided the primary leadership and support for the emerging unions, partially because many had brought socialist values as well as work skills with them from Europe and Russia. Newspaper reporters and other observers of the scene described the ferocity and eloquence of the Jewish girls who led the strike of twenty thousand shirtwaist workers on November 22, 1909, as Irving Howe summarizes:

> As the evening dragged along, and speaker followed speaker, there suddenly raced up to the platform, from the depths of the hall, a frail teen-age girl named Clara Lemlich. . . . She burst into a flow of passionate Yiddish which would remain engraved in thousands of memories: "I am a working girl, one of those striking against intolerable conditions. I am tired of listening to speakers who talk in generalities. What we are here for is to decide whether or not to strike. I offer a resolution that a general strike be declared—now. . . ." Thousands of hands went up: "If I turn traitor to the cause I now pledge, may this hand wither from the arm I raise."[16]

Paradoxically in the United States Jewish women had more opportunity for secular education and regular employment than they had in their countries of origin. Thus opportunity beckoned, and economic necessity drew them toward employment while the mores of the country discouraged them from pursuing it. Large numbers of Jewish women, especially unmarried Jewish women, did in fact opt for the world of education and work.

An emphasis on secular education for women is not new in modern Jewish life; there is evidence that levels of literacy among seventeenth- and eighteenth-century Eastern European Jewish women were higher than those in many surrounding societies, and with the coming of the emancipation in the nineteenth century, substantial portions of even pious Jews allowed their daughters to take advantage of educational opportunities. Indeed, in some communities secular education for girls was considered appropriate, while boys were expected to devote themselves to sacred texts.[17]

Nevertheless, rates of secular education for women increased strikingly with emigration to the United States. Even though sons were definitely favored when opportunities for secular education were limited, Jewish women were more likely to receive extended secular education than any other group of women. In New York in 1910, at a time when Jews made up about 19 percent of the population, 40 percent of the women enrolled in night school were Jewish; by 1916, 25 percent of the graduates of Hunter College were Jewish women of Eastern European origins; and by 1934 more than 50 percent of New York female college students were Jewish.[18]

Contemporary American Jewish women enjoy levels of secular education far more advanced than at any other time in Jewish history. More than 25 percent of younger (ages eighteen to forty-four) Jewish women today have earned degrees beyond the bachelor's degree: Twenty percent have M.A.s, and 8 percent have Ph.D.s or professional degrees. Thirty-eight percent have completed their B.A.s, and another 24 percent have attended or are attending college but have not completed their degrees. Only one in ten younger American Jewish women—compared to more than one in three in the older age groups—have not gone beyond high school.

Not only have levels of higher education increased among Jewish women today, but many report that their professors give them more encouragement and guidance than professors were likely to give women decades ago. A woman in her late forties who heads the Health Care Financing Administration in the U.S. Department of Health and Human Services, recalls, "Just before I finished graduate school, a professor warned me I would always lose out to equally qualified men. This is part of my strong drive—in terms of advancement and career, women have to be better." In her case this discouragement actually served to strengthen her resolve. Now a married mother of three grown children, she works from six in the morning until eight each evening, dealing with regulators and policy issues in cooperation with the legislative and executive branches of government and supervising a budget of $140 billion. She notes that the "atmosphere for women has improved, and the number of women working in professional areas with young children is large now. When I started, mothers and other part-time workers were not regarded as serious career players. It is much easier now to sequence and not lose ground."

In the past even highly educated and talented women were far less likely than they are today to focus their energies and use their education on a clearly defined career path. For decades much in the American culture worked to convince women that they could not "have it all," that they must choose between marriage and family on the one hand or work and career on the other. In the early 1900s some women who had attained professional status through the pursuit of education deliberately remained unmarried because they felt that work and family were mutually exclusive. In the 1940s, 1950s, and 1960s, the vast majority of American Jewish women worked only until they married or became pregnant with their first child and then abandoned work for decades.

Indeed, more than any other ethnic group, Jewish women in the 1950s and 1960s were likely to attend and finish college, to enter the workplace in disproportionate numbers in the "helping" professions, such as teaching or social work or in lower-level management—and then to drop out of the labor force when they became pregnant with their first children. Such women were convinced that in devoting themselves to homemaking they were doing the best thing for their husbands and children and behaving like "real Americans." Their husbands were convinced that in discouraging their wives from working, they were giving their families the best opportunities that golden America could offer.

Most Jewish women did not work after marriage unless there was dire financial need. Consequently even women who completed college often had no specific career preparation; the pursuit of a liberal arts degree was used as a kind of intellectual finishing school. If a wife worked it might indicate that her husband was an inadequate provider; therefore even women who were trained as teachers or librarians somehow hesitated to return to the job market. A Jewish communal professional now in her sixties remembers, "My husband pleaded with me not to take the job, even though only a small salary was involved. He said he would be embarrassed in front of his friends. So I didn't, even though it would have given me a lot of pleasure." However, many women admitted in later years that they missed the stimulation and independence they once experienced as working women. As one Jewish homemaker said in an interview when she was over seventy years old: "If a wife worked, the husband couldn't dominate as much as he could with a girl who depended on him for all her income."[19]

The high educational level of Jewish women, before feminism encouraged paid employment, was most often utilized on behalf of voluntarism, especially on behalf of Jewish organizations. Voluntarism by both men and women was important to the Jewish communal world. However, voluntarism by women has historically had particular significance. Women for many decades viewed Jewish voluntarism as "their" Jewish activity, analogous in some ways to men's communal role in the synagogue. They also viewed voluntarism as "their work"—thus as at once a sacred and a secular and often very satisfying activity.

For most of the twentieth century, the health of American Jewish organizational life was greatly enhanced by untold millions of hours of free labor and organizational ability donated by women. Many of these women were relatively highly educated for their socioeconomic and generational status; they had fewer children than their gentile cohort; and, at least from the 1950s until relatively recently, they tended not to work for pay, devoting themselves with professionalism and passion to Jewish organizations.

Any one Jewish woman often participated in several Jewish organizations or causes. Women who volunteered for Hadassah, ORT, Na'amat, Jewish federations, synagogue sisterhoods, and scores of other local, national, and international Jewish organizations did indeed "work for" those organizations, despite the fact they received no remuneration for their efforts. Jewish organizations, for their part, gave Jewish women a religiously and culturally approved, nonthreatening outlet for their intellectual, organizational, and social energies. And because of women's work, Jewish organizations achieved levels of accomplishment that were admired and emulated by many in the non-Jewish world.

The same qualities that might have equipped women for successful paid careers promoted their advancement in the Jewish volunteer arena. Being the national president of Hadassah has much in common with being president of a major corporation. Not only the highest leadership roles in Jewish communal work are analogous to paid employment, but so are lower levels of management. June Sochen comments, "An experienced volunteer in a major social service agency or national Jewish organization would be paid $75,000 a year if she were in private industry."[20]

As Jacqueline Levine, who has served in leadership capacities in a number of major Jewish organizations such as CJF (Council of Jewish Federations and Welfare Funds), NJCRAC (National Jewish Community Relations Advisory Council), and the American Jewish Congress (AJC), accurately puts it: "My husband works professionally for pay. I work professionally not for pay." Her lively, politically astute, and self-confident nature made her a leader almost from the beginning of her involvement. When she was twenty-eight years old, her second child had just been born and she had received her B.A. from Bryn Mawr. Levine recalls:

> One day my husband came home from work and saw me sitting and reading a newspaper. "What are you going to do with your brains and your talent?" he said to me. I started to look for organizations which were doing what I considered meaningful, political work. I got in-

volved with the American Jewish Congress because they were actively
fighting against Senator Joe McCarthy. I soon moved into leadership
positions. I led the American Jewish Congress in the civil rights march
in Selma. I went to every march against the war in Vietnam from 1963
on. I picketed against the anti-Israel mural in the United Nations Pa-
vilion in 1964, and I was arrested for that—I went to jail with Theo-
dore Bikel. Not bad!

For women who have been aristocrats in the world of Jewish organizational work, and for hundreds of thousands of Jewish women
who worked many hours each week in the lower echelons of Jewish
organizations as well, such work was truly their life's vocation.

Anecdotal evidence reveals that, for many Jewish women, meetings and other activities held on behalf of synagogues, schools, and
other Jewish organizations provided a chance to get out of the house
and to socialize with like-minded women, as well as to engage in
good works. The important role these organizations played in the
social, cultural, and religious lives of American Jewish women is
amply attested to by veteran volunteers, who describe not only hours
of hard work but also hours of friendship, plans mapped out and
goals attained, and warm feelings of accomplishment. Even such rote
and labor-intensive tasks as preparing mailings and organizing bake
and rummage sales could be experienced as enjoyable and worth-
while in such a context.

Female volunteers often worked for many years for the Jewish
organizations of their choice, beginning with pedestrian tasks early
in their organizational "careers" and proceeding up the ranks to
more challenging and responsible positions as they gained experience and became more affluent. In many Jewish organizations the
most common pattern for Jewish volunteers was that positions of
power and prestige went to those who were able to (and did) donate
substantial amounts of money and who had worked for years as foot
soldiers for the cause. In other organizations, such as synagogue sisterhoods or school parent-teacher associations, however, hard work
and competence were often more significant factors than affluence,
and even Jewish women of modest means could, with diligence and
dedication, attain leadership positions. These positions, in addition
to providing satisfaction, were often an avenue to communal prestige. Thus for many decades Jewish institutions and organizations
thrived along with their female volunteers.

* * *

Feminist attitudes toward traditional female activities and trans-formed life-styles have changed this pattern. In the 1960s and 1970s female voluntarism came under the critical scrutiny of the feminist movement. To some feminist critics, voluntarism was a subterfuge, an escape from the emptiness of the homemaker's existence. The female volunteer was denigrated as a mere pawn, an unpaid slave laborer who made it possible for paid male organizational employ-ees to achieve their goals. Not only did male communal professionals exploit the labor of female volunteers, feminists charged, but even male volunteers were culpable: Male but not female volunteers had the opportunity to rise through the ranks to decision-making posi-tions of prestige and power, while women were contained in low-ranking, powerless organizational ghettoes. Furthermore, those women who did enter Jewish communal work professionally were kept in the most subordinate, least lucrative slots, while their male counterparts rose to executive posts.[21]

One of the most critical and articulate observers of voluntarism among Jewish women was Doris Gold, now a publisher of feminist books, many on Jewish topics. Gold lambasted a system that ex-ploited "more than a million volunteers who 'work' for no pay at all—a virtual underground of antlike burrowers in our social welfare institutions." Calling female voluntarism "pseudowork," Gold won-dered, "Why have trained, educated 'aware' women opted for vol-untarism, instead of structured work or creativity, during or after childbearing years?"[22] Similarly, in "The Sheltered Workshop," Aviva Cantor asserted that Jewish organizational work was nothing more than "a placebo" or "a distorted form of occupational ther-apy," designed to keep Jewish women "busy with trivia and involved with a lot of time-consuming activities."[23]

Such characterizations of women's Jewish organizational activity do not match the way the participants experience it. Many lifelong activists in the Jewish communal world have charged that feminism, by pushing Jewish women into the paid work force, and through its strong critique of voluntarism per se, has discouraged younger gen-erations of women from volunteering for Jewish organizations. "These young Jewish women work and don't give us any time," they assert. However, research contradicts speculations that the return of Jewish women to a more active, lifelong role in the labor force has a negative impact on women's desire to volunteer for Jewish organi-zations. Contrary to popular assumptions, full-time homemakers and unemployed women are not the most likely to volunteer, and full-time labor force participants are not the least likely. Instead part-time workers are the most likely to volunteer for Jewish causes (32 percent), rather than women who called themselves homemakers (21 percent), students (13 percent), full-time workers (18 percent), or retired or unemployed (27 percent).

Despite widespread anxiety about the impact of higher education and careerism upon the communal activities of American Jewish women today and tomorrow, high levels of educational and occupational accomplishment are not contradictory to Jewish communal life. In fact low levels of participation in Jewish communal causes are found among Jewish women who have generally weak ties to the Jewish community. To put the matter in the simplest terms: The "enemy" of women's vibrant involvement in American Jewish communal life is not higher education or careerist aspirations. Rather, it is a weak Jewish life in other areas as well—social, cultural, and religious—regardless of educational or occupational profile.

Perhaps the most definitive outcome of the organizational profile of American Jewish women is that mixed marriage—rather than education, occupation, age, presence of children in the home, or any other factor—marks the single greatest difference in levels of voluntarism for Jewish causes. Jewish women who are married to non-Jewish men have drastically lower rates of voluntarism for Jewish causes than other married Jewish women: Only 6 percent of born-Jewish women married to non-Jewish men volunteer any time for Jewish causes—compared to one-third of Jewish women married to Jewish men (either born Jews or converts) and more than half of women who are themselves Jews by choice. The differences in voluntarism between inmarried and mixed-married women are even more dramatic among younger American Jewish women, age forty-four and under: Five percent of young mixed-married Jewish women volunteer for Jewish organizations, compared to 42 percent of Jewish women who are married to Jewish men.

The women who now most frequently volunteer for Jewish organizations are married women age forty-four or under living in in-married and conversionary Jewish households. The prevalence of mixed marriage, rather than raising rates of careerism, provides the greatest single challenge to levels of Jewish voluntarism and is the most significant factor contributing to perceptions of inadequate voluntarism among younger women. Those who are critical of the phenomenon of working Jewish mothers have sometimes charged that careerism leads women away from a Jewish social life—and ultimately away from Jewish involvements. Friendship circles are a very significant factor in whether or not Jewish women volunteer for Jewish causes. Women who do not have predominantly Jewish friendship circles are far less likely to volunteer than those who do. Jewish women who say that none of their best friends are Jewish almost never volunteer for Jewish causes, although 40 percent of them volunteer for non-Jewish causes only. Thirteen percent of Jewish women who have some Jewish friends volunteer for Jewish causes, and 40 percent volunteer for non-Jewish causes only. Among Jewish women who have mostly Jewish friends, however, 35 percent volunteer for Jewish causes and 19 percent volunteer for only non-Jewish causes.

In the past popular impressions were that the most traditional Jewish women would be at home with their children and have predominantly Jewish friendship circles, while less traditional Jewish women would work outside the home for pay and have more non-Jewish friends, presumably people they may have met at work. However, data on American Jewish women aged eighteen to forty-four does not support these stereotypes. The religious makeup of women's friendship circles is not dependent on employment status. Within each of these groups, between half and two-thirds of the women are employed either full- or part-time for pay. Indeed, labor force status remains relatively similar from volunteer group to volunteer group within each group of friendship-circle types. Among women who have no Jewish friends, 48 to 55 percent work; among women who have some Jewish friends, 61 percent to 66 percent work; and among women who have mostly Jewish friends, 48 percent to 57 percent work.

Feminism has not driven women away from Jewish organizations and friends, but it has profoundly changed the attitudes of women toward the choices they can make about the uses of their education and time. The nature of voluntarism has also changed as a result. Volunteering for Jewish organizations used to be the one outside activity allowed women. Now that they can choose to work for pay, to volunteer, or both, they often look for different emotional rewards than women did decades ago. Few women today join and work for half a dozen Jewish organizations; they are far more likely to choose one or two that have special meaning for them. Contemporary volunteers for Jewish causes often say they like to work for causes that make good use of their talents. A lawyer enjoys using her legal skills for Jewish causes, a writer her writing skills. Highly educated women working in professional capacities are often unwilling to enter the volunteer realm as "privates" and often expect to go directly into leadership positions instead. It is harder to find women to prepare mailings and participate in bake and rummage sales but easier to find volunteers who can deliver a stimulating class or lecture. They expect the causes they work for to be considerate of their time constraints and special needs; many ask that meetings be held during the evening. If meetings are held on weekends, they often ask that child care be provided on site, because, as one working woman puts it, "On Sunday afternoons I don't want to drive away from home and leave my toddlers with a baby-sitter yet again, as I must do all week long."

Feminism made women aware that they need not fear the world of paid employment, so long portrayed as "the jungle out there" in contrast to the supposedly safe haven of home life. Feminism insisted that, given appropriate education, savvy, and courage, women could take their place in every occupational realm. Jewish women, partially because they were among the most highly educated American women,[24] and partially because they came from a culture that in other historical periods had supported their marketplace activities, were predisposed to take advantage of growing opportunities for women.

In the past women often did not take their own potential seriously. They were unlikely to plan their education so that it could open up career paths for them. As one woman recalls, "I didn't take myself seriously. I didn't think much about careers. I would have gotten a liberal arts degree and would have taken more math. I was good in math and physics. Maybe a career in neuropsychology. I was hired as a 'girl Friday'—male counterparts were hired as account executive trainees. There was little mobility for women. I didn't realize it at the time but I had 'been had.' " Even those who earned higher degrees often were not aggressive enough to rise within their fields.

One of the most ubiquitous experiences of older Jewish women who worked when paid employment for women was less common was that they felt grateful for what were in essence exploitative situations. Entire generations of older working Jewish women can relate to Gladys Rosen's rueful recollection: "When I was a young married woman with small children at home, I was thrilled that anyone would give me a chance to work. I was grateful to be exploited—

and Jewish institutions had no qualms about exploiting Jewish women." At a time when the presence of women in esoteric fields of Jewish scholarship was very unusual, Rosen wrote a distinguished doctoral dissertation on Arabic-Jewish literature, entitled "The Samaritan Commentary of Meshalma Ibn Murjan: The Joseph Cycle," completed in 1948 at Columbia University's Department of Semitic Languages and Literature. She taught at Brooklyn College and Rutgers University before her children were born. While raising her family, despite the self-admitted naïveté with which she approached salary and benefits negotiations, she established a solid, impressive career in Jewish communal life, serving for decades in research and administrative capacities in the offices of J.T.S. and the American Jewish Committee. Now in semiretirement, Rosen is quick to point out that today young women with her education, talents, discipline, and drive would make very different demands and decisions.

Today's striking levels of higher education for Jewish women translate into shifting occupational profiles. The vast majority of Jewish college women today assume that they will be working for most of their lives. They plan and educate themselves to work; the days when college functioned as a kind of intellectual finishing school or exclusively as a preparation for intelligent motherhood seem to be past. Moreover, Jewish college women not only take for granted that they will work, they often assume that they have the right to choose and prepare themselves for work that will bring them maximum emotional and financial compensation. Thus it is not at all unusual for middle-class Jewish college women to be directly ambitious for themselves, where they once would have been ambitious for their husbands and only vicariously for themselves ("behind every great man . . .").

This ambition is reflected in the large numbers of Jewish women currently enrolled in professional programs. Silberman, for example, reports that "a 1980 national survey of first-year college students taken by the American Council on Education found that nine percent of Jewish women were planning to be lawyers—up from two percent in 1969. The proportion planning a career in business management increased by the same amount, and the number planning to be doctors tripled, from two percent to six percent. In this same period the number of Jewish women planning to be elementary school teachers dropped . . . from 18 percent in 1969 to six percent in 1980; those choosing secondary school teaching plummeted from 12 percent to only one percent."[25]

Nearly 40 percent of contemporary wage-earning American Jewish women who fall into the following categories—childless women, mothers with children aged eighteen or under, and women aged forty-four and under—are employed in professional capacities. Indeed, viewing Jewish women by family formation, and moving from the more mature to the youngest family groupings, the data indicate a dramatic decline in employment in clerical and technical capacities and a corresponding increase in those employed in professional capacities.

Employment in the generally more lucrative high-status professions, which have been accessible to women for the shortest period of time (physicians and dentists, lawyers and judges, professors, senior systems analysts, executive positions, etc.), increases from only 7 percent of Jewish women with children nineteen and over to 11 percent of women with children eighteen and under and 15 percent of women who have not yet had children. Employment in the helping professions (teachers below the college level, social workers, librarians, middle-level engineers and programmers, nurses, etc.), many of which require master's degrees but are not usually as lucrative as the high-status professions, increases from 16 percent of women with children aged nineteen and over to 28 percent of women with children aged eighteen and under, and declines slightly among women with no children (24 percent); this decline may be significant, because teaching, social work, librarianship, and nursing have traditionally been considered "women's professions," and the first two especially have historically been favored by American Jewish women. While the percentages of women employed in managerial or service positions remain stable from one family grouping to another, women with children aged 19 or over are far more likely to be employed in clerical or technical positions—56 percent—than women with children aged eighteen or under—37 percent.

Today college-age Jewish women often take the broad variety of professional opportunities available to them very much as a matter of course. Ironically many young women seem unaware of how much feminism has expanded their options. For example, an attractive and exquisitely dressed and groomed Jewish woman in her senior year at an Ivy League university insists, "I'm not a feminist!" She comments casually that her father owns a chain of retail stores. When asked about her career plans, she smiles. "I'm premed, and I'm not ashamed to say that I'm in the top 10 percent of my class. Now I have to choose between medical schools associated with New York

University and Washington University, in St. Louis." She plays with the heavy gold bracelet at her wrist. "It depends partially on where my boyfriend decides to go to law school. He's choosing between N.Y.U. and Ann Arbor [Michigan]. We've been living together for the past year. We've talked about marriage, and I'd rather not do a long-distance romance just now, but I'm not willing to compromise on my medical education either. So we'll just have to play it by ear."

Four decades ago college women with similar socioeconomic profiles almost never subjected themselves to grueling years of law school, medical school, or Ph.D. programs; for that matter, they were unlikely to be openly living with their college sweethearts, and they were extremely unlikely to entertain the idea of jeopardizing a promising romantic involvement by attending school half a continent away from a potential spouse. The intensity with which Jewish women pursued the goal of a secure marriage even as they acquired a higher education is satirized in Herman Wouk's *Marjorie Morningstar* (1955), when playwright Noel Airman dismisses the sincerity of Jewish women who say they want careers: "She'll tell you the hell with that domestic dullness, never for her. She's going to paint, that's what—or be a social worker, or psychiatrist, or an interior decorator, or an actress." However, says Airman, all this talk is just for show. "They're all married now—to dentists, doctors, woolen manufacturers, lawyers, whatever you please."[26]

Philip Roth puts wealthy Jewish college women in the worst possible light in his portrayal of Brenda Patimkin, heiress to Patimkin Plumbing (*Goodbye, Columbus*, 1959), who declares that she need not get a job because "Daddy could live off the stocks alone." That said, it should be noted that certain of Brenda's attitudes were actually quite common among middle- and upper-middle-class Jewish women in the 1950s and early 1960s. Jewish women—especially those in "comfortable" financial circumstances—assumed that any job training they acquired in the course of a college education would be used primarily in the brief number of years before they married and started a family. Jewish women were told that job training was also a good idea "just in case," as a kind of insurance policy against some future catastrophe. Few such women, however, assumed that they would spend the majority of their adult years in the work force. As a result, few planned coherently for meaningful labor force participation—and their lack of vocational training, conversely, reinforced their disinclination to return to paid employment.

Until very recently Jewish women were distinguished by the impact of family on their work lives—a pronounced plummeting pattern of their participation in the labor force. In 1957 only 12 percent of Jewish women with children under six worked outside the home, compared to 18 percent of white Protestants. As recently as fifteen years ago, it was true that Jewish women were likely to work until they became pregnant with their first child, and then to drop out of the labor force until their youngest child was about junior high school age.

Economist Barry Chiswick suggests that elevated rates of higher education among American Jewish women, coupled with their low rates of labor force participation, were instrumental for decades in producing generations of successful children. According to Chiswick, highly educated Jewish women became intelligent mothers who provided exceptionally nurturing and stable home lives for their developing children. He asserts that this arrangement was very effective in terms of economics because the financial and social benefits of higher education for women were thus always passed on to the next generation. The daughters involved would, like their mothers, plow their educational achievements back into the family unit.[27]

Feminism and other social and economic factors have ensured that American Jewish women today are much more likely to be paid employees than they were at midcentury, and the majority of them continue to work for pay outside the home throughout their childbearing and child-rearing years. Among contemporary married Jewish women, 56 percent work for pay (44 percent work part-time, and another 12 percent work full-time), one-quarter call themselves full-time homemakers, and 18 percent are unemployed or retired. Among Jewish women aged forty-four and under, 70 percent work for pay (59 percent work full-time, and another 11 percent work part-time), only 17 percent are homemakers, 11 percent are students, and 4 percent are not employed (1990 NJPS Jewish female respondents). Today women's labor force participation departs radically from patterns of the recent past. In most cities the majority of Jewish mothers continue to work even when their children are quite young. In Boston, Baltimore, San Francisco, and Washington, three out of every five Jewish mothers of preschool children are working.

The ubiquitousness of the working Jewish mother—one of the most concrete results of feminism—can be examined by looking at age group and comparing it with earlier data. In the 1975 Boston study, the labor force participation of Jewish women dipped lower than any other white ethnic group during the childbearing years. Among women, the number of working Boston Jewish women aged thirty to thirty-nine in 1975, fell to 42 percent, compared to about half of white Protestants, Irish Catholics, and Italian Catholics. Past forty, the percentage of Boston Jewish women at work soared higher than any other subgroup, with almost three-quarters of Jewish women in the labor force. In contrast the participation of other white cohorts, which tend to have longer childbearing spans, rose only modestly from the thirty-to-thirty-nine cohort to the forty-to-forty-nine cohort.[28] Data from the 1985 demographic study of the Boston Jewish population show a very different picture. The majority of Jewish women in every age group except for those over age sixty-five are employed, and the younger the age group, the more likely they are to be employed. Only about one-third of Boston Jewish women in the two age groups most likely to have young or school-age families— thirty to thirty-nine and forty to forty-nine—are not employed.

In addition to feminism, perceived economic need strongly encourages a large proportion of Jewish women to work outside the home. As has been widely demonstrated in the general American population, for middle-class families today, two incomes are often needed in order to attain and maintain a middle-class standard of living: that is, purchase of a single-family home in a desirable location, relatively new automobiles and major appliances, attractive educational options for one's children, including college and possibly private and/or graduate school, and summer camp and vacation options. It is also true that perceptions of what makes up a middle-class life-style have been significantly revised upward, so that more income is needed by "middle-class" families. These factors are especially significant for American Jewish families, who have traditionally had a strong ethic of providing their children with "everything."[29]

The emotional environment surrounding working women has changed significantly, and these changes have made an enormous difference. Younger women are likely to be surrounded by peer groups which urge them to work, rather than to become homemakers. They have matured with a feminist ethos that is more likely to make the nonworking wife feel defensive; among women forty and under, especially those who live in cities that have a strongly career-oriented atmosphere, even women with young children often complain that they are made to feel inadequate if they are not pursuing careers at the same time that they are raising their families. For them feminism has often seemed to mean not increased choices but a lack of respect for the choices they have made.

A significant majority of Jewish women, however, have begun to buck the tide of careerism, when they are financially able, and to devote themselves exclusively to family when their children are very young. These mothers have chosen to use the teachings of "sequencing"[30] rather than those of "juggling."[31] One such woman states, "I only have one child, and she is only going to be young a very short time. I was a successful career woman for a long time. I didn't give birth to my daughter until I was forty. I really enjoyed working, and I'm sure that in a few years—probably when she starts first grade—I'll go back to work. But in the meantime I'm enjoying this part of her life, when she really wants me to be near her. I can join her at nursery school plays, and share the progress that she makes. And I don't think there's any substitute for unplanned time together."

Other mothers agree, even when their financial status is not secure. "There's only one kind of quality time between parents and children, to my way of thinking, and that's the quality that emerges spontaneously from quantity time," says a woman who temporarily dropped scientific research work—for which her Ph.D. in biochemistry had equipped her—during her three children's infancies and toddler years. She and her husband, an engineer, endured ongoing financial struggles to maintain their household at the fringes of an affluent Boston suburban neighborhood. "I'd rather do without physical things, I'd rather strip the walls and paint them myself, than give up the early childhood of my children," she comments.

Such mothers often knowingly sacrifice career advancement as well as financial reward. "When I did my graduate degree at Brandeis," she recalls, "we were taught that science was our highest moral responsibility and commitment. I think my professors would have been horrified to see that I had a more important 'mistress' than science. I know that even though I will certainly go back to research, my career will never be the same. But I have the right to make this choice. And I don't think that anything in the world is more important to me than the healthy development of my children as Jews and as human beings. No one can do these things better than I can."

Just as mothers who stay home to raise their children sometimes feel that women who work outside the home do not respect their choices, mothers who juggle paid employment often feel that full-time mothers treat them with open hostility. As a teacher and mother of three commented, "Women have yet to learn to be nice to other women. There's still a war on! We care about our families and our children and the Jewish community as much as they do." The healthy development of children, both as human beings and as Jews, and the maintenance of strong Jewish marriages are probably the two major areas of concern to Jewish mothers—as well as to Jewish policymakers and planners—when they appraise the contemporary dual-income marriage. The attempt at this fusion has long historical antecedents in the Jewish family. Connections between work and family were the norm in many traditional Jewish families. In contemporary times, while some women reject traditional family life in the single-minded pursuit of a career, research has repeatedly shown that the vast majority of Jewish women want to have both careers and families. Indeed, unlike other religious and ethnic groups, Jewish women with extensive higher education and high-powered careers are likely to want as many or more children as the less educated Jewish women of a similar age.[32] Moreover, many Jewish women feel their familial and professional interests to be organically related. It is these women who are most likely to state that their traditional orientation helps them to balance dual responsibilities.[33]

Nonetheless a certain level of conflict is an intrinsic part of the context of their lives. Rabbi Lenore Bohm ruefully describes her toddler saying, "Don't you want to put your play clothes on?" when she sees her dressed in a suit. Bohm's feelings at such moments are shared by many professional Jewish women who are equally committed to their families and their vocations.

"My daughter is four years old now," says Professor Elissa New. "She was born when I was writing my dissertation, and she's gone through her infancy with a mother whose mind often drifts to literary ideas even when I'm supposed to be building Legos with her or paying attention to Kermit the Frog. She always knows when that happens, too. 'Mommy, stop thinking about work,' she'll say to me. She takes my face in her hands. Sometimes she comes into my study. 'Mommy, turn off the puter.' On the other hand, I'm already a role model for her, and that's very nice," says New. "She comes to school with me and meets my students. She's proud of me. I like that."

The conflict between career and family comes into play not only with children but earlier, with husbands. One woman recalls that in the early years of their marriage:

My husband's role in the home was more traditional than I would have liked. I spent many years battling with him. Actually, he does more than my father ever did—but not as much as other men I know. I still do all the cooking and cleaning—I've given up on fighting about those things because it's just easier to do them myself, although he's wonderful with our daughter and takes an absolutely equal role in child care.

Compromise and mutual supportiveness is typical of working families that work it all out: Things are often less than perfect, but both spouses are firmly committed to their relationship and to their children, so they compromise, roll with the punches, and usually emerge with arrangements that are satisfactory for them both. In a study of nearly five hundred married dual career couples, researchers discovered that the husband's character is the key to a successful dual-career marriage:

"The more supportive a husband is and the more supportive his wife perceives him to be, the higher the marital quality experienced by his wife." Examining the impact of "competitiveness, balance, gender-role identity, and support," these researchers found that:

By far the most important factor affecting husbands' perceived marital quality is sensitivity. The stronger his sensitivity, the more positive his perceived marital quality. The wife's perceived marital quality also rises with the increase in the husband's sensitivity. . . . The contemporary marriage is based on the emotional attachment of two persons, and that attachment is expressed by giving and receiving emotional support. People who lack the ability to form emotional attachments by expressing love and support obviously will experience a lower-quality marital relationship than people who have that ability.[34]

Some contemporary American Jewish women actually use the ritual gender divisions of traditional Jewish life as a means of balancing their marital relationships. "I have a much more forced personality than my husband," admits a Jewish communal professional, "and my career has taken a much more public turn than his. Although he makes twice as much money as I do, I'm in the public eye constantly. So I consciously play a supportive role in the household and encourage him to do all the traditional male Jewish things that establish him as king of the household. I know women who alternate with their husbands on reciting the *kiddush* over wine or the *motzi* over bread on Friday night, but I think it's better for our relationship and better for the kids too that my husband reigns in the religious realm."

One suspects that Jewish women historically have often engaged in such sometimes semiconscious balancing acts in order to preserve the emotional harmony, the *shalom bayit* of their households. It has been pointed out, for example, that in the *shtetl* women were hardly docile, ornamental flowers. They often managed "the fiscal affairs of the family. . . . The earning of a livelihood is sexless, and the large majority of women . . . participate in some gainful employment." Furthermore women were expected to voice their opinions far more boisterously than men both in the marketplace and at home. However, in such homes men were established as the rulers of their households in no small part by their exclusive gendered roles in Jewish ritual.[35]

Despite the historical precedents of Jewish husbands and wives sharing wage-earning responsibilities, today's younger dual-career couples face a new set of problems. Sheila Kamerman notes that in the past even working women "shaped and fitted their work around their families and their family responsibilities while men have shaped and fitted their families around their work and job demands. Some of the tensions now emerging are a consequence of some women adopting men's attitudes and behavior, while others are insisting that some modification is required of both men and women if the goal is for individual, family and child wellbeing."[36]

For Jewish couples who married before the impact of women's liberation, there was almost always a commitment to the primacy of the family. They did not wonder whether or not to have children, and postponement of the first child was likely to depend on the father's career—as many couples waited until the conclusion of a residency or other professional training—rather than the mother's. For those older dual-career couples, the difficulties were those of pioneers: trying to work out their own family arrangements in a society that operated on the assumption of clearly defined gender roles; facing down the disapproval of family and friends; overcoming skepticism on the job. An educational psychologist remembers that when she pursued educational goals in the 1960s in Detroit, she "felt like an iconoclast." Ironically the women who were "high school stars" now "live pedestrian lives," she says, while those who, like herself, were "willing to venture greater risks have often created interesting careers for themselves."

As a result of perceived disapproval of high-powered women, veterans of the business world often describe their careful attention to just the "right" feminine appearance. A woman who began her career decades ago by volunteering for B'nai B'rith and for political campaigns remarks that she was always careful to look feminine but not seductive. She founded an ad agency and public relations firm in 1966, which has grown into one of the most successful such enterprises in the Baltimore area. Now she recalls, "Women in business used to be a no-no. I had to be different than males in the way I looked—but similar in attitudes. I wore a hat and gloves—but acted like a man in the boardroom. I spent a lot of time listening. I was very well prepared and researched—but not pushy or assertive. Men sometimes used to be put off by women. Now there is lots of competition."

Today Jewish community disapproval is no longer a salient factor in a woman's decision whether or not to work. A recent survey found that only one-third of Jewish women currently believe that nonworking women make better mothers than women who work; while close to one-half of non-Jewish women think that working women are less effective mothers and that children are more likely to get into trouble when both parents work.[37] Couples now deciding to have children must face an entirely different set of psychological barriers. Rather than worrying about communal disapproval if working mothers decide to continue working, many are anxious about employer and peer group disapproval if they curtail their working hours and career advancement to make time for child care. Contemporary values—which emphasize holding a stimulating job, personal development and growth, and experiencing many of the pleasures of an open and vital society—make the decision to begin or enlarge a family a difficult one.[38]

Childless women who have devoted many years to higher education and professional training and then to establishing careers are often torn by conflicting desires. As they edge into their thirties and beyond, many long for a child but worry that the limitations imposed by pregnancies and maternity leaves will stunt their professional growth. Most are less willing than earlier working women to fall back temporarily on part-time or free-lance work and to risk jeopardizing career advancement.[39] In Baltimore, for example, more than half of married Jewish women who haven't yet had children are professionals, compared to one-third of the women with children at home and fewer than one-quarter of women with grown children. Again, women alone are not responsible for these decisions: Many potential fathers, too, are concerned that children will dramatically —and unpleasantly—change a very pleasant dual-career life-style by limiting their freedoms, diminishing their financial status, and imposing on them a portion of child care and family-related household tasks.[40]

Despite the problems associated with balancing the demands of family and career, many women find that that blend leads to general feelings of happiness, satisfaction, and fulfillment. The great majority of Jewish career women with large families studied were pleased with their lives on both a personal and a professional level. Almost 85 percent felt they were "successful" or "very successful" at child rearing; three-quarters described themselves as personally "extremely satisfied" or "very much satisfied"; and more than 80 percent said they were "successful" or "very successful" at work.[41] In the daily lives of such women, feminism is often practically combined with deep emotional ties to Jewish values. While some have attempted to identify the dual-career couple with an assimilationist, "egalitarian" family mode,[42] many of the women who aspire to combine work and motherhood are more committed Jewishly than either men or stay-at-home mothers.[43]

Dual-career couples today are the predominant group among young and middle-aged families in every wing of American Judaism. Many are deeply committed to Jewish life. Such women say that their Jewish values and life-styles have enhanced familial devotion, stability, and structure, and increased the family's ability to weather dual-career stresses and strains. However, some say that the Jewish community, which supposedly wants to strengthen families and encourage larger families, is not doing its part. They feel that the local Jewish community is sadly failing dual-career families. They voice the complaint that "the Jewish community is urging us to have more children, but it isn't willing to help us meet the cost." The area of largest dissatisfaction is that of day care and Jewish education. Mothers of young children complain bitterly about the lack of Jewish day-care centers. "Children should be raised in a Jewish environment, and day care is part of that," said one. Others complain that Hebrew schools, day schools, and Jewish camps are unwilling to lower tuition fees for large Jewish families unless their income is very low. They assert that Jewish organizations retain the attitude that Jewish women should have more children *and* that Jewish women should bear the financial and psychological burden of raising them.[44]

Many women reject the notion that they are uniquely responsible for the well-being of their households; rather, they seek to share responsibility for that sphere with husbands, paid household help, and family-support institutions. Dual-career families often find the most enduring difficulty lies in obtaining practical help: sitters, transportation, household help. Families cope with these difficulties by carefully scheduling activities and by creating living arrangements that best facilitate meeting the responsibilities of work and family life. One Jewish communal professional reports, "It tends to be a gender issue in terms of thinking about it." She "feels resentful, even though he was fairly equal, that I have to be the one to think about it. I have to be aware and plan. Men tend to take care of themselves. Women take care of the family and household." Their success in accomplishing these goals depends not only on their own intellectual, emotional, and physical resources but also on those of their marital partners. The pleasure of independence can often be offset by the discord that may result when a husband is angry and resentful about these changes and takes out his feelings on his wife and children.[45]

The stress of graduate education, followed by careerist life-styles when they are embarked upon after marital patterns are already established, can be contributing factors to marital unrest. A husband's unwillingness to support his wife's career with practical help in the house can be a factor in such breakups. One divorced woman remembers that when her children were young, her "first husband had almost no role in the home. It was certainly a major factor in our divorce." She confesses that she "marvels at the young mothers on the staff—I don't know how they do it." Indeed, many divorced Jewish women report that their ex-husbands resented their career ambitions. Another woman, who heads a Jewish institution of higher education, laughingly typifies her ex-husband's role in the home as: "King! Lord of the manor! Dominant! I used to ask my husband's permission to go places, to please watch the children. Occasionally he did it. When I was working and going to school he wasn't supportive in the home, but he put a good face on to the world. He always talked about 'obligations' and 'responsibilities.' "

Sometimes the birth of children is the additional stress factor that splits a relationship apart. A female rabbi recalls, "I wanted to be well established before my children were born. I was a rabbi for six years before they were born. I waited for Hillel to develop a reasonable maternity leave policy. My eight-year-old boy used to think all mothers were rabbis. My children loved being the rabbi's kids at Hillel, but it created tension between me and my husband—I was out a lot. My husband told my son I worked more than other moms worked." She says that after her husband's departure she had to face many "sore questions." She thinks her ex-husband would say "a lot of it had to do with my career." She disagrees: "I would never have chosen a career that made a marriage impossible. He was accommodating but didn't share my passion for Judaism. He resented my work schedule. This has meant the end of a twenty-year relationship. My son said, 'God wants Mom to keep kosher, but God doesn't care what Dad and I do.'"

Husbands with traditional attitudes toward gender roles often provoke guilt feelings as well as resentment in their wives. The director of a Jewish education agency talks about the conflicts that rocked her marriage and still trouble her as she tries to find room for all the difference pieces of her life: "My husband was very traditional. We didn't share housework. He remarried and divorced. I'm always pulled and have always been pulled. The worst stress is finding time to study, which always looks like extra. I always make sure to have fixed time to study three to four hours a week—speak Hebrew, Bible with Rashi [leading commentator on the Bible, 1040–1105 C.E., Troyes, France], with a teacher."

Many women whose marriages have come apart regret that they did not put career goals first. One says, "I should have finished school and gotten my doctorate before marriage. On the other hand at forty my kids were big, I had a good job and one master's. I was still a kid when I had and raised my kids. I would have been a better parent. I would have had a different career path."

Children can feel angry about a mother's career. Many mothers reported that daughters had more mixed feelings about their mothers' careers than did sons. One rabbi remembers, "When I finished my MA I was having coffee with a girlfriend. My daughter was nine years old. She walked by and said snidely, 'Now she's going to be a mother for a change.'" A Hebrew professor describes the difference between the reactions of her fourteen-year-old son and those of her six-year-old daughter: "My son is proud of me. It gives him great pleasure. My daughter sees my work as her enemy, and she also has a sense of pride. There's a sense of competition, too—it's always a contest." Indeed, sometimes daughters and husbands share a bond of resentment against the preoccupied professional mother. One woman notes, "Both my daughter and my husband sometimes express animosity toward my writing. Not just time but my state of mind. When I write, writing is the focus of my being. It is hard for me to shut off the writing me and put on the cooking and wifing me.

When it became clear that I really had to write I said, 'Either you help me now or I'll forever be lost.' It became almost a business deal."

Women themselves, as well as their husbands and children, can feel conflict about ambition and career achievement. One Jewish communal executive winces as she recalls "One of my daughter's first complete sentences was, 'I'm going to a meeting at Angela's,' with a bag slung over her arm. I've worked full-time since they were born. Very occasionally they would complain about my being places. I didn't see myself getting to where I am now—it became a career and profession over period of time. It started as a job—at some point I became aware of the fact that I'm ambitious. This was troubling to me because of my values. I have undergone a lot of soul-searching about my ambitiousness. Also, many women think they're putting something over on people. I feel timid. I look at some of my male colleagues who speak out fearlessly and without compunction— sometimes just to get themselves noticed."

Reflecting on the impact full-blown careerism has on families, many older Jewish working women are grateful that they had the opportunity to sequence, rather than to juggle, their lives. As one woman put it: "I'm very glad that my professional life didn't take up as much of my life then as it does now. Every life choice has side effects. I see pain that [my] children endure when they leave their young kids. I work five to six days a week, often till ten at night. I'm glad I'm not cheating anyone."

Many other working Jewish mothers, however, are adamant that they and their children thrive as long as they maintain their flexibility, have a clear sense of priorities, and are willing to be patient about work goals while their children need their time. As one woman who has authored four books, taught on a university level, and mothered three children puts it, "These juggling acts we all do just don't work. We have to see ourselves as a continuum." She says her life fell into place when she stopped trying to accomplish everything perfectly all the time, cut back on her writing hours to spend time with her children when they got home from school, asked family members for help, and insisted on time for her husband and herself—and for herself alone.[46]

The issue of working women is of concern not only to individual family units but to the Jewish communal world. Jewish communal leaders have voiced concerns about the potential impact of new lifestyles among American Jewish women upon the Jewish organizational world. Perhaps one of the most burning practical issues for the contemporary organized Jewish community is that of attracting and retaining sufficient levels of Jewish communal activism to maintain institutional vitality, including belonging to synagogues and Jewish organizations, voluntarism, and participation in leadership tasks. Members of and volunteers for Jewish organizations have higher levels of Jewish activism and involvement in other areas of Jewish life as well, making it likely that a process of mutual reinforcement may be at work. In addition, the vitality of the wider Jewish community is to a very real extent intertwined with the vitality of Jewish organizations, which provide the contexts for viable communal activity.

Life has changed dramatically for today's American Jewish women. Contemporary trends in education, occupational choices, and labor force participation have changed patterns of family formation and communal activism. These changes cannot be regarded as ephemeral; they have been strong for at least two decades and show no signs of abating. But although the working attitudes and behavior of Jewish women at the end of the twentieth century are different from what they were in the middle, many women continue to be interested in major commitments to Jewish life, both on a familial and a communal level. Despite personal and communal anxiety about the potential impact of higher education and labor force participation on women's Jewish commitments and life-styles, large numbers of contemporary women are blending Jewish and feminist values within their daily lives. Among Jewish women aged eighteen to forty-four increased secular education and occupational opportunity do not go hand in hand with increased assimilation. Highly educated, highly achieving young women are more, not less, likely to work for Jewish causes than their less educated and ambitious sisters. Intensity of Jewish social, cultural, and religious involvement is the key to Jewish communal activism. The long-range lesson to the Jewish communal world seems clear: Anxiety about increased education and careerism among women is misplaced.

In those households where home lives and organizational activities show no appreciable Jewish flavor, weak Jewish commitments in general are at play—and not the increased educational and occupational opportunities open to Jewish women today. Jewish family members and communal leaders and planners, however, need to respond to the changing expectations, needs, and interests of women in order to discover how to attract increased numbers of women to Jewish communal causes.

Moreover, higher education and careerism among today's women do not obliterate their desires to establish a Jewish family. Better-educated, ambitious Jewish women are more likely as a group to want to get married and to want to have larger families than their less educated sisters. Dual-career families make up the majority of households with children who belong to synagogues and provide children with Jewish education; a significant proportion of Jewish children also live in households with working single mothers. Today, most mothers in households that are affiliated with the Jewish community work outside the home—and many feel the Jewish community has yet to acknowledge their numbers and to respond with adequate positive, supportive policies to the realities of their lives. In pursuing educational and occupational goals and raising Jewish families, contemporary American women are fulfilling the potential of work patterns established by previous generations of Jewish women in paid and unpaid employment. Jewish women at work today are a new incarnation of ancient and time-honored Jewish models of female competence and energy; they are contemporary women of valor.

Chapter Five

Broadening Sexual and Gender Roles

"When the Holy One, Blessed be He, created the first Adam (human creature), He created them androgynous, as it is written, 'Male and female He created them . . . and He called their name Adam."

—Midrash Genesis Rabbah, Genesis 1:27

FEMINISM OFTEN PROMOTES EGALITARIANISM as the path by which women can have the greatest freedom to accomplish their goals and achieve self-development. In such areas as education and employment, the positive impact of egalitarianism seems clear. However, much less clear is the impact of egalitarianism on elements of human psychology and behavior that are related to sexuality. The broadening of sexual and gender roles under the aegis of feminism and other social movements has evoked troubling questions.

Some questions focus on sexual activity. If society does not impose strict behavioral patterns on men and women, some ask, will sexual encounters become so casual as to be meaningless, driving people farther apart rather than drawing them closer together? If society does not assign a meaning to sexuality, will individuals invest their sexual activities with emotional depth and spiritual significance? Will marriage still be an attractive option, and will couples be committed enough to maintain marriages over the long haul if pre-

and extramarital sexual activities become the norm? In the words of Rabbi Manis Friedman, the Hasidic author of *Doesn't Anyone Blush Anymore?*, "If you help yourself to the benefits of being married when you are single, you're likely to help yourself to the benefits of being single when you're married."[1]

Other questions explore gender roles. In societies that clearly define gender roles based on perceptions of biological differences, both men and women may chafe under rigid role prescriptions. Sensitive men may feel oppressed, for example, when they live in societies that prefer stoic males, and aggressive women may feel devalued by societal preferences for docile females. However, even though they may rebel against such gender-role definitions, men and women in such societies have clear ideas of what is expected of them. Some fear that when gender roles are broadened or considered irrelevant, both individuals and societies can become profoundly confused. Ungrounded by sex and gender identification, individuals may feel less tied to concepts of family and community. Isaac Bashevis Singer suggests that women who, like his heroine Yentl, dress and study like men may become androgynous down to their very core: "Only now did Yentl grasp the meaning of the Torah's prohibition against wearing the clothes of the other sex. By doing so one deceived not only others but also oneself. Even the soul was perplexed, finding itself incarnate in a strange body."[2]

Although men and women are often urged, in liberal circles, to behave as though they were gender-blind, references to sexuality and sexual activity continue to permeate our literature, our media, and our lives. Ours is an age that both emphasizes and tries to erase the impact of sexual and gender differences, in realms as diverse as education and employment, physical appearance, and intellectual development. Controversy swirls around such blurring of gender roles. Many acclaim the new permeability of roles, but a backlash—authored by both men and women—urges a reinstatement of dramatically virile men and seductive women and a rediscovery of sexual shame.[3]

Adding to the controversy are indications that the broadening of gender roles has not freed women from some of the most egregious psychological burdens of femininity. With educational, occupational, and social freedoms that their grandmothers could only have dreamed to dream of, today's young women are more than ever obsessed by body image. Recent surveys show that even highly educated, ambitious young women—but not men—say that they would rather be thin than be successful or happy. Eating disorders such as anorexia and bulimia flourish among even the most privileged of young American women and are particularly widespread among college-age Jewish women. Naomi Wolf describes the chemical and surgical violence millions of women inflict on themselves in an attempt to attain standards of physical perfection. Despite feminism, despite higher education and careers, women today often regard the appearance of the normal, healthy female body as flawed, and they act to correct these "flaws" to the point of undermining their own health.[4]

Controversy as to whether, and in what ways, men and women are—or ought to be—different extends to intellectual as well as physical spheres. Some feminists urge women to minimize the constraints of biological sexuality. Others, in contrast, emphasize genetic differences between men and women and urge women to trust the wisdom of genetic coding. Carol Gilligan has argued that women and men have intrinsically different ways of thinking about moral issues and that the female moral voice is superior. She urges women to cease imitating male forms of thought and expression.[5] On the other hand, Carolyn Heilbrun has written eloquently about freedom from gendered thought patterns. She suggests that many women do not achieve intellectual, emotional, and spiritual freedom until menopause, because of the sex-based social tyrannies of our culture. After menopause, Heilbrun insists, women become virtually androgynous, and as a result they become for the first time their own persons.[6]

Traditional Judaism has had much to say about sexual and gender differences. Most modern Jews are only vaguely acquainted with the complexity of Judaic approaches to sexuality, hence misinformation abounds. As Jewish feminists study and explore these issues, they often find some rabbinic discussions deeply appealing and even liberating in their approach, but others at times comical, insulting, or repulsive. Some approaches and prescriptions diverge strikingly from contemporary sensibilities; others seem startlingly modern and illuminating. Moreover, Jewish feminists often differ among themselves as to the significance of particular rabbinic prescriptions. Biblical and rabbinic laws surrounding menstruation, for example, have evoked responses that are basically positive, as when Blu Greenberg sees them as a "catalyst" to both passion and female autonomy,[7] and negative, as when Rabbi Sally Priesand declares them "senseless and irrelevant to modern society."[8] Halakhic prescriptions defining sexual behavior and gender roles are perhaps most salient to those Jewish feminists who model other aspects of their lives on traditional approaches as well. However, even those who do not necessarily feel bound by traditional thinking often find the dialogue of Jewish thinkers through the centuries a provocative springboard for discussion and exploration.

Biblical texts seem to accept social divisions between men and women and often describe women utilizing the ploys common to persons of subservient status as they try to manipulate people and events. However, as Tikvah Frymer-Kensky points out, biblical texts pointedly do not suggest that women think differently than men do—only that society limits their options.[9] In contrast, many rabbinic authorities assume—like Carol Gilligan—that women's minds are likely to work differently than men's. Rabbinic authorities assume that men and women differ from each other in more than physiology and reproductive roles. Jewish law suggests a sweeping array of gender-based differences that seem designed to emphasize those qualities that distinguish and differentiate women from men. Interestingly, however, many rabbinic texts share the assumption that such gender distinctions are open to question, arising from the limitations of the human condition. A midrash on Genesis 1:27 states that the original human creature breathed into life by God was androgynous; only the creature's loneliness precipitated the separation into two distinctive sexes with two distinctive gender roles.

The purpose of sex and gender distinctions among human beings, according to Jewish tradition, is to enable men and women to enjoy companionship, pleasure, and creativity with partners who complement and complete them. Halakhic literature, which calmly and dispassionately discusses a broad spectrum of sexual activities, often differs from one text to another and from one issue to another as to the impact of sexuality and gender on the optimum form of acceptable behavior. However, despite rabbinic differences of opinion, the halakhah consistently prescribes that adult Jewish men and women should live in marital unions in which male-female genital sexual activity occurs on a regular basis.

According to most Jewish interpretations of the Hebrew Bible, sexuality did not cause the "fall." Adam and Eve correctly cohabited together on the first Sabbath eve after their creation, according to the rabbis; it was their disobedience to the divine decree regarding the tree(s), not their sexual activity, which displeased God.[10] Judaism regards sexuality as a good and sacred aspect of life within the marital framework and at the proper time and place. An erotic life that satisfies both husband and wife was seen by the rabbis as an important component of *shalom bayit,* the serene and orderly household perceived as the basic building block of Jewish society. As one rabbinical aphorism puts it, "Sexual desire brings peace between husband and wife" (Midrash Ecclesiastes Rabbah 13:5). According to the thirteenth-century Jewish scholar Nachmanides, when a husband and wife unite sexually "in a spirit of holiness and purity," their union is seen as mirroring and reinforcing the union of masculine and feminine aspects of the Divine Creator. Significantly, within Judaism the Sabbath was seen as an especially appropriate time for sexual union.

Within both the Hebrew Bible and rabbinic law, sexuality was viewed as a key element of human nature, a drive that had the capacity to enhance or to destroy life, to be put to positive and constructive or to dangerous uses. Female sexuality was viewed as a powerful force for either good or evil. Female eroticism, sensuality, and nurturing qualities were viewed by the authors of such biblical books as Proverbs and the Song of Songs as part of the arsenal used by the good and wise woman to attract a man and to keep him on the productive and moral path of life.[11]

This positive attitude toward heterosexual eroticism within marriage was retained within much of later Hebrew literature as well. Medieval Hebrew wedding poems, for example, drew heavily on "the prelapsarian love of Adam and Eve in the Garden of Eden and the love of the bride and groom in the Song of Songs."[12] Deliberate celibacy was considered to be an aberration, and both unmarried men and women were regarded with pity or suspicion in much of Jewish literature and in many Jewish societies. Homosexual erotic activity was forbidden for men, based on the biblical prohibition against "lying with a man in the manner in which one lies with women." The prevalence of homosexual activity in some surrounding cultures, such as that of classical Greece, did nothing to soften the Jewish distaste for such sexual orientation; if anything, it stiffened Jewish opposition.[13] The possibility that women might be homosexuals was largely ignored within much of Jewish law, whether out of rabbinic unawareness that such sexual orientation existed or out of apathy is unclear; when it is discussed, it is disapproved of and considered a product of the influence of foreign perversions.[14] (Perhaps for similar reasons, male masturbation is discouraged;[15] that of females ignored.) However, despite the dictates of Jewish law on the subject of male homosexuality, a number of non-halakhic sources indicate that homosexuality existed, however closeted and disapproved of, in traditional Jewish societies.

Once a woman married, her sexuality was consecrated to her husband. Married women were sexually off limits for any man except for their husbands, and according to biblical law the punishment for extramarital intercourse involving a married woman was death for both the man and the woman. The child of an extramarital affair was a *mamzer,* a bastard, and was forbidden to marry into the legitimate Jewish community for ten generations. The product of a premarital affair, however, was *not* a bastard, according to Jewish law, and had the same legal status, including the right to marry, as any other Jewish child. Premarital sexuality per se is not forbidden by the Hebrew Bible, although it instructs girls and their fathers not to falsely claim virginity where it no longer exists, and it prohibits Israelite girls from becoming prostitutes. However, the social sanctions against premarital sexuality for girls were very strong in every traditional Jewish community. Traditional Jewish communities approved of and sanctified only one context for sexual activity for women—within marriage.

Jewish law also recognized women's sexual rights within marriage. First, a married woman had the right to sexual fulfillment. The rabbis assumed that women desire sexual activity just as men do but that women may be shy about initiating it; they also assumed that men who had certain life-styles, such as men who travel or are scholarly types, might occasionally be so distracted that they neglected their wives' emotional well-being. For this reason rabbinic law stipulated the minimum frequency with which husbands should offer their wives sexual activity.[16] Second, within Jewish law every woman had the right to refuse sexual advances that did not please her. Jewish law recognized the reality of marital rape and forbade it. The author of *Iggeret Ha-Kodesh,*[17] for example, advises husbands:

> You ought to engage her first in matters which please her heart and mind and cheer her. . . . And you should say such things some of which will urge her to passion and intercourse, to affection, desire and lovemaking. . . . And you shall not possess her against her will nor force her because in that kind of a union there is no divine presence [shekhinah[18]] because your intentions are opposite to hers and her wish does not agree with yours. And do not quarrel with her nor beat her for the sake of having intercourse.[19]

Despite these positive injunctions, biblical taboos against cohabitation with a menstrual woman contributed to the image of women as creatures delimited by their sexuality. An elaborate rabbinic complex of laws of menstrual purity, *taharat hamishpakhah,* prohibited sexual relations between husband and wife while she had the ritual status of *niddah,* for a minimum of twelve days a month (an assumed five-day menstrual period and an additional seven "white" days following); it also discouraged as well any physical contact between husband and wife during that time. Elaborate precautions were suggested by some writers to prevent any inadvertent breach of the laws by a forgetful spouse. Within the context of the way Jewish law approaches all appetites, this preoccupation with detail is not unusual: Traditional Jewish law provides systems of discipline for all human appetites, and to modern sensibilities these laws can easily appear arcane. However, human beings internalize feelings about sexuality in a mode more intense and complicated than those they use to deal with other areas of life. Therefore, although it is quite true that the laws of *kashruth* are at least as complex as the laws of *taharat hamishpakhah,* their psychological impact may have been quite different.

The sexual depictions of women within Jewish law and literature had a far-reaching social impact. For much of Jewish history women were denied access to the intellectual life of the community, which centered around the study of sacred texts, primarily the Talmud, and they were denied a public role in Jewish worship. These exclusions were based on certain assumptions in Jewish rabbinic law about the nature of women. The rabbis assumed that, as a practical matter, the vast majority of women would be absorbed in domestic responsibilities for most of their adult lives. They also assumed that men as a group were easily inflamed into sexual thoughts, and that a woman's uncovered hair, her arms or legs, or even her voice could—perhaps unwittingly—distract a man from such sacred tasks as prayer or study. One of the rationales for the exclusion of women from study and public worship was that women's physical attractions were perceived as a sexual snare for men.

Men's sexual impulses were thus controlled by limiting their access to women in many arenas of life. Sublimation of strong emotions into spiritual and intellectual fervor was more easily effected by carefully preventing sexuality from intruding into the worlds of study and prayer, and sexual thoughts were minimized by preventing women from entering into those worlds.

This does not mean that study and prayer were considered to be "sacred" while sexuality was considered to be "profane." Nevertheless, since women's sexuality presented a "problem" for men when they were engaged in study or prayer, women were barred from two activities that not only were central to the intellectual and public religious life of the society but provided access to communal power and prestige as well. Rabbinic law had the effect of creating an extremely stable society, a society that in many ways protected and respected women and celebrated certain aspects of sexuality[20] but also in many ways stereotyped the image of women, especially in regard to perceptions of their intellectual and leadership capacities.

In societies where few women learned the intricacies of Jewish law and the nuances of talmudic descriptions of female nature, the image of the woman was sometimes telescoped and distorted. Thus, female sexuality, which some rabbis saw as "dangerous" in that it might distract men from sacred tasks, was sometimes (albeit mistakenly, from the standpoint of Jewish law) seen as being simply dangerous. Some men leaned toward asceticism and attempted to minimize the impact of sexuality on their environments even more than stipulated by Jewish law. Some Jewish communities, in addition, were much affected by notions of menstrual contamination drawn from the superstitions of surrounding cultures.

For women married to men who feared female sexuality or living in communities in which such fears were rife, it was little comfort that in other households or communities different attitudes prevailed. Similarly, while women were initially released from many time-based commandments (such as blessings limited to certain hours of the day) because it was assumed that their maternal responsibilities would take priority, the popular image of women sometimes indicated that they were incapable of such activities or that such activities would be unseemly for women. Thus, women's subordinate and limited position in Jewish life was linked to their sexuality and to their perceived sexual nature.

For hundreds of years Jewish women's attitudes toward their own sexuality and the appropriate roles for their gender was shaped by Jewish law and by the tightly knit Jewish communities in which they lived. With the advent of modernity, strictly defined sexual mores began to loosen for many Jewish women, along with greater education, mobility, and access to more open societal roles. Among women who left their homes to live far from family in the big cities—especially those who lived among the writers, actors, painters, and the intelligentsia in artistic enclaves in cities like Warsaw—among highly assimilated upper-class Jewish women, and among women absorbed in socialist revolutionary activities, sexual restrictions were often cast off along with other vestiges of bourgeois Jewish life. Their new life-styles are described in detail in contemporaneous memoirs and fiction.[21]

Unmarried Jewish women often emigrated to the United States alone, some as young as twelve years old. Some had already absorbed the messages of socialism or other modern, secular movements before they came. Others traveled to the United States with their families but soon gravitated toward peer societies and threw off parental influences and religious restrictions.[22] The advice columns of the *Jewish Daily Forward* and fiction by writers like Abraham Cahan describe not only unmarried working women but also married women left alone with male boarders falling into sexual involvements. In environments where many young unmarried immigrant women were separated by actual and/or emotional oceans from family and familial control, and later with the impact of Jazz Age morality, freer moral standards were seen not only among bohemians and the upper classes of assimilated Jews but among some emancipated working Jewish single women as well.

Interviews with second-generation American Jewish women who came of age during the 1920s and 1930s reveal that sexual activity, contraception, and abortion were part of the everyday landscape of life for some of them, especially those who had ceased to be formally religious, long before the sexual revolution and the advent of the latest wave of feminism. Although anxious Jewish parents expected and urged their daughters to remain virginal until marriage, and although the double standard for men and women had certainly not disappeared, some American Jewish women did not wait for marriage to become sexually active—although many consciously avoided promiscuity.

One woman explains:

Each night I was going out. I had a boyfriend, it lasted for six months. It lasted for two years. It lasted for eight months. It had a depth to it, it had a meaning to it, it had a caring to it. And a love to it. And that I think is absolutely true. And in two instances, I had every intention of marrying them. In both instances, they paid a good deal of attention to me. Real personal attention. I had a need for love that was so great, so intense, that other things didn't seem to matter. And I found myself pregnant again. Now, in all honesty, I knew that both the first time and the second time my boyfriends used contraceptives but once they didn't and we got caught. My boyfriend had a friend who was a doctor—actually, he had just graduated medical school—and he arranged for me to have an abortion.[23]

While the vast majority of American Jewish women got married eventually, during the years of the Great Depression they often married late, in their late twenties or their thirties. This left a number of mature years for them to be working outside the home with male coworkers, often struggling with overt or subtle sexual overtures and sometimes harassment in those environments. Memoirs and novels depicting Jewish women in the 1930s and 1940s sometimes describe a work-related initiation into sexual activity, followed by a series of sexual involvements before marriage. One woman comments, "It was not that unique. We tend to think of that in our day nobody ever did things, but it is not true. I went off on a weekend with Jack before we were married, and he wasn't the first one either. I had gone off on a weekend with another boy before I was married; it was not the invention they think it is."[24]

After World War II Jewish women, like their gentile counterparts, were influenced by the trend toward early marriage and large families, and by the reemergence of strong social sanctions against pre- or extramarital sexuality. A rigid double standard, reflected and reinforced by films and women's magazines, expressed American preconceptions with gender roles. Among middle-class Americans in the 1950s and early 1960s, males were expected to be virile before and after marriage, and premarital sexual initiation was part of that virility; females, however, were expected to be virginal—but sexually appealing—before marriage and maternal and monogamous—and still sexually appealing—afterward.

Although Jewish women sometimes had sexual experiences before marriage in the decades after World War II, they felt guilty about their activities because of the disapproval expressed in Jewish and middle-American society. Herman Wouk described the feelings of a young Jewish woman toward her own sexual adventures in his 1955 novel, when Marjorie Morningstar confesses her one affair to her fiancé—whom she assumes is not himself a virgin:

Twentieth century or not, good Jewish girls were supposed to be virgins when they got married. . . . For that matter, good Christian girls were supposed to be virgins too; that was why brides wore white. . . .

the story somehow broke from her in a stammering rush of words; every word like vomit in her mouth. That ended the evening. . . . Then he drove her home. She remembered that drive for years as the worst agony she had ever endured. It was like being driven to a hospital, dying of a hemorrhage."[25]

While middle-class Jewish and non-Jewish women in the 1950s and 1960s experienced enormous conflict over the initiation of sexual activity, in the 1970s the antiauthority environment of the Vietnam years and the ease of contraception made possible by birth control pills played their roles in turning sexual standards on their head as well. Together with these forces, the insistence of many early feminists that women's sexuality belonged to them and should be enjoyed by them without worry about societal or religious sanctions worked together to devalue virginity. Many women have reported that, instead of being the prize it was to Marjorie Morningstar, virginity past a certain age became a kind of albatross, something to get rid of so that a woman could be "normal."

In the years before the emergence of, and common knowledge about, a spectrum of sexually transmitted diseases, sexual intimacy became a part of the dating scene and was expected in most "serious" and long-standing relationships. Novels, memoirs, and interviews with women who were single during the 1970s and 1980s reveal that sexual activity became a "given" for most women by the time they reached their early twenties. A survey of one hundred thousand American women in 1977 revealed that sexual activity among women under age twenty-five was widespread: 94 percent of Jewish, Protestant, and Catholic women reported that they were sexually active before marriage. Strong religious feelings among Jewish women in that survey, however, had more of an inhibiting effect vis-à-vis premarital sexual activity than among non-Jewish women: Forty percent of Jewish women who described themselves as "strongly religious" had premarital sexual experience, compared to 73 percent of "strongly religious" non-Jewish women.[26]

Even within some "modern Orthodox" communities, sexual expressions of affection became more common in the 1970s and 1980s than they had been in earlier decades. A variety of sources indicate that some self-defined Orthodox Jewish singles did not place prohibitions against premarital sexual intimacy in the same category of binding Jewish law as, for example, desecrating the Sabbath.[27] This was especially true in enclaves of older single Jewish professionals living in their own apartments in major metropolitan areas. Some assert: "There is a Jewish injunction against premarital sex, but there is apparently little difference between the secular and the Orthodox world in this regard. . . . You might go to bed one date later." Several women told stories about Orthodox men who arrived for dinner dates with a *tefillin* bag—needed for morning prayers—in hand.[28] Rebecca Goldstein's novel *The Mind-Body Problem* chronicles the experiments in blending contemporary and traditional sexual mores devised by women and men in such societies, including potential visits to the *mikvah* by single Orthodox women involved in long-standing sexual relationships.[29]

Today, when asked about the impact of feminism on sexuality and gender roles, American Jewish women tend to be positive. Many of them speak quite vehemently about being released from the tyranny of the double standard or a societal obsession with physical virginity in women. Usually beginning with the proviso, "Except for AIDS and other sexually transmitted diseases," many women go on to talk about the ways in which women's lives have improved. Their approval ranges from older women who have bitter memories of back-room abortions in their youth, to middle-aged women who talk about how long it took them to get beyond their sexual inhibitions even after they were married, to younger women who speak enthusiastically about the emotional freedom to be sexually active they enjoyed during their single years.

Many women are pleased that feminism and other social and medical factors have broadened women's reproductive options. Almost universally they reiterate their commitment to family-planning education and to the preservation of reproductive choice in the United States. Even those Jewish women who have very mixed feelings about abortion tend to agree with the woman who said, grimly, "I may feel distaste about some of the excesses of abortion choices, such as abortion used for gender selection and as birth control, but I would fight with every cell of my being to keep men like Senator Orrin Hatch from gaining control over women's bodies." The personal commitment Jewish women feel about reproductive choice is reflected in their organizations. The vast majority of mainstream American Jewish women's organizations have publicly supported legislation that makes family planning and abortion available to women on demand.

Among the sponsors of a Washington, D.C., "March for Women's Lives," organized to "send a strong pro-choice message to candidates" in the 1992 elections, for example, were the American Jewish Committee, American Jewish Congress, Hadassah, the

Jewish Labor Committee, Na'amat, the National Council of Jewish Women, Women's American ORT, the Union of American Hebrew Congregations, and the Women's League for Conservative Judaism. The Union of Orthodox Jewish Congregations of America chose not to join the effort "because of this issue's complex halachic ramifications."[30]

American Jewish women have been among the most motivated and reliable users of birth control since the earliest decades of the twentieth century, and the use of birth control is almost universal among them today. Modern Orthodox, Conservative, Reform, Reconstructionist, and "just Jewish" women use birth control as a matter of course. Because rabbinic law prefers birth control methods that do not divert semen from the vaginal canal (a preference based on biblical injunctions against a man wasting his seed), pills, contraceptive foams, and diaphragms tend to be the methods most commonly used by traditional Jews who practice family planning.[31]

Even the right-wing Orthodox world has been influenced by the availability and ubiquitousness of birth control. A study comparing women in very right-wing (Kollel), right-wing (Agudah), and centrist (Young Israel) Orthodox communities in a largely Orthodox suburb of New York found that in the Agudah community, in which nine out of ten women covered their hair, more than 70 percent of the women reported using birth control after they had given birth to at least one child. Several of these women said they had not told their husbands that they were using birth control. One said, "My husband doesn't know I use birth control. He thinks we have been unfortunate. . . . I had three children in three years. I didn't feel I could discuss it with my husband." Another woman said, "I think I asked my husband once. I got the impression not to talk too much to my husband about it." Among the ultra-Orthodox women many would not answer the question, having been instructed by their husbands not to talk about "personal" issues; some said they used birth control after the birth of several children—although each Kollel wife who used birth control said she was doing so for health rather than "personal" reasons.[32]

In some overseas countries, abortion is used by many women as the primary form of birth control. However, in the United States, it is very unusual for Jewish women to think of abortion as just another form of birth control; rather it is considered an unusual—but crucial—emergency measure, to be used when birth control measures fail or in case of grave fetal abnormality or maternal illness.

Perhaps their attitudes toward birth control and abortion are influenced by the fact that the approach of Jewish law toward these subjects is not black and white.

Jewish law regards abortion performed in order to safeguard the mother's physical health as acceptable, and some rabbis include mental anguish as an appropriate justification for abortion. According to Jewish law, until the unborn child begins to emerge from the birth canal, his/her life is not considered coequal to the mother's.[33] Only at the moment of birth does the mother's health cease to take precedence over that of the fetus.

Nevertheless traditional Judaism does not take abortion lightly. It allows abortion when the fetus endangers the life of the mother, and the fetus is not considered a full human being until birth.[34] Jewish law does not allow abortion for feminist reasons, nor does it believe that a woman has the right to control her own body in that sense. (Jewish law prohibits tattooing, for example, because that is considered a mutilation of the body.) Neither men nor women are thought fully to own their own bodies, and their behavior toward their own bodies is governed by Jewish law. As Robert Gordis notes, "It is basic Jewish teaching that no human being is master of his own body, because he did not create himself; male and female alike have been fashioned by God in His image."[35]

Many American Jewish women like the idea that they—and not outside forces—will decide not only how to control their reproductive lives but also when and with whom they will have sexual relationships, and what the nature of those sexual relationships will be. Many women expressed satisfaction that they and their daughters might not be as sexually "inhibited" as the generations that came before them. "I'm not really sure how my mother felt about sex," said one woman in her fifties:

> She didn't talk about it. But my daughter and I did, and she knows how important a joyous sex life has been to me. She knows that my husband and I have always scheduled time to be alone. She didn't always like being left out and left behind, when we had a romantic evening together. But I've noticed that now that she has children of her own she does the same thing. It's one of my greatest hopes that her sexuality brings her joy.

Despite early speculations that careerist aspirations among women might threaten men and impair sexual enjoyment in dual-career marriages, the opposite seems to be the case. "My husband gets turned on when he sees me in a suit or working at the computer," says one woman:

> I think that the contrast between the woman the working world sees—the crisp, efficient woman with a briefcase—and the woman that only he knows in bed adds a kind of mystery and eroticism to the relationship, even after two decades of marriage and four children. We exploit the costume-party aspect of our complicated lives—it's like our version of the shepherd and the shepherdess.

In recent research as well, increased levels of education and career aspiration among women have been linked to improved enjoyment of sexual activity among dual career couples. According to a recent study of three thousand couples, "A working mom who shares financial decisions with her husband is far more likely to have a satisfying sex life and happy marriage." Moreover, two-thirds of the "women in these new egalitarian marriages are more likely to think of their husband as their best friend," compared to only one-third of women in male-dominated marriages.[36]

Both Jewish men and women tend to express attitudes that seem strikingly liberal, especially in comparison to an often-conservative middle-American population. A 1985 study of Jewish and non-Jewish women living in the Middle West found that Midwestern Jewish women are far more liberal than non-Jewish women in attitudes toward pre- and extramarital sexuality. More than three-quarters of the Jewish women studied said that sex before marriage was acceptable, while fewer than half of the non-Jewish women approved of premarital sex. Perhaps even more startling, given Jewish religious and cultural prohibitions against adultery, 28 percent of the Jewish women said they "could envision situations when sex with someone other than one's spouse is not wrong," compared to only 12 percent of the non-Jewish Midwestern sample, who said they might sanction extramarital sex in certain circumstances.[37]

The sexual liberalism of American Jewish women is often part of a larger package of strongly profeminist attitudes. Jewish and non-Jewish women were compared on a composite scale that measured attitudes toward *"feminism, or . . . the modern version of women's roles and rights."* Nearly half of the Jewish women surveyed scored "high" on this scale, compared to only 16 percent of the non-Jewish women. Another one-third of Jewish women, and one-third of non-Jewish women, measured "medium" on the scale. Twenty percent of Jewish women surveyed scored "low" on the scale, compared to 40

percent of the non-Jewish women. An overwhelming 91 percent of
Jewish women—compared to 56 percent of non-Jewish women—
agreed that "every woman who wants an abortion ought to be able
to have one."[38]

Some radical feminist thinkers promote sexual freedoms which
may be perceived as destructive to the salience of the traditional
Jewish family. Judith Levine, a journalist and critic who writes for
the *Village Voice,* is representative of those feminists for whom sexual freedom is the key to feminism. She vehemently renews her commitment to the individualistic sexual orientation of "the early
women's movement":

> I believe in destabilizing traditional sexual setups and struggling, as
> we did in the 1960s and 1970s, with the emotions that go with such a
> cultural upheaval. But you can't do this without asking fundamental
> questions about sex. Questions like, is monogamy better? (My an-
> swer: not necessarily.) What's wrong with kids having sex? (Often,
> nothing.) Why is it worse to pay for sex than to pay for someone to
> listen to your intimate problems or care for your infant? (You tell me.)

Levine insists, "We shouldn't be looking for meaning in sex at all, in
fact, but rather trying to slip implicit meaning from sex."[39]

Interestingly, Jewish students today may be more sexually conservative than were students twenty years ago. A thirty-eight-year-
old woman, now a professor and the mother of two, credited
feminism with "giving me the artillery to resist my mother's pleas
that I remain sexually inactive during college." She continued:

> My mother had a real double standard: It was okay, even expected,
> for my brother to acquire some sexual experience, but not for me.
> Feminism freed me from that and made me feel independent. I was
> just as active sexually as the Jewish guys around me, and I had a great
> time. I felt good about being a sexual being. I had two abortions, and
> while I was upset I didn't feel stained or sullied. Now I'm married, and
> neither one of us believe[s] in open marriage, but I'm sure glad that I
> had the chance to be adventurous and free when I was young.

She is convinced from discussions with her students, however, that
female Jewish students today are more cautious than she was and
place a greater stress on emotional commitments as part of a sexual
relationship. Few today are attracted to the idea of physical promiscuity. Linda Gordon Kuzmack, who leads workshops on Jewish attitudes toward sexuality among college students, agrees:

They don't take sex lightly. They feel that part of being Jewish is being serious and responsible about sexuality. Most of them aren't going to "save sex for marriage," as so many women in my generation did, but they say they aren't going to "waste" it on someone they don't care about, either. Many of them are smart enough to insist on a reciprocal, caring relationship as a context for sexual activity.

Many Jewish college women are quite willing to make commitments, but insist they must be reciprocal. "Faithfulness in marriage is great," says one. "I'm all for it—otherwise why get married? But no differences between 'his' and 'hers.' Men should be just as married as women. And as for what I did before I got married—well, as long as I don't bring a medical condition with me, it's none of his business."

As they assess the impact of feminism and other social movements on contemporary sexual mores, however, women of all ages refer to differences between the impact of the sexual revolution on men and on women, which they see as more troubling and open to question. Commonly mentioned is the idea that the social movements of the 1960s and 1970s not only opened up doors for women but also made their lives more difficult; feminism gave women more options in terms of sexuality and gender roles, but it also created new social pressures. "When everybody knew that nice girls didn't, it was easy to say no—that was the answer men expected. How do you say no today? They accuse you of being frigid or gay," one recently widowed woman complains. "I don't want to sleep with everyone I date a couple of times, although I would like to continue a relationship with some of them. Now even nice men often think you have to have a specific reason for saying no—instead of having a specific reason for saying yes. I think in certain ways life was simpler when sexual and gender roles were clearly defined."

Women who choose to remain virgins report they are often hassled about their status. A twenty-two-year-old virgin said she was often asked if she was "Catholic or a born-again Christian or a lesbian." She said some people "just can't imagine somebody my age not having sex," especially when they discover that she is "a Jew going for a graduate degree in public health." She angrily resents such lack of respect for her choice.[40]

A professor of psychology at a women's college says that male and female students seem to experience sexual freedoms differently:

For young men sexual activity is often primarily recreational, and sexual freedom often expands recreational opportunities. It's much easier for young men now than it was thirty-five years ago to find bright, attractive, healthy, interesting sexual partners. Women, however, often come to a sexual relationship expecting caring, sensitivity, companionship, and some level of personal commitment. At the conclusion of early sexual experiences, men are often satisfied while women often feel cheated—angry, disappointed, devalued—and sometimes hostile toward men and sexual activity with men.

Some people who work in university settings think that university communities provide an environment that encourages sexual experimentation, including alternative forms of sexuality. A professor of history and women's studies in a Midwestern college says:

> In certain circles lesbian orientation is politically correct. I know that I'm not being politically correct in saying this, but I'm convinced that in certain cases some young women who would have been contentedly married if they had been born a hundred years ago, today are subjected to miserable experiences with exploitative men and then wander into lesbian relationships. The men they have met use them, then drop them, or are callous, or disillusion them in some other way. They meet young women with whom they have a lot in common— their relationship has all the warmth and caring and ease that women's relationships with each other often have. And the sexual logistics aren't that difficult to work out—people's sexual needs can be satisfied in lots of ways. By then they are convinced that they have a lesbian sexual orientation.

Jewish lesbian women with a strong Jewish consciousness often want to meet and create a relationship with a "nice Jewish girl." For many of them, such a relationship is a reinforcement of their own positive feelings about being both Jewish and female.[41] Many strongly committed Jewish lesbians yearn to have Judaism sanctify their monogamous relationships, feeling that in choosing a Jewish partner, and often raising Jewish children, they are indeed establishing a faithful home in Israel.[42] One student commented wistfully that an earlier generation of Jewish lesbians had it "easier. They couldn't come out of the closet, so they married and they had children. Then they came out of the closet and left their husbands—but they had their children already. I want to have children, and I want to honor my own sexuality, but it's a lot more complicated now."

Professor Evelyn Torton Beck, however—a middle-aged woman with grown children who now lives happily with a Jewish woman she describes as "my life's companion"—recalls a personal journey of change and discovery that makes it clear that confronting lesbian sexual orientation was never simple. She warns that confining Jewish experience to the "mainstream community" is bound to alienate and exclude Jews who have a lot to contribute to contemporary American Jewish life. "Traditional Judaism doesn't speak for all Jews," she said. "We have to stop thinking about Judaism as monolithic, as all Mom, Dad, and the kids. We have to make space for all committed Jews if we are to survive as a strong community."

Jewish women of lesbian orientation are often delighted to see an easing of gender and sexual definitions; many feel that this process has not yet gone far enough. Several Jewish lesbians said that the Jewish community puts them in a "double bind: while it is not likely to go in for overt and violent gay-bashing, it does not want homosexual or lesbian . . . orientation openly declared either. According to Adina Abramowitz, a Hillel rabbi told her: "No Jewish community should reject me as long as I didn't go around proselytizing. I asked him if that meant I should stay in the closet. He said yes. He had no answer to the obvious question of how I was supposed to meet a Jewish woman to be my partner."[43]

Many Jewish lesbians have strong ties to Jewish culture; some have lived in, or frequently visited, Israel. Living in Israel, however, they also encounter far-more-vehement homophobia than is common among Jews in the United States.[44] As a doctoral student at HUC-JIR in Los Angeles comments about being a lesbian growing up in Israel, "The negative feeling about lesbians in Israel made me feel that I wanted nothing to do with religion. But in the more open atmosphere of the United States I have discovered Judaism. I found a synagogue with active outreach to gays and lesbians, and I have discovered Jewish prayer. Judaism has become the blood of my life."

Lesbianism remains a vital force in certain wings of the Jewish feminist movement. Indeed, Professor Anne Lapidus Lerner notes, "One is struck by the degree to which lesbianism, in particular, has become an accepted fact of life" at the Reconstructionist Rabbinical College.[45] Rabbis in Reform and Conservative congregations have been urged to incorporate fully their homosexual congregants and to sanctify their unions by some sort of religious marriage ceremony, according to other sources.

Judith Plaskow is among several prominent Jewish feminists who propose a more accepting attitude toward alternative sexual orientation, based on a new theology of sexuality. Plaskow agrees with Jewish tradition that sexuality can include a powerful spiritual component, and also that sexuality can be a disruptive and destabilizing force: "There is no question that the empowerment that comes from owning the erotic in our lives can disturb community and undermine familiar structures." Jewish feminists should use both the spiritual and the disruptive potential of sexuality to expand sexual options for contemporary Jews, Plaskow urges.[46]

Rejecting a hierarchy of permitted and forbidden types of sexual expression, lesbian feminists such as Plaskow insist, "The same norms that apply to heterosexual relationships also apply to gay and lesbian relationships." She urges contemporary American Jews to "see sexuality as part of what enables us to reach out beyond ourselves," and to value most highly "that place within ourselves where sexuality and spirituality come together." Plaskow admits that "historically, this vision has been expressed entirely in heterosexual terms." But such limitations, she warns, categorically exclude the sexuality/spirituality of other Jews, who can find it "only in relationships between two men or two women. Thus what calls itself the Jewish path to holiness in sexual relations is for some a cutting-off of holiness—a sacrifice that comes at high cost for both the individual and community. Homosexuality, then, does not necessarily represent a rejection of Jewish values but the choice of certain Jewish values over others—[and] where these conflict with each other, the choice of the possibility of holiness over control and law."[47]

Betty Friedan, on the other hand, has recently spoken out strongly on behalf of the family, urging feminist sympathizers not to be put off by what she sees as the sexual theatrics and exhibitionism of the radical left wing of the movement. "Jews have always known that a strong family is important for both Jewish and human survival," says Friedan. "The family is not the enemy. That came from a subversion of the women's movement. What we need now are real choices having to do with love, marriage, children," Friedan declares. "The sexual issues are used as diversionary devices now, to take attention away from the really serious issues, like the distribution of wealth, economic survival. . . . The ones who now want to take away the rights of women are using antifeminism and abortion and the sexual issues to divert people from their economic exploitation."[48]

Perhaps the strongest negative reactions to the redefinition of sexual and gender roles come from those women who have participated in new life-styles and then rejected them. Debra Kaufman and Lynn Davidman have both recently published books on female *ba'alot teshuvah,* women who have returned to strictly Orthodox life-styles, often from life-styles that were previously quite removed. One of the primary forces driving many of their subjects into more traditional life-styles was a deep disillusionment with contemporary sexual norms, combined with an attraction to what they perceived as a cherishing of the woman within a Jewish marriage. One woman said:

> For all the sexual freedom I felt in my late adolescence and early adulthood, I can tell you that it was more like sexual exploitation. I felt there were no longer any rules; on what grounds did one decide to say no? If the rule was casual sex and if you engaged in it on what grounds did you say no. . . . What rules did you use? If you see what I'm saying, without overriding rules, or without protection of some sort, the sexual liberation meant that women were free to be exploited more by men . . . the laws of taharat hamishpacha . . . make so much sense. For instance, I am not a sex object to my husband; he respects me and respects my sexuality. Because he does not have access to me anytime he wishes, he cannot take me for granted. The separation restores our passion and places the control of it in my hands."[49]

Another woman revolted against "one-night stands." She pooh-poohed the exaltation of orgasm in modern culture, saying the overall attitudes toward women and sexuality have a much greater salience to a woman's quality of life: "Orgasm alone was just that, an orgasm—masturbation could and did fulfill the same function. I didn't want moralizing; I wanted to know how sexuality would fit into my life; you know, over the long haul. Orthodoxy had an answer to that . . . when I learned about the family purity laws . . . they immediately made sense to me. In fact, my boyfriend and I practiced taharat hamishpacha while we were living together. Neither of us could take our sexuality or me for granted."[50]

Interestingly, most of the newly Orthodox women were in other ways full participants in the changing life-styles of American Jewish women. Fifty-one percent currently work, and "almost all intend to participate in the paid labor force at some time. . . . Almost all of the women who did not have advanced degrees intend to retain and/or obtain more education before returning to the labor force."[51] Although they overtly rejected feminism and feminist goals, "They used feminist rhetoric and emphases to describe their Orthodox lives. Contrary to the common assumption that nonfeminist women are unable to identify as women and to act in their own interest, these *ba'alot teshuvah* are quite conscious of their status as women and defend that status." In addition, many of them share a feminist conviction of female superiority of moral development:

The familial and the feminine provide a counterbalance for them to a world "run amok" with masculine notions of success, achievement, and status acted out through competitive individualism and self-aggrandizement. They view themselves not merely as passive reflections of male imagery, but rather as moral agents for positive action. They not only believe in gender difference, they celebrate it."[52]

One does not need to be a "born-again" newly Orthodox Jewish woman to have redefined and found new meaning in Jewish attitudes and rituals surrounding sexuality. One of the greatest contributions feminism has made to contemporary Jewish life is to revision Jewish sexual attitudes. Jewish young women today often have more positive feelings about a variety of Jewish attitudes toward sexuality than did their mothers or grandmothers.

Seldom does one see the kind of automatic rejection of Jewish customs that was often typical of Jewish intellectual women in the past.[53] Many young women today have absorbed pro-Jewish feminist spiritual interpretations of Jewish laws and customs surrounding sexuality like those advocated by Rachel Adler in her pivotal reinterpretation of the laws of *mikvah* purification,[54] and that of Wechsler on *niddah* and women's spirituality: "The women who can enter this ritual and participate in such a fullness of meaning may experience an affinity and a powerful reconciliation with the source of all that is. This is, at a deep level, the dynamic of atonement. Rather than being outside the sacred circle, this dynamic oscillation places her firmly within it."[55]

As the twentieth century draws to a close, the sexual choices of American Jewish women have been greatly expanded. Most women are pleased that they have sexual options, and few would willingly choose or return to a closed society with narrow boundaries. Nevertheless, the sexual scene in contemporary American life is hardly idyllic. Sexually transmitted diseases—to which women are often more vulnerable than men—have complicated nonmonogamous relationships, diminishing the exuberance that once typified the singles culture. Nor is the disparity between men and women in sexual matters exclusively a matter of greater vulnerability to disease. Women complain about cavalier attitudes frequently encountered among men who view sexual activity as part of casual dating; the women describe themselves, in contrast, as searching for compassion and companionship. While many such women emphatically do not wish a return to societal insistence that marriage be the universal precondition for intimacy, they also feel that sexual "liberation" has often liberated men to behave irresponsibly.

To many observers the unswerving relegation of sexuality to married heterosexual unions seems unworkable in a culture in which significant numbers of women are unmarried (single, divorced, widowed), for a significant portion of their lives. Indeed, avoidance of premarital sexuality is the norm today only among those (primarily Orthodox) women who marry relatively early, in their late teens and early twenties. Nevertheless, many women feel that Jewish guidelines are useful to them in charting their course through newly complex sexual territory. Single women often say that Jewish emphasis on commitment is an important component of their sexual decisions. They see sexuality as one aspect of a broader relationship, and they believe that loyalty is an important part of premarital relationships. Some single Jewish women devise their ethos of monogamous, nonmarital sexuality with the help of contemporary scholarship, which explores precedents for nonmarital relationships in rabbinical writings that diverge from codified Jewish law.[56] Although Western Jewish societies in the past did not sanction nonmarital unions, some rabbis thought them permissible, and social conditions today make such categories appealing to many women, who are neither ready for marriage nor for completely casual approaches to sexuality.

Married women who have deep ties to Judaism report that the structures of Jewish belief and behavior not only help them juggle their daily routines, but also give them the strength to find private time for the people they love, including husbands as well as children and parents. Some also speak of the strength which Judaism has given them to resist extramarital affairs, which often seem ubiquitous in the workplace. "If feminism teaches me that I am the sole owner of my own sexuality," says one, "Judaism teaches me that I have chosen to dedicate my sexual activity exclusively to my husband. That was a choice entered into freely, which is now a solemn personal as well as religious commitment."

Such commitments, interestingly, seem to enhance rather than diminish sexual pleasure. A recent survey found that "most religious women of all faiths were consistently more likely to report being happy most of the time, to describe their marriages and their sex lives as very good, to be satisfied with the frequency of intercourse, to discuss sex freely with their husbands—and even to be more orgasmic."[57] Analyzing these data and their connection with the sexual lives of Jewish women, researchers suggest that "caring and commitment derived from deep religious feelings can lead to behaviors that contribute to sexual satisfaction."[58]

Many women feel that committed relationships are undermined not by feminism's insistence that women must control their own sexuality, but instead by an individualistic society's incessant emphasis on personal freedom and happiness. While rigid prescriptions limit personal freedom, they also prevent the worst excesses of exploitative behavior in interpersonal and sexual relationships. Prohibitions against premarital sexuality and marital rape, for example, may not make men genuinely kinder or more compassionate to their sexual partners, but they do prevent a singles ethos of "scoring" sexually and a marital environment in which women have no sexual voice. In the absence of externally imposed, religiously or socially structured standards of sexual behavior, the personal ethics of each individual become the exclusive curb on self-serving impulses. In the current climate of self-involvement, in which, in Woody Allen's words, "the heart wants what it wants,"[59] scores of books, articles, films, and television programs glorify a romantic preoccupation with ephemeral passions rather than enduring mutual commitments.

Jewish feminists wish to retain constructive Jewish approaches to sexuality. They see in traditional Jewish life a respect for women and for female sexuality that was often not fully appreciated by critics who concentrated on obliterating rigid boundaries. Conversely they observe in modern life an overt espousal of sexual freedom for women that sometimes masks callous exploitation and is often at its basis antifeminist and antiwoman. The only lasting solution to the problems of establishing meaningful sexual relationships in contemporary Western societies, according to numerous Jewish women, is to inculcate in both men and women the capacity to respect, care for, and be loyal to sexual partners. As long as men or women regard sexual partners with a predatory eye, unkindness will abound, both outside and inside marital unions. When the media and popular culture reinforce an individualistic ethic, the family becomes the primary inculcator of the desire and ability to relate the others in an empathetic, even altruistic manner: "Until Jewish parents teach their sons to treat women as considerately as they would like their own daughters treated, and until neither men nor women regard each other as trophies, things are not going to get any better," says one observer.

Every major ancient religion and every modern school of psychological thought have focused on the power of sexuality in the lives of human beings. More often than not, the basic physiological differences between the sexes have been extended to or confused with the differences in gender roles that societies assign to women. Frequently such gender-role differences have been defined not as societally but as biologically determined. In some cultures women have been rather forcefully encouraged to extend their biological childbearing and nurturing activities into lifelong domesticity; these same cultures then describe women as lacking in ambition, energy, or aggression—by virtue of the fact that they are willing to be confined to domestic enterprises. Women in many cultures have been deprived of equal educational opportunities and then derided by those cultures for not being equally intellectual.

The tendency to blur the lines between sexuality and gender roles has continued into modern times and is even sometimes championed by feminist theorists who, in Susan Jacoby's words, "have stood the old argument about sex difference on its head. The concept that women are different and therefore inferior has been replaced, in many instances, by the idealized notion that women are different but *superior* beings." Thus women are sometimes said to have innately a more subtle, people-oriented moral development than do men, or to think in networks of meaning rather than in a linear mode. Critics of the different-but-superior theories warn that such formulations can easily back-fire. "The compensatory impulse to worship a woman's 'menstrual powers' that supposedly link her to Nature and Life" can serve not to empower women but to "restore the familiar pronatal pressures on women who cannot or choose not to have children. They make women who have a difficult time with menstruation or childbirth feel guilty," says Carol Tavris.[60]

Indeed, assertions that women are different and superior have been used for generations by apologists for patriarchal systems, who wish to maintain the exclusion of women from men's intellectual, spiritual, and physical turf. Many a traditional rabbi, for example, has insisted that women do not need to participate in public prayer or Torah learning because women are innately spiritual, or they are intrinsically closer to God and therefore do not need the paraphernalia that men use. Issues coalescing around sexuality and gender pervade the biblical and rabbinic prescriptions of the Jewish religion, much of the impetus for change in contemporary social movements, and much of the institutional and personal resistance to suggested change.

Gender bias continues to play a role in Jewish and American life.

Jewish women have been active in the political realm in trying to make the American government more inclusive of and responsive to women's issues. Most are firmly committed to the process of erasing employment biases based on gender and on giving women a legislative voice. Many are especially concerned with issues such as ensuring reproductive choice, controlling sexual harassment and violence, and increasing support for family units, universal medical care and education, and a more wholesome environment.

In the Jewish world as well, American women have worked to diminish the ways in which a gender bias based on sexuality has distorted their image and has excluded them from public participation in their own birthright. Traditional Jewish law ruled that women must be unseen and unheard because women's voices would incite men to lustful thoughts, distracting them from prayer; today's Jewish women are learning to pray out loud in their own voices. Jewish culture seldom sanctified and celebrated life-cycle events that were peculiar—and profoundly significant—to females; today's women are breathing Judaism into the momentous events of their lives. Jewish communities seldom taught women as thoroughly as men because they believed that women were generally frivolous and lightheaded; today's Jewish women are acquiring the intellectual tools to master the most complex Judaic texts. In a communal system that kept power, leadership, and decision making in male hands, relegating women to auxiliaries and female ghettoes, Jewish women are fighting to break through ceilings. Confronting a literary and media culture in which the ambivalences and angers of Jewish males were projected onto satirical caricatures and grotesque portrayals of Jewish females, women are creating their own literature and films and learning how to see themselves anew.

American Jewish feminists today believe that individuals and societies can cherish and respect sexuality without using sexual differences as a scaffolding to construct spiritual, intellectual, and social hierarchies. As they re-vision their roles within Jewish religious, communal, and cultural life, feminists are not attempting to become "more like men," and they do not necessarily wish gratuitously to blur the lines between the sexes. They are, instead, preventing stereotypes of femininity (from whatever source) from being utilized artificially to limit their development—and their contributions—as human beings and as Jews.

Chapter Six

Sanctifying Women's Lives

Blessed are You, O Lord our God and God of our foremothers and forefathers, who has set the moon in its path and has set the order of the cycles of life. Blessed are You, O Lord, who has created me a woman.

—Prayer for the onset of the menses (1972)[1]

ALL CIVILIZATIONS, societies and religions have devised rituals and ceremonies to mark passages in the lives of their citizens and adherents. Participants find such observances meaningful for many reasons. Perhaps most important, they confirm the communal significance of personal experience; they assure the individual that she or he does not celebrate or mourn alone, because the community as a whole shares the joy and the grief. Ceremonies legitimate not only the life-cycle event itself but, by extension, the individual who celebrates and mourns as well. The message of a life-passage ritual is: Your happiness and your sorrow are real; your friends rejoice and grieve with you; your life and its events are important to all of us. In addition, when the ritual or ceremony is part of a religion, it has another layer of significance—it is sanctified and marked as an event that is important to God as well as human beings.

Although Judaism has historically provided powerfully meaningful ceremonies to sanctify the life-cycle events of Jewish males, Jewish women have found many of the most profoundly moving events

121

of their lives unmarked and unsanctified. Female life-cycle events have largely passed without formal communal, ceremonial responses and even without provision for personal rituals that might express the sacredness of the moment, as the individual woman herself experienced it.

In traditional Jewish societies, differences between men and women in Jewish law and life begin at birth. Ceremonies surrounding the birth of a son are extensive, long sanctified by Jewish law and community custom. The first Friday night after the birth of a son, Ashkenazi fathers traditionally host a *shalom zachor,* literally "welcome to the male," an informal, festive after-dinner gathering at their homes, at which songs are sung, homilies set forth, and refreshments served. Eight days after the birth of a son, the *brit milah,* ritual circumcision, provides an occasion at once solemn and festive for the celebration and sanctification of the child's birth. In addition, if the first child is a male, thirty days after his birth his father participates in a *pidyon ha-ben* ceremony, "buying back" his son from the service the child would otherwise be obligated to render to the priestly class, according to biblical law.

It is difficult to overestimate the deep, complex feelings of communal solidarity and personal joy created by communal celebrations of the *brit milah,* both among the parents and among the community members. The very name of the circumcision ceremony—*brit*—means covenant and recalls the original covenant God made with Abraham. The ritual circumcision conveys the male child into the historical destiny of the Jewish people, not only by duplicating the "mark upon his flesh" first practiced by Abraham but also by evoking the concept of the chosenness of the Jewish people. At the ceremony the parents are blessed with a wish that they may be privileged to escort their son as he matures into the study of the Torah, the marriage canopy, and the doing of deeds of lovingkindness. In traditional Jewish communities the *brit milah* is far from a private affair; an indirect announcement is made in the synagogue to the entire community as to the time and place of the event, because no Jewish male may refuse a direct invitation to such an auspicious occasion.

The circumcision ceremony evokes not only the joyous acceptance of a Jewish destiny but also a courageous leap of faith, with both religious and nationalistic overtones. Because of the antisemitism of many societies in which Jews lived historically, the *brit milah* has come to symbolize each parent's willingness to expose his child to the dangers being Jewish might entail. A circumcised male child is marked forever as a Jew, in both good and evil times. Thus Nathan Zuckerman, in Philip Roth's novel *The Counterlife*, confronts his own ineradicable Jewish soul, his pledge to the future of his people, when he determines:

> I know that touting circumcision is entirely anti-Lamaze and the thinking these days that wants to debrutalize birth and culminates in delivering the child in water in order not even to startle him. Circumcision is startling, all right, particularly when performed by a garlicky old man upon the glory of a newborn body, but then maybe that's what the Jews had in mind and what makes the act seem quintessentially Jewish and the mark of their reality. Circumcision makes it as clear as it can be that you are here and not there, that you are out and not in—also that you're mine and not theirs. There is no way around it: you enter history through my history and me. . . . The heavy hand of human values falls upon you right at the start, marking your genitals as its own.[2]

Many Jewish males, including those who are quite removed from Jewish ritual observances and synagogue life, have indeed seen circumcision as "quintessentially Jewish and the mark of their reality." Professor of Literature Ann Shapiro describes a conversation she had following the presentation of a paper on American Jewish writers at the annual Modern Language Association of America meeting: "This male professor kept insisting that circumcision was the universal symbol of the Jew," she said. "I kept trying to convince him that it's only universal for half the Jewish people—that Jewish women can only relate to circumcision vicariously. And he acted as though I was crazy. He just kept repeating the same thing again and again. Circumcision is the universal symbol of the Jew."

Much as Jewish mothers, sisters, and daughters may empathize, rejoice, and identify with the *brit* ceremonies, bar mitzvahs, and other life-cycle passages of their sons, brothers, and fathers, such ceremonies do not sanctify the specific life-cycle events of women. Jewish feminists work to rediscover and create modes of sanctifying those things that happen to women personally. The creation of sacred rituals, however, is a complex task, and one that often touches on sensitive issues. Suggestions for new ceremonies or liturgical responses to such events as the birth of a daughter, the onset of menses, a girl's religious coming of age, childbirth, miscarriage or abortion, or menopause can seem to some observers to be alien intrusions into an ancient tradition. Some Jewish feminists are very alert to religious sensitivities, well educated in Jewish texts and attitudes, and careful to make use of materials that are clearly in the spirit of Jewish tradition. Others, however, freely incorporate materials from other cultures, which serve as additional irritants to those who oppose Jewish feminist innovations. Opponents of such innovations sometimes accuse feminists of criticizing and rejecting two thousand years of Jewish religious observance, history, and thought through the introduction of woman-oriented ceremonies and prayers.

Jewish feminists certainly have no desire to diminish the significance of ceremonies with ancient authority and deep historical and spiritual significance. However, they are insistent that the lives of Jewish girls and women should be accorded deep spiritual significance as well. In contrast to the communal joy and profound feelings evoked by the circumcision ceremony, in the past ritual responses to the birth of a girl were pallid. The child's father was one of several men in the synagogue called to make a blessing on the Torah, and there he would recite a prayer for the health of the mother and child and name his daughter. The blessing was similar to that given the father of a son—with one significant exception: "May you be blessed to lead your daughter to the marriage canopy and to doing deeds of lovingkindness," by implication leaving the study of the Torah to male children alone. Some families would also mark the occasion by serving simple refreshments after Sabbath services, but neither the mother nor the infant herself was necessarily nor customarily brought to the synagogue for the occasion. As recently as twenty-five years ago, a lavish kiddush reception after services could arouse the sarcastic comment: "You're doing all this for a girl?"

Today, however, the birth of a Jewish girl in Jewishly aware circles is likely to be the occasion for meaningful ceremonies and celebrations. The Sephardi custom, *seder zeved habat*,[3] "celebrating the gift of the daughter," has been adapted in many communities into the more commonly entitled *shalom bat*, "welcoming the daughter," or *simhat bat*, "rejoicing in the daughter." Once a little-known concept, the *shalom bat* has become popular in many Jewish communities. In the home or synagogue, with mother and daughter present, friends gather to listen to talks, eat, sing, and celebrate together. It is very common to announce the child's name at this ceremony and to discuss the origin of the name, with time often devoted to recalling and honoring the person after whom the daughter has been named.

Some parents use traditional Sephardic prayers; others compose new prayers for the occasion; others make use of printed materials that have been written and disseminated in liberal Orthodox, Conservative, Reform, and Reconstructionist circles.[4] Roselyn Bell, reviewing the many methods now in use for welcoming a Jewish daughter, notes that "the Reform movement includes a 'Covenant of Life' ceremony in its *Gates of the Home* prayer book for home usage. There is also a naming prayer in the Reconstructionist prayer book. The Conservative Rabbinical Assembly has a printed certificate that can be presented upon the birth of a daughter . . . and some Orthodox synagogues, such as Lincoln Square Synagogue and Kehilath Jeshurun of Manhattan, have printed procedural suggestions for a *simhat bat*."[5]

Less commonly, this ceremony of dedicating a female infant to her Jewish destiny may be referred to as a *britah*, that is, "her covenant." Sharon and Michael Strassfeld have suggested a *brit mikvah*, a ceremonial immersion of the baby girl in a *mikvah*, as the appropriate counterpart to *brit milah*, and Rabbi Julie Cohen insists on the suitability of the word *brit*. "I don't call it *simhat bat* but *brit banot* [a covenant for girls]," Rabbi Cohen says of a ceremony she created for the birth of her niece, "because I think the word *brit* should be used. We want to welcome a girl into the covenant—not in the sense of copying what boys do, but because bringing a child into the covenant is so important, and you would want to do it in front of family, friends, and community."[6] However, perhaps because they remind some people of female circumcision, terms making use of the word *brit* are far less popular than variations on *shalom bat*.[7]

Ceremonies for the sanctification and celebration of a Jewish daughter's birth have proliferated. A brief summary of one such ceremony is instructive because it illustrates the syncretic nature of Jewish feminism and shows how Jewish feminists of both genders are drawing on the past to create new forms that are both traditional and innovative. When a daughter was born to Rabbi Ruth Langer, who received her Reform ordination from HUC-JIR (Cincinnati) in 1986, and Professor Jonathan Sarna, Braun Professor of American Jewish History at Brandeis University, they consecrated their daughter's birth together with a mixed congregation of more than 150 family members, friends, and professional colleagues on Sunday morning in the Orthodox synagogue at which they regularly worship.[8] One grandmother carried the infant into the synagogue and up to the *bimah* (central lectern), where the child remained for the duration of the ceremony. Professor Sarna first described the history of such ceremonies, including the German Jewish *Hollekreisch,* a secular naming for both boys and girls at the age of one month, and the Sephardi *seder zeved habat.*[9] He spoke about each of the liturgical ingredients in the traditional *zeved habat* and chanted each of them together with the congregants, including a verse from the Song of Songs,[10] a midrash suggesting that God appreciates women's prayers and supplications,[11] a unique *mi-shebarach* prayer (prayer asking for blessing) written especially from a woman's perspective,[12] and Psalm 128, the Song of Ascent.

Sarna than yielded the pulpit to his wife, Rabbi Langer, who spoke with her infant daughter, Leah Livia, in her arms. Langer provided a history of the two great-grandmothers after whom the child was being named, and expressed her "fervent prayer that our daughter will have the merit of coming to embody—and in that way give an added measure of immortality to—the two great women whose memories we cherish." Both grandfathers and two Orthodox rabbis added greetings and good wishes from the *bimah* before the ceremony concluded with a sumptuous brunch, at which the emotions of joyfulness, gratitude, and accomplishment were freely expressed by those assembled.

Daughters like Leah Livia Sarna will presumably never feel—as so many Jewish women feel today—that the great moments of her life, from birth onward, went unsanctified and uncelebrated. Birth ceremonies for Jewish girls honor the newborn daughter and the women who came before her; such ceremonies—like the *brit milah*—focus on the chain that connects contemporary Jewish children to their historical past.

An even more pressing issue than the neglect of the Jewish daughter is the spiritual neglect of the Jewish mother. The ritual invisibility of the Jewish mother—except as her presence affects her husband—is one of the most egregious aspects of childbirth in traditional Jewish societies. When rabbinic law turns its attention to women after childbirth, it is only to stipulate how long the new mother is sexually unavailable to her husband. Today Jewish women are reclaiming and composing sacred ceremonies that celebrate their unique roles in the reproductive process. Many of these ceremonies make use of ancient blessings, quotes, and other materials. Indeed, one of the great challenges to contemporary American Jewish feminists is to ground innovative ceremonies in the traditions of the past, so that they will evoke a sense of deep connectedness with Jewish women and communities throughout the ages.

In many synagogues today the mother recites aloud *birkat ha-gomel,* the traditional prayer of thanksgiving for deliverance from a potentially dangerous situation, when the Torah is read at the first Sabbath service after childbirth. The new mother recites the prayer either standing at her place after her husband's Torah reading (in Orthodox synagogues) or after she herself receives an *aliyah* (in non-Orthodox services). This custom of a woman coming to synagogue and saying the *birkat ha-gomel* marks a change from the past, when the husband recited this prayer on his wife's behalf because a woman's voice was seldom raised for herself in a public setting. It is also indirect testimony to the less restricted lives of today's young mothers, who, barring complications, are hospitalized only a short time after childbirth and soon resume their customary activities.

However, while certainly appropriate and forward looking, this custom does not alter the fact that although Judaism has created a plethora of blessings for almost any situation affecting men, no official blessing has ever been accepted as ritually incumbent on the new mother. The father is encouraged to recite a prayer for the hearing of good tidings if the child is a boy. The *birkat ha-gomel* is an all-purpose prayer that is also recited when an airplane doesn't crash or one falls off a ladder and survives. By the same token, Judaism has created a rather beautiful and insightful blessing praising the Creator of operational orifices (*asher yotzar*), which is recited by Orthodox Jews after completing defecation and washing their hands—but there is no blessing for completing childbirth for a woman, despite the fact that childbirth is, for many women, without doubt one of the most profoundly spiritual occasions possible in human experience.

Jewish feminists are actively involved in composing, recreating, and reclaiming blessings that attempt to fill that vacuum. Some blessings are a century or more old, examples of the *tekhinnes,* Yiddish prayers for women—sometimes authored by women—passed down from mother to daughter, which were earlier attempts to fill the lacunae of Jewish women's spiritual experiences. A century-old prayer for the birthing mother, for example, reads:

> Oh, my God! Soon approaches the great hour when I shall give birth to another human being, according to thy wise ordination. . . . I call upon Thee, from the depths of my soul. Fortify me with strength and

courage in the hour of danger, God of Mercy! Grant that the life of my child may not be my death! . . . Convert, O God, my pain into delight at the lovely sight of a living, well-formed and healthy babe, whose heart may be ever dedicated to Thee.[13]

Tekhinnes illuminate the lives of pious Eastern European women who reached out for ways to express their spirituality.

More recently authored women's blessings also often draw heavily on biblical and traditional materials. Thus, one modern prayer for a woman who has just given birth—"Blessed art Thou, our Creator, for making me Thy partner in the creation of a new Jewish soul"[14]—is actually based on the biblical Eve's declaration when she had just given birth to Cain: "I have acquired a man-child with the help of God."[15]

Several articulate observers of contemporary American Jewish life believe that powerful vehicles for and expressions of Jewish women's spirituality were lost in the transition from Old World to American forms of Judaism. Women as different as Reform Professor Ellen Umansky, radical Orthodox feminist Rifka Haut, and Miriam Klein Shapiro, president of the right-wing Conservative Union for Traditional Judaism, emphasize the rich spiritual lives of women in many pre-American traditional Jewish communities.

Shapiro, for example, finds meaningful spiritual outlets in some old Yiddish prayers, and she has used them to construct new prayers as well for such moments as pregnancy and birth, which she describes as "the most religious episodes in my life. Five times from an act of love I have felt life growing inside of me. I know what a miracle is. Crossing the Red Sea is nothing compared to that. Traditional Jewish feminists are using old materials, retrieving them for new settings, such as Rosh Hodesh celebrations and ceremonies for girls getting their period. Why shouldn't the life cycle of women not be given proper treatment? In fact, they were given much fuller treatment before immigration to the United States, but life-cycle materials were lost when men and women were brought together in the synagogues. I'd like to retrieve and reuse many of these beautiful, traditional prayers. Thus the *techinot* utilized by our grandmothers can provide us with at least the beginnings of liturgical responses to our own bodies."

When Jewish tradition seems to ignore important life-cycle events, feelings of emptiness and puzzlement are voiced by many women. Rabbi Laura Geller remembers that when she began menstruating at age thirteen, she ran to tell her mother. Her mother told her "that when she got her first period my grandmother slapped her. I could almost feel the force of my grandmother's hand on my mother's face, the shame, the confusion, the anger. . . . And as I thought back to that time, I understood that there should have been a blessing. . . . Thank you, God, for having made me a woman—because holiness was present at that moment."[16]

Old and new blessings and prayers that reflect women's experiences are used at ceremonies which mark and sanctify other previously ignored and unsanctified major events of a woman's life. Rabbi Lynn Gottlieb, spiritual leader of Congregation Nahalat Shalom in Albuquerque, New Mexico, describes an all-female initiation ceremony for menarche held on Rosh Hodesh—the "blessing way"—in which mothers and pubescent daughters (twelve and thirteen years old) sit in a circle and share their thoughts and feelings about the onset of menstruation and sexuality:

> When we did a ceremony for becoming a woman prior to Bat Mitzvah, everybody dressed in red and sat under a red *chupah* with their mothers. We passed a bowl around with necklaces the women had made for their daughters. Each woman told the story of her first period and how it was received. They shared wisdom they've learned about being a woman. I worked with the girls. They each wrote a blessing for themselves, blessing seven parts of themselves they felt good about—eyes, athletic ability, drama, ability to get all A's in school. For some of them it was very hard to do. They all got a lot of positive feedback and love, which is very important for adults as well as children. Many adult women had no memories of menarche being marked, or they had only negative memories. Many women remembered getting slapped, which created fears of their own bodies and their own sexuality. Adults also talked about taking care of their own bodies, only sleeping with people they wanted to, and protecting themselves.

Feminists have focused not only on the onset of menstruation at the beginning of adulthood but on midlife and menopause experiences as well. They create ceremonies to sanctify these moments, often addressing the *shekhinah*, traditionally the female and nurturing aspect of the Creator, and referring—like the *tekhinnes*—back to the examples of biblical women.[17] Rabbi Laura Geller, director of the Jewish Feminist Resource Center in Los Angeles, has composed several prayers and ceremonies which use the waters of the *mikvah* "for healing processes," including a ceremony for women who have undergone abortions. The Jewish Women's Resource Center in New York has published, among other ceremonies for women, those which give Jewish sanctification to such events as menstruation, marriage, and weaning a child.[18]

Perhaps the most widespread result of the religious efforts of Jewish feminism is the popularity of the bat mitzvah celebration. Reconstructionist founder Mordecai Kaplan, who was also closely associated for many years with the Jewish Theological Seminary, may have been the first to suggest the concept of bat mitzvah,[19] and Conservative Judaism made popular the actual celebration of this event. At first few families chose to celebrate the bat mitzvah,[20] and during the 1950s and 1960s many Conservative synagogues limited the celebration to the less problematic Friday night services, when the Torah is not read. Moreover, Reform congregations did not take the lead in mainstreaming bat mitzvah ceremonies because at the time when they were gaining popularity many Reform congregations had substituted the concept of confirmation ceremonies at the completion of Sunday school studies for the concept of bar mitzvahs. It was not until some time later, when the Reform movement was reincorporating a number of more traditional rituals into its services, that it also reincorporated the bar mitzvah ceremony—and with it the bat mitzvah as well. By the late 1980s, however, most Conservative and almost all Reform congregations had made bat and bar mitzvah ceremonies virtually identical, including calling girls to the Torah.

For women who missed having a bat mitzvah in their youth, such a celebration at a later stage of life provides the opportunity for both a renewed commitment to Judaism and a feminist assertion of personhood. Susan Gilman, who opted for an adult ceremony, says, "In the midst of our Jewish lives, there was a void—something that was not quite okay for us. One of us said she wanted to stand where her husband and four children stood and read a *haftarah* from the same bimah. Two of us are making up for being denied the chance years ago when we were told in our *shuls* there was no such thing as girls being *bat mitzvah*."[21]

Suzanne Reisman, a potter and grandmother from Long Island, states unequivocally that her recent bat mitzvah at her Reform temple was one of the great events of her lifetime: "I would say that three kinds of days were the highlights of my life—the day I got married, the days when my four children were born, and the day in which I had my bat mitzvah, read from the Torah, and helped to put the Torah back into the ark. Every time I handle the Torah I want to weep with joy. I realize how much it means to me. All my life I have been Jewish, and at last I have a way to express my Jewishness."

Recently, the woman who was the first to be called to the Torah for a bat mitzvah celebrated her seventieth anniversary of that event. As eighty-two-year-old Judith Kaplan Eisenstein recalls her bat mitzvah when the Torah was read by men, she was allowed to stand below the platform "at a very respectable distance from the scroll of the Torah" and recite from her own copy of the Five Books of Moses. "It all passed very peacefully," she recalled. "No thunder sounded. No lightning struck." At a recent ceremony Eisenstein—a noted musicologist, composer and author—was honored by prominent Jewish feminists, including Betty Friedan, Letty Cottin Pogrebin, Blu Greenberg, and Rabbi Rachel Cowan.[22]

Orthodox practitioners have slowly responded to the pressure to celebrate a girl's religious majority. Some congregations have established a format for celebrating bat mitzvah on Sunday morning or Shabbat afternoon at a special *seudat sh'lisht,* the traditional festive "third meal." At these occasions the girl typically delivers a *d'var Torah,* a homiletic address marking the seriousness of the occasion. Other congregations leave the mode of celebration up to the discretion of the child and her parents. These celebrations have become commonplace in many Orthodox circles, with families sometimes traveling great distances to be at a bat mitzvah, just as they would for a bar mitzvah. Much feminist commentary on this phenomenon has tended to concentrate on the disparity between limited Orthodox forms of bat mitzvah, on one hand, and egalitarian Conservative, Reform, and Reconstructionist modes of bat mitzvah on the other. This, however, misses the point that Orthodoxy has in fact traveled a farther road than other wings of Judaism in breaking away from previously prevailing norms.

Divergence in the treatment of women in Orthodox congregations even in the same locale can be striking. A study of bat mitzvah ceremonies in two suburban Orthodox communities found differing patterns in attitudes and behavior among the clergy, bat mitzvah girls, and their families.[23] Neither age nor religious intensity could predict how feminist or antifeminist rabbis and congregants were. A more restricted role for women was enforced in the synagogue with fewer ritually observant families. On the other hand, the congregation with almost universally "Orthoprax" ritually observant families had a much more liberal attitude toward female participation.

The difference between the two "modern Orthodox" congregations reveals much about contemporary American Jewish life and the factors that do—and do not—influence the position of women in the religious community. Congregation Darchei Noam has been described as "havuroid"—that is, it has an egalitarian ethos and is highly participatory. The rabbi's talks alternate with those of congregation members, and women are among the congregants giving talks from the *bimah* at Darchei Noam Sabbath-morning services, although their talks, unlike those of the male congregants, are delivered at the conclusion of the services rather than between the Torah reading and the *musaf* (additional) service. Coed classes are taught by members as well, and teachers have included both men and women. Women can and do serve as synagogue officers and make announcements from the *bimah* at the end of the service. Darchei Noam allows women's prayer services in the synagogue building on Rosh Hodesh (the monthly new moon, traditionally a festive holiday for women), on the holiday of Simhat Torah, and for special occasions such as bat mitzvahs. The celebration of bat mitzvah at Darchei Noam can consist of a women's prayer service, if the family chooses to do so, complete with a Torah reading and talk by the bat mitzvah girl. A significant proportion of women at Darchei Noam have liturgical skills learned at day schools or Hebrew-speaking camps; the congregation also offers courses in cantillation to both men and women.

At Congregation B'nai Shalom, on the other hand, the thirty-five-year-old rabbi strictly limits female participation. He does not allow women's prayer services in the synagogue and exercises tight control over the forms the bat mitzvah celebration can take. No women are allowed on the *bimah* on the morning of a regular Sabbath service. Thus the bat mitzvah girl may speak at a celebration following a Sabbath service in the social hall. She is allowed to give a *d'var Torah* from the pulpit at a nonservice gathering in the synagogue during the week, often followed by a celebration in the social hall. In addition some families celebrate the occasion at home. Most of the girls study in preparation for their bat mitzvahs with the rabbi or a teacher in their day school, so the bat mitzvah involves more than a party. Nevertheless the restricted bat mitzvah ceremonies and parties at B'nai Shalom are described as not especially meaningful, even by girls from observant families who attend services regularly. One girl said that she had a party near her twelfth birthday because "there was a lot of pressure from the family" and "that was the thing to do." At a later reception at the synagogue she gave a *d'var Torah* on the *parsha* (appropriate reading from the Five Books of Moses) of the week, but "it never really was my *parsha* anyway, it's not my birthday . . . if you asked me what the *parsha* was, I wouldn't be able to tell you." She laughingly admitted that her father gave her the sources to write her speech from and she wrote it two days before the reception.[24]

Strikingly, some of the bat mitzvah girls at B'nai Shalom believed that only "irreligious" girls would have more-participatory bat mitzvah celebrations. One said that bat mitzvah was not significant to her Jewishly "because I'm not a boy, or like girls who are not religious, so I don't read the Torah. It's not like anything's different, although when I was younger, I waited three hours between eating milk and meat, and now I wait six, but it's not such a major difference. Maybe if you're not religious, and this is your religious thing, it makes a difference."[25]

In contrast, almost universally the girls who have had bat mitzvah celebrations in the context of a Torah reading in a women's prayer group describe the experience as profoundly spiritual and moving. Perhaps the most eloquent was Yaffa Leah,* an Orthodox day-school student:

> I know on Shabbes when I was *davening* [praying, here—leading the female group in prayer] and I was *layning* [chanting the portion of the week from the Torah], I felt when people talk about being close to *Hashem* [the Name, respectful Hebrew term for God], this is what they mean. I felt awe. It was really a wonderful feeling that I'm doing something here that I don't usually get to do, but it's still a meaningful thing. . . . A bat mitzvah's about taking a new role in Jewish society. Since then, I've been a lot more aware of what I should and shouldn't do. It used to be that I wouldn't care too much if what I did was right and wrong. Now I know that this is my responsibility, not anyone else's. No one else is watching me, no one's going to fix my mistakes. It's become more important to me to do the right thing, both to be nice and kind, and also to look at the Torah more carefully, to learn, and to fulfill all the commandments.[26]

---

* Asterisk indicates pseudonym.

Yaffa Leah looks forward to using her skills at future women's prayer groups: "We have the women's Torah reading on Simchat Torah, and I *layned* there. Each time, it's something so special that it makes me wish that I could do this more often." She feels sorry for classmates at her day school who had less meaningful ways to mark their bat mitzvahs: "A lot of them didn't have anything, or something small. It was really different. I don't know why they see things so differently, but they do. I didn't discuss it with them at the time because we didn't talk about such serious things. Most of my friends didn't go into such depth with their learning. I think that's a really meaningful thing to do, because before you become a Jew, you should really know what you're doing." However, she is very clear that she does not want to pursue these activities in an egalitarian setting: "To become Bat Mitzvah in a way that is not approved by the Torah defeats the whole object."[27]

Without conferring with any of the bat mitzvah girls who mark their religious maturity in a women's prayer group, the rabbi of B'nai Sholem scornfully rejects both their motivations and indeed the whole concept of such a prayer group. "A woman's service is deceptive. The attempt to simulate a minyan is insulting and inappropriate," he said, although participants and researchers never called the women's prayer group a minyan. The rabbi added that "there is nothing to be embarrassed about in the traditional roles for men and women," and that he does not like to "give credence to the notion that ancient Jewish traditions are based on prejudice or the degradation of women." He thought that "these new ideas are 'just to make a statement,' and that is the problem with them, rather than the issue of women *davening* together which they do in Orthodox day schools."[28]

Nicky Goldman, a Brandeis University graduate student who interviewed the bat mitzvah girls, was especially impressed by "the involvement of the mothers" at Darchei Noam. "They were called up to the Torah that their daughters were reading from. They gave talks during the service. They felt intense pride in their daughters' learning and performance. I felt that this was a tremendous experience for the mother and daughter to share." She feels it is crucial for people to understand that "the women were serious, that this was not the result of a fad, and that it was part of a process, not an outcry. . . . Here a way has been found of pushing out the parameters of Jewish law—yet remaining in it—so that young women, and for that matter, their mothers also, can have a positive, meaningful experience to celebrate their Bat Mitzvah, and to mark the start of their responsibility to fulfill the *mitzvot.*"[29]

The one event of Jewish women's lives which has been vigorously celebrated for hundreds of years in both Ashkenazi and Sephardi societies is the transformation of a girl into a bride. The *kallah* (bride) has always existed on a plane in which she for a short but glorious time is a special person indeed. Providing an attractive trousseau for a bride was a matter of such importance that, according to Jewish law, if she was an orphan or the daughter of poor parents, the entire community was responsible for endowing her with the things she needed (*hakhnassat kallah*). In Sephardi societies the bride was accompanied to the *mikvah* at some point shortly before her wedding by a lively group of female relatives, who showered her after her immersion with candies, good wishes, and the characteristic Oriental ululation (a series of trilling cheers); in Ashkenazi societies the same errand was usually performed with considerably less public spectacle by the bride, her mother, and the ritual bath attendant alone. As in all female immersions in the ritual bath, the bride recited the specific prayer referring to the commandment of immersion, following the second of three complete immersions into the "living" waters (water at least partially from a natural source).

On the day of the wedding the bride was to have a *shomeret,* a female attendant (wisely, generally not her mother), to watch over her and to provide for her needs. Before the wedding ceremony, while the groom presided at a table in a separate room (the *khossen's tisch*), the bride was enthroned on a special chair, where well-wishers could approach her and the two mothers; immediately before the marriage, dancing men escorted the groom to the bride, and he ascertained that he was in fact marrying the correct woman (unlike the biblical Jacob) before placing the traditional bridal veil over her face. As the personage of honor at the ceremony and following dinner, the bride was never left alone. If she was an orphan, someone would be delegated to walk down the aisle with her. At the dinner, even in pious communities where all the men and women sat separately, the bride was usually allowed to sit with the groom. It was a special good deed to dance and sing before the bride, to perform amusing stunts, and to entertain her, and both men and women competed (albeit in separate circles) to bring a smile to the bride's face.

Contemporary Jewish feminist brides often retain many of these traditional practices, while supplementing them with additional events of an overtly spiritual or scholarly nature. Thus some Jewish feminist brides prepare a prenuptial scholarly talk, the result of some months of study, to be delivered at an engagement party, on a Sabbath before the wedding (sometimes in combination with a bridal *aliyah* to the Torah), or in a bridal room that closely parallels the groom's room before the traditional veiling ceremony.

Interestingly, the prenuptial visit to the *mikvah* has been championed by many Jewish feminists, most of whom have no intention of regularly maintaining the family purity laws after marriage. Orthodox Jewish law requires brides and married women to bathe thoroughly and then to immerse themselves in the *mikvah* following menstruation and seven "white" days, prior to initiating or resuming sexual activity. Much to the surprise of older American Jews, many of whom regarded the *mikvah*—if they thought of it at all—as a quaint relic of outmoded attitudes and life-styles, interest in the *mikvah* has had a renaissance of sorts in feminist circles. A key factor was Rachel Adler's positive discussion in the first *Jewish Catalogue*.[30] Feminists exploring Jewish women's spirituality and religious expression, together with well-educated younger generations of Orthodox women who take religious obligations seriously and newly observant women who seek the structured environment and sexual limits of Orthodoxy, have revitalized *mikvahs* in many communities.

Positive articles about *mikvahs* have appeared in several publications, including the *Reconstructionist* and *Hadassah* magazine. Two female rabbis wrote an article while students at the Reconstructionist Rabbinical College about how *mikvah* ties in to their search for Jewish feminist spirituality:

> It appeals to the individual on the many levels of her spiritual existence and relationships. First, it addresses her relationship with her future husband—that intimate, binding relationship of two people who at times fuse in body and soul. Next, it addresses her relationship with other Jewish women, who have ancient and current ties to her through water. Finally, it addresses her relationship with all Jews, through Torah and its folkways.[31]

Their "Ceremony for Immersion" includes prayers and blessings in Hebrew and English, some drawn from traditional sources and some newly composed. Some years later Rabbi Barbara Penzer is still enthusiastic about the role of *mikvah* in her life:

The *mikvah* is a very positive experience for me personally and in my marriage. During a year when we were in Jerusalem and lived only a block away from a *shul* [synagogue] with a *mikvah*, I went every month. How could I live in Jerusalem and not go to the *mikvah*; it just fit in so naturally. Here I go less often, but I strongly urge every bride whom I marry to at least begin her married life with this beautiful experience.

A large number of female rabbinical candidates observe the laws of family purity and visit the *mikvah* regularly, according to Professor Anne Lapidus Lerner, dean of List College at the Conservative movement's Jewish Theological Seminary in New York. "These are women who have a lot of integrity and who are very serious about their spiritual and religious lives," she says. "They are taking on many additional obligations, such as time-bound prayer three times a day. They feel deeply that they should maintain those obligations which Jewish women have maintained—sometimes with great difficulty—throughout Jewish history."

In addition, as alluded to earlier, the *mikvah* has taken on importance as the locus of new, specifically feminist ceremonies, such as ceremonies for healing after rape, miscarriage, or abortion. These events are often powerfully significant to women, and they yearn for the acknowledgment and amelioration religious ceremonies can offer. One woman remembers bitterly, "When I discovered that despite physically and emotionally agonized days in bed I had miscarried and lost the baby, the doctor scheduled me for an outpatient procedure. I was already in my fourteenth week, and the procedure was very painful, and when it was all over they let me rest in a lounge chair for twenty minutes, gave me a glass of orange juice, and sent me home. My whole world had fallen apart, and it was like it hadn't happened—no one noticed. My husband was very supportive, but what I really craved was some kind of ceremony which said, 'This matters, this is important, you have suffered a real loss.' "

According to Jewish tradition, one does not mourn for a child under one month old, and no ceremony marks fetal death. Some creators and practitioners of ceremonies that aim to give women spiritual strength at such uniquely feminine moments feel that there should be available a *mikvah* that is not funded by and tied to the Orthodox community. "I would feel dishonest," says Rabbi Laura Geller, "if I would have to bring a woman in for a postabortion healing ceremony and walk past the *mikvah* attendants in their head coverings. It's true that they don't ask me what we're doing there. But I have no doubt that they wouldn't be too thrilled if they knew. My wish is to build a special *mikvah* which would serve as a communal resource, the physical and spiritual focal point of the Jewish Women's Resource Center."

Some life-cycle events, of course, revolve around the lives of others. The death of a parent, in particular, is a momentous event for surviving children. Traditional Jewish law treats mourning sons and daughters identically in many ways. Both men and women are required by Jewish law to exhibit public and private mourning behavior: During the period of *shiva,* for seven days after the funeral, they are expected to wear torn clothing, to avoid bathing, to cover their mirrors, to sit on low stools, and to avoid commerce and such daily tasks as food preparation. The practical effect of the latter prohibition is that even the mother of a large young family is prohibited from kitchen tasks during the week of *shiva.* These tasks must be assumed by nonmourners, thus allowing the female mourner to work through her grief with the same intensity as does a male. For a month after the funeral it is customary for neither men nor women to cut their hair. For a year after the funeral, avoidance of joyous celebrations (except for their own children's weddings and bar/bat mitzvahs), particularly those with live music, is equally incumbent on both males and females. However, in one respect men and women are treated quite differently in traditional Jewish circles—men are required to recite kaddish (prayer in memory of the dead) and women are not.

Many women are deeply offended by their exclusion from public prayer after the death of a parent or relative. The recitation of kaddish (which is actually a paean to God's greatness and does not refer to death) has attained a powerful symbolism for many, perhaps most, Jews. Among those of Eastern European cultures, a male child was often referred to as a *kaddish'l,* a guarantee that kaddish would be recited after one's death. According to some strands in Jewish tradition, survivors recite kaddish to aid the soul of the departed as it attempts to rise from a limbolike state into heavenly existence; when no male survivor was available, a (preferably pious) male was paid to recite the prayer. For most American Jews, however, kaddish is significant because it is a way to publicly honor and show devotion to a departed parent and to express one's commitment to the totality of the Jewish people, linking the values of the past with an as-yet-unknown future.

Even Jews who are in many other ways rather removed from formal prayer and religious rituals are often punctilious about reciting kaddish during the mourning period and on the *yarhzeit* (the anniversary of a loved one's death). Many women report that they simply assumed that they would recite kaddish at mourning services each day—only to be told in no uncertain terms by male synagogue regulars that women were not welcome and that no one would answer amen to their recitation. When these women arrived at their local Orthodox or Conservative synagogue—Reform congregations by and large do not hold daily services—they learned for the first time that many synagogue regulars regard daily prayer services as kind of privileged male turf, regardless of that particular congregation's official stand on female participation in Sabbath-morning services.

Traditional synagogues are the most likely to have daily prayers, and they are also the most likely to be unwilling to count women for a minyan, posing a serious problem for the would-be female kaddish reciter. Greta Weiner recalls entering one Conservative synagogue only to be pushed to the back of the chapel by a man who insisted that her presence would be "disruptive of the men trying to pray." Refusing to count her and her teenage daughter for the minyan, the congregation that evening had only nine men and did not include kaddish in its prayers.[32] Ruth Seldin, coeditor of *The American Jewish Year Book,* tells a similar story about a friend who was in mourning:

> She came regularly, in fact, not just to say kaddish, though that was obviously important to her. An older man was sympathetic. "Listen," he told her. "You've got a brother—why don't you tell him to say kaddish for your father?" The woman looked at him, barely able to control her anger. "My brother doesn't give a damn—I want to say kaddish, don't you understand?"

Seldin comments, "When nine men and a duet or trio of women would sit gloomily in an empty sanctuary, unable to pray because a male body was missing, the emotional toll on the women, and on some of the men, was high. When it strikes you suddenly that your presence in the synagogue counts for nothing, that you are for all intents and purposes a lump of useless protoplasm or when you consider the possibility that God will listen to words only from the mouths of half His creatures, the *other* half, how can you react except in shame and rage?"[33]

The first shock of exclusion comes only a few hours after the funeral. A forty-five-year-old suburban New Yorker who works as a paralegal says:

> We were sitting *shiva* in our living room, my mother and I on low chairs, our guests sitting in a circle on couches and easy chairs, when all of a sudden there was this invasion of men in suits and ties, sweaty, on their way home from work, men from our conservative *shul* I hardly knew and my mother had never met. They ordered my mother and me and all our female friends out of the room—and I mean *ordered.* "We have to *daven,*" they said. "Your husband has to say kaddish." "What do you mean, my husband?" I asked them in tears. "My father was buried this morning. My husband's parents are alive and well. I'm saying kaddish for my father." "No you're not!" barked the *gabbai* [sexton]. "You can say kaddish til you're blue in the face but it won't count. If you want your father's soul to go to heaven, you better get a man to say kaddish for him three times a day."

Such brutal exclusions during a time of extreme vulnerability evoke strong feelings among many women. As one professor remembers, "For me feminism started when I was ten and was not allowed to say kaddish for my father. Each morning I dragged my crying little brother to shul—but I was not allowed to go in with him." A similar experience estranged *Ms.* magazine founder Letty Cottin Pogrebin from Judaism for fifteen years. At age fifteen she was unceremoniously ejected from the room when sitting *shiva* for her beloved mother. Her bitter feelings toward Judaism as an organized male religion were not healed until she led a congregation in prayer on the High Holidays fifteen years later. Pogrebin, who says she was raised in a "high Conservative" home with extensive holiday observances and frequence synagogue attendance, insists that the communal experience of Judaism—most commonly represented by communal prayer—is crucial:

> Until you've converted the I of Judaism to the We of Judaism, you haven't really found the center of Judaism. When I was fifteen and wasn't able to be counted in the minyan at the shiva for my mother I was alienated from the patriarchy of Judaism. It excises women from the healing of Jewish mourning rituals and prevents closure. I turned my back on it all. For the next fifteen years I did nothing except for celebrating holidays in my house to honor my mother's memory.

What brought me back to the We of Judaism was an unexpected communal experience which began a new spiritual journey for me. I came back when I was enlisted to be the *hazzanit* at the community Rosh Hashanah service on Fire Island. I stood in front of 350 people at an enormous converted church. I sang Kol Nidrei. My legs shook. That was the beginning of my spiritual breakthrough. I came back spiritually through feminism through the capacity to lead.

Indeed, strong feelings around the issue of saying kaddish for a parent are among the most universal experiences in the formation of Jewish feminist commitments. Many women feel anger and resentment toward the Jewish religious establishment vis-à-vis the treatment of women in the synagogue. It is clear that for decades untold numbers of Jewish women drifted away from Jewish tradition and Jewish institutions because they perceived Judaism as being indifferent or even hostile to their spiritual and emotional needs. By bringing sanctification and spirituality into American Jewish women's life-cycle experiences, and by bringing American Jewish women more centrally into the world of public Judaism, including prayer, feminism is breathing new life into the American Jewish community.

Each of these areas of Jewish feminist activity has evoked a corresponding—and sometimes vituperative—backlash. In perhaps no other spheres of Jewish feminist striving have the oppositions been as organized and vehement as in those of religious exploration, education in Judaica and scholarly development, and Jewish communal leadership. Some aspects of this creative renewal—such as Jewish life-cycle celebrations for females—affect huge numbers of American Jewish women. Other aspects—such as female ordination, the practice by women of traditionally male-focused rituals, and the creation of new, female-oriented prayers and rituals—directly affect only highly committed and involved women. However, even women who are not directly involved in the more intensive forms of Jewish feminist spirituality are reenfranchised by an environment in which women have increasingly become public Jews.

Chapter Seven

Praying with Women's Voices

My heart's song is eternal Sabbath.

—Kadia Molodowski[1]

FROM BIBLICAL TIMES ONWARD Judaism has always recognized that women have souls and that they can and should communicate directly with God. Rather than suggest that women need intermediaries in their relationship with God and their own spirituality (as in Milton's *Paradise Lost*—"He for God only, she for God in him"), Jewish tradition indicates that each woman, like each man, has her own personal connection with her Creator. Indeed, the biblical Hannah's heartfelt prayer was considered by Talmudic sages to exemplify correct and effective communication with God (Berachot 30b–31a). However, the assumptions and the language of Judaism, its narratives, laws, and liturgy—with a number of noteworthy and deeply significant exceptions—have largely been framed in the language of men to reflect the experiences of men. Those passages of biblical, rabbinic, and liturgical literature that do reflect the viewpoint of Jewish women have received scant notice in traditional Jewish settings, in comparison with the far-more-numerous passages drawn from an all-male world view.

Contemporary Jewish feminism has turned a systematic spotlight on the religious souls of Jewish women. Jewish feminism has gone back to the biblical, rabbinic, and historical wellsprings of Judaism

143

to rediscover, reemphasize, and reinterpret women's roles in the development of Judaism as a religion, an ethical system, and a culture. It has opened the doors of classical Jewish learning to women of all ages. It has worked toward reinvesting major female life-cycle events with formal, Jewishly significant spiritual import. It has rediscovered old prayers and created new ones both to transcend patriarchal attitudes and to give expressions to female Jewish spirituality, and it has moved women into more public positions in prayer services themselves.

According to rabbinic law and Jewish tradition, the religious obligations of Jewish males are incumbent on them except in cases of extremity, such as life-threatening situations, while many of the religious obligations of women are modified by their obligations to other human beings. Although women are legally obligated to obey all laws except those that are time-dependent, females' religious obligations have been placed in the context of relationships to their parents,[2] husbands,[3] children,[4] and the community at large.[5] According to Jewish custom, and in some cases according to Jewish law as well, women's opportunities to communicate with God and to express their spirituality have often been considered secondary to their responsibilities to family members and to the sensibilities of the community.

The estrangement of Jewish women from prayer is in many ways a particularly American phenomenon, which reflects the overall U.S. shift during the twentieth century from home-based to institutional religion. In the European Jewish settings from which the vast majority of American Jews derive, women typically prayed in the home. The *tzibbur,* the worship congregation, is defined as a group of at least ten men. The presence or absence of women is irrelevant to the *tzibbur* in rabbinic law. Group prayer was desirable because certain prayers could only be said in the presence of a *minyan* (quorum) of ten men[6] but prayer was not seen as exclusively a group activity, especially in the recitation of prayers three times a day. Men prayed in the synagogue when they could, but many frequently prayed in the home as well.

In contrast, in twentieth-century American Jewish life increasingly small proportions of the population have prayed three times a day, and prayer services for the vast majority of American Jews have taken place almost exclusively in the synagogue. For most of the twentieth century, the American synagogue has been controlled and dominated by men, just as it was a male domain in the Old World.

However, few American Jewish women pray in the home as their grandmothers often did. As a result, for a very long time they prayed only sporadically. Many American Jewish men still felt connected to prayer because it was part of their synagogue connection; lacking that bond, many women felt estranged from Jewish prayer and spirituality.

Traditional Jewish authorities agree that women should pray; rabbinic differences of opinion center around the forms and frequency of prayers that may be required of women. Because the evolution of the traditional prayer services has evoked differing interpretations, womens' obligations to recite those prayer services have been the subject of dispute as well. In biblical times God was served through sacrifices under carefully specified conditions, but prayer was often regarded as the spontaneous service of the heart. Rabbinic law, however, stipulates particular prayers and prescribes the times for them, thus changing the legal status of prayer—and changing the relationship of women to prayer. The status of women vis-à-vis prayer was called into question when prayer services became determined and codified by rabbinic law. Many of the laws central to rabbinic Judaism are stated in some form within the Torah, the Pentateuch. Prayer, like many other aspects of Jewish life, began as a biblical imperative and underwent later development and refinements, as the legal system is developed and expanded in the Mishnah, circa 200 C.E., the Jerusalem Talmud, circa 400 C.E., the Babylonian Talmud, circa 500 C.E., medieval Talmudic commentaries, later codes and commentaries, and the responsa literature, which includes rabbinical rulings on specific cases.

According to rabbinic law, women were released from the obligation to pray at specific times because rabbinically required prayers at specific time periods might conflict with a woman's domestic duties. The law tried not to put women in the position of being in conflict as to whether to perform a child-care task or to complete a prayer service within the allotted time. They were encouraged to pray whenever possible and were obligated, in the view of Maimonides, Nachmonides, and many other classical commentaries, to pray at least once a day.[7]

The worship behavior of Jewish women in traditional communities differed widely, as did their levels of education and literacy, but some form of daily prayer was virtually universal among observant Jewish women. Better-educated pious Jewish women prayed formally in Hebrew at least once a day—and some recited the appropriate prayer services two or three times a day. In some communities women were given only the most rudimentary Hebrew education or no Hebrew literacy at all. Nevertheless, even women who were not well educated enough to read fluently from the Hebrew prayer book memorized and recited short blessings throughout the day, including those required when they performed those special rituals specifically incumbent on women, "women's *mitzvot.*" These included baking the Sabbath challah and burning a piece of the dough in commemoration of the Temple sacrifices in ancient Jerusalem, immersing themselves in the *mikvah* prior to resuming sexual relations with their husbands one week after their menses had ceased; and blessing the Sabbath candles.

Moreover, although some have mistakenly assumed that traditional Jewish women did not have the opportunity for rich spiritual lives, the religious expression of women in the observant Ashkenazi societies from which the majority of American Jews are descended was far from limited to challah, *mikvah,* and *narot,* the lighting of candles. Religious expression was part of the texture of women's lives as they performed their daily routines. Their private lives were suffused with homely—and home-based—religious expression, although they were not required to pray and study on the same rigid time-bound schedules as were their fathers, husbands, and sons. As they went about their chores and celebrated life-cycle events, women recited specialized Yiddish prayers that were passed down from mother to daughter.[8] There are *tekhinnes* for both daily events and major life-cycle events, for baking bread and giving birth. They often allude to biblical characters and stories, drawing analogies between women in their ongoing physical lives and their role models in the Holy Scriptures. When *tekhinnes* refer to God—and they often do— they speak more of God's warmth and nurturing qualities than they do of awesomeness and power. Women who were literate in Yiddish read books of homilies and interpretations of the Bible on Sabbath afternoons. Even those who were illiterate attended services on Sabbath mornings, where they could follow and respond to the devotions of more educated female *zoggertes,* or prayer leaders.

Nevertheless, Jewish women's formal obligations to prayer were seldom stressed in traditional Jewish communities. Often they were discussed so little that eventually they were forgotten or even denied in the popular culture. Thus, even though women do have an obligation to read the Purim Megillah and to participate fully in the recitation of the Sabbath prayers on wine (kiddush), bread (*motzi*), and distinguishing between Sabbath and weekdays (*havdalah*),[9] these prayers were almost universally recited exclusively by men. Within a family structure, the father's recitation of the kiddush, *motzi*, and *havdalah* prayers corresponded to the mother's prayers on lighting of the candles and were part of a gender-based spiritual division of labor. However, even in situations where men were unavailable and women were obligated by Jewish law to read the Purim Megillah and to recite the prayers on wine, bread, and Sabbath's beginning and ending, women often mistakenly believed they were forbidden to recite some of these passages and prayers. As a result it was not uncommon for widows and divorcées to search for men to chant prayers for them, which they not only could but should have chanted for themselves, and to listen passively in fulfillment of their mistaken notion of Jewish law. Many women believed it was more virtuous and correct to listen to a male acquaintance recite the kiddush, for example, than to recite it for themselves.

Men and women prayed separately in both Sephardi and Ashkenazi synagogues, with the women behind a partition (the *mekhitzah*), in overhanging balconies, or even in an adjoining room. The rationale for the separation is based upon perceptions of the inexorably sexual presence of females. As Maimonides states, "One should not look at a woman, even at his own wife, while reciting the *Shema*, and if even a hand breath of any part of her body is uncovered, he should not recite the *Shema* in her presence." (Shulhan Arukh, Orah Hayyim 55:1) Scholarly debate continues over how ancient this separation of the sexes might be, with some scholars insisting that separation by sex goes back to the period of the Second Temple in Jerusalem and others finding evidence that such separation is of relatively recent origin—that is, only eight or nine hundred years old.[10]

However venerable the separation of the sexes, certainly since the Middle Ages most Jewish men and women prayed separately and accepted this arrangement as unshakable and appropriate. As a practical matter, except for Sabbath mornings and holidays the synagogue was almost exclusively a male domain, as synagogue attendance was considered primarily a male obligation. Only men were counted toward the minyan, and only men received such synagogue honors as reading from and handling the Torah. As many a little girl discovered, all the "action"—prayer accompanied by the wearing of the *talit* (prayer shawl), and during the week, *tefillin* (phylacteries), the taking out and reading of the Torah scroll, the blessing by the *cohanim* (priestly descendants) on Sabbaths and holidays, the parading and dancing with the Torah on Simhat Torah, and the marching with the *lulav* and *etrog* (four "fruits" of the autumn festival, that is, palm, myrtle, and willow branches and a citron) on Sukkoth—occurred on the men's side of the *mekhitzah*. Many women remember their childhood feelings of loss when they grew old enough to be forever banished to the women's section, where they could only peek over or through the *mekhitzah* to view the central activities of the prayer service.

With the growth of the Reform movement in Germany in the nineteenth century, and with the later creation and expansion of Reform and Conservative Judaism in the United States, the isolation of women in prayer began to change for the vast majority of Jews. However, these changes occurred very gradually. As long as Christian denominations by and large also treated women as somewhat less equal than men, both Reform and Conservative Judaism did not move swiftly to change the status of women in public Jewish life. Indeed, despite the attempts of some leaders to suggest substantive movement toward female equality in worship services, the majority of Jewish religious leaders edged away from the topic. Even in settings in which momentous change was taking place in other areas of ritual and prayer, women's issues were downplayed—tabled to committees or left to the end of agendas when they could not be avoided or ignored.

At a Reform rabbinical conference in Frankfurt am Main in 1845, for example, one of the speakers proposed that women ought thenceforth to be obligated to prayer and to be counted for the minyan. This subject, however, was not discussed at length but was tabled to a special commission for further study. Nevertheless the Frankfurt conference participants did have time to discuss and vote on many substantial changes in other areas of Jewish life: the rabbis voted unanimously to permit organ music in the synagogue on the Sabbath and to remove the traditional *musaf* services, which recall the sacrificial services in the biblical temple; a majority also resolved that petitions "for the restoration of a Jewish state should be eliminated from our prayers."

At similar conference in Breslau one year later, the rabbis vigorously debated the superiority of Sunday or Saturday observances of the Jewish Sabbath; they resolved that Reform congregations would be free to abolish the second day of festivals, that Reform Jews could resume the eating of bread on the eighth day after the beginning of

Passover, since this day was no longer considered a binding part of the Passover holiday for them, and that traditional forms of mourning—such as tearing the clothing, not shaving, or sitting on comfortable chairs—be abolished. When the subject of women's position was raised at the Breslau conference, the previously appointed commission on women's status reinforced the idea that women should have the same religious obligations as men and that the morning prayer thanking God "for not having made me a woman" should be eliminated. However, once again it is reported that "Unfortunately this important and interesting report could not be discussed owing to lack of time. It was merely read."[11]

In Germany at this time, separate seating for men and women remained in force, and the leadership of Reform congregations was exclusively male.[12] In the United States, the movement of women into egalitarian modes went forward somewhat more easily. Much discussion was devoted to women's participation in choirs at the dedication of the Bene Israel synagogue in Cincinnati in 1852. Those who opposed female participation said that according to Jewish custom, it was inappropriate to hear female voices in the public services. Philipson suggests, "Nowhere was the Orientalism of the synagogue more pronounced than in the inferior position assigned to women in the public religious life." However, by the convention of the Union of American Hebrew Congregations held at Baltimore in 1891, the delegation of the Berith Kodesh congregation of Rochester, N.Y., counted a woman as one of its number. American Reform Judaism gradually succeeded in eliminating many of the inequalities that had separated men and women in Jewish prayer. Reform congregations introduced mixed choirs, abolished the women's gallery, built temples with family pews, and substituted the confirmation ceremony for boys and girls in place of the bar mitzvah for boys alone.[13] In the spring of 1921 Martha Newmark, a seventeen-year-old student at Hebrew Union College, asked for and received permission to officiate at High Holiday services, could a willing congregation be found. (She was less successful in her quest to study for rabbinic ordination, and no American woman would be ordained within the Reform movement until fifty years later, in 1972.)[14]

Within the formal and highly structured services common in American Reform Judaism for decades, the position of women was in many ways not appreciably different from that of the male laity. Men did not wear head coverings or prayer shawls—indeed, until the 1960s, in many temples they were forbidden to do so. In some congregations neither men nor women were called up to recite the blessings and read from the Torah. Men and women sat side by side, and responded as instructed to worship cues issued by officiating rabbis. In many congregations for years English was almost exclusively the language of worship, "a source of culture and enlightenment,"[15] so the lesser Jewish education received by many women was not as much of an impediment to worship as it was in more traditional prayer services. However, as more Hebrew was incorporated into Reform services, with the infusion of Eastern European Jews into the Reform movement and the rise of the State of Israel, the gap between male and female levels of Hebraic literacy became more apparent. As one older woman put it, "I have to sit next to my husband or I can't follow what's happening."

Nevertheless, it was not until feminism changed women's feelings about their spiritual selves and their position in the worshiping congregation that numerous Reform women began agitating for more participatory roles. For some the first step began with bat mitzvah. The bar mitzvah ceremony, once virtually replaced by confirmation, began to be reinstated in some Reform congregations in the decades following World War II. Reform bat mitzvah ceremonies became popular in the 1970s and 1980s, and, as a prerequisite for the bat mitzvah, formal religious instruction for girls began to be more widespread among Reform Jews. Increased rates of formal education gave young Reform women levels of Jewish literacy that were often higher than those of their mothers and predisposed them to look for active participation in worship services as adults.

The involvement of women in prayer within the Conservative movement followed a somewhat different pattern, because of the more traditional nature of many Conservative congregations. Conservative Judaism first developed as a staunchly traditionalist counterforce, in opposition to the pressures of Reform Judaism rather than in contradistinction to Orthodoxy. Indeed, what we today think of as Orthodox Judaism was simply mainstream Judaism before the ideals of the emancipation, emerging in the more direct challenges of Reform Judaism, forced the crystallization of self-conscious, clearly defined traditionalist movements in response. One response to radical Reform was neo-Orthodoxy; another, ideologically more flexible reaction, was that of Historical, or Conservative, Judaism, in the late nineteenth and early twentieth centuries.

American Conservative congregations in the twentieth century aimed to offer an atmosphere that blended dignified, decorous worship services with traditional prayers and familiar customs. Initially many first- and second-generation American Jews of Eastern European backgrounds longed to pray like Americans and yet in a mode that was familiar and characteristically Jewish. They sought a modernity they did not find in Orthodox worship and yet felt uncomfortable in American Reform congregations. As a result, for decades Eastern European Jews were attracted to Conservative congregations, in which men wore head coverings, were called to the Torah, and recited a substantially traditional service primarily in Hebrew.[16]

Although most American Conservative congregations abolished separate seating fairly early in their history, the role of women in Conservative congregations remained quite modest for years after mixed seating became the norm, in keeping with other traditionalist tendencies. In 1955 Jewish sociologist and chronicler of the Conservative movement Marshall Sklare could still accurately report that women had almost no formal role in Conservative worship services during which the Torah was handled. He noted that women were much more likely to be included on Friday nights, when the Torah was not brought out. Despite the fact that the exclusion of women might seem "to indicate an inconsistency in the Conservative approach," Sklare concluded at that time, "there has been no widespread agitation for perfect equality. Conservative women have generally been satisfied with their limited status, a great advance over the age-old segregation. Furthermore, the pattern of formal equality coupled with limited participation follows the model of many Christian denominations where the rites central to worship are also performed largely by males."[17]

Nevertheless, change was already afoot. In 1955, the same year that Sklare's monolithic work on Conservative Judaism was first published, the Rabbinical Assembly's (Conservative rabbinical organization) Committee on Jewish Law (CJL) considered the issue of women being called up to read the Torah. At that time the majority opinion, voiced by a consensus of ten rabbis, suggested that women should be given honorary *aliyot* (Torah readings) on special occasions after the requisite seven Sabbath *aliyot* had already been given to men. Five dissenting rabbis, however, urged that women be given *aliyot* on an equal basis with men. Only one rabbi on the 1955 committee rejected the notion of women's *aliyot* outright.[18] A 1962 survey of Conservative congregations showed that few congregations had acted on the CJL's suggestions. Of 254 congregations responding, 77 percent did not give women *aliyot* under any circumstances, 20 percent gave women *aliyot* under special conditions, and only 3 percent honored women in this way on an equal footing with men. As Anne Lapidus Lerner notes, the restrictions set up by the 20 percent are particularly interesting:

> The late Rabbi Louis Levitsky thought it should be granted to "only those to whom it has deep religious significance and who can recite the *berakhot* by heart easily—never more than one on any Shabbat." These are restrictions which are never applied to men. According to Rabbi (Aaron) Blumenthal, "a number restrict it to girls at their Bat Mitzvah." This is a rather odd approach to religious training, but one which recurs. The bar mitzvah ceremony marks a young man's entrance into adult Jewish responsibility and privilege—the first, it is hoped, of many such occasions. But a Bat Mitzvah would mark a young woman's *exit* from participation. It would be the only time she was permitted to go up and read the *haftarah*.[19]

In the 1970s and 1980s, however, the picture changed dramatically. It was precisely the disparity between the literacy in and love of Judaism that many girls gained as they trained for bat mitzvah and the absence of participatory roles for women post–Bat Mitzvah that motivated Conservative activists within the Ezrat Nashiim women's study group to agitate for change. In September 1973, partially as a result of the efforts of Jewish feminists, the CJL voted nine to four that women should be counted for a minyan, basing the majority decision on the changing "contemporary position of women in society." The minority group opposing insisted, "There is no halakhic support." However, they did not limit their objections to those based on Jewish law. The Conservative rabbis who wished to prevent women from being counted in a minyan also cited economic reasons, which have no particular connection with Jewish laws in this area—"the *minyan* should consist of heads of households who support the community"—and reasons of sociological expediency—"Only a small pressure group wants it and it is a passing fad." According to Lerner, after the 1973 decision was reported in a front-page article in the *New York Times,* it evoked "a storm of comment, both positive and negative."[20] It should be noted that throughout this period prayer services at the Conservative Jewish Theological Seminary remained segregated by sex, with a *mekhitzah* separating the two groups. Indeed, even today the seminary offers students and faculty two services, one fully egalitarian (with the proviso that female participants must be fully halakhic and "serious" about prayer) and one traditional, sex-separated service with *mekhitzah.*

The battle over women's status in Conservative synagogues was still unresolved in the middle 1970s. A questionnaire distributed to Rabbinical Assembly members in 1975 revealed that almost half of Conservative synagogues at that time gave women *aliyot* on occasion and almost 40 percent counted women in the minyan.[21] This marked a substantial change in conservative life, which was deeply moving to many women. Ruth Seldin remembers that when the CJL voted to include women in the minyan, "Amen v'amen, we said to each other, with tears in our eyes. . . . I have been catapulted from one world to another; from a world in which women sit as passive observers of worship conducted by men, to a world in which women are able to share as equals in that responsibility." Nevertheless, she notes that the process has been at all times far more complex and controversial than she would have ever expected.[22]

The diversity of congregational attitudes toward female participation was illustrated in a 1978 study of 470 congregations representative of different branches of the Jewish religious community, and distributed among the various geographic areas of the United States.[23] Mixed seating and women leading the congregation in English readings were almost universal among Reform and Conservative congregations. Almost all Reform congregations allowed women to chant the service; slightly less than 50 percent of the Conservative congregations counted women for a minyan or allowed them to lead services; none of the Orthodox did. Nearly all Reform congregations and about 50 percent of Conservative congregations honored women with *aliyot* to the Torah, while none of the Orthodox congregations did. Women gave sermons in almost all Reform congregations, more than 75 percent of Conservative congregations, and 7 percent of Orthodox congregations. Most Reform congregations and almost 66.6 percent of Conservative congregations had women opening the ark and chanting kiddush and *havdalah,* but only 2 percent of Orthodox congregations did so.[24]

Opposition to egalitarian status often has little to do with religion and more to do with the "old boy" clubbiness that exists in many synagogues, primarily where there is an older population. Seldin suggests:

> As those who have spent their lives around synagogues know, a kind
> of Tammany Hall clique can concentrate great power in its midst; it
> may control the financial affairs of the synagogue as well as ritual
> matters, and it may either support the rabbi uncritically—or hound
> him at every step with criticism and complaint. Since people who hold
> power are rarely eager to give it up or to share it, in a synagogue where
> such a power group reigns, women's search for equality may be seriously blocked.[25]

The egalitarian prayer model is championed outside established synagogues in many Havurot. Prayer and study groups that often involve relatively small numbers of Jews, who are frequently fairly knowledgeable and/or committed Judaically, Havurot have a participatory and egalitarian ethos. Usually eschewing the materialistic trappings of institutional Judaism, they have been the locus of much creative ferment in the American Jewish community—ferment that has often filtered out, eventually influencing more established synagogues and temples. Because Havurot have no rabbis, cantors, or other professionals to lead services, read from the Torah, deliver sermons, and teach classes, and because they rely on group members to undertake these responsibilities, they have been pioneers in providing opportunities to women in these areas.

Even within Havurot, however, egalitarianism did not always arrive without conflict and confrontation. One particular Havurah, the Kelton Free Minyan,* located near a large California state university in Los Angeles, illustrates the practical elusiveness of egalitarianism in worship environments. Although the Kelton Minyan formally and officially gave women equal status relatively early in its history, female members felt they were "invisible" in prayer and study sessions. Part of their low profile could be traced to dramatically lower rates of Jewish education: The most active and vocal participants of both tended to be traditionalist males with strong Jewish education. However, men with poor Jewish educations did not feel self-conscious and effectively "silenced" in the same way the women did. Even after women with stronger Jewish educations became more prominent in the minyan, women felt invisible much of the time. Consciousness-raising groups seemed to accomplish nothing except the airing of grievances.[26] Finally, after a Simhat Torah celebration degenerated into a male-controlled, somewhat ribald event, reports Riv-Ellen Prell, the women decided to plan a females-only worship service at which "women sought and achieved (if temporarily) the social and symbolic visibility that allowed them to link the self and the text."[27]

Over the years, a mixed genre of synagogues developed that resolved mixed-seating issues by providing several different modes. Often called "traditional" synagogues, this model thrived especially in the 1950s and 1960s in the Midwestern United States where some congregations affiliated with the Orthodox movement separated men and women but provided no physical barrier between them, some had a large mixed section of men and women separating two separate sections of men and women (thus, a human *mekhitzah*), and some did away with separations altogether, adopting mixed seating but continuing to call themselves Orthodox. In 1960 about 250 Orthodox synagogues had some type of mixed seating, and in 1954 "90% of the graduates of the Chicago Hebrew Theological Institution, which is Orthodox, and 50% of the graduates of the Yeshiva, the Orthodox institution in New York," had positions with exclusive or optional family seating. Orthodox rabbinical institutions, however, especially Yeshiva University, continued to oppose their graduates accepting or remaining in positions where mixed seating had become the norm, unless they could convince the congregation to reestablish a woman's gallery or a *mekhitzah*. As the decades have passed, the opposition to mixed seating within the Orthodox movement has actually become more forceful along with general Orthodox triumphalism, and the creation of new so-called "traditional" congregations has ebbed.[28]

Women coming from egalitarian environments sometimes react with shock and horror on encountering the separation of the sexes typical in Orthodox environments. For example, a poet and translator of Yiddish poetry who grew up in a Reform environment and is now strictly observant of both the Sabbath and *kashruth*, finds herself far more comfortable in an egalitarian than in an Orthodox setting:

> I identify my return to traditional Judaism with my relationship with my husband. I don't like climbing stairs to get to a balcony. There is no community of women in the Orthodox synagogue near our house. I refuse to cover my hair except when it's snowing. The first time I went to an Orthodox Yom Kippur service I felt so angry, a curtain

separated me from men. I couldn't follow, I wanted to be there, I couldn't see page numbers. The women were a well-dressed, emotionally closed group with lots of kids, and were not very open or helpful to me. I felt like an outsider.

Some feminists are deeply disturbed by prayer with separate seating. A Sephardi novelist says:

The first time I went to a Sephardi synagogue, I was flooded with feelings of both profound joy and profound anguish. I wept. It was wonderful to be worshipping in my own tradition—a Sephardi tradition—at last. And yet I was furious at being stuck up in a balcony. To me feminism is crucial. It gives me self-respect and pride. Sitting up in the balcony of that synagogue gave me a different concept of the nature of sin. Do you know what sin is? It is the hypocrisy of men. Women are locked away and segregated in synagogues so that men don't have to deal with their fear. Religion is a social construct based on society, economics, political and sexual customs of the surrounding community. This treatment of women is not divine law. It is human, fallible, subject to change. Sephardi Jews lived in and resemble Moslem society. I was always enraged growing up. I always had been a rebel. Father said, you're rebelling against nature. Because of feminism I began to understand not just why I was angry but what I could do about it. For me the medium was language.

Others, however—even some who are not especially observant religiously—feel more comfortable with the traditional synagogue. Many find themselves caught betwixt and between, full of conflict, with no comfortable, politically correct spot to rest. A literature professor says that when she worships in settings where women get *aliyot* she is disturbed: "I'm not used to it. It looks fake to me. I find it peculiar sitting with men. It doesn't feel so holy. And the women with *yarmulkes*—ridiculous. Yet I can't handle women wearing *shaitels* [wigs worn for purposes of modesty by some Orthodox women] either. I want to see full recognition. Yet I'm uncomfortable with this. Just like I can't eat pork."

Some Jewish feminists have found the separation of the sexes so offensive that they have made it a moral principle never to pray in a setting in which men and women sit on opposite sides of a partition. National Havurah activist Esther Ticktin, for example, called for all like-minded Jews at least to boycott and preferably actively to op-

pose such arrangements.[29] Some Reform Hillel rabbis will participate in almost any type of Jewish prayer service, such as the campus
Jewish society of gays and lesbians, but will pray alone either before
or after participating with the Orthodox student prayer service, so
that they do not actually worship in a gender-separated setting, "on
moral grounds." While students who share these egalitarian senti-
ments often describe their rabbis as heroic, some of the Orthodox
students, including females who consider themselves to be feminists,
have complained that such a boycott by the person whose job it is
officially to provide for their spiritual needs puts them in the position
of being religious and social pariahs.

Today a curious situation has developed: Because of the conflu-
ence of Jewish feminism and general demographic trends, those Jewish feminists who are most devout in their observances are often
thrust into conflict with traditionalist Jewish communities that are
resistant to feminism and to women in leadership positions. This is
often the case because except among Orthodox and traditional Conservative Jewish households, the observance of Jewish ritual laws
has declined over the last half century from generation to generation
throughout the United States. When women who are in the thick of
Judaic learning and increased ritual practice look for a community
that shares their practices and values, they usually have no choice but
to turn to traditional communities.

Jewish educator Miriam Klein Shapiro points out some of the iro-
nies of this situation. It is primarily in congregations that do not
count women for a *minyan,* she asserts, that an actual quorum of ten
men gathers for three services a day. In many congregations which
count both men and women for a *minyan,* the generally less rigorous
observance of Jewish law among the congregants often results in the
fact that even counting both genders fewer than ten people show up
for services. Contributing to this problem is the fact that some traditional Conservative men, who have no objection to praying together with women as a group, refuse to pray with a quorum that has
fewer than ten men; in other words they don't require a *mekhitzah*
for group prayer but they do require a halakhic minyan of ten men.
Such men sometimes leave their regular congregation for daily prayer
when they see that their congregation is counting both men and
women, and they go to another congregation, frequently Orthodox,
which counts only men, for daily prayer—thus exacerbating the cycle of inability to obtain a minyan of any kind at more liberal congregations.

Orthodox Jewish feminists often feel as though they are in the position of being ostracized from both sides of the religious spectrum. The exploration of female participation in worship takes place not only in an egalitarian context, but in an all-female context as well. In all-female prayer groups, women have the opportunity to lead prayers and read the Torah, to be vital participants in a context in which for millennia they were nonessential auxiliaries. Even in all-female groups, however, conflicts arise between Orthodox and non-Orthodox women. While some non-Orthodox women welcome the all-female context so that they may read, lead, and pray without the potentially intimidating presence of men, Orthodox women need the all-female format because they will only perform in this way if men are not present. Furthermore, many Orthodox women will not recite the 20 percent of the prayer service reserved for a quorum of ten men unless they receive permission to do so by a recognized male rabbinical *posek* (person recognized as a competent formulator of Jewish law). Thus, non-Orthodox women welcome the women's prayer group because it allows them complete freedom of exploration, but Orthodox women are limited in the extent of exploration they feel able to pursue. As Steven M. Cohen notes, feminist religious styles "are predominantly determined by differences in approach to Jewish life rather than differences in approach to feminism."[30]

Although prayer is one of the most ancient concepts in Judaism, and one might imagine that a group of women praying together would inspire only positive comments, the fact is that women's prayer groups have become a *cause celebre* in American Jewish life. In many ways the formation of these groups and the reactions they have caused are both symptomatic of the accomplishments of Jewish feminism and the fear such success evokes. Group prayer by women is not per se controversial, as it is a regular occurrence in many Orthodox girls' yeshivot; moreover in European settings (and in certain ultra-Orthodox male yeshivot today) women were relegated to small rooms totally separate from that of the men, where they prayed devoutly, often led by a female leader. The two new phenomena that seem to have infuriated certain Orthodox rabbis were: (1) Women themselves have chosen to pray separately, rather than being relegated to separation by men; and (2) women are carrying, and reading from, the Torah scrolls.

In the world of Orthodox Judaism, formal daily prayer is still a serious requirement for a large proportion of practitioners, and weekly prayer is the norm for the vast majority—and it is in the world of Orthodox Judaism that the battle over women and prayer still rages. Moreover today it is in issues over group prayer that the most public opposition to Orthodox feminism has come to a head.

Indeed those two words—*Orthodox* and *feminist*—might seem to be in direct opposition, and some Orthodox Jews who have attempted to blend the values of feminism and Orthodoxy have encountered bitter conflict. Their struggle is worthy of close attention because the confrontation between feminism and Orthodox Judaism is in many ways emblematic of the antagonism between Judaism and modernity. "Feminism is an ugly word in the Orthodox community," says a feminist activist in Manhattan's dynamic Lincoln Square Orthodox congregation. "Anything that smacks of contemporary political movements is automatically suspect to most Orthodox leadership." Feminism is by definition a political movement which aims to transform society so that gender does not define behavior or limit opportunities. It requires widespread and ideally rapid changes, either through augmented evolution or through revolution, to accomplish its goals. Orthodox Judaism, on the other hand, is by its nature very resistant to change, because it is committed to the *halakhah*, which governs every aspect of human behavior.

Orthodox Jewish feminists of both genders not only face conflict from without, in the form of resistance from the majority of Orthodox rabbinic leaders; they also often experience inner conflicts. Orthodox feminists believe deeply both in the authority of Jewish law, on one hand, and in expanding and enhancing opportunities for spiritual expression for women, on the other hand. Unlike feminists who identify themselves as Conservative, Reform or Reconstructionist Jews, who generally believe that the force of morality is on the side of egalitarianism, Orthodox feminists often find themselves psychologically split at the root. They champion simultaneously, and must somehow reconcile, both the spiritual equality of women and a fundamentally androcentric Jewish tradition.

Their hopes for reconciliation—like their difficulties—arise from the nature of rabbinic Jewish tradition. Rabbinic tradition is not inevitably synonymous with stasis: indeed, the Jewish legal system has been in a state of cautious flux for more than two thousand years. In each of the postbiblical discussions of Jewish law, many differing possible interpretations are explored. Sometimes, the rabbis discussing a specific issue suggest that one particular interpretation is preferred. However, that interpretation is frequently challenged by rabbis of a later generation or even a later century, and new interpretations are seen as preferable.

Ironically, in some ways the challenges of modernity seem to have made the Orthodox legal world more resistant instead of more amenable to change. Modern movements that emancipated first the Jews of Germany and later the Jewish communities of Eastern European and Russia not only opened the way for Jews to express themselves in secular modes, such as non-sectarian higher education, socialism, and nationalism, but also opened the door for changes within Judaism itself. In Germany and later in the United States, Reform Judaism rejected the claims of rabbinic Judaism, positing universalist goals of social justice and welfare as the basis of Judaism. American Conservative Judaism attempted to blend a deep respect for the halakah with a willingness to make changes appropriate to modern life. In many contemporary Orthodox Jewish circles, a siege mentality prevails, because the vast majority of American Jews have abandoned the strictures of *halakhah* and have attached themselves instead to the more flexible standards of Conservative, Reform, and Reconstructionist Judaism or have disaffiliated with organized Jewish life altogether.[31]

Of all the major wings of American Judaism, only Orthodox Judaism has retained its belief that Judaism is synonymous with the *halakhah,* a divinely given and inspired way of life. However, Orthodoxy itself is far from monolithic. To right-wing Orthodox practitioners and rabbinical leaders, modernity is an evil that has succeeded in fragmenting Jewish religious life. Left-leaning Orthodox thinkers see another side of the issue: To them modernity has provided unparalleled blessings as well as problems. Left-leaning Orthodox Jews approve of the acquisition of higher secular education and familiarity with the intellectual worlds of modern science and Western humanism.

Most of the overt dialogue between feminism and Orthodox Judaism has taken place in left-leaning Orthodox circles—although even right-leaning American Orthodoxy has been deeply (and often unwittingly) influenced by feminism. In terms of education and occupation, for example, all but the most sectarian adherents of Orthodoxy have absorbed widespread cultural values. In most American Jewish communities today, the majority of Orthodox women under the age of fifty, like their non-Orthodox sisters, have attained college degrees and are employed outside the home. Orthodox women with wigs or other head coverings work as computer systems analysts and accountants in Gentile-owned corporations; many of these same women vigorously deny that their lives have been in any way influenced by the feminist movement.

Substantial numbers of Orthodox women seem to compartmentalize the nontraditional aspects of their lives from their traditional roles.[32] Others find ways to rationalize, to defend the religious status quo, and to make all the pieces of their lives fit together. An Orthodox female accountant, who attends law school four evenings a week, who modestly tucks her hair up under a hat when she goes to work, and who prays every day—even on the subway if she has no time to do so at home—has found a way to remove the implied inferiority of women from the morning prayers:

> Some people object to the fact that Orthodox Jewish men say a prayer in the morning in which they thank God for not making them women. The men's blessing doesn't bother me. . . . I don't think it is meant to demean women. When I pray, I don't concentrate on the blessing men say; instead, I meditate on the prayer women are supposed to say. We thank God for creating us "according to His will," and that seems like a much greater compliment to us. . . . A positive statement is always much stronger than a negative one. Our prayer might also imply that women are created more in the image of God. Hashem [one of God's names] is the epitome of sensitivity, and women are more sensitive than men.[33]

Some Orthodox feminists, on the other hand, routinely substitute the Conservative movement's reworking of these passages in their private prayers.[34] Many of the difficulties which Jewish feminists have faced in trying to effect change have been due to the peculiar sense of anxiety and inferiority that often afflicts the so-called "modern Orthodox" world. Orthodox Jews who do not reject modern values and life-styles often find themselves looking over their shoulders at the right wing to make sure that they do not delegitimize themselves through overly bold or revolutionary decisions. Administrators of coeducational Orthodox day schools in the Midwest and on the East Coast, for example, have reported that some teachers who have no personal convictions prohibiting coeducation still may refuse to teach at their schools, because once they have taught in a coeducational school they can be blackballed by rabbinic authorities from teaching at all-male yeshivot, religious educational institutions.

However, despite the intrinsic conflict between Orthodoxy and feminist goals increasing numbers of women are finding it possible—although not easy—consciously to synthesize feminism with traditional Jewish life and law. The advancement they have accomplished—and the struggles they have endured—are poignantly symbolic of the progress and provocation that have marked contemporary American Jewish feminism over the past twenty years. Members of a new hybrid community, Orthodox Jewish feminists are in many ways a heterodox group, spanning a wide spectrum of ages and religious and educational backgrounds. Their ranks include a few forward-looking Orthodox rabbis who research legal precedents for expanding women's spiritual expression and work with women, both individually and in groups, to implement their findings. Yeshiva University Professor Rabbi Saul Berman, for example, strongly distinguishes between the positive aspects of traditional Jewish gender distinctions and the negative, societal outgrowths of these distinctions—outgrowths that have often been mistakenly sanctified and are detrimental to the spiritual lives of women. He feels that the rejection of women's prayer groups by Orthodox rabbis and Jewish communal leaders is a result of their confusion about what is essential and what is a negative side effect of the law:

Judaism has many prescriptions for role differentiation. These role differentiations are necessary, but they can and have created many undesirable side effects or consequences. We must differentiate between what are the necessary aspects of role differentiation and what are the undesirable consequences—and eliminate them. Halakhic women's Tefillah (prayer) groups eliminate the unnecessary by-products of gender role differentiation. We have a responsibility to do whatever we can to expand spiritual opportunities for women within the framework of Jewish law.[35]

Several pro-feminist Orthodox scholars and rabbis have published books, articles and papers strongly defending women's prayer groups. The lengthiest and most extensively developed is Rabbi Avraham Weiss's *Women at Prayer: A Halakhic Analysis of Women's Prayer Groups*,[36] a careful and sympathetic exploration of the issue in both ancient and modern sources. Rabbi Weiss has been a true pioneer in the area of women's issues within traditional Jewish life, because he not only researches and writes about these issues but actively provides forums for women to expand their spiritual and religious horizons. His congregation, the Hebrew Institute of River-dale, N.Y., is one of the few Orthodox congregations in the world that houses a monthly women's *tefillah* group, which has been operating on a regular basis for more than a decade. He refutes the accusation that such female prayer groups are destructive to Orthodox Jewish life by declaring that, on the contrary, "Our women's *tefillah* group is part of a larger vision of Torah, Israel, outreach and activism" which he and his congregants have developed.[37]

Rabbi Aryeh A. Frimer, a professor at Bar-Ilan University in Israel, produced a heavily documented defense of "Women and Minyan" in a recent edition of the Rabbinical Council of America's scholarly journal, *Tradition*. Frimer shows that women are allowed by highly respected rabbinical authorities to constitute a worship quorum at such times as they read the Purim Megillah of Esther for each other or when a group of three or ten women recite the *birkat ha-mazon,* the grace after meals.[38] After carefully discussing opinions both for and against female quorums, Frimer goes beyond those who have argued only for the acceptability of female prayer groups by stating that under certain conditions women's minyanim are allowable by Orthodox law.

"Many contemporary authors have concluded that in this instance ten women or nine women and one man do indeed constitute a valid *minyan,*" Frimer states. Moreover, he adds, the presence of "a *mekhitza* does not prevent men and women from joining together to form a *minyan* quorum" for certain specific purposes. While "women cannot constitute a *minyan*—either alone or together with men—for the purpose of public prayer which includes *kaddish, kedusha, barehku,* repetition of the *shemoneh esreh* or the reading of the Torah and the *haftarah,*" he warns, they can without objection constitute a *minyan* for a wide variety of special occasions: the reading of the *megillah* and the benedictions that follow it, in cases of public martyrdom, to recite the special blessing said after escape from a life-threatening situation—including childbirth—*birkat ha-gomel,* at a circumcision ceremony, and at a Hanukkah candlelighting in the synagogue.[39]

Orthodox women who are involved in feminist activities such as prayer and study groups range in age from new bat mitzvah girls and college students to middle-aged and even elderly mothers and grandmothers. "One of the myths I would like to shatter is that single or divorced women make up the bulk of women exploring Orthodox feminism," says a strictly Orthodox Manhattan computer systems analyst in her thirties who worships once a month with an all-female prayer group; the other three Sabbaths in the month she prays in an Orthodox *shteibel,* a small, highly Orthodox congregation with, as she puts it, "a floor-to-ceiling *mekhitzah"* separating the men and women:

> On the contrary, the vast majority of Orthodox women who search for a wider, more uplifting role in prayer and Jewish study lead or plan to lead very normative Orthodox Jewish lives. Most are married women with larger-than-average families. If they are unusual in any way, it is that they tend to be highly educated, both religiously and secularly. They probably include a larger-than-average number of talented professional women.

Almost universally, Orthodox feminists insist, "Whatever arguments they have with traditional Judaism will have to be resolved within Orthodoxy, not in some other wing of Judaism." One woman points out that Jewish feminism is one aspect of the general struggle between tradition and modernity that preoccupies modern Orthodox Jewish women:

> My search for understanding includes, but is certainly not limited to feminist issues. I am bound with my deepest being to traditional Jewish life. I am not only a woman, and, I suppose, a feminist. I am also a Jew in a non-Jewish society and an Orthodox Jew within the diverse sphere of American Judaism. In all of these areas I'd like to work for acceptance of my human dignity.

Orthodox feminists are especially incensed by what they perceive as a slanderous public relations campaign waged against Orthodox feminists by some rabbinic authorities. Rabbinic detractors have sometimes portrayed them as a radically feminist collection of marginal malcontents, whereas in truth they are largely composed of mainstream, Jewishly committed Orthodox women with very typical Orthodox life-styles. Many women in women's prayer and study groups would not characterize themselves as feminists. "Twelve women serve on the Lincoln Square Women's Tefillah Group," notes one Orthodox activist, "but only two of the twelve are self-proclaimed feminists. Only two of them are members of the National Organization of Women and read *Ms.* magazine. All of the steering committee members are employed outside the home, and all of them are interested in creating spiritual opportunities for women. But most of them would not want to be called feminists."

Some feminists charge that Orthodox rabbinical rejection of the concept of a group prayer for women is based to some extent on a wish to keep women isolated from each other, as though women in groups might veer into disruptive activities. The fear of the disorder that might be brought on society by women in groups is an ancient one: Rabbinical commentaries on the story of the biblical Dinah, who ventures out into a field and is raped by a non-Israelite from a nearby tribe (Genesis 34), include the speculation that Dinah had been seeking out a group of non-Israelite female friends for companionship and unknown activities. They also link Dinah's putatively provocative behavior to that of her mother Leah, who brazenly went out into the fields to acquire the aphrodisiacal mandrakes from her sister Rachel in a vain attempt to win their husband Jacob's love (Midrash Rabbah 80:1–12, Vayishlakh).

Women were at least as isolated—and frequently more so—in the societies that surrounded the Jews down through history, such as those of classical Greece and of Islamic Spain, according to such scholars as Orthodox rabbi and writer Eliezer Berkovits. The mistrust of women was a commonality of many ancient cultures, including, but hardly exclusive to, Judaic cultures. While fears of disorderly social women may have been merely tolerated by Jewish tradition, neither essential to nor reflective of the true message of timeless Jewish morality, it seems clear that "the seclusion of women was also a form of control exercised by their husbands," Berkovits notes:

> At least one midrashic opinion attempts to find a basis for such control in the Torah itself. When God created Adam, through him He blessed the future male race and said: "Multiply and fill the earth and subdue it." [Genesis 1:28] If the word in the Hebrew original, *khivshuha*, were to stand by itself it may be understood as "subdue her," i.e., the woman. On it follows the explanation: "The man subdues (i.e., controls) his wife, so that she should not walk about the marketplaces . . . and not fall into disgrace (or sin) as happened to Dinah."[40]

Indeed, the image of women banding together to accomplish their goals is unsettling even to some modern religious leaders who consider themselves pro-woman.[41] There seems to be a very real attempt on the part of religious men to ignore, deny, or denigrate the female bonding, friendship, and real supportiveness that goes on the women's side of the *mekhitzah* and, even more so, in women's prayer groups. One woman asserts that rabbis "know that male bonding is part of what motivates men to wake up at the crack of dawn and get to a daily minyan. But they don't want to admit that women can form the same kinds of bonds in a prayer setting. Few of them will acknowledge that women's *shtiblach* [small prayer circles] existed among pious Jewish women throughout Europe. They try to paint women's prayer groups as something totally new in order to delegitimate them."

Many Orthodox feminists have mixed feelings about feminism, Orthodoxy, and the role of women in traditional Jewish life. "The future of women in Orthodox Judaism is a difficult issue," says a family therapist and mother of four grown children and former member of the Teaneck Women's Tefillah Group, who has since emigrated to Israel. "I go to the Tefillah group, but I haven't taken an *aliyah* yet. I like to prepare *divrei Torah* [Sabbath lectures] for the group. It's an intellectual challenge, and I get a lot out of choosing the topic, preparing the research, and sharing it with the group, but I haven't resolved my feelings."

Blu Greenberg, a mother of five grown children who has described herself as a "mild-mannered yeshiva girl," has done much to articulate the keen conflicts felt by feminists whose primary commitments are to the survival of the Jewish people and the preservation of the Jewish tradition; hers is probably the name most often associated with feminist efforts within Orthodoxy.[42] Working for understanding and compromise between proponents of two opposing worldviews, Greenberg has come under attack by the right-leaning Orthodox, many of whom would like to strip her not only of any claim to Orthodoxy but also of satisfaction and joy in her role as a wife and mother. When Greenberg's 1981 book, *On Women and Judaism: A View from Tradition*,[43] came out, urging reevaluation of women's status in Orthodoxy, she asked a friend who edited an Orthodox paper to excerpt it. The friend replied that to do so would be as if the American Cancer Society ran a cigarette ad.[44]

The work of feminism in the Orthodox community is impeded by the fact that many Orthodox women have internalized negative attitudes toward public prayer for women that sometimes go even beyond the letter of the law. One forty-eight-year-old mother of eight, the wife of a university professor, comments that she no longer joins her family in the singing of traditional Sabbath prayer melodies (*zemirot*) at the table. "I feel it's not in the spirit of *tsniut* (modesty) for a grown woman to sing out loud in front of her husband and children," she says, although she admits that her husband did not request and was somewhat bemused by her decision. Large groups of Orthodox women are indeed totally unaccustomed to hearing their own voices, either individually or in a group, lifted in prayer.

Nevertheless, Orthodox feminists continue to work to make traditional Jewish communities more responsive to women's spiritual needs. Greenberg feels, "I do not believe for a single moment that the divine plan for this world was to have women eternally consigned to second-class status, or not at all, in significant areas of our religious and cultural life. Nor do I believe that the system will crumble and shred if women are given first-class status." Women such as she embody the seemingly inconsistent but living and vital growth of contemporary modern Orthodoxy. "Orthodoxy is a great gift to me," she says. "I'm willing to make some tradeoffs in my feminist views for what is an extremely rich, rewarding texture in my life. In that way, perhaps I could be considered a failure as a feminist, and I've taken some criticism in feminist circles. But the reality is, I wouldn't want to relinquish one single *Shabbat* as we observe it, for all of the new ideas."[45]

Despite internal and external controversies which hover around the subjects of women and prayer, Orthodox feminist activist Rifka Haut sees much about which all Jewish feminists can be hopeful and proud. She speaks with particular passion about the women's prayer services that began in the winter of 1985 at the *Kotel,* the remains of the Western Wall of the Temple in the Old City of Jerusalem. "While men struggled bitterly, torn by denominational differences over the 'Who is a Jew?' issue," Haut remembers, "Jewish feminists resolved their religious and philosophical differences and worked together to create a united women's prayer service, complete with Torah reading, at the *Kotel.*"

The participants in the women's prayer services at the *Kotel* have spanned the religious spectrum from Orthodox women who cover their hair to self-described radical feminists affiliated with the Reform and Reconstructionist wings of Judaism. In order for women to conduct a halakhic service in which Orthodox women could participate, the non-Orthodox agreed to make difficult and serious concessions. Reform Jews oppose praying behind a *mekhitzah*. Many stay away from the *Kotel* or pray in the plaza just behind the divided area that fronts on the wall. So that all women could pray together, they accepted the fact that they would not constitute a minyan and therefore would not recite such prayers as *kedushah* and *kaddish,* for which ten men are necessary. As Rifka Haut recalls, "Women who philosophically oppose prayers which include the desire to reinstate animal sacrifices agreed to use the traditional prayer book, which includes such references. The women, in a display of true sisterhood, graciously and with understanding, accepted all the limitations that an Orthodox, non-*minyan* service implies."[46] Yet the Orthodox women were making enormous sacrifices at home and were often regarded with great suspicion by the mainstream Orthodox community. Haut insists, "Women who have participated in our services and in other Orthodox feminist activities are often vilified in the communities, schools, and synagogues in which they live and work and pray. Sometimes their children are vilified as well. It takes enormous courage for Orthodox women to 'come out' as active feminists."

The services at the Wall brought women from differing backgrounds together in a true union of intense prayer and cooperation and were organized so that women from all denominations participated equally.[47] Regardless of their religious orientation, many of the participants provide vivid descriptions of the personal, religious, spiritual uplift their prayers at the Wall gave to them. "Overcome with emotion, I approached the *Kotel,* leant on the ancient stones, and wept," said one woman. "Surrounded by the group, I was nevertheless able to pray my own, private prayers, with a depth and feeling never before experienced. The sense of private prayer and group prayer merged completely for me at that moment. Drenched in tears, I finally rejoined the group."[48]

However, the intense spirituality of the experience was interrupted from the very first service onward by violent reactions from both male and female "regular" worshipers. Although the combined voices of the women, uplifted in prayer, reflected the harmonious resolution of differences, Haut recounts,

> when we began the Torah reading, a woman, a habitual "resident" of the Kotel, began screaming at us, insisting that it is *asur,* forbidden, for women to read from a *Sefer Torah.* She ran to complain to the rabbi of the *Kotel,* Rabbi Getz, who informed her that what we were doing was not against *halakhah* and we could continue. She returned, and was quiet. However, by this time, the men praying on their side of

the *mekhitza* had been made aware of our presence. We were now in the midst of our Torah reading. A group of men began screaming at us, rhythmically, cursing us, warning us, shouting *asur*, pigs, and *tameh*—unclean. For them, the sight of women reading from the Torah was more than they could bear. I lifted my eyes from the words of the Torah for a moment to glance at them. They seemed garbed in darkness, in intolerance. I forced my eyes back to the Torah scroll, the holy black letters suspended on the white parchment. We women assembled were like the letters of the Torah, each one individually different, yet creating meaning in our unity, surrounded by the whiteness of the ancient stones.[49]

The participants faced an enormous challenge whether to continue with and finish their prayers. Haut remembers,

> Despite the frenzied shrieking of the fanatics, who were by then shaking and banging the *mekhitza* up and down, attempting to terrorize us, we heeded Deborah Brin's plea to "focus, focus" on the prayers. We continued the Torah reading, correctly and with feeling. The women had already formed a tight protective circle around the Torah, so that no one could harm it or take it from us. By this time, however, Norma Joseph, who had been given the task of judging the mood of the people, decided that we should quickly conclude our service and leave. We rolled the Torah and finished *Shacharit*. Those who wished to form a minyan for the women who wanted to say *Kaddish* separated themselves briefly from the group, as had been planned, and said *Kaddish*. Maintaining a very tight circle, and again singing "Oseh Shalom," we walked back to our buses, and left. We had certainly made our presence, the presence of women, felt.[50]

Later attempts by women to pray in a group at the Wall met with even more violent reactions. For young women, especially, the crudity of the attacks came as a kind of loss of innocence. Judith Green remembers,

> It was really completely innocent. We were completely taken by surprise. First the [ultra-Orthodox] women started screeching at us, shoving us around and trying to grab the prayer books out of our hands . . . it didn't really happen [the month before] because it was an international conference that was covered by the press. We had no press, no police, nothing. It was like a pogrom. The men just broke right through the *mechitzah*. They grabbed us and people were

thrown to the ground. They were trying to get the *Sefer Torah* out of our hands. We were in the middle of reading the *Torah*. I remember we just started screaming, "They are trying to get the *Sefer Torah!*" We put our arms on each other's shoulders and made a kind of wall around the table with the *Torah* on it, so we could get out of there. They wouldn't have cared if they had thrown the *Torah* on the ground. They probably thought that it was *pasool* anyway because we had touched it. It was unbelievable.[51]

Barbara Gingold comments that the ultra-Orthodox men seemed inordinately threatened:

They are afraid of women taking things into their own hands. They are afraid of women having knowledge. They are afraid of being dispossessed in the synagogue. Somebody fifteen years ago called the Orthodox synagogue the last remaining exclusive men's club in the world. That's what it still is very much in Israel. It's their last fortress. It is very much a man's world. They are totally free there to make the laws, make the codes of behavior, and dictate what is going to happen there and how.[52]

However, the women were sometimes angrier and more abusive than the men—and they often incited the men to violence. Elana Raider remarks:

The ultra-Orthodox women . . . were screaming, "You cowards! Are you going to defend our religion? They're killing our tradition." The religious women tried to tear the prayer books out of the hands of the women who were praying. The men banged on the *mechitza,* once again, screaming. But, instead of just screaming, some of the men came into the women's side. They threw women to the ground as well as attempting to steal the *Torah* and turn over the table that the *Torah* was resting on.[53]

A later service on the Fast of Esther "was terrible," and very frightening, according to Julie Fischer and Rachel Levin. The police of the Old City threw tear gas because the levels of violence were so great. Ironically:

the religious women were the ones who saw us praying together and praying with the *Torah*. They were the ones who riled up the men.

They were the only ones who could get close enough to see what we were doing. The men could only get as close as the *mechitzah*. One student got hit on the head with a chair, and I almost got hit with a glass bottle. The violence was terrifying. I have never felt like that in my life! Those people had so much hatred for us. The things we were called were unbelievable, as if, God Forbid, we were not Jews, or, God forbid, we were not humans on the same level as the ultra-Orthodox males. It was really sad.[54]

The violence against the group, which has come to be known as "the women of the wall," has continued to escalate, despite the fact that the women have agreed not to bring a Torah scroll with them when they worship. Women worshiping together at the Wall, quietly but in unison, have been attacked verbally and physically by onlookers. For many it is this vision of Jew attacking Jew that is the most disturbing element of all.[55]

Jewish feminist efforts in the area of spiritual experimentation in many ways epitomize both the broad range of Jewish feminism and aspects of Jewish feminism that make onlookers fearful. In addition, rather than simply appropriating for women roles and behaviors that were previously primarily male—such as study and prayer—Jewish feminist spiritual exploration seeks to *transform* study and prayer so that they speak from and to female experience. The entry of women into previously male domains agitates many; changing the rules of the game, as Jewish feminist exploration often seeks to do, agitates traditionalists even more.

One of the most common feminist changes involves the inclusion of the matriarchs and other biblical women in the appropriate liturgical settings. Such changes, while appealing, are not always easily accomplished, even by religious leaders and practitioners who devoutly wish to depatriarchalize Jewish prayers.[56] Furthermore, many committed and knowledgeable Jewish feminists have worked to create prayers and rituals that express women's spirituality within the context of Jewish tradition. Arlene Agus describes the Jewish feminist attraction to the celebration of Rosh Hodesh, the festival of the New Moon, which "traditionally held unique significance for women perhaps dating back as far the Biblical period." The Rosh Hodesh celebration was appealing to traditional-minded yet creative feminists, says Agus, precisely because "it offered unlimited opportunities for exploration of feminine spiritual qualities and experimentation with ritual, all within the framework of an ancient tradition which has survived up to the present day." Within the Rosh Hodesh ceremonies suggested by Agus, women wear new clothes, give charity, recite prayers, poems, and a special kiddush, recite a *shehechiyanu* (thanksgiving prayer) at the eating of new fruits, have a festive meal featuring round and egg-based foods, and include the *shir hamaalot* and *yaaleh veyavo* in the *birkat ha-mazon* (grace after meals). All these activities are quite consonant with traditional Jewish life yet offer "an opportunity for spiritual development, and occasion for speaking to the Creator and experimenting with the dialogue," and "a pause in which to thank God for creating us women," says Agus.[57]

The Passover seder has provided another opportunity for creative feminists. In describing the evolution of the first of her feminist Haggadahs, Aviva Cantor deals with both the strengths and the limitations of feminist transformations of Jewish ritual. Cantor adapted a *Jewish Liberation Haggadah* she had written with a group of socialist Zionists in the New York Jewish Liberation Project and made it suitable for a feminist seder. She rewrote the Haggadah, "first taking care of the minor changes." These were, she continues,

> making God "ruler of the universe" instead of "king," adding the names of Jacob's wives to the Exodus narrative, and changing "four sons" to "four daughters." The major change was to utilize the four-cups ritual and to dedicate each cup of wine to the struggle of Jewish women in a particular period. The Haggadah's aim was to provide connecting links between Jewish women of the past and us here in the present. A great deal of material came from Jewish legends and historical sources, some only recently discovered.

Although the feminist seder experience was quite enjoyable for the participants, Cantor reports, she missed the heterogeneity of the traditional seder: "As much as I loved a Seder with my sisters, what gnawed at me was the memory of the Seders I had at home, in my parents' house, Seders of men and women of several generations, with children running underfoot and spilling the wine. The Seder has always been a family celebration and, for me, a Seder just for women seems incomplete." Cantor seems to capture much of the spirit of the feminist centrists when she concludes that in the ideal seder "women could be as 'visible' as men, but neither men nor women would be the entire focus of the Seder."[58]

Another feminist seder tradition brings together Letty Cottin Pogrebin and her daughters Abigail and Robin in a group that includes some of America's most talented women—much-published psychologist Phyllis Chesler, columnist Michele Landsberg, novelist E. M. Broner, filmmaker Lilly Rivlin, artists Bea Kreloff and Edith Isaac-Rose, and their "spiritual leaders," writers Grace Paley and politician Bella Abzug and her daughters Eve and Liz.[59] These women combine tradition and feminism by holding this seder service on the third night of Passover. For them, unwilling to forgo the very special feeling of a family seder or the deep emotional, spiritual, and intellectual significance of a feminist seder, the third-night seder is an attempt to incorporate both. "When my daughters have their own homes," says Pogrebin, "a feminist Seder will be a time-honored part of their childhood tradition. It will be a familiar aspect of their Jewish roots."

The intensive role of women in private, domestic spheres of Judaism and their near invisibility in public Jewish prayer are reflected in many familiar rituals and ceremonies, including some that take place in a family context. Passover seder observance provides one such significant example of the status problem faced by contemporary Jewish feminists. Preparations for a traditional Passover are extensive and exhausting, and, because they relate to domestic areas, they have always been largely relegated to female hands. Throughout the eight-day Passover holiday, baked goods containing leavening are scrupulously avoided in traditional Jewish homes, to the extent that year-round dishes and kitchen utensils are locked away and special Passover items, which have never come into contact with leavened materials, are used exclusively. Like many women *Ms.* magazine founder and active Jewish feminist Letty Cottin Pogrebin remembers that prior to Passover her mother engaged in "attic-to-basement housecleaning to rid every surface of *chametz* (leaven products), and [did] a complete change of dishes, and because she kept a mostly-kosher kitchen, she had to pack away two sets of everything (meat and dairy), and unpack all their Passover equivalents right down to the can opener. The typical Passover menu included gefilte fish, chopped liver, chicken soup with matzo balls, potato pudding, tzimmes, macaroons—all made from scratch without a pressure cooker, electric mixer, food processor or microwave." All of this work resulted in a splendid "seder table: the damask cloth with dim pink shadows from red-wine spills of meals past; the ceremonial plate with separate compartments for the parsley, *haroset,* gnarled horseradish root, roasted shank bone, and charred hard-boiled egg; the cut-glass bowls for salt water; two pairs of candlesticks, chrome and brass; the silver goblet for the Prophet Elijah" and a grotesquely exhausted mother. When the seder night arrives, however, men and boys become the focal point.[60]

The disparity between the male and female experience of the traditional seder is especially powerful to many Jewish women. In Pogrebin's childhood household the women "served the meal and cleared the dishes while my father reclined in an oversized chair at the head of the table, ennobled in his *kippah* (skullcap) and *kittel* (white ceremonial robe). Year after year, the Haggadah, the retelling of Israel's liberation from bondage, came to us in my father's voice, annotated by the symbols, songs, and rituals that he brought onstage like some great maestro conducting the solo parts of the seder symphony."[61] To some women in traditional homes, the juxtaposition of female servitude and male kingliness felt like oppression in the midst of the profoundly evocative festival of freedom.

The female preoccupation with preparations for Passover and the seder, contrasted with the male posture of regal ease at the seder table, has spawned ironic muttering among women for generations. In the contemporary United States, this disparity seems all the more egregious. Many Jewish feminists have expressed interest in taking upon themselves the ritual obligations to recline on a pillow during the Passover seder ceremony.[62] In traditional communities for most of Jewish history, it has been widely accepted that while men must recline at the seder table (to indicate that each of them is a free person as important as a king taking his ease), it is inappropriate for women to recline in the same way.[63] The observance of the custom of reclining on a pillow at the seder table is an evocative symbol both for Jewish feminists and for the rabbis who oppose them. It symbolizes Jewish feminists' attempts to make Jewish tradition more sensitive to women and more cognizant of their contemporary leadership roles. It is also symbolic of some rabbis' resistance to seeing women in positions of leadership and power.

Female exclusion from reclining at the seder table can be traced back through Talmudic literature and followed up through contemporary Orthodox rabbinic commentaries.[64] Some rabbinic commentators explore the concept that specific women, or specific groups of women, may indeed be required to recline. What makes a woman so important that she is required to recline like a monarch (as is every male over the age of thirteen, *regardless* of his importance)? A religious authority in thirteenth-century Germany, Rabbi Mordekhai ben Hillel Ashkenazi, makes a rather revolutionary, pro-woman statement, which was picked up and reiterated by Rabbi Moshe Isserles in sixteenth-century Poland: "In our community all the women are important."

The implication of the Mordekhai's and Rabbi Isserles's statements is that the quality of "importance" is culturally relative rather than absolute. Therefore, in certain communities, women as a group may live and behave in such a way that it is customary and appropriate for them to recline. The Vilna Gaon, in eighteenth-century Lithuania, retained the concept of cultural relativism but interpreted it as an issue of economic determination applying only to singular women, and not to women as a group: "An important woman (is wealthy enough so that she) doesn't need to busy herself with the needs of the household or the preparation of food."[65] Although the *Shulhan Arukh*[66] does leave open the loophole for "important" women, the notion that a reclining woman is somehow an insult to her husband and the other "free persons" (read "men") has persisted. It has been and remains unusual for Orthodox women to recline at the seder table.[67]

Today, however, Jewish feminists argue that the contemporary American community is one in which women occupy positions that socially coequal those of men. The vast majority of American Jewish women have levels of both secular and Jewish education unthinkable in earlier periods of history. They occupy positions of importance and prestige in the professional and business worlds. They most certainly are "free persons." Since cultural relativism is part of even the Vilna Gaon's strict interpretation of the law, many contemporary Orthodox Jewish feminists feel it is now time to declare, along with the Mordekhai and Rabbi Isserles, "In our community all women are important," and therefore required to recline, full participants in the Passover miracle retold and reenacted at the Seder.

Symptomatically some Orthodox religious authorities have resisted such halakhic logic and resorted to an old standby in the exclusion of women from public Judaism—sexual provocation. Thus Rabbi Chaim Karlinsky, discussing "Women and the Laws of Reclining at the Seder," comes to a conclusion more extreme—and far more misogynist at its core—than that of medieval rabbis. If women recline at the Seder, they will seduce the men, Karlinsky worries, "because of immodesty and wanton behavior. Women leaning in mixed company can lead to levity and infringements of the ways of modesty, especially when they get to the last cups and have already imbibed. The impression of such levity is as much to be avoided as the avoidance of even minute quantities of hametz (leavened bread or bread products) during Pesach." Not for legitimate Jewish legal reasons, therefore, but because he fears the supposedly irresistible effects of female sexuality, Karlinsky prohibits the reclining of women at the Seder table.[68]

Many expressed distress and outrage that women are put in the position of enabling observances—and then being shut out of full participation in them. An Orthodox public relations writer with one baby girl says:

> We are keenly aware of the fact that we are making Orthodoxy possible in today's United States. We know that very few households outside of those which are Orthodox or right-leaning Conservative worry about the *mitzvot* the way we do. Then to be told that we can't participate fully even when there's really no *halakhic* (legal) reason for us not to, to be told that we have to lead constricted religious lives just because we might turn some man on—well, it's outrageous! Our souls are just as important as theirs.

Feminism has motivated many women to seek out woman-oriented prayer settings, but once they are praying within those settings it is spiritual communication—not political posturing—that is the focus of participants' minds and hearts. For many contemporary women, prayer settings inclusive of, directed toward, or composed of women have become the locus of deep spiritual expression. Women from all wings of Judaism report that prayer that draws on—rather than ignores—their womanhood opens up an extra dimension to their prayer. Rather than an expression of a political "feminist" stance, prayer that incorporates womanhood gives their spirituality a wholeness that they find lacking in other settings. An Orthodox graduate of Columbia University comments that her participation in an halakhic women's prayer group during her student days "was not a political statement at all." Instead it was "a warmer way to be able to pray and feel closer to God." Women in a conventional synagogue often do not hear their own voices lifted in prayer, and they miss the reinforcing effect of group prayer that is the rationale for the creation of the *tzibbur*. When they pray together and participate fully, their links to other worshipers and to God are enhanced. As one woman says, prayer among women makes her feel "more of a connection spiritually to God and to the people" among whom she prays.[69]

For some women, such wholehearted, woman-oriented worship occurs when the birth of a child radically reshapes their spirituality. Rabbi Amy Eilberg expresses her encounter with a maternal God:

> The tenth day of Penina's life was Shabbat, and I was ready to pick up the *siddur* to *daven*. I was prepared, as always, to meet in my *davening* the God of Jewish law, the transcendent God of command and demand, of judgment of those who fail in their commitments. I would not have been surprised to encounter the angry, thundering God who could disapprove of the hiatus in my *davening,* or judge the way I understood it. Instead, I met a different God that Shabbat evening. I met a God of love and acceptance, of joy and celebration. As I lovingly turned the pages of the *siddur,* the old friend with whom I'd been out of touch for many days, I imagined a God who rejoiced rather than judged, who affirmed rather than legislated. This was the God of nurture, not just of command; of love as well as law. This God fully shared with me the overwhelming joyousness and miraculousness of my daughter's birth, and celebrated my own rebirth, as a mother.[70]

Following her daughter's birth, says Eilberg, both her vision of Godhead and her mode of prayer changed forever:

> My *davening* that evening was loving, gentle and deliberate, generated by the energy of caring and caregiving more than by the need to discharge a legal obligation. My encounter with the *siddur* and with God that Shabbat was suffused with the same spirit that had filled my days since Penina's birth, days in which tasks of caring for a newborn baby felt like acts of exquisite sanctity. The God that I imagined that night had not missed my *davening* those intervening days, understanding that my days had been filled with holiness, while I nursed the baby, rocked her, changed her and loved her. This God understood the intrinsic sanctity of acts of nurturance. This feminine God, after all, was the model of all human acts of creativity and caregiving. It was from Her that we had learned to create and nurture new life. Far from judging me in my hiatus in addressing Her, She rejoiced that I had instead found Her, and myself, in the midst of caring for my infant daughter. I am, I now know, forever transformed by that moment of encounter with the other dimension of God, the feminine God, for whom love and nurturing are of ultimate value. My relationship with God is forever changed and enriched by that extraordinary time when,

at a uniquely feminine moment of life, I found myself in touch with a feminine image of God.

Like other spiritually devout Jewish feminists, Rabbi Eilberg is sure that her prayers will never be the same, now that she has been able to expand her imaginative understanding of God and to pray to her Creator with the wholeness of a woman's voice.[71]

As startling as some may find Eilberg's assertions that motherhood can enhance one's relationship with God through special religious and spiritual insights, and that God has a definitive maternal aspect, her personal experiences echo passages from the Bible and from rabbinic literature. One definition of a person who has the wisdom to cleave to God's will, according to the *Sayings of the Fathers,* is the person *asher roeh et ha-nolad*—"the person who sees the newborn" (*Pirke Avot*). This verse is often interpreted to mean that true wisdom or discernment is impossible without the ability, like a parent who sees the newborn child and understands its potential, to see a situation and understand where it can lead. But in ancient civilizations, it was the female midwife and the mother who were in fact the first to see the newborn and to assess it. The statement that the person who can best cleave to God's way is the one who sees the newborn elevates female, maternal experience to a symbol of one of the primary conditions for wisdom and piety. Gifted mothers—and people who are like gifted mothers—have the capacity to enter into the potential of their children and of situations and the wisdom to guide both people and situations in the right direction. As Claudia Camp succinctly notes, the biblical metaphor of mother in Israel is "indicative of a complex of meanings associated with the mother," a role which "embodied the idea of the effective counsel of unity and shalom. The counsel of the mother was, metaphorically at least, Israelite counsel *par excellence.*"[72]

God is pictured as a mother in passages such as the one in which Isaiah tells the Jewish people that God undergoes all the stages of gestation in the process of revitalizing the Divine relationship with them: "Listen to me, Oh house of Jacob, and all the remnant of the house of Israel, You that are born from within my belly, you that are carried from inside my womb; I remain the same into old age, and even when my hair grows white I will carry you; I created you, and I will bear you, I will carry you, and I will deliver." (Isaiah 46:3–4) In another passage in Isaiah, appropriately read each Rosh Hodesh, God tells the Jewish people that He will provide nurture like that provided by a mother who nurses her baby and caresses it on her knees. (Isaiah 66:12–13).

When Jewish women draw on their own deepest experiences and discover the maternal aspect of Godhead in their prayers, when they participate fully in prayer either in egalitarian or in women's prayer settings, when they reach out for the warmth of communal solidarity and mutual inspiration which has always been part of Jewish group prayer in the *tzibbur,* they are not making a break with the past. When they lift their voices in prayer, they are building on the legacy of the past. They are not, through their activities, deriding or diminishing the extent and power of women's prayers in the past, as critics such as Rabbi Ilan Feldman charge:

> It is very superficial thinking when women begin to think of themselves as the first intelligent generation of women in 2,000 years. . . . Do women of today really believe that their grandmothers and great-grandmothers and great-great-grandmothers were less spiritual and less attuned to their own spiritual needs?[73]

Jewish women who pray out loud in their own voices today are not rejecting the devotion of traditional Judaism but embracing it and making it their own. They are following in the footsteps of the biblical Rebeccah, Miriam, Hannah, Deborah, and others. They are continuing the traditions of those very great-grandmothers of whom Rabbi Feldman speaks, women for whom prayer was part of their daily breathing. No doubt many Jewish women a hundred years ago found meaningful spiritual outlets which grew out of the contexts of their lives. Many of them devoutly recited the three daily services at home and uttered the appropriate *tekhinnes* as they went about their domestic tasks as well. Many took deep pleasure in the religious activities of their husbands and sons, and took joy as well in training their daughters to carry on these feminine traditions. The ritual bath was often connected to the women's bathhouse, and thus provided an additional context for women to blend their religious obligations with informal interactions with other girls and women.[74] Living in close-knit communities in which women bonded with women easily in daily activities around a family courtyard or in the marketplace, the fellowship of the synagogue and the study hall may not have seemed lacking from their Jewish lives.

But as the contexts of women's lives in every wing of Judaism today are different from those of the past, so the contexts of women's prayers are different as well. The existence of *tekhinnes* for baking bread or completing a garment are no spiritual answer for women who purchase baked goods and clothing in a shopping mall. While the *mikvah* continues to be a meaningful personal spiritual outlet for some women, it usually is no longer connected to the socializing of a communal bathhouse. There are no family courtyards in which female religious and social solidarity can be reinforced, and the workplaces in which the vast majority of Jewish women are employed today are profoundly secular environments.

Jewish feminism has rediscovered opportunities for women to pray in Jewish ways that fit the contexts of contemporary life. Numerous precedents for such prayers exist in rabbinic literature and in previous Jewish communities. In past centuries, perhaps because of lack of Jewish education and liturgical skills, in addition to the overwhelming burden of raising large families and participating in breadwinning activities, these precedents often did not blossom into widespread formal group prayer by women. Today, however, women's Jewish and secular education, life-styles, and social expectations groom them for levels of participation in worship founded on the prayers of Jewish women in the past. Jewish feminists, rather than walking away from Jewish traditions and following powerful tides of assimilation, seek out a more complete relationship with their spiritual heritage.

Chapter Eight

Educating the New Jewish Woman

We run the danger of defining women's religiosity only in terms of feelings, mysticism, or intuition, of stereotyping women as they were stereotyped for centuries as creatures of emotion and instinct. No. I want women to be learned in law and text, to combine spirituality with intellect, and to walk with confidence in the paths of the Torah.

—Francine Klagsbrun[1]

AN APPRECIATION of the extraordinary strides feminism has made possible for American Jewish women need not distort the position of Jewish women in the past. In traditional Jewish cultures, women had important, multifaceted roles in the home and the community, and Jewish law prescribed for women levels of respect and safety unmatched in neighboring cultures for centuries. However, until the twentieth century, full and rigorous Jewish education was only available to women who established themselves as being "exceptional." The importance of intensive Jewish education in helping women to achieve feminist goals within the religious sphere—especially for women who wish to take leadership roles within the community and those who wish to encourage congregations and communities to be more responsive to women's issues—can hardly be overestimated.

As Rifka Haut puts it, "part of the reason that many of us aren't treated as equals yet is that many of us aren't equals yet, at least when it comes to Jewish learning." A new chapter is opening up in which Jewish education for women is almost as common as Jewish education for men. Today an extensive and intensive Jewish education is potentially open to all.

A brief look backward at the evolution of attitudes toward Jewish education for women shows that it was uneven. The concept was somewhat controversial and continued to be so until very recently. Traditionally study was valued for its own sake, and it was forbidden to use Jewish learning "as a spade to dig with." However, in reality learning was one key to communal status and power. Because within Judaism, the religion of action, no activity was more revered—or more Jewish—than learning, the ability to learn—to be a *lamdan*—made a scholar "somebody." In many communities learning brought celebrity and prestige. More important, learning provided the tools to understand the intellectual and legal underpinnings of a religion in which stasis and change were vitally linked to intellectual and legal decision making by accomplished scholars, *poskim.*

One of the primary responsibilities of the Jewish father, according to rabbinic interpretations of biblical law, is to teach his sons Torah—that is, traditional Jewish texts. Ideally it was expected that all Jewish males would learn enough Hebrew to be devotionally competent, praying three times daily and on Sabbaths and holidays, and to understand selections from the Pentateuch and the Prophets read each week in the synagogue. This education was provided to male children from an early age in formal classroom settings, in Europe called the *cheder* and *yeshiva ketana.* Those males deemed to be intellectually superior received lengthy and rigorous Jewish education in one of a number of talmudic academies, the *yeshiva gedola,* for adolescents and adults, learning Aramaic and mastering skills that would enable them to read and understand the Talmud and rabbinic commentaries spanning many centuries and cultures. Women, however, seldom had access to these most extensive forms of Jewish education. Men as a group had levels of knowledge that were, with notable exceptions, unavailable to women.

Rabbinic attitudes toward teaching the Torah to women were diverse but tended to be negative. The rabbis looked at biblical passages such as the pivotal commandment in Deuteronomy (11:19): "And you shall teach your sons." They discussed whether the Hebrew word *b'naikhem* actually meant "sons" exclusively, or whether the gendered Hebrew commandment used the male form to mean "children" generically, including sons and daughters. While discussion ensued pro and con across the centuries of midrashic, talmudic, and responsa literature (rabbinic answers written in response to specific inquiries regarding Jewish law), the mainstream conclusion was repeatedly that women as a group are inappropriate candidates for serious study of the oral law (postbiblical texts), and possibly for the written law (biblical texts) as well. Fathers were commanded, the rabbis concluded, to "teach their sons but not their daughters."[2]

Since female children and adults were exempt from the obligation to study Torah, they could not be obligated to teach Torah to their children.[3] This posed something of a logical problem, since a number of biblical and postbiblical passages mention the mother's role as a source of wisdom (Proverbs 1:8 and 31:26, for example). Traditional sources often resolve this apparent contradiction through a gendered division of pedagogical tasks. The mother is expected to provide her children with a deep emotional commitment to Judaism and appropriate moral teachings, and to train her daughters in the legal and practical intricacies of managing a devoutly Jewish home. The father, on the other hand, is obligated to transmit the intellectual tools and information that will enable his sons to study Jewish texts on the highest level possible for their innate talents and economic status.

Talmudic options on the advisability of teaching daughters ranged from those of Ben Azai, who ruled that a father is obligated to teach Torah to his daughters, to those of Rabbi Eliezer, who believed that Torah learning might undermine a woman's moral fiber, saying, "He who teaches his daughter [Torah, the oral law] it is as if he taught her licentious behavior" (Sotah 21a). Rabbi Eliezer's opinion has been much quoted both by those who wish to prevent women from studying the Talmud and by feminists who wish to present talmudic thought in its harshest, seemingly most misogynist light.[4]

The most influential discussion of Torah study for women is found in Maimonides' *Mishneh Torah* (Hilkhot Talmud Torah 1:13). When Maimonides discusses teaching women, he rules that the rewards for Torah study are greater for men than for women because of the general principle in Jewish law that one is rewarded more for performing deeds one is obligated to do than for those one does voluntarily. (Psychologically the rabbinic attitude was that required behavior is likely to seem onerous, therefore fulfilling such obligations garners the greatest rewards.) A father is not directed to teach his daughters Torah, although women will indeed be rewarded if they study it. This produces an obvious inconsistency. Maimonides reconciles these two views by suggesting: "Most women are not equipped to study and will distort the words of the Torah according to the whims of their minds." He then argues that this is the true meaning of Rabbi Eliezer's statement—that the man who teaches his daughters the oral law is exposing it to distortions or trivializations by the feminine mind. However, while it is preferable for a father not to teach his daughters biblical texts, such education is not prohibited and will not result in such distortions.

These general guidelines were judged to hold true for the majority of women, most of whom, it was assumed, would not want to take on further obligations in the area of Torah study. But what of the father who wished to teach his daughters as well as his sons, and what of the daughters who wished to learn? In several discussions a category of women is created who are considered "exceptional." These exceptional women, unlike the putatively typical run of feminine types, do not have "frivolous minds." They have emotional and intellectual qualities that make them appropriate candidates for Torah study, because they will not trivialize or distort the words of the text or use them for questionable purposes. One can recognize an exceptional woman, said some rabbis, by the very fact that she articulates a desire to study. Thus a father is not obligated to provide a formal Jewish education for daughters as a group, but given an "exceptional" female for a daughter, he may certainly educate her and she will be rewarded for her learning.

Women who acquired intensive knowledge of biblical and talmudic texts were often regarded with great admiration and respect by the rabbis and scholars in their communities. Although their activities were considered unusual, those who managed to acquire expertise in Torah studies were lauded, not marginalized. However, as Shoshana Zolty notes in her recent research on women and Torah study, though in several instances women were described as being erudite in an early edition of a given work, as publishers or typesetters "corrected" the text, their erudition was edited out in later editions. Thus a husband's original elegy for his saintly wife reads that she "sits and expounds" for a public audience on Sabbath afternoons; however, in a later edition it is the husband who lectures and the wife sits and listens.[5]

One famous example of rabbinic ambivalence on the subject of learned women is that of Beruriah, a woman who dared to overstep her bounds and steep herself in the study of learned texts. Beruriah is both lauded and treated with disturbing harshness within rabbinic tradition. The wife of the celebrated Rabbi Meir, and the daughter of Rabbi Hanina ben Teradion, Beruriah was said to have studied three hundred laws from three hundred teachers in one day (Pesachim 62b)—a hyperbole that nevertheless testifies to the quickness and retentiveness of her mind. In a variety of anecdotes, she was described not only as brilliant and insightful but also as a paragon of pious belief in God's wisdom as well (Brachot 10a, Eruvim 53b, and Midrash Proverbs 30:10). However, according to some accounts Beruriah came to a sordidly bitter end. Annoyed by Beruriah's insistence that women were not truly frivolous, Rabbi Meir persuaded a student to try to seduce her and prove her wrong. Eventually Beruriah weakened, and when she realized what had transpired, she committed suicide. According to some accounts, her husband was also devastated and fled into exile (Avodah Zarah 18b).[6] This tendency on the part of some rabbinic commentators to delegitimize Beruriah has itself become a compelling focus for Jewish feminist exploration.

The transmission of the legend about Beruriah's tragic ending, seemingly so out of character for both Beruriah and Rabbi Meir, transposes her brilliant life into a morality tale about the inadvisability of educating women, argues Judith Romney Wegner.[7] In reality, a sort of double standard seems to have developed in medieval and postmedieval Jewish societies, which follows Maimonides' dictum (*Mishneh Torah* [Hilkhot Talmud Torah 1:13]) almost to the letter. Jewish fathers and Jewish communities were discouraged from providing formal Jewish education for their daughters. Where such education was provided, however—and it was almost always provided by fathers and other male relatives—the brilliant and articulate female scholars who resulted were admired, consulted for legal advice, and encouraged to give classes to others. Although they were promised a reward in the world to come, their erudition was generally rewarded in this world as well.

Despite the rabbinical treatment of Beruriah's demise, it is clear that Beruriah did not stand alone and that other female scholars are treated in an unambiguously positive fashion by their male colleagues and by history. A number of erudite women are mentioned in talmudic literature.[8] Documents describe Sephardi women such as: "the daughter of Rabbi Nissim ben Jacob of Kairouan (Tunisia, 11th century)"; "three daughters of Isaac of Basra, Iraq" (12th century); "the distinguished daughter of Rabbi Samuel Ben Ali of Baghdad"

(1180), a woman so proficient in Talmudic studies that she gave classes through a lattice; "Asenath, the daughter of Rabbi Samuel Barzani of Kurdistan (16th–17th centuries)," later the wife of Rabbi Jacob Mizrahi of Amadiayah in Northern Iraq who lectured at and maintained a yeshiva; and the grandmother of Rabbi Joseph Hayim ben Alijah Al-Hakam, who according to her grandson in his book of responsa Rav Pe'alim, "would study 18 chapters of Mishnah [at midnight]. . . . Also during the night of [the holiday of] Hoshaha Rabbah the women would remain awake and would study Mishneh Torah, Psalms, the prayers of Kortei ha-Brit."[9] The names of numerous female scholars, in both Sephardi and Ashkenazi societies, are described in a variety of texts, letters, travel literature, wills, elegies, and diverse other forms.[10]

The pattern for educating women in elite families seems to have been established by Rashi (acronym for Rabbi Solomon ben Isaac, eleventh-century France), indubitably the most famous and arguably the most respected commentator on the Bible and Talmud in Jewish history. Rashi, who had only daughters, apparently did not cut them off from the scholarly learning that permeated their household, as his daughters demonstrated in later life; their own daughters were also known to be knowledgeable. Each daughter and granddaughter married esteemed scholars, the intellectual leaders of their generation. The opinions of these women are often referred to in rabbinic texts.[11] After Rashi, many rabbinic families apparently followed suit. As a thirteenth-century tosaphist (commentator on talmudic texts) later summarized, "We can rely on the testimony of the daughters of the leaders of the generation."[12]

Women who attained Jewish intellectual greatness were often the daughters, wives, and granddaughters of the greatest Jewish scholars. No doubt these women evinced their interest in Judaica early in their lives, and, according to rabbinic dictates found in the Talmud and responsa literature, such interest in itself was evidence that they were "exceptional" women—and thus appropriate candidates for the study of sacred texts. By the thirteenth century, Rabbi Judah he-Hasid's work *Sefer Hasidim* had suggested that men should teach Torah to their wives and daughters and even hire a teacher for them, as long as he was not a bachelor.[13] We do not know in which direction the influence went—whether liberal attitudes made Torah study for women more accessible in some families, or whether contact with brilliant and sincere God-fearing women made some rabbis more liberal. It is likely that the influence went in both directions, so that scholars such as Rabbi Joshua Falk, who wrote his commentaries in turn-of-the-seventeenth-century Poland, indicated that talented women—like his own compassionate, devout, and brilliantly learned wife, Bella, and his mother—may be taught any sacred text, albeit in a private setting to preserve their modesty.[14]

Despite rabbinical suggestions that women not be instructed in the intricacies of the oral law, some women—primarily from rabbinical families—persisted in achieving intellectual heights. In the eight centuries following Rashi, scores of women of distinction are mentioned in European communities such as Worms, Vienna, Posen, Brody, Mayence, Breslau, Prague, Bonn, Frankfurt, Braunschweig, and Fürth (Germany), Vitebsk, Lemberg, and Minsk (Russia), Cracow and Belbirsk (Poland); Vilna (Lithuania), Bolechow (Galicia), Sophia (Bulgaria), Bohemia and Moravia. That such women achieved what they did speaks volumes about a thirst for knowledge which knows no gender. The very existence of these women—who provide a continuous albeit little recognized tradition of female learning—enhances the Jewish feminist struggle for female access to rigorous learning by providing a series of impeccable role models. However, down almost to present times, the accomplishments of learned women have seemed in traditional circles to require explanation. One relatively modern text encouraging the education of the exceptional woman, for example, begins by reinforcing the idea that most women are generically incapable of such study:

> Perhaps the words of our Sages, i.e., "Whoever teaches his daughter Torah is as if he teaches her *tiflut*" referred to a father teaching a girl when she is young. This is so even if through her actions it can be recognized that she acts in a pure and upright manner. Certainly under such conditions there may be cause for concern since most women are presumed to be light-headed, wasting their time on nonsense. Since the majority of them are so, they sin from their impoverished minds. However, the women who dedicate their hearts to approach the service of God by choosing good for its own sake will surely rise to the summit of the mountain of the Lord and dwell in his holy place, for they are exemplary women. The scholars of their generation should treat them with honour and respect and encourage them.[15]

In most Jewish communities, for most of Jewish history, in contrast to the elite succession of "exceptional" women who studied and taught and were cherished for their brilliance, learning was generally available to women only on very basic levels in informal contexts.[16] Responsa literature from many communities, ranging from the twelfth to the nineteenth century, specifies the materials that were to be off limits to women. It was almost universally understood that women were obligated to be taught and to study those laws that pertain directly to them and to the management of a Jewish home, but many rabbis continued to express unease with the idea of women trying to learn the complicated minutiae of rabbinic logic and legal materials. Within postmedieval European and Sephardi communities, rabbis differed on whether that instruction should be formal or informal, in Hebrew or in the vernacular.

Contrary to popular expectation, perhaps, rabbinic opinion did not necessarily move in the direction of liberalism as the centuries passed. Perhaps the most extreme attitude was voiced by the Hatam Sofer—the Hungarian rabbi Moses Sofer—who, at the turn of the nineteenth century, spearheaded negative reactions to modernity in general. He commented that girls may only read "German works in the Hebrew letter [Yiddish], based on *aggadic* [narrative rather than legal] tales from the Talmud, but nothing else."[17]

Some sort of literacy among Jewish women seems to have been fairly common in most Jewish communities.[18] The Cairo *Genizah* (a storage area for sacred documents that served as an unofficial archive) contains many texts that refer directly and indirectly to levels of Jewish education ranging from the basic to the impressive, among women in many locales.[19] Substantial numbers of Jewish women received a simple Jewish education, from their parents or tutors, and supplemented their Jewish education as adults through texts written for women. In Sephardi cultures, a variety of texts existed in Ladino or the appropriate vernacular. In Italy perhaps more than any other society Jewish education for women seems to have been widespread during, and for hundreds of years after, the Renaissance.[20] The synagogue also often served as an important site of Jewish education for women. Ashkenazi girls and women in communities such as thirteenth-century Vienna, for example, are described as attending the synagogue on a daily or weekly basis to listen to rabbinic sermons. Some of these women were knowledgeable enough to lead other women in hymns and prayers. In addition at least sixty women functioned as printers, publishers, and funders of publications in European communities.[21]

Indeed, even though it is clear that most Jewish women were not intensively educated, higher levels of education probably existed than is generally recognized. Female-authored works, such as Rebecca Tiktiner's *Maineket Rifkah* (Prague, 1609; Cracow, 1618), instructs mothers: "when your children lie down to sleep you tell them stories from the Torah and from the Gemara." Tiktiner has no doubt that the typical woman in her society will be familiar enough with materials from the oral law to be able to incorporate them easily into her own home-based education of her children.[22]

Ashkenazi women frequently spent Sabbath afternoons at home reading from such Yiddish texts as the *Ze'enah u-Re'enah,* which translated and interpreted stories from the Bible. Some contemporary readers see the *Ze'enah u-Re'enah* as a "feminist Bible," because the work often championed women and their viewpoints; for example, after commenting (on Exodus 15:20) that Sarah, Abigail, and Hannah were each prophets, the commentary concludes: "Women should be honored, because when they are pious, they are pious without limit."[23] Some, but not all, of women's *tekhinnes* (devotional prayers that often make reference to biblical figures and incidents) were authored by women who themselves possessed impressive levels of learning; others, especially in the eighteenth century, were authored by men.[24]

As intellectual tools, however, these sources were severely limited. Not only were the masses of Jewish women deprived of intensive learning and the world of intensive learning deprived of the masses of Jewish women—sometimes there were psychological tolls as well. Many Jewish men used their knowledge with kindness and integrity. However, in the hands of men with character flaws or misogynistic impulses, Judaic knowledge could be used as a weapon against ignorant wives or daughters. Yiddish writers often depict the role unequal education for men and women played in impoverished, dysfunctional Eastern European households.[25] In I. L. Peretz's story "A Woman's Wrath," a prematurely aged mother is verbally brutalized by her husband. Because she has interrupted his study session, he threatens her: "Hell! Everlasting flames! You'll be hung by your tongue—you'll receive all the four punishments of the supreme tribunal!" Because of her vastly inferior Jewish education, the wife is unable to recognize her husband's threats as a cruel, rancorous lie.[26]

The bitterness engendered by such episodes and attitudes drove many superior women away from Jewish life in the past. In nineteenth-century Europe some Jewish women became poets, actresses, and mistresses of intellectual salons, the self-proclaimed atheistic leaders and followers of socialism and other modernist movements. Some of them actually converted out of Judaism; others simply drifted into estrangement from Jewish life. Ironically, these very defections provided a critical rationale in helping proponents of Jewish education for women to change the habits of centuries and to offer universal Jewish education for girls as well as boys. To some extent, the potential defection of uneducated Jewish women is still an effective argument assisting those who try to expand Jewish women's intellectual and spiritual horizons.

A common misconception is that Orthodox Jews have lagged far behind liberal Jews in the effort to provide women with a rigorous Jewish education. This is historically inaccurate, and to some extent the opposite of the truth. An unwillingness to provide women with more than a rudimentary Jewish education was one vestige of traditional Jewish and non-Jewish attitudes which some very liberal Jews retained even after they had discarded other forms of traditionalism.

Widespread formal Jewish education for women is a relatively recent development, although some formal Jewish education for girls certainly predated the nineteenth century. Rabbi Ephraim Hayyot (early eighteenth-century Galicia) comments that in Germany, Italy, and Poland separate teachers were hired for boys and girls, and Rabbi Jacob Emden (eighteenth-century Germany) advises sending girls to female teachers or educating them in the home.[27] The slow, cumulative growth of Jewish education for women is linked to the process of emancipation and acculturation to Western society. In Germany, where the Jewish community was profoundly affected by the ideals of the Haskalah (Jewish Enlightenment) in the late eighteenth and early nineteenth centuries, both the burgeoning Reform movement and the enlightened neo-Orthodox movement of Samson Raphael Hirsch sponsored formal Jewish education for girls. In Eastern Europe, where the Jewish community proved more resistant to Westernization, such schooling came somewhat later. After World War I some secular Jewish schools, both Yiddishist and Hebraist, provided formal Jewish education for girls.

Most important, Sarah Schnirer established the Bais Yaakov movement, which revolutionized Jewish education for girls. The daughter of a Belzer Hassid, Sarah Schnirer was born in 1883 and received minimal Jewish education as a child, but pursued her education on her own and later with neo-Orthodox teachers in Vienna. She returned to Crakow determined to "rescue Judaism for the new generation" by providing intensive Jewish education for girls in an

Orthodox setting. In 1917 she opened a school with twenty-five girls; the school expanded rapidly and new branches were established. Schnirer's educational work won the support of such leading Orthodox figures as the Hafetz Hayyim and the Belzer Rebbe, who pointed out that women receiving sophisticated secular education but rudimentary Jewish education were likely to abandon Orthodoxy. In 1937–38, a total of 35,585 girls were enrolled in 248 Bais Yaakov schools in Poland alone.[28]

The Nazis destroyed not only the lives of millions but also the rich Jewish culture in which Sarah Schnirer's schools were growing. It was a long time before the all-day religious school movement would take root and flourish on American soil. For decades after the mass immigration of Eastern European Jews to the United States (1880–1924), the vast majority of American Jews were passionately committed to the concept of public schools, and many actively opposed the parochial school movement. This meant that most American Jewish education took place in a congregational context in Sunday schools and afternoon schools, often called *cheder,* and supplementary school, or Talmud Torah. Due to the disruption of Jewish life, the American supplementary schools were often substandard both in pedagogues and pedagogy.

By and large, until very recently only the most Orthodox families sent their children to all-day Jewish schools. By the post–World War II period, as day schools were more extensively established, American Orthodox families began to send girls and boys to day schools in almost equal numbers. However, during this time period, boys were enrolled much more frequently and for longer periods of time than girls in Sunday and afternoon schools. In many non-Orthodox families, the primary rationale for enrolling boys in Jewish schools was to provide them with training for the bar mitzvah. Until the bat mitzvah ceremony acquired a similar popularity, Conservative, Reform, and Reconstructionist parents were much less likely to enroll daughters along with sons in Jewish schools.

Thus, among American Jewish women over fifty-five (1990 NJPS), Orthodox women are the most likely to have received some formal Jewish education and nonobservant or "just Jewish" women the least likely. Although significant numbers of older Orthodox women did not receive any formal Jewish education—reflecting the opinion of some Orthodox thinkers that girls need not know the holy tongue, the Orthodox as a group were more likely to use Jewish all-day schools, private tutors, Yiddish schools, or other means of education for both boys and girls. In fact Orthodox Jews are more likely to provide their daughters with a rigorous Jewish education than are members of any other wing of Judaism. Half of all born-Jewish respondents ages eighteen to forty-four who were raised as Orthodox Jews received day-school education—and among these Jews the percentages of boys and girls in day school were virtually identical. Contrary to popular expectations, the gender gap in Jewish education today is seen primarily among supplementary-school students and primarily among persons whose households of origin were Conservative or Reform/Reconstructionist.

Despite the popular notion that the Reform and Conservative movements have consistently been relatively egalitarian, in the area of Jewish education they have lagged dramatically behind Orthodox behavior. Recent statistical studies definitively refute assertions of such observers as Prell that Jewish education for boys and girls in the 1950s and 1960s was increasingly equal, and that "the more traditional the denomination the more persistent was educational inequality."[29] Orthodox standards for what comprises religious literacy and Orthodox willingness to devote large amounts of time to religious subjects have always—and continue to—far outstrip that of Conservative, Reform, and Reconstructionist families as a group. Rifka Haut asserts, "the average twelfth-grade Yeshiva girl often has a more extensive and deeper knowledge of traditional Jewish texts than the typical Reform rabbi."

Jewish education for girls rises in Conservative and Reform settings among women ages thirty-five to fifty-four, who are presumably more likely to have been affected by the growing popularity of the bat mitzvah ceremony. Reform is the most likely of the three denominations to limit a girl's education to Sunday school only. The testimony of women such as Sara Lee, now the director of the Reform Rhea Hirsch School at Hebrew Union College–Jewish Institute of Religion in Los Angeles, is especially poignant: "I received no Jewish education as a child. My brothers went to Hebrew school. My Jewish education really began with Young Judea and a trip to Israel—all my formal Jewish education came after I was sixteen years old."

Although its vitality in Europe was brutally cut off during World War II, the basic assumptions underlying the formation of the Bais Yaakov schools have now been accepted by even the most ultra-Orthodox groups in the United States: The education of girls is widely viewed as a necessity for the preservation of a traditional

Jewish way of life. In day schools ranging from the Satmar school, Bais Rochel, which eliminates the twelfth grade to make sure its graduates cannot attend college, to coeducational Orthodox schools such as Ramaz in New York and Maimonides in Boston, which provide outstanding secular education and teach their boys and girls Talmud together, the crucial necessity for providing girls with a Jewish education has become an undisputed communal priority. During the past decade it has also become increasingly popular for Orthodox young women to spend a year of religious study in Israeli yeshivot between high school and college. In addition Stern College for Women, an undergraduate school of Yeshiva University in New York City, now offers courses in Talmud, as do a growing number of Orthodox synagogues.

In a startling development the Lubavitcher Rebbe recently stated that women should be taught the Talmud in order to preserve the quality of Jewish life, and in order that the tradition should be passed down from generation to generation. If he had forbidden such study, every right-wing Jewish paper internationally would have publicized his opinion. However, since he strongly urges the kind of study that still makes many in the "black hat" world of the right-wing academies very nervous, his statement has received almost no publicity whatsoever.

In an article in Hebrew, following much the same line of reasoning as did Rebecca Tiktiner in the *Maineket Rivkah,* the Lubavitcher Rebbe urges that women be taught the oral Torah so that they, who provide the most consistent presence in the home, can supervise and guide their children's religious studies. Contradicting much classical Jewish thought, Rabbi Schneerson asserts that all women are capable of learning the oral law. He notes that in the past the group of women who did in fact study the oral law was limited because such study was entirely voluntary. Today, however, he urges, women may and should be taught the complete range of talmudic texts. They should study with their husbands subjects even including the "fine, dialectical" points of law that most previous rabbis posited as being inappropriate for women. These study sessions are necessary, says Rabbi Schneerson, because without them women can easily be seduced by the charms of secular studies. He says: "It is human nature for male and female to delight in this kind of study. Through this there will develop in them [the women] the proper sensitivities and talents in the spirit of our Holy Torah."[30]

Indeed, schools of advanced Jewish education that either cater to women or are coeducational are flourishing both in the United States and in Israel. Philosopher Vanessa Ochs, in a moving and powerful memoir of her year of study in Israel, describes a number of schools and a number of individual women who give classes often frequented by American women. Significantly, the vast majority of the learned women Ochs met in Israel, like Rashi's daughters, had studied with their fathers—all learned men who had no problem in providing their brilliant daughters with rigorous higher Jewish education. "In the drama of learning Torah, the mothers hovered like benevolent shadows. When the women recalled their father's teachings, it was gratitude not so much for the material they taught as for the concrete expression of love." Chana Safrai, daughter of Hebrew University Jewish history professor Samuel Safrai, for example, said:

> As far as my father was concerned, my learning Torah as a woman was not an issue. Never! My father never differentiated between me and my brother Zeev, who is two years younger and is now a professor of geographic history of Israel at Bar-Ilan University. We were the same in his eyes. He always made sure I had the opportunity to study. When I was thirteen, he almost cancelled his sabbatical abroad because he feared he wouldn't find someone to teach me in his place. He went only because he found a teacher willing to teach both me and my brother. . . . At ages eight and nine, we learned a chapter of Mishnah by heart (every Saturday morning). . . . By eleven years old, we'd study a whole page of Talmud during the week and by the end of the week, we'd know it by heart. At twelve, we learned the whole of tractate *Taanit* by heart, and then *Sanhedrin*. . . . Our father's teaching didn't alienate us. It encouraged us. We have both followed in his footsteps.[31]

In her exploration of educational institutions, Ochs interviewed Rabbi Chaim Brovender, the founder of some of the more liberal Orthodox schools for men and women. One of the women's schools is named Bruria, after the learned woman cited in the Talmud. Rabbi Brovender spoke openly to Ochs about the advantages women enjoy—and the disadvantages they suffer—in their pursuit of rigorous Jewish studies. On the one hand, said Rabbi Brovender, "in religious circles, women are not taken seriously." This is not an unrelieved disadvantage. "Whether he likes it or not, a man is pushed by peer pressure to study Talmud," which some of them dislike and some are not suited for. On the other hand, "For women, there is no peer pressure. She can face her reactions. Does she like Talmud, does she want to learn it? Men don't have the opportunity to ask those questions." Indeed, *"because* women are not taken seriously, they can do creative things. I'd like women with backgrounds in music, art, and literature to establish an integrative position between their competence in these fields and Torah in order to create new Torah enterprises."[32]

The positive role of schools such as Bruria, Pardes, and others in the education of American Jewish women is attested to by women such as Rabbi Rona Shapiro, a Harvard literature graduate who originally went to Israel to try kibbutz life and decided to enroll in Pardes, which was "the only place I could get the depth and intensity of study without the compulsory observance and the single-mindedness that other yeshivas seem to demand."[33] After two years, she fixed her goal on the rabbinate and has just received ordination from the Jewish Theological Seminary of America.

During her year in Israel, Ochs studied at several institutions and with several individuals. Their variety as people and in terms of teaching techniques testifies to the vitality and growth of serious learning for women.[34] Ochs has special praise for Professor Nechama Leibowitz, the first contemporary woman to publish a rigorous analysis of Torah texts, calling her "the source, the real thing. . . . To have studied with Nechama is to have been in analysis with Freud, to have been educated in nursery school by Maria Montessori, to have been inoculated against polio by Dr. Salk. In many communities Nechama's biblical interpretation has complete authority. . . . Her studies, placing Bible in the context of ancient and modern Jewish Bible commentary, have been edited into the best-selling and widely translated six-volume *Studies in the Weekly Sidra.* . . . Rabbi Pinchas Peli once referred to Nehama, now in her eighties (although you wouldn't know it from her rigorous teaching schedule, which could wipe out a much younger person), as Israel's most outstanding living rabbi. This was long before the ordination of women. . . . He was referring to the original meaning of the word rabbi. A rabbi is, above all, a teacher of Torah."[35]

In the United States as well as in Israel, new programs of study have been created that supplement existing institutions of higher learning. These new schools for girls emphasize mastery of the intellectual tools that will enable their students to pursue further independent study. As Chana Henkin, founder and director of the Nishmat School for Women in Jerusalem, says, women have traditionally been "taught to record and digest someone else's preformu-

lated thoughts, while men grapple with texts."[36] The Drishna
Institute has provided outstanding classes and study opportunities
for New York Jewish women for many years.[37] Recently, in Hill-
crest, N.Y., Jewish educator Esther Krauss has created a school
where adult women receive not only formal classes (*shiurim*) but
then participate in vigorous, extended, hands-on study sessions with
a regular study partner (*b'chevruta*) just as men have done in yeshivot for centuries. This form of lively, interactive learning has been
the hallmark of the highest levels of traditional study, but was in the
past considered off limits to women. Called *Shalhevet:* A Torah Institute for Women, the school aims to "sharpen learning skills
through intensive textual study."

Mrs. Krauss, who served previously as the associate director of a
girls' yeshiva high school, has written frequently about her belief
that contemporary Orthodox women should be required to pray and
study as rigorously as men. She believes that until such requirements
are egalitarian, neither women nor men in Orthodox spheres will
ever regard women as fully serious spiritual adults. The fact that this
type of leadership in high-quality Jewish studies for women is emerging out of the most mainstream Orthodox elements should not be
underestimated. Such schools illustrate the fact that although Orthodoxy is widely perceived (both internally and externally) to be un-
changing, and although many elements within Orthodoxy are
implacably hostile to feminist stirrings, mainstream Orthodoxy has
been cautiously receptive to changes in communal standards vis-à-vis
Jewish education for women.

In general young American Jewish women today are far more
likely than their grandmothers were to receive some formal Jewish
education. One chapter is ending for American Jewish women and
another is beginning. The concept of widespread Jewish education
for women was for centuries regarded with profound suspicion. Today it is accepted both in principle and de facto throughout the Jewish community. The issue of Jewish education for women is an area
in which Jewish feminist concerns and Jewish survival concerns are
synonymous. Without much exaggeration, it might be said that the
continuity of the American Jewish community and the presence of a
Jewishly educated and committed generation of children tomorrow
depend on universal Jewish education for American Jewish girls and
women today.

Changing the landscape of Jewish education for women is a matter not only of bringing more women into Jewish educational set-

tings, but also of bringing women more into the subject matter of Jewish education itself. Curricula vary widely from denomination to denomination and even from school to school, but common elements of Jewish educational curricula often include (1) liturgical literacy—providing students with enough familiarity with the prayer services so that the will feel comfortable in a synagogue or temple; (2) Bible basics—conveying at least the more salient highlights of biblical narratives and religious injunctions; (3) Jewish law and customs—grounding students in the ritual norms for daily, Sabbath, and holiday celebrations and other occasions for each particular denomination; (4) cultural manifestations—familiarizing students with some aspects of Jewish cultural expression, such as music, dance, and artifacts; (5) Hebrew language and literature—giving students, to a greater or lesser extent, depending on the educational setting, some proficiency in the spoken, written, biblical, and liturgical Hebrew language; (6) Jewish history—conveying the sweep of Jewish history, often with a special emphasis on such cataclysmic recent events as the Holocaust, the creation of the State of Israel, and Israeli history; and (7) Jewish peoplehood—creating an emotional bonding and sense of responsibility for Jews worldwide, especially in Israel and in communities where Jews are oppressed or threatened.

Such curricula, while certainly ambitious, have often been notoriously incomplete in that they focused on the experiences and needs of the male half of the Jewish people. Without overt ill intent, but simply because the male Jewish experience was considered the norm, Jewish educational texts have historically focused on men. This androcentric focus of Jewish studies has extended from the most rudimentary to the most elevated settings. From nursery children in Jewish Sunday schools to university students in graduate programs, Jewish studies have, until very recently, been by and about men. Even when women were the focus of a particular course of study—when, for example, students of rabbinic Judaism might be studying portions of the talmudic tractates dealing with women—women were seen in these texts through male eyes.

For the past two decades, however, Jewish feminist scholars have turned their attention to women in Jewish history, civilization, culture, and literature from the Bible through contemporary times. The writings of Jewish feminist scholars have spanned the gamut from highly accessible articles and tools meant to reenfranchise the broadest spectrum of English-speaking Jewish women to highly technical, esoteric dissertations. Conversations with women who teach and study in these areas can often be inspirational. Again and again one hears the stories of one who has been drawn deeply into an interaction with her Jewish past—often from a childhood that was only marginally committed to Jewish life. But no matter what their initial background, for a sweeping number of women in Jewish studies, Judaism has become the passionate intellectual and spiritual calling of their lifetimes.

Before the emergence of Jewish feminism, Judaism was deprived of the full spectrum of intellectual, spiritual, and imaginative talents of Jewish women, and Jewish women were deprived of the full scope of Judaism as an intellectual, spiritual, and imaginative force in their lives. Tradition discouraged most Jewish women from complete participation in their religious heritage, and the Jewish culture itself was robbed of creative minds and hearts that would surely have enriched it immeasurably. Contemporary American Jewish writers such as Cynthia Ozick and Rebecca Goldstein have written powerfully of the impoverishment of the Jewish intellectual tradition resulting from the exclusion of women in the creation of Jewish law and literature; Ozick notes that such exclusion has meant "a loss numerically greater than a hundred pogroms; yet Jewish literature and history report not one wail, not one tear."[38] Esther Singer Kreitman, sister to the brilliant literary Singer brothers, illustrates in her thinly fictionalized autobiographical novel just how marginalized intellectual Jewish women were often made to feel.[39]

Women who attempted to train themselves or to make careers in Jewish communal life or Judaic studies were often severely discouraged. Carol Diament, the first woman to receive a doctorate in Judaica from Yeshiva University, remembers that in the 1970s women who were clearly the stars in their classes in Medieval Jewish Studies were discouraged so firmly that not one of them finished her degree. Diament, who specialized in modern Jewish history—a more acceptable field for women—made it through. Some women were told that "only rabbis need apply" for particular positions or courses of study—and that females could not become rabbis. Not until the mid-1970s did legitimate and comfortable positions for Jewish women who wanted to focus their energies on Jewish achievements gradually begin to appear, and to this day some Judaic studies departments are haunted by a kind of vague mistrust of females as faculty and graduate students in traditionally male areas of Jewish scholarship.

Today, through Jewish education, Jewish feminism is providing Jewish women with the intellectual tools with which to fully appreciate, participate in, and understand the richness and complexity of their own heritage. By providing women with new spiritual opportunities, Jewish feminism is giving them a religion that touches their contemporary lives both broadly and deeply. By opening up public Judaism and leadership roles, Jewish feminism is investing women with an enthusiasm for Jewish life and a respect for themselves as fully enfranchised Jews. Because of the conjunction of feminism with other historical forces, Jewish women play a crucial role in the revitalization of spiritual and intellectual American Judaism. In the past massive waves of immigration renewed and revitalized American Jewish life. Some Eastern European Jews in the two decades before and two decades after the turn of the century, and Holocaust survivors after World War II, brought to the United States a religious intensity that infused American Jewish communities, places of worship, and other institutions. Today feminism is providing a new wave of immigration. Feminism is bringing newly ardent Jews—women—into the fold. Feminism is the new American Jewish immigration.

Chapter Nine

Breaking Through Jewish Ceilings

It's the same old story. Everyone is in favor of women rabbis—until it comes time to hire one. A congregation would rather take an incompetent man than a woman. Women are picked last.

—Rabbi Paula Reimers[1]

ONE OF THE MOST VISIBLE RESULTS of Jewish feminism has been the emergence of women into strata of Jewish communal leadership previously occupied exclusively by men. By the fall of 1992, about 280 women had been ordained as rabbis by Reform, Reconstructionist, and Conservative rabbinical seminaries. Jewish organizations in most major metropolitan areas had appointed or hired female leaders to executive-level positions. From the outside it seemed as though feminism had been extremely successful in breaking through the glass ceilings of the Jewish communal world and giving women an equal opportunity to serve as leaders within the Jewish community. However, women who aspire to leadership positions have often encountered great resistance.

Resistance to female leaders seems to be linked to nostalgic images of leadership patterns in historic, traditional Jewish societies. Before emigration to America, rabbis and communal leaders functioned in what was basically an all-male world. Leaders of the *kehillah*, the

201

organized Jewish community, were politically skilled men who negotiated with the all-male power structures governing the countries in which Jews lived. On the skills of such Jewish leaders the fate of entire Jewish communities often depended. Rabbis, produced by the all-male European yeshivot, were esteemed primarily for their devotion to learning, their ritual piety, and their scholarly brilliance. Hasidic *rebbes*, members of a male dynastic succession, were respected and loved by their followers as charismatic leaders.

In contrast, contemporary American rabbis, while they may incorporate some of the qualities of their predecessors, such as scholarship and charisma, are hired to fill jobs that demand other skills as well. Today's rabbi serves as an orator, teacher, social worker, personal counselor, youth group coordinator, and consensus builder. Similarly today's Jewish communal leader does not have to bargain for Jewish communal survival with hostile princes, but must instead often function as a CEO, fund-raiser, director of volunteers, and liaison worker with Jewish, non-Jewish, and government agencies. Women today have the opportunity to acquire extensive Jewish and secular education equal to that of men, and they are often gifted in other areas salient to rabbinical and communal leadership positions. Jewish women have trained and worked for leadership positions, and the tasks involved in rabbinical and other types of communal leadership are not gender-specific within the modern American context. But women who prepare for jobs as contemporary rabbis and Jewish communal leaders are often confronted by opposition fueled by memories or impressions of Jewish life in the past.

The idea that significant numbers of mainstream "good Jewish daughters" would be caught up in issues of female leadership in the Jewish communal, scholarly, and religious worlds marks a major break with Jewish tradition. Public leadership was seen as inimicable to the modesty that was becoming to adult Jewish women; they should not desire, it was felt, to thrust themselves into the public eye. Tellingly, even some of the women whose spectacular Judaic learning attracted large audiences are reported in rabbinic literature as having lectured behind a thick curtain[2] so as not to go beyond the bounds of modesty—hardly a mode that could be used on a regular basis by public leaders. Although the leading figures of the Hebrew Bible include an impressive number of forceful women, throughout medieval and postmedieval Jewish history women as a group were encouraged to remain modestly behind the scenes or to assume a subservient posture in most public religious settings, especially in

Jewish communities located within Muslim host cultures. The ancient exclusion of women from serving as the heads of communities (Sifre, Deuteronomy 157) was expanded by Maimonides to a recommendation that women not serve in any public communal office (*Mishneh Torah,* Hilkhot Melakhim 1:5).[3]

Even nonritual related communal leadership roles were deemed inappropriate for women—that is, at odds with requirements for feminine modesty. In general Jewish women were taught that their glory lay in the domestic realm; according to the biblical verse, "the honor of the king's daughter is all within," *k'vodah bat-melech p'nimah* (Psalms 45:14). The extreme isolation of women in some traditional Jewish societies is spelled out in a frequently cited passage:

> For every woman has the right to leave her home and to go her father's house in order to visit him or to a house of mourning or even to a wedding as an act of loving-kindness to her friends or relatives, so that they may also come and visit her. She is not like a prisoner that she should neither come and go. But it is shameful for a woman to leave her home continually, at times outside her home and at others even walking in the streets. A husband should prevent his wife from doing this. He should not allow her to leave the house more than once in a month or twice, according to the need. For the beauty of a woman consists in her staying withdrawn in a corner of her home, for this is how it is written: All the honor of the king's daughter is within [her home] (Ishut 13:11).

This sequestration of women had an inevitable impact on the development of their intellectual and social skills, as the rabbis recognized. They commented that preadolescent girls as a group often seem brighter and more disciplined than boys of the same age; they puzzled over the reversal of those qualities in mature males and females. Orthodox Rabbi Eliezer Berkovits critiques and summarizes the rabbinic conclusions:

> The question, of course, is: What happened to the female's superior intelligence? Tosafot explains that ... the boys' natural intelligence develops because he is so often in the house of his teacher, which is not the case for girls. The opinion is formulated more explicitly in a midrash: "The way of a woman is to sit in her house; that of a man, to go out into the marketplaces, and thus he learns wisdom from other peo-

ple" (Genesis Rabbah 18a). . . . Women are by nature of superior intelligence, but . . . their intelligence cannot mature because of their lack of education and exclusion from social and economic activities. They had no experience in legal matters, such as the legal forms of property transfer, or in monetary evaluation of everyday objects.[4]

Indeed, some early sources go so far as to state that because of religious and social gender-linked differences between men and women, the life of a male acquires a value beyond that of a female:

"The man has precedence over the woman to be maintained" (Mishnah Horayot 13a). This means that if both are in danger of their lives, e.g., if both are in equal danger of drowning, the man is to be saved first. Maimonides explains that since the man is obligated to observe more mitzvot (divine commandments) than a woman, his life is of greater sanctity than the woman's (Maimonides, Commentary on Mishnah). . . . Not only does woman, at this stage, not have equal status with man in this male-built society, but she is really outside of it.[5]

Much of public leadership was off limits to women for halakhic reasons: Jewish law forbade women from fulfilling certain ritual requirements for groups that included men, and was ambivalent as to whether they might fulfill others. Rabbinic law noted that it was inappropriate for women to perform some functions, such as reading from the Torah for the congregation, because the female performance of such a function might detract from the "honor of the congregation," k'vod ha-tzibbur, shaming the men by indicating that none of them were sufficiently well versed to perform the Torah reading. Sometimes these interpretations are expanded beyond a strict reading of the law. When rabbinical authorities cannot find a specific legal reason for preventing women from assuming a role that implies public status, they often fall back on sexual innuendo— women may not participate in a given role because their participation may lead to sexual improprieties.

Complaints that decisions about female participation, prominence, and leadership roles are based more on received cultural norms than on the law are not limited to Orthodox women. Indeed, Conservative-raised Letty Cottin Pogrebin reflects the feelings of many women when she asserts that she abandoned Jewish ritual observance for many years because of her perception that women were basically servants and had no public leadership roles in traditional Jewish life. Since she had a vision of Judaism as "a male-run religion personified by my Daddy," she felt, as a female, that she could only receive bits and pieces of Judaism as a favor from men—that is, it was not her birthright. Ironically, Pogrebin observes, she left Judaism because of what she now realizes were feminist considerations, and she returned to Judaism because changing mores and the impact of feminism made it possible for her to take a leadership role as the cantor of a prayer group.[6]

The changing status of women within American Judaism has been at least as influenced by transformations in the surrounding culture as by evolving religious beliefs. The expectations of congregants and indeed of rabbis and religious thinkers as well have responded to the tenor of the times. This is clearly seen in the struggle of women to attend, be ordained by, and eventually to teach in American Jewish rabbinical seminaries. In the fall of 1992, one female professor taught at each of the Reform Hebrew Union College's three campuses, three taught at the Reconstructionist Rabbinical College, and the Conservative Jewish Theological Seminary employed three female faculty members and five teachers of Hebrew (not considered an academic specialty).

Hebrew Union College (HUC) ordained the first American Reform woman rabbi, Sally Priesand, in 1972. Fifty years earlier, in 1922, Rabbi Jacob Lauterbach had voiced the opposition of Reform rabbis in the HUC Board to the ordination of women. Rabbi Lauterbach's objections are worth looking at closely because they vividly illustrate the impact of secular communal norms on religious thinking and pronouncements. Rejecting the Central Conference of American Rabbis' (CCAR) reluctant conclusion that women "cannot justly be denied the privilege of ordination," Rabbi Lauterbach asserted that no woman can be both a mother and homemaker and also a good rabbi. He based his objections on four sequential axioms that seem dated to the modern temper but that once were accepted by large segments of American society: First, women would be unable to make a true career commitment. Female work was a temporary arrangement at best, and women could hardly be expected to give many hours of each week and many years of their lives to any career. Second, any woman who truly desired a career could only do so by forgoing husband and family. Third, the marital relationship required one dominant and one subordinate partner; any woman who wanted a real career would need a subordinate husband to enable her to fulfill her career aspirations. Fourth, the notion of a dominant wife and a subordinate husband was unwholesome and antithetical to traditional values. While Lauterbach made a case for the rabbinate being more difficult than other vocations, his objections were really not religious but cultural: He clearly was writing out of a context that did not include women who were simultaneously wives and mothers—and professionals: female surgeons, trial lawyers, physicists, and astronauts.[7]

Since Priesand's ordination in 1972, Hebrew Union College has ordained almost two hundred female rabbis and has invested seventy female cantors. Dr. Alfred Gottschalk, president of HUC-JIR, notes that in 1992 "fully half of the Colleges-Institutes enrollment is comprised of capable women . . . in our rabbinic, cantorial, education, communal studies and graduate programs." Moreover the movement is training women in the Israeli Progressive Movement and is planning to ordain its first Israeli rabbi in the summer of 1992.[8]

Most Reform congregations however, continue to express a preference for a male primary rabbi; women rabbis are still far more likely to find employment as assistant rabbis, chaplains, and Hillel clergy.[9] Now that the earliest female rabbis have attained some seniority within the Reform movement, it remains to be seen if they will also attain rabbinical posts with the prestige and salaries commensurate with their senior status. Sally Priesand, who began her career as an assistant rabbi at the Stephen Wise Free Synagogue in New York, has served for over a decade as the rabbi of Monmouth Reform Temple in Tinton Falls, New Jersey. Many Reform female rabbis commented on the sexist attitudes and sexual politics that prevail in hiring and later in their pulpit practice. Some male congregants behave in a condescending or hostile way toward female religious professionals although the men may themselves be Jewishly illiterate.

Rabbi Laurie Coskey, who holds an assistant rabbinical position in a large Reform temple in Southern California, regards the sexist attitudes of some congregants with humorous resignation:

Some of my congregants see me as the Mommy and Michael [the "senior" rabbi] as the Daddy—even though we're pretty close in age. They are happy for me to give sermons, provide classes for them and their kids, do marital and other kinds of counseling—but they don't want me to have anything to do with money. Only Michael is allowed to play financial hardball with the big boys.

Overall she feels very accepted by most of the congregation, says Rabbi Coskey, although "some individual males continue to test my abilities all the time. Some of them deliberately attempt to discredit my expertise—and always in front of other people, especially their own families. It's as though they have to reassert masculine prerogatives, as though my presence makes them feel threatened in their family's eyes."

Female Reform cantors, on the other hand, have found much more widespread acceptance and have obtained employment in many prestigious congregations. In 1986 the entire entering class of cantors at HUC consisted of women. Halakhically, women cantors pose as many problems—although somewhat different ones—as do women rabbis, and there is no halakhic difference between a primary and an assistant rabbi. Therefore the bias against women primary rabbis but for women cantors and assistant rabbis would seem once again to be a cultural one. Cantors may be perceived as assistants to rabbis or even as a species of religious entertainers—employees, rather than leaders, of the congregation. Chaplains and Hillel rabbis have less prestige and much lower salaries than full Reform pulpit rabbis; their work has a very high social work or counseling component and is usually focused on the young, the old, or the ill, rather than on affluent and powerful community lay leaders. Thus, despite Reform assumptions of full egalitarianism, a substantial number of Reform congregants seem content to relegate female clergy to subordinate positions. Moreover, this preference seems to be related to persistent cultural and prestige-oriented prejudices rather than derived from traditional religious laws.

The Reconstructionist Rabbinical College included women as soon as its doors opened in 1968 and ordained the first woman, Sandy Eisenberg Sasso, in 1974. As of fall 1992, fifty-one women have received ordination from RRC, and the college has been home to much important Jewish feminist scholarship, including explorations of women in the Bible, liturgy and rituals, gender and power. Because the RRC's ordination of women predated by a decade that of the Conservative movement, some women who considered themselves primarily Conservative by conviction studied for ordination at RRC and obtained positions at Reconstructionist congregations. The school's Jewish Woman's Study Program continues to attract female rabbinical candidates who are especially interested in exploring feminist issues within their rabbinical training. The class of 1993 consists entirely of women.

The struggle within the Jewish Theological Seminary (JTS) in moving toward the Conservative ordination of women provides a well-documented case study of the evolution of women's roles within American Judaism. The way toward considering such an idea was first opened by the votes to give women *aliyot* and later those to count them for a minyan by the Rabbinical Assembly's Committee on Jewish Law and Standards in 1973. During the late 1970s there was strong pressure within the Conservative movement to change the policy of the Jewish Theological Seminary and to begin to ordain women as rabbis. Seminary chancellor Dr. Gerson D. Cohen and Rabbi Wolfe Kelman, executive vice president of the Rabbinical Assembly (RA), were strongly in favor of the change, as were many younger, seminary-educated pulpit rabbis.

As support for Conservative female ordination of women was building, so was the opposition to it among both Conservative pulpit rabbis and scholars. Some organized their opposition along halakhic lines; others used psychological or sociological arguments. A special issue of the journal *Conservative Judaism* in 1974 explored topics connected to "Women and Change in Jewish Law." Among the articles was one that became a hallmark of Jewish antifeminism. In it psychiatrist Mortimer Ostow characterized Jewish feminism as an attempt to obliterate "the visible differences between men and women" and "a possible encouragement of transsexual fantasies." Even if this were not a conscious or unconscious aim of Jewish feminists, Ostow warned, the end result of fully empowering women within public Judaism would be to emasculate Jewish men, producing a society where women dominated the synagogue but suffered frustration in the bedroom as a result.[10]

Ostow's article evoked a flood of profeminist responses from both men and women, which were collected in a second special issue of *Conservative Judaism*, titled "Women and Change in Jewish Law: Responses to the Fall 1974 Symposium." In a detailed statement leading off the collection, Arthur Green answered Ostow's objections to Jewish feminism point by point, noting that the "gentleness of a loving mother-God might serve as a good counter-balance to the sometimes overbearing austerity of God as father, kind and judge.

Mother Rachel, Mother Zion, and widowed Jerusalem have done much to add to the warmth of our spiritual heritage."[11]

Green's defense of the feminine persona of the Jewish people in Jewish literature was hardly the last word on the subject of the possible damage to the Jewish male psyche which might be done by feminist aspirations to public Jewish life. Five years later, in *Conservative Judaism*'s "Open Forum" column, Rabbi Richard M. Yellin stated flatly that by definition only men could be rabbis:

> Can a woman become a rabbi? I believe asking a question like that is like asking: Can a Jewish woman become a Jewish man? The rabbi is an identity model for men, implicitly saying to them: Channel your energies in similar fashion. Get married; have children; study Torah; be loyal and faithful to your wife, children and community. And if you wish recognition, if you want status in the Jewish community, then do it through your study, your knowledge and your efforts in producing a more viable community. We Jews have survived in history not because of the power of our warriors or businessmen, but because of the piety of our fathers and husbands, who are commanded to marry women who freely choose to opt for family and children.[12]

Yellin scolded women who did not conform to his ideas of the Jewish norm: "Anyone who feels that getting married or having children is oppressive or gets in the way of realizing identity reflects a posture that cannot exist normatively within the Jewish system. . . . Those who created Jewish tradition felt that the woman's role model was inherent in every mother who had a family." Women are sensitized by their roles as mothers, Yellin asserted. As they care for children, they become good human beings.[13]

But where, Yellin wonders, is the Jewish man "to get the same kind of sensitization? If you send him to his mother he becomes 'mommified.' You emasculate him. He becomes a Portnoy." In fact, suggests Yellin, Judaism is a system of laws created to create kinder, gentler men without emasculating them. The purpose of the system of Jewish laws is to create a males-only "support system" that will create a man "who takes responsibility for his children, who channels all his aggressions into charity, voluntarism, and all the things we customarily call 'feminine.' . . . **The task of Judaism is to bring the male into the more traditional female role without feeling threatened, sissified, emasculated and rendered impotent**" (my emphasis).[14]

In Ostow's and Yellin's words lingers an overt fear of the sexual female—and an assumption that women's spiritual and religious needs can be fulfilled in the domestic arena and the privacy of the home. Men have ambitions and aggressions that must be channeled in Jewish fashion; women don't have the same kind of impulses, and in any case motherhood will provide for their spiritual needs. "It's the male who needs the *minyan* more because his natural tendency is to prove himself in the world. The woman, who is more easily drawn to normative family life, is reinforced by the fruits of her biology," he insists. Men are attracted by power and affluence—thus only men need to put on the *tefillin*. Only men need to come into close contact with the Torah, because dressing the Torah is a lot like dressing a child—something that women get to do all the time! The rabbi must be a man because he needs to be a role model for other men. Other men need a rabbi because he can show them how to love his wife and children and care for the community and still be manly. This is no job for a woman, Yellin firmly concludes.[15]

At the annual convention of the RA in May 1977, the majority of rabbis voted to ask for the formation of an interdisciplinary commission "to study all aspects of the role of women as spiritual leaders in the Conservative Movement." This report was to be presented first to the Executive Council of the RA in the spring of 1978 and to the RA at the 1979 convention. The final report of the commission minimized both halakhic difficulties and the strength of feeling of dissenting rabbis. It stated that it would be morally wrong for the Conservative movement to continue to deny ordination to qualified women. A majority of Conservative congregations, said the commission, were ready to accept female rabbis, and three-quarters of rabbinical students expressed support for the admission of women to the rabbinical school. The commission strongly recommended "that the Rabbinical School of The Jewish Theological Seminary of America revise its admission procedures to allow for applications from female candidates and the processing thereof for the purpose of admission to the ordination program on a basis equal to that maintained heretofore only for males," and that the seminary "educate the community" properly "so as to insure as smooth and as harmonious an adjustment to the new policy as possible."[16]

However, the commission's premises and recommendations were opposed by several older and world-renowned seminary professors—devout men who had studied at Orthodox yeshivot—and were intensely committed to traditional halakhic Judaism. The ordination of women was opposed by a substantial group of Conservative pulpit rabbis as well. The commission's report recommending ordination for women appeared in January 1979. Shortly after this Charles Liebman, then visiting professor of Jewish sociology at JTS, and Saul Shapiro, an active Conservative layman and a senior planner with IBM, prepared "A Survey of the Conservative Movement and Some of Its Religious Attitudes, Sponsored by JTS, for the Biennial Convention of the United Synagogue of America" in November 1979. The aim, focus, methods, and conclusions of this survey differed significantly from the commission's report.

Liebman and Shapiro claimed that Conservative Judaism had become stagnant and was losing its youth. They showed that the Conservative laity could be divided into a large group that had little if any commitment to the halakhic process and a small, loyal core who took halakhah seriously. Although the more liberal far outnumbered the more traditional group, they said, the children of the larger, less traditional group often defected into Reform congregations or simply did not affiliate, while the children of the smaller, more traditional group were both more likely to affiliate and to stay within the Conservative wing.

At one time, the authors cautioned, Orthodox Judaism lost large numbers of its youth to Conservative congregations, but Orthodoxy had been so reduced in numbers that Conservative congregations could no longer look to it to replace congregants who had drifted to the left. Liebman and Shapiro suggested that the traditional minority might well represent Conservative Judaism's best chance for a viable and vital future. And since the liberal left was most likely to accept female rabbis, while the traditional right seemed to oppose them on halakhic grounds, a vote to ordain women rabbis might drive the most loyal of Conservative youth farther right into the modern Orthodox camp.[17]

Liebman and Shapiro's suggestions did not deflect the agenda of the proordination factions at JTS and in the RA. Meanwhile Conservative rabbis opposed to female ordination tried to rally their forces. A group of pulpit rabbis, together with some seminary faculty, convened a conference on halakhic process in December 1979. They asserted: "A further example of the move away from a serious commitment to *Halakhah* is indicated by the handling of the ordination of women. The fact that it has been defined as a non-halakhic issue when it should be clear that this decision will affect basic halakhic norms, indicates that this question is not being considered through Halakhic process." According to the authors of the conference, "registration requests began pouring in just 48 hours after our first mailing and the number of co-sponsors has almost tripled (to 120 thus far)."[18]

Apparently enraged by this attempt of the Conservative right to form "a new dissenting group," Wolfe Kelman, executive vice president of the RA, sent a "Memorandum" to Saul I. Teplitz in which he castigated the "political strategists who conceived this new letterhead and organization . . . against the established policies and elected officials of the Rabbinical Assembly." Dividing them into groups, Kelman questioned the integrity and/or importance of all participants. Of those with reputations, he implied that they themselves had participated in changes that conflicted with established legal codes. Others, he pointed out, were not JTS graduates and for some reason "were panting" to flaunt their zeal for halakhah. And in any case, he noted the congregational rabbis involved were distinguished by their "relatively small number and obscurity."

While pulpit rabbis and seminary professors were engaged in vehement and sometimes vituperative debate, a group of women who wanted to become Conservative rabbis had been studying at the seminary in hopes of a positive outcome to their career goals. On December 6, 1979, they wrote to the seminary faculty urging them to support the ordination of women:

> We are a group of women who have been graduated from or are presently enrolled in academic programs at the Jewish Theological Seminary, and we are interested in entering rabbinical school. Each of us has come to this decision in her own way. Several weeks ago, we began meeting to discuss our common goals and feelings. This letter is to indicate our interest and to share with you some of our concerns. We are seriously committed to Jewish scholarship and to the study of Jewish texts. Although some of our specific practices vary, we are all observant women who are committed to the halachic system. We wish to serve the Jewish community as professionals in a variety of educational and leadership capacities. We are interested in teaching, writing, organizing, counselling and leading congregations. Although we realize that these tasks can be performed by people who are not rabbis, we desire to receive rabbinical training, and the title "rabbi," because we feel that with this authority we can be most effective in the Jewish community. We believe that our efforts are sorely needed and that there are many communities where we would be fully accepted and could accomplish much towards furthering a greater commit-

ment to Jewish life. We are fully aware that there are a number of complicated halachic issues related to Jewish women. We feel that these issues should be addressed carefully, directly and within the scope of the halachic process. This process, however, should not delay the admission of women to the Rabbinic School. We wish above all to learn and to serve God through our work in the Jewish community.[19]

In 1979 the Faculty Senate of JTS voted to table the question of ordination, and in the spring of 1980 Gerson Cohen announced the initiation of a new academic program for women that would be parallel to the rabbinic program but would not involve the same emotional issues. In 1980, however, the Rabbinical Assembly voted 156–115 in support of women's ordination. The entire senior faculty of the seminary's Talmud department continued to oppose ordination, as did a large minority of pulpit rabbis, but in 1984 the seminary faculty voted to admit women to the rabbinical program. The first women to enter rabbinical school at JTS entered in September 1984; the class included eighteen women and twenty-one men. Amy Eilberg, the first woman to receive Conservative ordination, graduated in 1985. By 1992 the Jewish Theological Seminary had ordained thirty-two women as rabbis.

For rabbis, teachers, and students who lived through the decision-making process on Conservative ordination of women, the period is variously recalled as a thrilling or a profoundly disturbing time. Judy Kanfer, who is now a teacher of Jewish subjects in a variety of settings in Columbus, Ohio, was studying Talmud and rabbinics at JTS during the upheaval over the ordination of female rabbis. She remembers that Professor Saul Lieberman, who vehemently opposed female ordination, was one of her most attentive and encouraging professors. Her experiences with him convinced her that Professor Lieberman was a vigorous supporter of women's learning—but that he opposed the ordination of women on the grounds that it would further tear the Conservative Jewish movement from its traditional roots and its links with the observant community.

Many women struggle with the issue of how fast the change concerning women in Judaism should occur. Some feel that to become normative and endure, change must be gradual. Kanfer, for example, insists, "What I witnessed at the seminary—the first vote—was so filled with bitterness and acrimony that it made me feel too much was being done too soon. I was mourning about what had happened to my beloved institution. The rabbis and professors were locked in a shouting match in the middle of the *aleynu* (a prayer that looks forward to the universal worship of one God). Instead of unifying people, ordaining women has led to more and more *Sinat Hinam* (causeless hatred, discouraged by Jewish tradition). I worry and I wonder, what will be the outcome?"

The "Final Report of the Commission for the Study of the Ordination of Women as Rabbis," together with papers on the halakhic and policy aspects of JTS's decision-making process and final decision, were gathered together in a volume entitled *The Ordination of Women as Rabbis: Studies and Responsa*. Published in 1988, the seminary's centennial year, the volume includes a plea by Robert Gordis for peace and for moving on to meeting the challenges facing the Jewish community. "One may hope," he writes, "that when passions cool and calm consideration of the issues prevails, those who have been doubtful on the issue or opposed to it, like those who favor it, will recognize that the goal to which all energies must be directed is *lehagdil Torah ulha'adir*, 'to magnify the Torah and make it glorious.' "[20]

A dissenting group of Conservative scholars, pulpit rabbis, and laypersons broke off from JTS and the RA to form a new organization, first called the Union for Traditional Conservative Judaism and then abridged to The Union for Traditional Judaism, UTJ. The founders hoped that UTJ would attract left-wing Orthodox Jews as well, who they felt had no comfortable home within the Orthodox world and would be natural allies. However, one element standing in the way of this alliance, is the fact that many left-wing Orthodox Jews are liberal on feminist issues. Thus, although the UTJ is far from a single-issue organization, and works for increased intensity of Jewish life on many levels, the issue upon which its birth was precipitated is precisely the issue upon which some potential Orthodox allies might wish the UTJ to be more flexible.

The Conservative Jewish Theological Seminary program for rabbinical ordination now attracts many young women from backgrounds ranging from Reform through Orthodox, who enjoys the rigors of a strictly halakhic lifestyle and intense spirituality which the ordination program imposes on them. One typical such woman, who grew up in a very relaxed Reform Jewish home, has taken on a full range of halakhic observances, including strict observance of Kashruth and Sabbaths and holidays. She prays daily and has recently begun to use a *talit* and *tefillin* when she prays. These practices are intensely meaningful to her, as she explains:

I put on a *ta'alith* for the first time this Rosh haShanah. The *ta'alith* enveloped me, wrapped me in prayer, in communion with God. After Succot I starting *laying* (putting on) *tefillin* too. It felt so right—putting on *tefillin* each morning focuses my mind completely on the prayers. The *ta'alith* and *tefillin* shut out all distractions. In ten years I hope to be a rabbi for a Hillel congregation of college students. I hope to be married and to have between two and four children. Judaism and feminism came into my life at the same time and are part of each other for me. I don't do anything Jewish that's not feminist and I don't do anything feminist that's not Jewish.[21]

The Orthodox movement could hardly be untouched by all this, despite the denunciations of many Orthodox leaders. Some Orthodox leaders, however, responded to feminist ferment within the Conservative movement positively, suggesting that eventually something similar might happen even in certain Orthodox camps. Rabbi Avraham Weiss, for example, proposed that the Orthodox movement initiate a parallel course for study for women that would enable them to carry out roles as teachers and counselors on an equal level with men, much as the seminary had done in 1979 when it seemed to have reached an impasse over the subject of ordination for women. "There are aspects of the rabbinate such as public testimony, involvement in a *bet din* and leading a public liturgical service that women may not, according to Jewish law, be involved in," said Weiss. "However there are aspects of the rabbinate—the teaching of Torah and counseling—in which women can fully participate in on the same level as men . . . A new title must be created for women to serve this purpose."[22]

Significantly Weiss has also been among those few Orthodox rabbis who have publicly championed the appropriateness of female participation in rituals connected with the handling and reading of Sefer Torah. He urges that "sensitivity is required for the many women who sincerely feel that holding the Sefer Torah would allow them to feel much more a part of communal tefillah. Indeed, we must ask ourselves whether the common practice of banning women from carrying the Torah justifies the numerous benefits that would accrue from adopting this practice."[23]

Currently there is a good deal of ferment within some segments of the Orthodox community for women to be *poskot*, deciders of Jewish law, particularly on issues relating to women's lives, such as *kashruth* (dietary laws) and *niddut* (sexuality and purification). Orthodox feminist Blu Greenberg has gone one step farther. In an article entitled, "Will There Be Orthodox Women Rabbis?" she answers in the affirmative:

> Will it happen in my lifetime? I am optimistic. At this moment in history, I am well aware that the Orthodox community would not accept a woman as a rabbi. Yet we are moving towards a unique moment in history. More than any other, the Orthodox community has widely educated its women in Torah studies. Thus, though it rejects the formal entry of women into rabbinic studies, de facto, through the broad sweep of day school, yeshiva high school education and beyond, it has ushered them, as a whole community, into the learning enterprise. At the very same moment in time, Reform, Reconstructionist, and Conservative Judaism are providing us with models of women as rabbis. At some point in the not-too-distant future, I believe, the two will intersect: more learned women in the Orthodox community and the model of women in leadership positions in the other denominations. When that happens, history will take us where it takes us. That holds much promise for the likes of me.[24]

For the female rabbis themselves, working in the rabbinate has been in many ways a mixed blessing. One rabbi who prefers to remain anonymous is convinced:

> Female rabbis are smarter, sharper, better than male rabbis in the Reform movement. Although feminism is clearly a source of energy in contemporary Judaism, the older men in the community say that it is divisive and that we shouldn't worry so much about gender. However, when they are asked to come up with coherent objections to feminism they can't say anything serious. What it's really about is that people in power don't want to give up the power they hold.

Rabbi Margaret Mayer agrees that power struggles underlie much rabbinical behavior, adding that male rabbis often speak in a patronizing manner or even ignore the contributions of female rabbis at rabbinical meetings. Most enjoy rabbinical tasks immensely while they perform them. Rabbi Laurie Coskey articulates the feelings of many when she says, "I love Judaism. I love making people more Jewish. I try to help people explore what God wants and expects from them. I see my work as a kind of holy quest." Rabbi Coskey, who was nine months pregnant at the time of her interview, dislikes the impact of pregnancy on the way congregants treat her: "They get very protective," she says, "and their protectiveness can interfere with my effectiveness. They concentrate on my comfort instead of their struggles. Even when I counsel a mourning family, they worry about my sitting down."

While some female rabbis complain about the obvious preference for male clergy in large, powerful congregations, others insist they themselves would avoid the largest temples. Rabbi Lenore Bohm, who was serving as a solo rabbi in a smaller congregation outside San Diego at the time of her interview, for example, chose a new, developing congregation rather than aim for a number two position in a very large, established congregation because, "I'm not a mover and a shaker." Ironically, she comments, under her leadership the congregation has grown by leaps and bounds.

Initially, says Rabbi Bohm, she was considered to be "a novelty—I was constantly hounded by groups to come talk. But now that has died down. Women rabbis are not new anymore. When young people come in to talk to me, they are obviously unfazed by it." Rabbi Bohm thinks that congregations now like to hire women rabbis as a kind of appealing "perk" of membership in their congregation—but that they still resist having the only rabbi be a woman.

However, a growing proportion of women rabbis attest to the fact that combining the rabbinate and a home life can be exceptionally difficult. Those women who have left the pulpit rabbinate have primarily done so because of growing families. Two—Rabbi Eilberg and Rabbi Bohm—published moving essays on their experiences in the rabbinate and their reasons for leaving. Rabbi Bohm had earlier indicated one of the problems: "I don't want my son to associate religion with Mommy leaving him," she said. "I don't want him to be raised in the temple or by my congregants. When I get into my suit, he says to me, 'Don't you want to put your play clothes on?' with a little quivering chin." Difficulties arise from aspects of the occupational structure of the American rabbinate, such as the constant spotlight as a religious leader and the nightly meetings that are part of the rabbinate.

The increased access of women to public roles in the Jewish community, both in religious and Jewish communal spheres, has been fraught with controversy and strong feelings. Women who have stepped into religious leadership positions, such as rabbis and cantors, have been barred from professional associations, in some cases, and from the most lucrative and prestigious senior and solo positions in other cases. Women who have pursued careers in Jewish communal life have often found access to top positions far more freely ceded to males. Arguments continue that women who are too prominent in Jewish life will discourage men from taking leadership positions, or that they will inveigle male leaders into illicit sexual liaisons, or simply that they are indulging in ambitious and forward behavior that is unbecoming to a Jewish woman.

Moreover, many women who have succeeded in acquiring positions of leadership in Jewish communal life have found that their competence and/or their executive methods are frequently challenged. Both female rabbis and female federation executives have found that their fiduciary skills, especially, are the subject of skepticism from male congregants or colleagues. Female rabbis report ongoing paternalism from some congregants, which sometimes expresses itself in a kind of avuncular, protective stance and sometimes in continuing "testing" of the rabbi's Judaic knowledge and professional skills. Additionally, female rabbis seem to experience fairly high rates of divorce, with husbands resenting the demands of a rabbinic position more than they might the demands of a legal, medical, academic, or business career—perhaps with the subconscious notion that religion should not take a woman away from her husband and family.

Jewish communal and organizational leadership, such as that of Jewish federations, welfare boards, community centers, synagogues, and national organizations, like other spheres of Jewish life in America, has been strikingly affected by feminism. In the 1960s and 1970s female voluntarism came under the critical scrutiny of the feminist movement partially because Jewish communal organizations often denied women access to positions of decision-making and power. Jewish women who have attained positions of power in Jewish organizations have joined in the critique, confirming the impression that women have been consciously excluded from opportunities for power. One of the first publicly to voice distress over inequities in the Jewish communal world was Jacqueline Levine, then vice president of the Council of Jewish Federations and Welfare Funds (CJF). Stating that she had frequently been included as "the only—and therefore the token—female representative" in Jewish communal leadership settings, Levine cited leadership figures as they existed in 1972; in three of the top ten cities, 13 percent of the combined boards of directors and 16 percent of the persons serving on federation committees were women. The percentages of women involved were somewhat larger in the medium-size and smaller cities.[25]

"The status of female leaders in Jewish organizations has improved—but not as much as people think, and may actually get much worse in the near future," Levine says now. "I have statistical data that go back to 1965. At that time, there were few women on boards and very few were officers. Now we have many women officers—but there are still very few presidents. All along, the smaller federations, having exhausted their stock of even mediocre male leaders, have been willing to take on an occasional outstanding woman as chief executive. But to date, many federations have never had a female president—including my own federation, MetroWest, New Jersey. And even where a woman does serve as president, the powers that be make very sure that the next couple of presidents are not women, even where they have to go to great pains to achieve that goal." Levine sees few women being groomed to take the place of female leaders, and she is convinced that "tokenism is and will continue to be the name of the game."

Shoshana Cardin, chair of the Conference of Presidents of Major American Jewish Organizations, the first female president of CJF and a highly regarded and articulate spokesperson for the American Jewish community, disputes charges of sexism. She states that volunteer leadership positions require the same fierce dedication as do high-powered careers—and that few young women today are willing to make the time and financial commitments that are necessary if one wants to rise to positions of decision making and power. "Jewish communal leaders have to have the time and money to travel extensively," she says. "They have to be at a point in their own personal lives in which their commitment to Jewish communal life is their highest priority. Mothers of young children and even older school-age children should have other priorities. At later sequences in their lives they can rise to positions of power in Jewish communal life."

Moreover, Cardin cautions that some feminists discourage leadership in the voluntary sphere. The hostility of some Jewish feminists toward "careers" in voluntaristic activity was one major reason why Cardin, one of the most powerful female leaders in contemporary American Jewish life, says she "parted ways" with feminism: "The point of departure between me and the feminist movement is very strong. . . . "When the 1975 International Commission for Women took place I wrote a paper with two agenda items—the role of women as mothers and as volunteers. From my perspective motherhood and family and citizen participation were critical, and they were eliminated."

One vivid symbol of institutional resistance to change is the UJA's policy of sexual exclusiveness in some local leadership cabinets, which groom future leaders of federations. Because only men are allowed in many cabinets, feminists charge that they serve the function of perpetuating a patriarchal hierarchy of power. UJA leaders cite "intense male camaraderie" as a primary reason for excluding women from the cabinet: It has been claimed that men in leadership positions bond together in intense personal and idealistic relationships, and that women would disrupt male bonding; it has also been feared that the presence of women in the pressured and deeply involved atmosphere of weekend retreats and working weekends would entice men into extramarital relationships.[26]

From a feminist standpoint the situation improved during the 1980s but is still far from equitable. Women from the baby-boom generation "want more power than the older women and the men think they deserve," succinctly comments Barry Kosmin. These younger women are less willing to be "passive front men," he observes, and demand real authority.[27] Women now make up between one-quarter and one-fifth of federation board members, executive committee members, and campaign cabinet members. Women have been federation presidents in Baltimore, Boston, Dallas, Houston, Los Angeles, Milwaukee, New York, Omaha, Toledo, San Jose, and other cities. The percentage of women on the boards of federations and federation-funded agencies rose from 14 in 1972 to 40 in the mid-1980s.[28] According to a 1987 JWB study, women comprise one-third of all Jewish community center board members.[29] Ironically, perhaps, as Chaim Waxman observes, even among Jewish women's organizations, all of whose chief executive officers might be expected to be women, a substantial number of male directors are to be found.[30]

Some women are startled by the enormous emphasis the Jewish communal world places on the ability and willingness to give. One female volunteer leader who has held several executive positions in the Los Angeles Jewish community says that the difference in the Jewish communal world is really money. "There is a very tight old boy's network in the upper echelons of the federation world, and very few women make it to the highest levels of leadership. In fact, few women make it to the top unless their husbands are significant givers," she says. Suzanne Cohen, chairman of the board of the Baltimore Jewish Associated Charities, agrees that the ability and willingness to give probably constitute the primary reason why women have had difficulties in getting ahead. During her first weeks as chairman of the Associated, she recalls being ignored with a kind of benign conspiracy of silence until she made it clear—with both her checkbook and her business acumen—that she had financial power:

> Women have to prove themselves even more than men do. They have to show that they are able to make the kinds of gifts which propel a campaign. When I first took over, many of the men assumed that I couldn't understand finances. I had to prove that they were wrong. Also, they expect women to be very emotional. They were worried that because I am a widow I wouldn't be able to withstand the pressure.

Cohen notes that her decision to continue to work in a volunteer capacity—even in an executive volunteer capacity—was an unpopular one. "I consider myself a feminist—whatever that means" she says, "but some of my feminist friends looked down their noses at me. Work for pay was in vogue. One of my daughters insisted that had I been a man I would have gotten this position ten years earlier, and asked me why I [didn't] get a real job. I told her the truth: I've worked hard to get where I am in the Jewish communal world. I've spent untold nights in meetings for years. It hasn't been easy, and I've endured a lot of stress, as people always do when they work in public and put a lot of emphasis on achievement. In this position I have more power than I ever could starting out in the professional world."

Sometimes women can attain a position for which they are eminently qualified but be prevented by their colleagues' sexist behavior from doing their best at the job. After many years of working in the Jewish communal sphere, one professional female executive took a sabbatical because of the high levels of frustration she experienced. "In our federation," she says, "no female volunteers are taken seriously in terms of leadership capacity. There was a female president who had worked so hard and so long that after a major fight they gave her a turn—but they didn't take her seriously. There is truly a boys' club; they spend time together at Jewish clubs where the men swim naked together. Just a few years ago the woman president had to enter through a different door. The club has a WASPy, elegant, old-fashioned male feel—and that's where federation business is transacted!"

A significant number of Jewish communal workers struggle optimistically for years but later report feelings of discouragement and burnout. Others are finally so exasperated by sexist behavior that they confront it openly. A director of development and alumni relations at a school that trains Jewish communal workers notes that "little has changed to move women into the top echelons in federation leadership in major national agencies during the last twenty years." She says that the "boys' club" environment that freezes women out is sometimes subtle:

> When you walk in on Monday morning and it's all men around the table and all the "boys" are talking about football, it's hard to know what to do. At first I thought you just have to be a "big kid," that it's not so important. But then I realized that they were speaking another language, and part of what was happening was that they also shared facts that I wasn't privy to. Once I stood up and said, "Obviously I'm in the men's room!"

A locker-room environment functions very effectively as a way to eliminate women from discussions. The director of lay leaders and professional personnel at a major metropolitan federation says, "They start talking about the game last night, and then the office door closes. Ironically most men at the top think that they have no issues. Most men, even nice men, don't see the issues when they occur." One symptom, she thinks, is that while men feel free to talk not only about such outside interests as sports but also about personal considerations, women are afraid to talk about either: "A male leader feels comfortable admitting he'll be late for a meeting because he has to drive his daughter to school. A woman won't talk about needlepoint, and she won't admit that her family conflicts with her communal responsibilities."

Recent research on the types of women who take positions as volunteer leaders in Jewish communal affairs shows that in terms of Jewish involvement and affiliation they are an elite group in many ways. Like contemporary Jewish volunteers per se, they tend to be far more Jewishly educated and active than the average American Jewish woman. Those who have children are likely to have larger families than average, about three children per completed family.

Women who serve in leadership roles in Jewish organizations are equally divided between ages 44 and under and ages 45 and older, according to data from the 1990 National Jewish Population Survey.[31] About half of them have served as leaders for non-Jewish organizations as well during the past two years. About half of them have children over age 19, 39 percent have children under age 18, and 12 percent have not yet had children. Like other American Jewish women, they tend to be highly educated: about one-third have finished college and another 35 percent have graduate degrees; only 13 percent have not gone beyond high school. More than half work outside the home for pay; only 13 percent describe themselves as homemakers.

Perhaps one of the most striking attributes of contemporary female volunteer leaders of Jewish communal organizations—unlike many of their predecessors—is that relatively few of them could be identified as secular Jews. Activist Elaine Winnick remembers that when she began traveling decades ago to promote the Council of Jewish Federations Women's Division, "In all of my travels I never once stayed in a kosher home." Jewish communal work was considered an alternative to synagogue attendance and home-based rituals in expressing one's Jewishness, rather than an activity which was complementary to specifically religious behavior.

Today, in contrast, nine out of ten female Jewish communal leaders belong to synagogues. Only 3 percent of them are married to non-Jewish men—compared to a national average for Jewish women about ten times higher. Surprisingly, more than half have never visited Israel—but one in eight has been in Israel at least four times. Contemporary American Jewish women who take leadership positions in Jewish communal organizations tend to be both more interested in Jewish spirituality and more assertive than women in the past, bearing indirect testimony to the pervasive effects of Jewish feminism.

Feminism has affected Jewish communal life not only through its volunteer leaders but through its professionals as well. Jewish communal service is a field increasingly populated by women; the 1992 enrollment of the Hornstein Program in Jewish Communal Service at Brandeis University, for example, consists of twenty-two women and fifteen men. Still, despite the presence in the field of qualified women, many of whom hold graduate degrees and many of whom have more seniority than the men they work with, very few women are promoted to executive positions. One recent article noted that "a

1981 survey of over 200 professional staff in 273 agencies, conducted by the Conference of Jewish Communal Service (CJCS), indicated that although women constituted over half (58 percent) of the total staff, they made up only eight percent of executive directors and assistant directors." A great majority of professional women (92 percent) were in the two lower job categories: 32 percent as supervisors and 60 percent line staff.[32]

Those women who do achieve executive positions frequently earn salaries far lower than those of their male colleagues. Thus a report by the Jewish Welfare Board in 1984 noted that 112 men were employed as executive directors, compared with 4 women. In a similar 1984 CJF report, among the 80 male executive directors, the average salary was $53,179, while among the 8 female executive directors the average salary was $25,294. Some of the reasons cited for not promoting women are the same as those given in the nonsectarian world: Women are reluctant to relocate; women get married and pregnant and are therefore unreliable employees. Other reasons are peculiar to the world of Jewish Communal Service. It is a constant struggle to find high-caliber persons interested in the field, therefore attention cannot be "wasted" on efforts for equal opportunities for women; if women flood the executive strata of Jewish communal service, salaries in the field will automatically be depressed.[33]

While some who oppose women in Jewish communal leadership positions say that women are inappropriate candidates because they resist relocation, others see their alleged lack of mobility as just one more sexist excuse. The executive director of a Jewish vocational service feels that all Jewish communal professionals, male and female, would benefit if less stress were placed on willingness to relocate. Women who hold executive positions in Jewish communal service report another type of job discrimination: a hostility to female "styles" of management that consider human factors and feelings to be significant in the daily routine. Another executive director of a large metropolitan-area agency complains that men in federation-sponsored agencies often feel uncomfortable with female management styles, such as relationship-driven process, discussion and consensus building; they deride such tactics as time-wasting and "wishy-washy." On the other hand, the same men bitterly dislike women who use such "male" techniques as autocratic decision making and assertive articulation of opinions. One woman with a long career in Jewish communal service spells out some gender differences: "Men need to play the game through the way they talk.

Women are task and detail oriented and much less likely to repeat things once they are said. I think I can bring something to organizations that men don't—an understanding of process. Male entrepreneurs like to decide things on their own, do not think about involving others."

Some executives find that they must juggle and work around male sensitivities and sensibilities. As one complained, "Many board members come to a certain point in the dialogue when they feel that I'm getting too influential, and they try to diminish my prominence by patting my head or behaving in other totally inappropriate ways. Or I have male volunteer executives who can't bear the thought that I as a female—even though I'm a professional in this area—know more than they do. We'll be voting on very complex decisions involving a lot of money, and I need to operate around people to get anything done." Even more infuriating, many women in second-tier executive positions described incidents in which they had coached virtually unprepared CEOs on the issues to be discussed for a particular meeting, only to have the male executive not only ignore their contribution to the proceedings but actually forget how he acquired his information and ideas. One noted, "Men will highjack ideas without any compunction and present them as their own. I'm not a shrinking violet, but that kind of outright piracy has left me speechless, frustrated, and on the verge of tears."

During her years as a Jewish communal professional, said one woman, the differences between male and female management styles were striking:

> My male CEO treated all female staff, no matter how highly placed, as his secretaries. The females concentrated on process and on the details of individual tasks, while he behaved as if the federation were his own personal entrepreneurial project. As an entrepreneur he tried to make quick, daring decisions without involving others in the decision-making process. He'd get impatient with female concerns about the workability of particular ideas.

Sure that "men use language so differently than women that sometimes it's comical," she continues:

> Men love to hear themselves talk. I would hear male colleagues make the same point over and over again just to hear themselves. My male colleagues would talk just to keep themselves "on the playing board

and in the game." Women executives, on the other hand, generally don't say anything unless they have a specific point to make, and they are much less likely to repeat something once it has been said. Also, women tended to be "invisible" at staff meetings—that is, a woman could make a point very articulately, but her male colleagues would act as though nothing had been said. Then some man would repeat the very same thing and the other men would act as though they were hearing it for the first time. They would only pay attention if another man was talking.

Several women who hold professional positions in the Jewish communal world admitted that "female styles" of management can and sometimes are taken too far. One woman said that female managers often stress inclusion—involving as many Jews as possible in a given project—to a cumbersome point: "Women sometimes think their job is to take care of everyone and to include everyone. When they can't do that and maintain a working level of efficiency, they sometimes feel overwhelmed and unsuccessful," she comments.

Age differences and the expectations that went with them added to divisions between Jewish professionals. One young executive says that older women in the field often respond to challenges or stress in "an extremely emotional or unprofessional way. This mode of response has actually worked well for them for years, but younger colleagues look at that sort of behavior differently. When you see an older woman getting 'hysterical' in a meeting or crying, that tends to play into stereotypes of Jewish women and to discredit female leaders in general." Older professionals, for their part, sometimes complain that younger female managers lack compassion. One asserts that women in their fifties and sixties, whether lay leaders or professionals, are much easier to work with. "Young corporate women are just as tough and abrupt as men. When I was their age, I think I managed to be both maternal and efficient. People told me I was very talented—I know I had a good time doing my work." Another highly placed female academic speaks even more strongly:

Don't quote me by name, but I have a feeling about some of my younger colleagues that if you needed something and you went to them for it, they would only help you if it were very convenient for them or if they thought that ultimately they would get something out of it. They are so busy protecting themselves and looking out for themselves—which they think is the definition of a "professional"— that they have lost many of the best qualities of women. I think the best female leaders can be efficient and forceful without adopting some of the limitations of male leadership styles.

Some felt that younger female executives had "lost their Jewish hearts."

Despite these caveats female professionals almost universally feel that women bring high-quality leadership to the Jewish communal field. Lois Rosenfeld of Baltimore's American Jewish Committee speaks for many when she says, "Women work twice as hard as men. When men hire women they know that women will work twice as hard. A woman who is second in command will work as hard as a department head—but she will seldom be promoted to department head."

Sexism, including sexual harassment, continues to be a salient issue in the Jewish communal world. Reporters Diana Aviv and Gary Rubin gathered the following examples of the victimization they claim is "rife within Jewish communal organizations":

A high ranking professional was invited by the agency's president to review policy papers relating to an upcoming meeting. The papers were in his hotel suite, and thus he requested that they hold their discussions there. In the middle of their discussion, he grabbed her and attempted to pursue a sexual relationship. A mid-level worker was having a substantive debate with her supervisors over a policy matter when he asked whether they could stop arguing and have her sit on his lap. A worker at a Jewish camp was approached by a rabbi to go out with him. When she refused, he persisted in asking her in ways that included sexual innuendoes. She complained to the camp administration, which did nothing. The situation became so unpleasant that she, rather than he, felt forced to leave the camp. A young Jewish worker applying for a grant necessary to running her program discovered that she would receive money only in return for sexual favors. An entry level professional was working in her office when the agency executive came in, stood behind her and massaged her shoulder and her arms. The woman was not only appalled, but at a loss to know how to respond in a way that did not jeopardize a career that was just beginning.[34]

Some men in positions of power in the Jewish community, whether in the rabbinate, as federation executives, or as chairs of Judaic studies departments, obviously do find disturbing the entry of women into their male domains. Both men and women in power have indicated that feminist goals in the Jewish communal world will be achieved only when women learn to be more aggressive in furthering their own cause. Thus, Irving Bernstein, former UJA executive, discussing the underrepresentation of women on the National Executive Committee and the Campaign Cabinet of the UJA, states that women's progress is impeded by their discomfort with the idea that they must forcefully assert themselves and their views in the face of opposition.[35] Naomi Levine, former executive director of the American Jewish Congress, urges women to study job descriptions, salaries, and promotions and to take legal action where necessary to eliminate discrimination. Anne Wolfe, who served as national staff director of the AJC's committee on the role of women, says that "nice conferences" change little; "a much more revolutionary push by women" is needed to achieve feminist goals.[36] Sue Stevens, director of the Women's Division of the Council of Jewish Federations, urges women to free themselves of "the cotillion mentality," in which women "wait to be invited to dance." She feels that women need to pursue career opportunities aggressively on their own behalf, rather than waiting for sympathetic men in power to clear the way for them.

In short, women have been advised not only to learn how to give financially—but also to learn how to "give as good as you get" in terms of confrontational techniques if they wish to achieve equity in leadership positions in the Jewish communal world. Women have traditionally shied away from confrontations, but it is clear that Jewish leadership positions will not fall into their hands without a willingness to stand and fight. This is complicated by the fact that when women do adopt male styles of management and confrontation, some within the Jewish communal world accuse them of being unwomanly. As Bernardo Blejmar, director of the Latin American Center for Training and Research for Jewish Institutional Leadership said in a Fall 1991 interview at Brandeis University, "Men have a word for women who are too prominent in public, especially in things having to do with business or money. These male attitudes make Jewish women uncomfortable with taking leadership roles in our Federations and Jewish institutions. Men call females who are too strong 'phallic women.' "

Jewish feminism has broken many barriers to female participation in public and leadership positions in religious and communal life. Perhaps ironically, the so-called secular Jewish communal world has proved even more resistant to change than the religious world. In both worlds feminist perseverance is clearly needed. And in both worlds, curiously enough, the specter of female sexuality as somehow threatening to an exclusively male hegemony recurs. As long as the isolation of women into ghettos of privacy and powerlessness is used as a principle of sexual control, women will not able to contribute their full measure to a vital American Jewish life.

Despite chronic problems, enormous changes have been effected vis-à-vis the role of women in Jewish public life in the past 25 years. For the first time in recorded Jewish history, women as a group can aspire to positions of power and prominence in the Jewish religious, scholarly, and communal worlds. Many observers comment that women in the rabbinate and in leadership positions within the Jewish community have humanized and energized these fields. "The Seminary is a fresher, more revitalized place," says Rabbi Gordon Tucker, dean of JTS's rabbinical school. "There's a realization that we're serving a constituency," and "God is being discussed more."[37] As one female executive in the Jewish communal world comments wryly, "Jewish men may not truly have any more confidence in women than they used to—but they sure have learned how to hide their feelings and veil their comments more effectively. They know the way they are supposed to feel and act, even if they don't feel and act that way all the time."

Chapter Ten

Balancing Jewish and Feminist Goals

Without doubt, we need to reinterpret Jewish tradition, literature, and liturgy, which are written from men's points of view and reflect different times. But we must be careful to safeguard ancient and meaningful traditions at the same time. I would never want to lose the refrain, Hakadosh Barukh Hu, "blessed be He," at the end of so many prayers. That's like changing someone's signature. And reimaging God in general, while necessary, is fraught with problems. Fertility goddesses are an abomination in the Jewish religion. Do we want to get rid of an old man only to substitute for him a fertility goddess or a nursing mother? And who wants a God who is a neutered "It"?

—Rabbi Margaret Meyer

DESPITE ITS EMERGENCE AS AN ENDURING SOURCE of enrichment and energy in contemporary American Jewish life, Jewish feminism poses acute challenges to the Jewish community. Feminism asks hard questions about the role of religion in people's lives and the role of people in the life of a religion—questions many in the Jewish community would prefer to leave unexplored. But reluctance to deal with difficult issues is not unique to leaders of the Jewish "establishment." Jewish feminist thinkers also frequently shy away from confronting the impact of feminist change on American Judaism and on the Jewish people worldwide.

231

Certain trends within feminist thought must be recognized as antithetical to the survival of Judaism as a distinctive culture, religion, and peoplehood. Without becoming part of an antiwoman backlash, and without demonizing feminism as a movement, it is necessary to define innovative ideas that contribute new vigor to American Jewish life and to demarcate them from trends that are not supportive of Judaic systems of belief. Neither American nor Jewish feminism actually encourages "women to leave their husbands, kill their children, practice witchcraft, destroy capitalism and become lesbians," as TV evangelist Pat Robertson so scurrilously charged when he campaigned against the Equal Rights Amendment (ERA) in Iowa in September 1992. Jewish feminism, a powerful force for positive change and renewal, will be strengthened by isolating and rejecting ideas that clearly contradict the historical thrust and moral imperatives of Jewish civilizations of the past. Conversely, by not distinguishing between those ideas that are and are not consonant with Judaism in feminist thought, Jewish feminism may compromise its own religious and moral appeal within mainstream Jewish communities.

Some feminists see "establishment Judaism" as essentially patriarchal and propose sweeping changes in regard to Jewish communal life, theology, class issues, the Middle East and Israel, Jewish education, and liturgy. They insist that their innovations do not blur or distort Judaism but instead reclaim and reemphasize elements that were erroneously suppressed. Some have called for the replacement of what they see as outmoded religious guidelines by those that are new and relevant, and some have called for the total abolition of structured constraints. Despite the revolutionary nature of such suggestions, they insist that forethought about the valid or viable "Jewishness" of particular feminist innovations is not necessary, because history will decide for them. "Some feminist changes will endure because they are appropriate, because they speak to felt needs within the community and ring true to the Jewish imagination. Others will fall by the wayside as eccentric, mechanical, or false. To try to decide in advance which will be authentic is to confine our creativity and resources; it is to divert energy needed to shape the kind of Jewish community in which we want to live," Judith Plaskow believes.[1]

But advising the Jewish community blithely to ignore questions of authenticity denies the fact that change and transformation can as easily result in disaster as in revitalization. Jewish history has included not only successful transitions, such as the transition from ancient, cultic forms of Israelite Judaism, based in the Temple and operating through animal sacrifices, to the more familiar synagogue-study-hall- and home-based Judaism of the past two thousand years. Jewish history has also endured less successful and even disastrous attempts at revolution that tore the Jewish people apart and left permanent scars. Initially the messianic messages of Sabbatai Zvi (1626–76) and Jacob Frank (1726–91) movements filled the hearts of huge numbers of Jewish people with hope and renewal. However, Sabbatai Zvi and Jacob Frank and their followers ended in apostasy, humiliation, and despair. The Sabbatian and Frankist debacles did not succeed in renewing Jewish life and thought, despite the vitality they at first inspired. Instead they created among mainstream Jews a profound and arguably unfortunate fear of mysticism and innovation that endures in many Jewish communities to present times—and that, ironically, is probably one psychological factor in communal resistance to feminism itself.

American Jewish life is in desperate need of revitalization, as illustrated by rising rates of intermarriage, falling rates of affiliation with Jewish communal activities, and increased numbers of Jews who do not identify Judaism as "very important" to their lives. Jewish feminism has already proved itself to be a source of great moral vigor and religious vitality. However, extreme care is necessary if Jewish feminism is to fulfill its potential in the positive reconstruction of American Judaism. It is necessary to distinguish those elements that are so intrinsic to mainstream Judaisms that to lose them would be to lose the integrity of the religion and the culture, from those that are incidental and nonessential outgrowths of Jewish life in a variety of societies. The Jewish community—including Jewish feminists—cannot afford passively to "let history decide."

If one sees Judaism as nothing more than a patriarchal system best demolished and discarded, such judgments and balances are irrelevant. If one agrees with those feminists who reject ethnicity and religion, then the conversation is over before it starts. Some believe that a lack of "cultural baggage" will lead to a better world: "My parents had not believed in God either, nor had my grandparents or any other progenitors going back to the great-great level. They had become disillusioned with Christianity generations ago—just as on the in-law side my children's other ancestors had shaken off their Orthodox Judaism. . . . Because what was the past, as our forebears knew it? Nothing but poverty, superstition, and grief."[2] However, if one sees in Jewish tradition far more than superstition and grief, an ongoing process of honest evaluation is necessary. This new balancing act is not an easy or uncomplicated task, and on its success depends much of the future vitality of American Jewish life.

Jewish feminist spiritual explorations run the gamut from the very traditional to the boldly experimental. Some explorations are grounded in and grow out of traditional Jewish life; for example, Jewish feminist emphasis on rigorous Jewish education for women, participatory involvement in prayer, and a reclamation and reinterpretation of *tekhinnes* and traditional women's observances. In contrast, the most experimental feminists seek a radical reformation of Judaism, beginning with the removal of hierarchical categories from Jewish prayer and thought, eliminating references to God as an arbitrary ruler who metes out reward and punishment. Such feminists often have extensive links to feminists among other religious groups, and they feel free to utilize ideas and agendas borrowed from other cultures. They often seem anxious to bring Judaism into line with feminist reforms of other religions. As one such feminist states: "Feminism is having a tremendous impact on all major religions. I have dialogues with Christian, Buddhist, and goddess feminists. Feminism is transforming the world."

Jewish feminists who urge that contemporary Judaism should take on more "inclusive, feminist, non-hierarchical" attitudes sometimes charge that the traditional Jewish Sabbath incorporates and sanctifies hierarchical divisions.[3] Traditional Judaism posits several different gradations of holiness, *kedushah*, distinguishes between them, and arranges them in hierarchical order. As one example of this detailed hierarchy, on those occasions when a Jewish festival starts just as the Sabbath ends, the *havdalah*—dividing or distinguishing prayer—praises God for instructing Jews "to distinguish between the holiness of the Sabbath and the holiness of festival days." In contrast feminist thinkers are often deeply suspicious of hierarchical structures, because they have so often been used to justify the oppression of women and of the lower classes in traditional societies. The so-called "great chain of being" has often been used as an excuse to enchain groups of people. Reacting to the abuse of hierarchical structures by oppressive patriarchal power structures, some suggest that a feminist reworking of the concept of Shabbat would reject Judaism's "system of hierarchical distinctions," which are central aspects of the traditional Jewish Sabbath both conceptually and within its complex ritual and celebratory symbolism.[4]

Within the transformed religion of radical Jewish feminists, dualisms or hierarchical categories such as Jew versus non-Jew, male versus female, even Sabbath versus weekday would be excised or dramatically revised. Says Rabbi Laura Geller of the Jewish Feminist Resource Center in Los Angeles:

> Believing that some creatures and some people are more important than others underlies all of our social injustices—class, race, age. It also skews our relationship with other species. Judaism has a strong sense of social justice as well as a patriarchal system. I believe it is time to emphasize the social justice and do away with the patriarchy. I want to rearticulate the relationship so we can repair the model and repair the universe.

Nonetheless, such a reformulation, however noble, obliterates concepts that are basic to Jewish life and thought. The hierarchies represented by the division between God and humanity, Sabbath and weekday, are the bedrock of Judaism, beyond which it cannot be reduced and still remain itself. Intrinsic to the Jewish vision of the universe is the belief that physical and moral order are created by separating the elements and creating for them complementary but distinctive roles. Without distinctions, the earth—and human life—is chaotic and formless. Each element is necessary and celebrated and none can exist without the others. According to the biblical text, God creates man-and-woman as his penultimate act of creation; he creates the masculine and feminine principles simultaneously and then separates them. God's final act of creation is to provide the Sabbath day and to distinguish it from the working days of the week, both of which are necessary to help humanity perfect themselves and the world. The importance of the Sabbath as a day of holy retreat from creative work, distinguished from the other days of creation, begins with the first chapter of Genesis and is forcefully reasserted at pivotal points in biblical literature.[5]

Judaism rests on the principle that belief is not enough to create a compassionate, spiritually significant life. Traditional Judaism has taken the approach that people need structured guidelines to live well. It celebrates permissible pleasures and encourages human beings to see the spiritual potential of those pleasures, but it also says that not every pleasure is permissible in every circumstance. Food, alcohol, sexuality, sleep, companionship are each sanctified at some times—and prohibited at others—in traditional Jewish life. The desire for a life undemarcated by hierarchies may well be feminist, but it is antithetical to historic Judaism as a religion and a culture.

A major challenge facing Jewish feminists is to find vehicles for female spirituality that are in keeping with historic Judaic attitudes. One tendency that is disturbing to many is the trend within some strands of contemporary feminism to incorporate pagan elements into Judaism. Leading feminists have written about the need for feminine images of Godhead, and some have subscribed to the belief that the exclusion of goddess imagery in Judaism was a brutal, patriarchal act, a historical error that must now be rectified. Kim Chernin has written movingly of envisioning in the land of Israel a huge, dancing, naked female figure in which she found profound spiritual meaning.[6] In E. M. Broner's novel, *Weave of Women*,[7] Israeli women exorcise demons with magic oil and incantations and devise strange and mystical new holy days and religious rituals involving female spirits. Another example of the yearning back toward paganism as a naturally matriarchal, benignly female-focused epoch in human history is the goddess-sculpting of Reconstructionist Rabbi Jane Litman.[8]

Some feminists accuse the authors of ancient Judaism of ruthlessly eradicating a benign and loving matriarchal cult of goddess worship while maintaining male imagery of the divine. But in biblical literature, goddesses are not more hated than alien gods. Instead biblical Judaism is described as despising and laboring to eradicate all polytheistic impulses and all plastic representations of corporeal images of godhead. Exhortations to avoid the worship of male gods such as *baal* and *Moloch* are more numerous and vehement than those to avoid female goddesses such as the *ashtarot*. Frequently cited in biblical texts as reasons for this suppression is the fact that worship of these gods and goddesses involved the sacrifice of children, and sexual rituals that were anathema to the moral direction of Judaism.[9]

Rather than representing a repressive development, worship of the Judaic monotheistic God can be seen as a liberating movement in many ways. Leaving behind the worship of multiple deities of fertility and war, light and darkness, meant asserting that human beings had the capacity to be more than the sum of their physiological parts, that their lives might have more meaning than that imparted by historical accident. Worshiping one noncorporeal God meant that destiny was more than biology. Thus Jews were instructed from the Bible onward to celebrate but not to worship fertility, to engage in offensive or defensive wars when necessary but not to worship war, to rejoice in the light and the darkness and the seasons of the year—but to worship none of them.

Instead of worshiping a group of deities—deities who could be played off against one another—biblical Jews were taught to worship one God. Those who worship one God believe themselves and all mankind to be subject to one divine and ultimately meaningful—although often unknowable—plan. By insisting that one God created the universe and guides history, Judaism has since biblical times also insisted that history and individual life have meaning. Traditional Judaism insists that as surely as the stars and the seasons move inexorably according to a pattern created and effected by God, the lives of human beings and nations follow patterns as well. The Jewish God is a God of history and of personal destiny—although those patterns are sometimes not apparent and often painful to human beings.

It is important to remember, too, that although some Jewish feminists may be taking unconventional approaches by looking to mystical elements, feminists did not invent the incorporation of mysticism into Judaism. One may chose to reject feminist mysticism in whole or in part without succumbing to the mistaken belief that feminism created such mysticism and foisted it on an otherwise "pure" rational Judaism. American Jews often think of mainstream Judaism as a superrational religion that errs perhaps in favor of legalism and intellectualism. However, strands of mysticism and magic have been woven through Judaism since the earliest times. Much of rabbinic thought was profoundly suspicious of the nonrational beliefs that repeatedly surfaced in Jewish life and thought; nevertheless numerous renowned scholars believed in magic even as they condemned it. Just as the biblical King Saul forbids using the skills of witches and necromancers but clearly believes in their actual abilities (Samuel I 28: 3–23), many rabbis eschewed the use of magic without disbelieving in it.[10]

Perhaps a safety factor in these intellectual explorations is the fact that, while ideas may be provocative, they often have limited impact on the everyday Jewish lives of mainstream Americans. An area that has much more potential practical impact on American Jewish life is revisions of Jewish liturgy. Traditional Jewish prayers refer repeatedly to God in male imagery and continually recall the interaction of God with male biblical figures. Numerous American Jewish feminists feel that worship services should incorporate feminine attributes of Godhead and references to the matriarchs in order to reflect and express the spiritual lives of women. The nature and extent of desirable changes in Jewish liturgy has been the focus of much animated, sincere, personal, and scholarly debate among Jewish feminists. Indeed, one can learn much about the positive power of American Jewish feminism in revitalizing spiritual attachments to Judaism by observing the care and concern, as well as the passion, with which these debates about liturgical reform are conducted.

Many women who feel deeply tied to Judaism believe, "Jewish women are not subordinate, and if their relationship with God is every bit as intimate as the relationship of men, then let us change the liturgy to reflect this awareness." Jewish historian Ellen Umansky expresses the feelings of many when she points out that Jewish tradition includes ample precedents for female imagery, such as the *shekhinah*:

> How many times can I praise God as the Shield of Abraham or the Shield of Our Fathers without feeling that if He left out our mothers, surely He must be leaving out me. . . . The image that dances before me is of a male God who blesses His sons, those human beings (our fathers) who were truly created in His image. To Jewish medieval mystics, God was not simply a King and a Father but also *Shechinah*, She-Who-Dwells-Within. The *shechinah* represented the feminine element of the Divine. It was She who went into exile with the people of Israel, She who wept over their sorrows, She they yearned to embrace. The Kabbalists, then, knew God as Mother and Father, Queen and King. Might we not incorporate these insights into our worship service?[11]

Some committed Jewish feminists, however, are cautious and even suspicious of newly created liturgy and rituals and prefer to find significance in tradition. As a rabbinical student at the Jewish Theological Seminary, speaking to an audience that included many Jewish feminist spiritualists attending an Ivy League divinity school, Debra Cantor stunned her audience when she responded to a question about changing Jewish liturgy:

> I really get nervous when I hear people praying to the "Queen of the Universe." I understand the motivation, but to me it sounds like a slide down the slippery slope toward paganism. "Queen of the Universe" reminds me of Diana, not of the God who created the world.

But I'll tell you what does resonate for me—going to the *mikvah*. I feel that I'm linked to the community of Jewish women since the beginning of Jewish history.[12]

Other, equally committed Jewish feminists nevertheless insist that "to talk of God as Mother is not the same . . . as talking about a Mother Goddess." Rather, with the male-oriented liturgy as it stands, one-half of the Jewish people is excluded from feelings of spiritual community. Their hope for a revised liturgy is "that the prayers we say together will soon reflect the experiences of *Klal Yisroel* as a whole."[13]

The dialogue about revising liturgy takes place not only within the academy but among practioners on the "front lines" of Jewish life, women who serve as rabbis and religious educators. Rabbi Julie Spitzer of Baltimore Hebrew Congregation feels quite comfortable about changing male pronouns to such evocative words as *Creator* or *Eternal*. However, she warns against using female pronouns or the word *goddess*. She says that if contemporary Jews can get beyond the urge to envision God in human, corporeal terms, much of the problem can be solved: "The trouble with the word *goddess* is that it conjures up pagan imagery. In fact, Goddess is not the correct feminized name of God. I feel God present as energy, power, spirit—a simultaneously imminent and transcendent force." One thing feminism has done, she notes, is to "wake people up to the significance of what they're saying. No more sleepy recitation of meaningless words."

Some Jewish feminists believe that the most radical changes may be not only necessary but even salutary to the ultimate health of Judaism. Poet and translator Marcia Falk, author of a forthcoming work, *The Book of Blessings: A Feminist-Jewish Reconstruction of Prayer*, has written many new blessings to enrich the spiritual lives of women and men—blessings that have evoked "impassioned responses and dialogue from a wide spectrum of the Jewish community, from scholars to feminists to ordinary congregants." Falk continues:

Reconstructionist and *Moment* have printed long columns of letters and even symposia in response to my blessings and essays. Although some Jews are threatened by my work, many have expressed a great desire for it. I think of what I'm doing as deeply Jewish.

Some Jewish feminists prefer to limit their liturgical changes to English prayers, and others insist on effecting feminist revisions in

Hebrew. "I'm concerned with saving Hebrew," Marcia Falk says, "in recreating Hebrew liturgy. I use classical images from *Tanach* (Bible), *Midrash, piyyutim* (sacred poetry)." In fact, Falk sees her feminist efforts as a revitalization of the Hebrew prayers. She uses Hebrew precisely because it is deeply meaningful to her:

> Hebrew is not a mantra to me—it has meaning. I want the community to use Hebrew in a creative way. Jewish prayers are, and have always been, human products and creations. Now they must be recreated so that they reflect the Jewish spirituality of our times. My idea of Jewish feminism goes beyond mere access to old forms. I don't want an opportunity to lead a congregation in praising a male God.[14]

Much of biblical literature and traditional Hebrew liturgy is gendered—the stories told and the messages put forth, even when not specifically necessary, in gendered imagery and language. The God of the Bible is often described with anthropomorphic imagery: Most often, the imagery is strikingly male, including images of God as a man of war; the pronouns used for God in Hebrew are almost universally male. However, more often than is commonly recognized, the biblical God is pictured in clearly feminine imagery: God is compared to a gestating, birthing, and nursing mother, who nurtures the Jewish people. Often, especially in prophetic literature, when God is pictured as a man the entire Jewish people are pictured as a woman, and their relationship is that of lover and beloved, husband and wife.

Much of the effort of both Jewish and Christian liturgical reformers is currently devoted to creating gender-neutral liturgy. Some people engaged in rewriting the English translation for High Holiday prayer books are struggling with how to translate a prayer like *Avenu Malkeynu* (Our Father, Our King) in a nongendered way, leaning toward such translations as "Our Parent, Our Guide."

However, utilizing balanced, gender-specific imagery may in the end be a more effective, sensitive, and meaningful use of language than eliminating gender altogether. The balancing of gender-specific language and imagery is in some ways implicit in the structure of traditional Jewish Sabbath and holiday readings of the Hebrew scriptures. On the awesome first day of Rosh Hashanah, Jews traditionally address their Creator with such male images as "our Father, our King," but both the Torah and the Haftorah reading tell the vivid, viscerally gripping stories of women who passionately desire to be mothers in Israel and eventually succeed in their goals, against all odds producing a nation and the leaders of a nation. On Purim Jews read the Book of Esther, a fablelike story in which a beautiful woman outwits a demagogue and saves a nation by her wits. On Passover the service includes the Song of Songs, more than half of whose lyrics express the experiences and emotions of a voluptuous bride; rabbinic interpretation, calling the Song of Songs the "holiest of the holies" and forbidding exegetes from stripping it of its immediate human power, explains that the extravagantly female bride represents the entire Jewish people. On Shavuoth the Book of Ruth tells the story of two women upon whom rests the temporal and messianic future of the Jewish people. And on Tisha B'Av the reading of Lamentations focuses on the destruction of, and the exile from, Jerusalem in the personified figure of a woman—the vivid desolation of Bat Tzion, the princess of Zion.[15]

On given Sabbaths, the Torah and Haftorah readings contain powerfully feminine imagery of Godhead, such as Moses' declaration that it was God who conceived and gave birth to the Jewish people and who should therefore bear the burden of nurturing and raising that people; and yet, Moses complains, it is he and not God who must carry the Jewish people next to his breast. Prophetic selections depict God comparing himself to a nursing mother who suckles and soothes her child and caresses it on her knee. This imagery, and the stories of each of many biblical women, suggest that the Divine is experienced in human lives not only in a transcendental but also in an immediate, personal, and often gendered way. Human beings in biblical stories, like Rebecca, Tamar, Jochebed, Ruth, Deborah, Naomi, and Esther, carry out whatever they perceive as God's will in an immediate, personal way and as women. Contemporary human beings experience life and God's role in their lives as sons and daughters, as partners in loving sexual relationships, as mothers and fathers. Gender roles have powerful positive meanings.

It is those meanings that are evoked in gender-specific liturgy, and much would be lost if gender-specific language were to be excised from worship. Reformers in many religions, including Judaism, who tried to do away with "empty" ritual and to replace it with edifying rhetoric have learned through experience that most people need ritual. When rituals have been eliminated from religious expression, practitioners simply have replaced them with new—and sometimes bizarre—ones. Reformers have learned that if rituals seem empty the effective response is not to do away with but to revitalize them, to reinvest them with meaning. This is one of the reasons why many

American Reform congregations have reclaimed and rehabilitated some of the ancient rituals they once discarded.

Gender, like ritual, is basic to human life and experience, and humans experience life not as disembodied intellectual and spiritual entities but as physical, sexual beings. Eliminating gender from prayer language impoverishes it and robs it of power and immediacy. Given the putative patriarchal nature of traditional Jewish liturgy, it is striking that much positive maternal imagery has been highlighted at key moments of the Jewish liturgical expression. Without doubt, given male-dominated study halls, worship services, and sermon lecterns, little emphasis has until recently been placed on female aspects of Godhead and the role of women in aggressively and proactively carrying out the Divine will. But the way toward righting such suppression of female spirituality is not to strip worship language of its gendered inflections and imagery. It is instead to reclaim and celebrate what is female as well as what is male. Equality is best attained by viewing each gender as equally cherished, equally precious, in the sight of a Creator whom the Bible describes as creating humanity, simultaneously, *zachar u'nekayva*, male and female.

Part of the utopian agenda that animates many Jewish feminists is a commitment to the concept of *tikkun olam*, repairing the world. By definition *tikkun olam* includes the attempt to defend the rights of oppressed groups, women, and minorities—the most vulnerable members of society. A biblical aphorism that can be used to summarize the goals of Jewish feminist *tikkun olam* is the command, "Be kind to strangers because you were strangers in the land of Egypt." The traditional Jewish concept of *pidyon nefesh*, of rescuing enslaved and oppressed Jews no matter where they live, would be enlarged: Feminized Judaism would concern itself with peace and human dignity worldwide.

Some women have applied feminist perspectives to innovative efforts for peace in the Middle East. Politically active Jewish feminists sometimes use Jewish texts and history as their jumping-off point for criticizing Israel, asserting, for example, that "the Jewish experience of oppression has led not to the just exercise of power by Jews in power, but to the Jewish repetition of strategies of domination," and that the Jewish historical experience has not served as a lesson, but instead, "past oppression has even been used as a justification for the right to oppress others."[16] Many such feminists fault the Israeli government and society for their treatment of women, especially lesbians, Jews of Oriental extraction, and Palestinians and other Arabs. Similarly some Jewish feminists assert that Israel, a country set up as a refuge for the persecuted, "has now itself turned persecutor."[17] Jewish feminists sometimes accuse others of abandoning deeper feminist values: "In ignoring the exclusionist basis of Zionism and the racist practices of Israel (by pretending that Israel is just any other nation state), we fail to speak out against the most obvious oppressions being visited on our sisters. Where is our solidarity with Palestinian *women* . . . ?"[18] These feminists sometimes assert that a new kind of Jewish identity must be found whose basis is an uncompromising awareness of universal human values.[19]

Despite their protests to the contrary, such feminists seem to be primarily identified with worldwide feminism rather than with the Jewish people and their destiny. As a result they are sometimes puzzled when they encounter the firmly nationalistic attitudes of their Arab sisters, who often demonstrate that they are primarily and firmly committed to their own Arab brothers—not to Israeli and American Jewish women.[20] Other feminists who have themselves been involved in dialogue efforts have seen the uncompromising nationalism of Arab feminists as a warning signal. "Dialogue is a noble and important goal," says Blu Greenberg, who has been a member of one dialogue group, "but for Jews the viability of the state of Israel must be the most sacred principle of all." Honest commitment to Israel's best interests will no doubt occasionally put Jewish feminists in the position of being "politically incorrect," and unpopular among some other feminists. However, the exigencies of Jewish survival have often demanded particularistic decisions by Jews who in other ways thought themselves citizens of the world, and Jewish feminist universalists will have to think hard about their deepest loyalties.

American Jewish feminism encompasses, of course, many other ideological agendas besides "correcting" Israel's shortcomings. Some leaders delineate Jewish feminist goals that include ecological issues, world peace, and an end to hunger, along with the expansion of Jewish spiritual opportunities for women. Rather than dividing the Jewish people into elites and commoners, rather than rejecting specific behaviors, sexual and otherwise, this transformed Judaism would reflect the feminist principle of inclusiveness. This vision of a feminist Judaism espouses many new-age values. For example, some feminists suggest that the dietary restrictions of *kashruth* should be replaced by vegetarianism or another regimen, consistent with current knowledge about how human beings can show respect for their own bodies, the lives of other animals, and the well-being of the planet. Within these new definitions, the category of nonkosher "might take the form of prohibiting foods that are grown with pesticides or that contain carcinogens or hormones. The traditional blessings over food would be replaced by special blessings before or after meals and a commitment to set aside a proportion of the cost of all meals to feed the hungry." Also prohibited would be "foods that are the product of exploitation and oppression." This new *kashruth* would "turn the simple everyday act of eating into an aspect of the continuing quest for justice."[21]

Depending on one's religious and political orientations, one could choose to argue one or more points of individual Jewish feminist agendas. One might argue that a separation of Jewish tradition into a "prophetic tradition which esteems justice" and a "rabbinic tradition which esteems order"[22] is simplistic. Every system of justice depends on laws, and rabbinic law is intensely committed to justice. Jewish lawgivers knew better than to depend on the individual's good nature to see that justice would be done and assumed that without order there can be no justice. An earth-conscious, health-conscious redefinition of *kashruth* and additional emphasis on feeding the hungry are profoundly in the spirit of Jewish law, but Judaism already prescribes regular gifts to the poor; one wonders why the elimination of traditional *kashruth* is a necessary prerequisite for an ecological overlay. Health dictates seem to change from year to year and sometimes from month to month, so that introducing a therapeutic basis for revision of *kashruth* means introducing ephemerality as well. One might argue that few human beings (even few feminists) live life with the intensity and thoughtfulness implied by some Jewish feminists standards, and that ordinary, careless people do better with a more consistent structure of prescribed behaviors.

However, what is inarguable is the seriousness with which many Jewish feminist leaders approach Judaism. And this very seriousness is in itself stirringly hopeful and a sign of revitalization. For almost one hundred years the American Jewish community has been in the process of becoming more and more like other Americans, less and less distinctively Jewish. For most American Jews, each generation finds Judaism less central to its sense of meaning and life values. Jewish feminism has made Judaism as a religion a matter of critical attention and importance to more Jews than any other recent movement in American Jewish life.

Some have worried that, despite the many positive contributions of Jewish feminism, the movement may be working to destroy other positive Jewish values, such as the role of Jewish women in performing deeds of loving-kindness. Historically, women have often identified with and articulated the needs of others, especially the family and the community, while men have insisted on individual rights. Like other widespread social issues, the issue of a possible conflict between professionalism and *menschlichkeit* (kindness, concern for others, consideration), and the impact of feminism and changing life-styles on that conflict, have special implications for the Jewish community. "Who is going to do what the women used to do?" wonders Miriam Klein Shapiro:

> I look at my busy professional friends—I look at myself—and I know that none of us does the amount of *gemilat hasadim* [deeds of loving-kindness] that we used to do when those things were the primary responsibility of women. We worry about getting ahead professionally—but we lose track of our responsibilities to welcome newcomers to the community by inviting them over to the house. We lose track of our responsibilities to pay attention to sick people and their families. That's what Judaism was all about, and we've lost track of it. We are so worried about praying with *talit* and *tefillin* that we have forgotten about the things that Judaism did for people, which I think was the major message of Judaism. If women who are committed to Judaism neglect the human things, then what can we expect from the rest of society?

Such observations and concerns are legitimate, but only tell half the story when they assign the responsibility for compassionate behavior to women and when they condemn feminism for the demise of communal conscience. In point of fact rabbinic law does not place the responsibility for deeds of loving-kindness primarily on women but places it equally upon men and women. Both men and women are responsible, in Jewish law, to be hospitable to newcomers, to visit the sick, to comfort the mourning, to equip and celebrate with the bride, to behave with empathy and respect to the elderly, to see that the dead are appropriately prepared and buried, and to perform a host of menial, homely—and compassionate—tasks for others in their community.

Judaism requires both men and women to be enablers and to put the needs of others, when necessary, before their own. In contemporary society, however, such behavior is not only not encouraged, it often seems to be scorned and condemned. Yeshiva University professor Rabbi Saul Berman aptly captures the moral environment of our age when he states, "Contemporary secular America has taken the divine out of the center of experience and has moved the self in instead. Individualism has become the new religion." Significantly, Berman does not see the rise of individualism as the chief value of our society as a gender-related issue.

Separation, personal space, breaking codependencies—all these have been the buzz words of an individualistic, atomized society. A woman who moved to a young, affluent suburb of New York from Montreal ten years ago says that American values of self-centeredness and individualism have transformed all wings of American Judaism. "I'm convinced that even Orthodox Jews in the United States are profoundly assimilated and affected by the individualistic values of our society," she argues. "Among Jews in their forties and under, even those who are still very careful about eating kosher food, who go to the *mikveh* and wear sneakers on Yom Kippur, even Jews like that are American down to their inner souls. They have forgotten what Judaism is supposed to teach us about empathy for others and communal priorities."

The conflict between loyalty to the family and community and loyalty to oneself—to "being true to one's heart"—is not truly or at least not only a conflict between feminism and Judaism. It is a conflict between the values of a traditional, hierarchical religious system and those of an intensely individualistic society. In terms of the way this conflict plays itself out in the lives of American Jewish women, it has often felt like a conflict between Old and New World values. Thus, in Vivian Gornick's piercing memoir, *Fierce Attachments*, a middle-aged woman and her aging mother disagree about no less than what constitutes humanity:

> "It's no use. Say what you will, children don't love their parents as they did when I was young."
> "Ma, do you really believe that?"
> "I certainly do! My mother died in my sister's arms, with all her children around her. How will I die, will you please tell me? They probably won't find me for a week. . . ."
> ". . . .Your mother didn't die in her daughter's arms because your sister loved her more than we love you. Your sister hated your mother, and you know it. She was there because it was her duty to be there, and because she lived around the corner all her married life. It had

nothing to do with love. It wasn't a better life, it was an immigrant life, a working-class life, a life from another century."

"Call it what you want," she replies angrily, "it was a more human way to live."[23]

Feminism and Jewish feminism have not destroyed family values. Feminism does, however, participate in many aspects of the ambivalence and confusion on this subject which is endemic to contemporary American society.[24] The stakes for the Jewish community in this process of winnowing out the constructive and the destructive elements offered by feminist theory are even greater than those for American society at large. The American Jewish community not only shares in all the human consequences of feminism but also carries with it the additional responsibility of preserving three thousand years of Jewish history and culture and confronting the problems of a numerically challenged population as well.

The tasks of Jewish feminism cannot—and should not—be accomplished by women alone. In order for it to play its part in the great and crucial endeavor of revitalizing American Jewish life, the whole-hearted and responsible efforts of both Jewish men and women are needed. In each area of contemporary American Jewish life—family, education and occupation, religious ritual and liturgical expression, life-cycle events, spirituality, leadership, and political efforts—progress can only be enhanced when men and women work together in good faith. Jewish family life is enhanced when men share the responsibilities of the household and child care. Female achievement in education and occupation can coexist with smoothly functioning family households when men as well as women strive for family-friendly schools and workplaces, which do not pit career achievement against familial responsibilities. Synagogues and Jewish communal institutions can benefit from the spiritual expression and the talents of both men and women when men do not see female participation as a "feminization" of irrevocably male turf.

In order for men to participate in the challenge of making American Judaism a healthy environment for men, women, and children, a deep level of courage, commitment, and unselfishness is called for on the part of both men and women. For most of human history and in most cultures, men have enjoyed enormous privileges, which they have enforced through a variety of means. Some societies have suppressed women much more brutally than others, and in the scale of world cultures historic Judaism comes out rather well. Although men have without doubt been the privileged gender in Jewish life, Judaism has always insisted that women have souls and that their communication with their Creator is as direct as that of men. Judaism has insisted that women have sexual needs, and that women always have the right to refuse unwanted sexual attentions. Judaism has tried to provide a safety net for women in marginal situations.

However, Jewish religious and cultural expression have been almost exclusively authored by males, and thus reflect a male view of women and the world. The intellectual and leadership capacities of women have been largely ignored, downplayed, or discouraged in most Jewish cultures. Life events that affect only women have been invisible in the cycle of Jewish celebrations. Given the realities of contemporary American life, in which women are increasingly able to experience life as full human beings rather than as mere helpful adjuncts of an egregiously male world, the persistence of such blind spots and lacunae within Judaism is profoundly unwholesome. Undoubtedly the forces of inertia make the maintenance of the status quo a great temptation—especially when the status quo has granted one group dominance purely on the basis of biology. But organic entities—including religions and cultures—either grow and evolve or decline and decay. In order for American Judaism to continue to develop, its men have a great part to play in working together with its women to make females full partners in a vibrant, responsive, and authentic Jewish life.

Jewish feminist agendas are still a source of conflict, not only within the Jewish community but sometimes within diverging strands of Jewish feminism itself. Jewish feminists who define themselves as Orthodox, Conservative, Reconstructionist, and Reform sometimes regard one another with more suspicion than affection, forgetting that each wing of American Judaism has led the way in at least one area of Jewish feminist progress. Reform and Reconstructionist Judaism have pioneered in the ordination of female rabbis. Conservative Judaism has pioneered in training women with liturgical skills, which enable them to take participatory and leadership roles in Hebrew language worship. Orthodox Judaism has pioneered in providing women with an intensive Jewish education and familiarity with traditional texts. Jewish feminists make the best use of their united strengths when they retain respect for their mutual contributions and enhance cooperation between women with diverse backgrounds but complementary goals.

The task of distinguishing between what is truly Jewish feminism and feminist agendas that are antithetical or at least problematic to Judaism continues to require honest appraisal and discrimination. Jewish feminism has succeeded best where it has worked to bring women to the center of authentically Jewish activities. Thus formal group prayer is a Jewish value, and it is now an arena in which Jewish women occupy a central place. No longer marginal, new generations of Jewish women feel enfranchised and at home in the synagogue. Rigorous Jewish education is a Jewish value, to which Jewish women now can obtain equal access. The Jewish community now has the benefit of the intellectual and artistic Judaic contributions of women as well as men. Moreover, women's needs, thoughts, and experiences are in the process of being incorporated into the central activities of Judaism. Women's place in Jewish history is being reclaimed by Jewish feminist biblical, rabbinic, and literary scholars, historians, and social scientists.

As American Judaism enters a dramatically new and demanding era, Jewish feminists struggle to preserve the riches of historic Judaism while creating meaningful social and spiritual models, to balance the demands of individualism with those of societal needs and group survival. Fortunately Jewish feminism has not only posed keen challenges to American Jewish life but has also provided powerful new tools with which creatively to forge a vibrant future.

TABLES

List of Tables

TABLE 1
Marital Status of American Jewish Men and Women
in Selected Cities and Nationally

Location	Year Study Completed	Married	Single	Widowed	Divorced
Atlantic City	1985	67	13	13	6
Boston	1985	61	29	4	5
Baltimore	1985	68	19	9	5
Chicago	1982	65	23	6	6
Cleveland	1981	69	11	13	8
Denver	1981	64	23	4	9
Kansas City	1985	70	17	7	5
Los Angeles	1979	57	17	12	14
Miami	1982	61	7	23	8
Milwaukee	1983	67	14	9	10
Minneapolis	1981	66	22	7	5
Nashville	1982	70	17	8	5
New York	1981	65	15	11	9
Phoenix	1983	63	18	9	10
Richmond	1983	67	14	12	7
Rochester	1987	68	23	6	3
St. Louis	1982	68	9	17	6
St. Paul	1981	66	20	11	3
San Francisco	1988	69	19	4	7
Washington, D.C.	1983	61	27	4	7
Worcester	1987	69	14	--18--	
NJPS	1990	64	21	7	8
US Census	1989	64	21	8	8
NJPS	1970	78	6	10	5
US Census	1970	73	16	9	3

Source: Jewish community studies, 1970 and 1990 National Jewish Population Surveys, and White Americans, 1970 and 1989 U.S. census studies.

TABLE 2
Marital Status by Age and Gender
A. 1990 National Jewish Population Survey Respondents

	18-24		25-34		35-44		45-54		55-64		65+	
	F	M	F	M	F	M	F	M	F	M	F	M
Married	12	2	62	46	74	73	75	77	77	87	57	82
Never Married	88	96	30	50	11	17	7	9	2	6	2	3
Divorced/ Separated	1	1	7	3	14	10	14	11	14	6	4	3
Widowed	-	-	1	-	1	1	4	3	8	1	38	12

Source: Data drawn from 1990 NJPS, respondents born or raised Jewish. Totals may equal more or less than 100 percent because they are rounded.

B. 1989 U.S. Census of All Americans

	20-24		25-29		30-34		35-39		40-44		45-54		55-64	
	F	M	F	M	F	M	F	M	F	M	F	M	F	M
Married	35	21	29	49	72	66	76	74	75	80	75	81	68	83
Never Married	63	77	62	46	17	26	10	15	6	8	5	7	4	6
Divorced	3	1	8	5	11	8	13	11	16	12	14	11	18	8
Widowed	-	-	-	-	1	-	1	-	3	1	6	1	9	3

Source: 1989 U.S. Census, Bureau of the Census, *Current Population Reports,* series P-20, no. 445.

TABLE 3
Occupational Status by Age and Gender
(*unweighted percentages*)

Occupational Status Level	WOMEN		MEN	
	Under 45	45 & Over	Under 45	45 & Over
High Status Professions	14%	7%	22%	26% ˙
Helping Professions	29%	18%	18%	10%
Managerial Positions	14%	15%	16%	20%
Clerical/ Technical	31%	52%	27%	28%
Service Positions	9%	5%	14%	14%
Refused/ Other	3%	2%	4%	3%

Source: Data drawn from 1990 NJPS respondents born or raised Jewish.

TABLE 4
Occupational Status of Women by Family Formation Status

Occupational Status Level	No Children	Children 18 or Under	Children 19 or Over
High Status Professions	15%	11%	7%
Helping Professions	24%	28%	16%
Managerial Positions	13%	13%	14%
Clerical/ Technical	35%	37%	56%
Service Positions	9%	9%	7%
TOTALS*	96%	98%	100%

* Totals shown may be greater than or less than 100% because they are rounded.

Source: Data drawn from 1990 NJPS respondents born or raised Jewish.

TABLE 5
Labor Force Participation of Women by Age

Labor Force Participation Jewish Female Respondents Ages 44 & Under			Labor Force Particpation Jewish Female Respondents Ages 45 & Over	
Labor Force Status			**Labor Force Status**	
Homemaker	17%		Homemaker	19%
Student	11%		Student	--
Part-time Worker	11%		Part-time Worker	8%
Full-time Worker	59%		Full-time Worker	31%
Not Employed*	4%		Not Employed*	44%
TOTAL**	102%		TOTAL**	102%

* Includes unemployed seeking work, unemployed not seeking work, and retired.

** Totals shown may be greater than or less than 100% because they are rounded.

Source: Based on data from 1990 NJPS respondents born or raised Jewish.

TABLE 6
Labor Force Participation of Mothers of Children Under
Six Years Old

	Full-time	Part-time	Homemaker	Other
Boston	29%	36%	33%	2%
Baltimore	27%	38%	35%	1%
Kansas City	28%	21%	44%	7%
MetroWest	22%	26%	49%	4%
Milwaukee	18%	32%	36%	14%
Philadelphia	23%	14%	59%	3%
Pittsburgh	29%	25%	42%	4%
Phoenix	26%	21%	50%	3%
Rochester	22%	32%	42%	4%
San Francisco	36%	25%	31%	8%
Washington	34%	30%	30%	6%
Worcester	15%	34%	51%	1%

Source: Adapted from Gabriel Berger and Lawrence Sternberg, *Jewish Child-Care: A Challenge and an Opportunity* (Cohen Center for Modern Jewish Studies, Brandeis University, Research Report no. 3, November 1988).

TABLE 7
Voluntarism by Women for Jewish and Non-Jewish Causes by Age, Marital Status, Family Formation, and Labor Force Participation
(weighted percentages)

Category	Jewish Causes	Non-Jewish Causes
Married	23%	41%
Under Age 45	23%	46%
Over Age 45	24%	36%
Never Married	16%	47%
Divorced	16%	37%
Widowed	23%	24%
No Children Born	14%	44%
Children 6 & Under	22%	48%
Children 18 & Under	24%	46%
Children 19 & Over	27%	33%
Homemakers	21%	41%
Under Age 45	29%	49%
Over Age 45	13%	32%
Students	13%	54%
Work Part-time	32%	39%
Under Age 45	24%	43%
Over Age 45	45%	32%
Work Full-time	18%	43%
Under Age 45	18%	45%
Over Age 45	18%	39%
Unemployed	27%	30%

Source: Based on data from NJPS respondents born or raised Jewish.

Tables

TABLE 8
Voluntarism for Jewish and Non-Jewish Causes by Education and Gender

Educational Level Attained	Jewish Causes		Non-Jewish Causes	
	WOMEN	MEN	WOMEN	MEN
High School or Under	15%	11%	23%	20%
Attended College	22%	14%	39%	43%
Bachelor's Degree	23%	13%	47%	49%
Master's Degree*	27%	18%	57%	48%
Ph.D., M.D., Dds., J.D.	27%	19%	44%	47%
* Includes nursing degree				

Source: Based on data from NJPS respondents born or raised Jewish.

TABLE 9
Jewish Education by Age and Gender

	Both Sexes			
Index	18 - 24	25 - 44	45 - 64	65+
None	23.7	24.3	20.9	36.6
Less than 3 years	4.7	8.1	9.6	12.5
3-5 Sunday School	5.3	7.6	8.8	4.1
6+ Sunday School	7.0	12.9	14.4	6.9
3-5 Supplementary	17.2	17.9	17.7	18.2
3-5 Day School	5.7	1.1	1.7	1.6
6+ Supplementary	24.7	20.7	21.5	15.2
6+ Day School	11.9	7.3	5.5	5.0
Total Percent	100.0	100.0	100.0	100.0

Index	18 - 24		25 - 44		45 - 64		65+	
	Women	Men	Women	Men	Women	Men	Women	Men
None	28.3	19.2	34.2	13.5	30.1	11.8	51.6	21.9
Less than 3 years	4.1	5.2	8.2	8.0	9.0	10.2	7.6	17.2
3-5 Sunday School	5.9	4.9	9.1	5.9	10.3	7.4	6.3	2.0
6+ Sunday School	6.7	7.2	14.6	11.2	21.6	7.2	9.1	4.9
3-5 Supplementary	15.5	18.7	10.1	26.5	11.2	24.0	10.4	25.7
3-5 Day School	9.2	2.3	0.9	1.4	-	3.3	1.1	2.1
6+ Supplementary	20.0	29.1	17.2	24.5	15.7	27.1	12.9	17.4
6+ Day School	10.3	13.4	5.7	9.0	2.0	8.9	1.1	8.8
Total Percent	100.0	100.0	100.0	100.0	100.0	100.0	100.0	100.0

Note: Data in this and subsequent tables are based on NJPS respondents who were born or raised Jewish.

Source: Sylvia Barack Fishman and Alice Goldstein, *When They Are Older They Will Not Depart: Jewish Education and Jewish Behavior of American Adults* (Cohen Center for Modern Jewish Studies, Brandeis University, 1992).

TABLE 10
Jewish Education by Denomination of Parental Home, Age, and
Gender
(weighted percentages)

	Women					Men				
	18-24	25-44	45-64	65+	All Ages	18-24	25-44	45-64	65+	All Ages
Orthodox										
None	**	29.7	34.6	41.1	34.4	**	8.0	2.6	10.0	7.9
Minimal	**	7.6	12.3	12.7	10.6	**	10.0	6.8	8.5	8.0
Moderate	**	9.8	29.4	19.9	20.0	**	21.3	32.9	36.2	30.6
Substantial	**	52.8	23.7	26.3	35.0	**	60.7	57.7	45.3	53.5
Total %	**	100.0	100.0	100.0	100.0	**	100.0	100.0	100.0	100.0
Conservative										
None	19.6	33.1	27.1	61.9	35.7	24.3	10.9	17.5	19.2	15.2
Minimal	7.0	12.5	21.6	16.4	14.9	2.4	9.5	16.8	22.2	12.0
Moderate	31.9	28.6	33.3	16.3	27.8	24.6	39.5	35.6	47.7	37.9
Substantial	41.6	25.7	17.9	5.3	21.5	48.7	40.1	30.2	10.9	35.0
Total %	100.0	100.0	100.0	100.0	100.0	100.0	100.0	100.0	100.0	100.0
Reform										
None	37.1	29.6	17.5	60.9	31.4	10.3	8.6	2.5	38.2	10.2
Minimal	11.6	27.6	23.6	10.4	23.6	20.7	19.0	27.9	23.5	21.3
Moderate	36.8	32.8	48.5	28.6	35.6	39.8	48.8	40.3	32.7	44.8
Substantial	14.4	10.0	10.3	-	9.5	29.1	23.5	29.4	5.6	23.7
Total %	100.0	100.0	100.0	100.0	100.0	100.0	100.0	100.0	100.0	100.0
Just Jewish										
None	**	56.0	53.5	70.4	61.3	**	79.1	24.6	53.3	60.8
Minimal	**	7.8	32.1	9.6	12.5	**	7.4	34.6	33.6	20.9
Moderate	**	6.7	6.7	20.0	11.0	**	7.3	32.8	7.0	12.0
Substantial	**	29.6	7.7	-	15.2	**	6.2	8.0	6.1	6.4
Total %	**	100.0	100.0	100.0	100.0	**	100.0	100.0	100.0	100.0

Source: Sylvia Barack Fishman and Alice Goldstein, *When They Are Older They Will Not Depart: Jewish Education and Jewish Behavior of American Adults* (Cohen Center for Modern Jewish Studies, Brandeis University, 1992). Based on 1990 NJPS respondents ages 18–44.

TABLE 11
Current Volunteers for Jewish Causes by Jewish Education, Denomination Raised, and Gender

	Orthodox		Conservative		Reform	
	Women	Men	Women	Men	Women	Men
None	17%	4%	7%	5%	15%	5%
1-2 years Supplementary or Sunday School	--	--	4%	5%	4%	11%
3-5 years Sunday School	4%	4%	7%	5%	12%	--
6+ years Sunday School	4%	--	2%	2%	27%	37%
3-5 years Supplementary School	4%	4%	16%	16%	12%	5%
6+ years Supplementary School	17%	16%	54%	59%	31%	32%
1-5 years Day School	--	4%	4%	2%	--	5%
6+ years Day School	54%	68%	7%	7%	--	5%
TOTAL	100%	100%	101%	101%	101%	100%

Source: Based on data from 1990 NJPS respondents born or raised Jewish.

TABLE 12
Marriage Patterns and Jewish Education
(*percentages of respondents married to born Jews*)

Index	Age Group		
	25 - 44	45 - 64	65 + over
None	30.0	52.2	79.0
Less than 3 years	32.2	55.5	71.4
3-5 Sunday School	39.5	41.1	65.3
6+ Sunday School	44.6	59.3	81.2
3-5 Supplementary	56.7	81.9	87.2
3-5 Day School	55.6	45.8	100.0
6+ Supplementary	50.7	64.8	84.8
6+ Day School	79.6	79.0	76.0

Source: Sylvia Barack Fishman and Alice Goldstein, *When They Are Older They Will Not Depart: Jewish Education and Jewish Behavior of American Adults* (Cohen Center for Modern Jewish Studies, Brandeis University, 1992). Based on NJPS respondents who were born or raised Jewish.

NOTES

Preface

1. Structured interviews were conducted from January, 1990, through September, 1992, with 120 women living in the following communities: Albuquerque, Ann Arbor, Atlanta, Baltimore, Berkeley, Boston, Brooklyn, Bronx, Cambridge (MA), Cherry Hill (NJ), Chicago, Columbus (OH), Columbia (MD), Denver, Encinatas, Gainesville (FLA), Los Angeles, Manhattan, Miami, Norfolk (VA), Orefield (PA), Philadelphia, Pittsburgh, Portland (OR), Providence, New Haven, Newton (MA), Queens, Rockland County (NY), Rockville (MD), San Diego, San Francisco, Sharon, St. Louis, Silver Springs (MD), Teaneck, Tucson, and Westchester County (NY). Women were selected from interviews using "snowballing" and other techniques, with the aim of providing maximum diversity among women who have a connection to and interest in some aspect of contemporary Jewish Life. The women interviewed included 16 female rabbis and Jewish educators, 20 students, 30 writers and professors of Judaica, 12 Jewish communal professionals and 12 Jewish communal volunteers, 14 professionals in non-sectarian spheres, and 16 women's prayer group participants. Although I constructed and used a questionnaire as a guideline for these interviews, our discussions were designed to and did range far beyond the standard questions, following each woman into her own special area of concern and expertise. Several outstanding questions were added to the questionnaire at the suggestions of the interviewees themselves. Some of the names and identifying facts have been changed in transcriptions of a particular situation, at the interviewee's request, but the details of each life are discreet and unmerged; in no case have I constructed a "composite" character, and the dialogue reported consists of direct quotations.

2. National data are drawn from computer tapes of the 1990 National Jewish Population Survey supervised by the Council of Jewish Federations (CJF) and the Mandell–Berman Institute–North American Jewish Data Bank of the Graduate School & University Center of CUNY. Unless otherwise indicated, tables referring to data from the 1990 National Jewish Population Survey have been prepared by the author, with the assistance of the staff of the Maurice and Marilyn Cohen Center for Modern Jewish Studies at Brandeis University. Unless otherwise noted, data from individual city studies are drawn from the following sources: Sherry Israel, *Boston's Jewish Community: The 1985 Demographic Study* (1987); Gary A. Tobin and Sylvia Barack Fishman, *A Study of the Jewish Population of Greater Dallas* (Dallas Jewish Federation

and the Cohen Center for Modern Jewish Studies, 1989); Gary A. Robin and Sharon Sassler, *Bay Area Jewish Community Study* (Bay Area Jewish Federations and Cohen Center for Modern Jewish Studies, 1988); Paul Ritterband and Steven M. Cohen, *The 1981 Greater New York Jewish Population Survey* (New York, 1981); Bruce A. Phillips, *Los Angeles Jewish Community Survey Overview for Regional Planning* (Los Angeles, 1980); Allied Jewish Federation of Denver, *The Denver Jewish Population Study* (Denver, 1981); Lois Geer, *1981 Population Study of the St. Paul Jewish Community* (St. Paul, 1981); Lois Geer, *The Jewish Community of Greater Minneapolis 1981 Population Study* (Minneapolis, 1981); Population Research Committee, *Survey of Cleveland's Jewish Population, 1981* (Cleveland, 1981); Ira M. Sheskin, *Population Study of the Greater Miami Jewish Community,* (Miami, 1981); Gary A. Tobin, *A Demographic and Attitudinal Study of the Jewish Community of St. Louis* (St. Louis, 1982); Bruce A. Phillips and William S. Aron, *The Greater Phoenix Jewish Population Study* (Phoenix, 1983–94); Bruce A. Phillips, *The Milwaukee Jewish Population Study* (Milwaukee, 1984); Nancy Hendrix, *A Demographic Study of the Jewish Community of Nashville and Middle Tennessee* (Nashville, 1982); Ann Shorr, Jewish Community Federation of Cleveland, and Jane Berkey and Saul Weisberg, United Federation of Greater Pittsburgh, *Survey of Greater Pittsburgh's Jewish Population,* 1984; Gary A. Tobin, Joseph Waksberg, and Janet Greenblatt, *A Demographic Study of the Jewish Community of Greater Washington* (Washington, D.C., 1984); Gary A. Tobin, *Jewish Population Study of Greater Baltimore,* 1986; Gary A. Tobin and Sylvia Barack Fishman, *Jewish Population Study of Greater Worcester,* 1987; Gary A. Tobin and Sylvia Barack Fishman, *Jewish Population Study of Greater Rochester,* 1987. All nationwide figures for the American Jewish population in 1970 are derived from the 1970 National Jewish Population Study (NJPS). Percentages have been rounded from .5 to the next highest number; as a result, totals may not equal 100 percent.

Chapter One: *Discovering Jewish Feminism*

1. Raquel Shira Kosovske, "Dialogue on the Beautiful: Lesbian Poetry and the Dutiful Daughter" (Manuscript, Brandeis University Women's Studies Senior Project, May 1991).
2. Adrienne Rich, "Split at the Root," *Blood, Bread and Poetry: Selected Prose* (London: Virago Press, by permission of W. W. Norton and Company), pp. 110–11, discusses the images of ladylike "gentile" behavior and "loud, pushy" Jewish behavior which were common in Southern society during her growing years. Her feelings of conflict between her Jewish and gentile roots were an important component of her experience of being "split at the root."
3. Sara Evans, *Born for Liberty: A History of Women in America* (New York: Free Press, 1989), pp. 266–67.
4. Betty Friedan, *The Feminine Mystique* (New York: Norton, 1963; 20th anniversary ed., 1983).
5. Gloria Steinem, "Humanism and the Second Wave of Feminism," *Humanist* (May/June 1987): 11–15, 49.
6. Shulamith Firestone, *The Dialectic of Sex* (New York: Morrow, 1971).

7. Evans, *Born for Liberty*, p. 279.

8. Further writings on women of color and feminism include: E. Francis White, "Listening to the Voices of Black Feminism," *Radical America* 18, 2–3 (Spring 1984); Gloria I. Joseph and Jill Lewis, *Common Differences: Conflicts in Black and White Perspectives* (New York: Doubleday, 1981); Alice Walker, *In Search of Our Mother's Gardens*, in which Walker coins "womanist" as an alternative to "feminist" for women of color; Gloria Anzaldua and Cherrie Moraga, eds., *This Bridge Called My Back: Writings by Radical Women of Color* (New York; Kitchen Table Press, 1981); Bonnie Thornton Dill, "Race, Class, and Gender: Prospects for an All-Inclusive Sisterhood," *Feminist Studies* 9, 1 (Spring 1983): 131–50; Audre Lorde, *Sister Outsider: Essays and Speeches* (Trumansburg, N.Y.: Crossing Press, 1984); Roslyn Terborg-Penn, "Discrimination against Afro-American Women in the Women's Movement," in *The Afro-American Women: Struggles and Images,* ed. Sharon Harley and Roselyn Terborg-Penn (Port Washington, N.Y.: Kennikat Press, 1978); Paula Giddings, *When and Where I Enter: The Impact of Black Women on Race and Sex in America* (New York: Bantam, 1985).

9. Evans, *Born for Liberty*, p. 297.

10. Trude Weiss-Rosmarin, "The Unfreedom of Jewish Women," *Jewish Spectator,* October 1970, pp. 2–6.

11. Rachel Adler, "The Jew Who Wasn't There," *Davka,* Summer 1971, pp. 6–11.

12. Conservative Judaism permits cautious change within the halakhah, the rabbinic legal system, while Reform Judaism considers halakhah nonbinding and Orthodox Judaism considers it always binding.

13. Steven Martin Cohen, "American Jewish Feminism: A Study in Conflicts and Compromises," *American Behavioral Scientist,* March–April 1980, pp. 519–58.

14. Elizabeth Koltun, ed. *The Jewish Woman: An Anthology* (New York: Schocken Books, 1987), Martha Acklesberg (introductory essay on the history of Jewish feminism, religious and social change), Judith Hauptman (Talmud), Paula Hyman and Judith Plaskow (women in rabbinic literature and law), Aviva Cantor and Jacqueline K. Levine (communal issues), Marcia Falk (biblical poetics), Charlotte Baum (American Jewish history), Rachel Adler (women in Jewish law and culture), and others. The work was later revised to include additional articles by other Jewish feminist thinkers, among them Arlene Agus (women's rituals), Blu Greenberg (feminist exploration within a traditional context), and Sonya Michel (American Jewish literature).

15. Charlotte Baum, Paula Hyman, and Sonya Michel, *The Jewish Woman in America* (New York: New American Library, 1976).

16. Ellen M. Umansky, "Females, Feminists, and Feminism: A Review of Recent Literature on Jewish Feminism and a Creation of a Feminist Judaism," *Feminist Studies* 14 (Summer 1988): 349–65.

17. For the place of Jewish identity in the larger construct of personal identity, see Herbert C. Kelman, "The Place of Jewish Identity in the Development of Personal Identity" (Working paper prepared for the American Jewish Committee Colloquium on Jewish Education and Jewish Identity, November 1974); and Peter Y. Medding, "Segmented Ethnicity and the New Jewish Politics," *Studies in Contemporary Jewry* 3 (New York and Oxford, 1987): 26–45.

18. Letty Cottin Pogrebin, "Anti-Semitism in the Women's Movement: A Jewish Feminist's Disturbing Account," *Ms.* June 1982, 145–49.

19. Ibid.

20. Ibid.

21. See, for example, Betty Friedan, *The Second Stage* (New York: Summit Books, 1981), pp. 162–66.

22. Pogrebin, "Anti-Semitism in the Women's Movement."

23. Susannah Heschel, "Current Issues in Jewish Feminist Theology," *Christian Jewish Relations* 19, no. 2 (1986): 23–32, 27–28.

24. Annette Daum, "Blaming Jews for the Death of the Goddess," *Lilith,* no. 7, (1980): 12–13.

25. Merlin Stone, *When God Was a Woman* (New York: Harcourt Brace Jovanovich, 1978). (Italics in original.)

26. Judith Plaskow, "Blaming Jews for Inventing Patriarchy," *Lilith,* no. 7 (1980): 11–12.

27. Ibid.

28. Courtney Leatherman, "Women's-Studies Group Hoping to Heal Wounds, Finds More Conflict," *Chronicle of Higher Education,* July 1, 1992.

29. Ellen M. Umansky, "Females, Feminists, and Feminism: A Review of Recent Literature on Jewish Feminism and a Creation of a Feminist Judaism," *Feminist Studies* 14 (Summer 1988): 349–65.

30. Sid Groeneman, "Beliefs and Values of American Jewish Women" (Report by Market Facts, Inc., presented to the International Organization of B'nai B'rith Women, 1985), pp. 30–31. The data were drawn from 956 questionnaires roughly divided between Jewish and non-Jewish informants. Of the women who completed the questionnaires 59 percent were ages twenty-five to forty-four, 41 percent ages forty-five to sixty-four. The study presents dramatic documentation of the transformation of values among American Jewish women under forty-five.

31. Lucy S. Dawidowicz, "Does Judaism Need Feminism?" *Midstream,* April 1986, pp. 39–40.

32. Susannah Heschel, *On Being a Jewish Feminist: A Reader* (New York: Schocken Books), p. xxiv.

33. I am indebted to Marshall Sklare and Jonathan Sarna, who have at different times and places commented on these analogies.

Chapter Two: Contemplating Marriage

1. Sheila Pelz Weinberg, "The Jewish Single-Parent Family," *Response* 14, 4 (Spring 1985): 77–84.

2. Many books and articles have been published on traditional Jewish family life. For a lucid analysis of the moral force of the traditional Jewish family, see Norman Linzer, *The Jewish Family: Authority and Tradition in Modern Perspective* (New York: Human Sciences Press, 1984); for a still-popular presentation of family life in Eastern European communities, see Mark Zborowski and Elizabeth Herzog, *Life Is With People* (New York: Schocken Books, 1952). For a partial bibliography of recent publications, see Benjamin Schlesinger,

Jewish Family Issues: A Resource Guide (New York & London: Garland Publishing, 1987).

3. William A. Percy, Warren Johansson, and Wayne Dynes, "Of Paul, Asceticism, and Homosexuality," *New York Times* (March 9, 1991); see also Steven D. Fraade, "Ascetical Aspects of Ancient Judaism," *Jewish Spirituality from the Bible Through the Middle Ages,* ed., Arthur Green (New York: Crossroad, 1988), pp. 253–88, for a discussion of the conditions under which temporary asceticism was allowed and an interesting exploration of the ongoing tension between abstinence and moderation within Judaism.

4. See Ellen Bernstein, "Jews and Drug Abuse," *Atlanta Jewish Times,* February 17, 1989; Ira Jay Rosen, *Jewish Social Work Forum* (Spring 1989): 58–71; David Margolis, "Helping Jews Overcome Drug Abuse," *Baltimore Jewish Times,* January 20, 1989; "Diagnosis, Alcoholic," *Moment* 11, 6 (June 1986): 45–47; Rabbi Dr. Abraham J. Twerski, "Denial," *Jewish Homemaker* (December 1989): 20–21; Faith Solela, "Family Violence: Silence Isn't Golden Anymore," *Response* 14,4 (Spring 1985): 101–6; Barbara Trainin, "Facing up to the Problem of Jewish Wife Abuse," *Jewish Week,* January 18, 1985; and Nadine Brozan, "Wife Abuse in Jewish Families," *New York Times,* December 6, 1982.

5. For an exploration of sympathetic, prowoman attitudes among Yiddish writers, see Sylvia Barack Fishman, ed., *Follow My Footprints: Changing Images of Women in American Jewish Fiction* (Hanover, N.H.: University Press of New England, 1992), pp. 15–23.

6. David Biale," Love, Marriage and the Modernization of the Jews," in *Approaches to Modern Judaism,* ed. Marc Lee Raphael (Chico, Calif.: Scholars Press, 1983), pp. 1–17.

7. Sholom Aleichem, *The Adventures of Menachem Mendel* (New York: G. P. Putnam's Sons, 1989).

8. Marshall Sklare, *America's Jews* (New York: Random House, 1971); see especially "Family and Identity," pp. 73–102.

9. Susan Glenn, *Daughters of the Shtetl: Life and Labor in the Immigrant Generation* (Ithaca and London: Cornell University Press, 1990), p. 77.

10. This tendency toward smaller families among Jewish women actually began at least as far back as the middle of the nineteenth century. According to Steven Martin Cohen and Paul Ritterband, "Why Contemporary American Jews Want Small Families," *Modern Jewish Fertility,* ed., Paul Ritterband, (Leiden: E. J. Brill, 1981), pp. 209–31, who work with figures from Prussia, with the loosening of the hold of religion and the introduction of family planning, birthrates for Protestants, Catholics, and Jews all declined, but the Jewish birthrate declined far more than the other two. Thus in 1924–26, Protestants were having 50 percent as many children as they had in 1842–44; Catholics were having 60 percent as many; and Jews were having only 36 percent as many children. Prussian Jewish women in 1924–26 were having just over two thirds as many children as Protestant women and just over one half as many as Catholic women were. As Cohen and Ritterband comment, "the shift from traditionalism to modernity had greater impact on the fertility behavior of Jews than of non-Jews" (210). Eric Rosenthal, "The Equivalence of United States Census Data

for person of Russian Stock or Descent with American Jews: An Evaluation," *Demography* 12, 2 (May 1985): 275–90, notes that in America as well, after the immigrant generation, Jews have had smaller families than other population groups. From the earliest comparative studies in 1889 through the most contemporary national and city studies, Jewish fertility tends to follow the curve of similar socioeconomic groups but to be significantly lower.

11. Married women report 20 percent more depression than single women, more nervous breakdowns, more physical symptoms of somatized mental disease, according to Walter R. Grove, "Sex Differences in Mental Illness Among Adult Men and Women" *Social Science and Medicine* 12B (1978); Mary Roth Walsh, *The Psychology of Women: Ongoing Debates* (New Haven, Conn.: Yale University Press, 1987); Judith Birnbaum, "Life Patterns and Self-Esteem in Gifted Family-Oriented and Career-Committed Women," *Women and Achievement: Social and Motivational Analysis,* ed. M. Mednick, S. Tangri, and L. Hoffman, (New York: Halstead Press, 1975), pp. 396–419.

12. In the 1972 thriller by Ira Levin, *The Stepford Wives* (New York: Random House), affluent husbands in Stepford, Conn., kill their wives and replace them with physically identical but much more subservient and obliging androids.

13. Diane Levenberg, "Single Jewish Women Ten Years Later," *Jewish Marital Status: A Hadassah Study,* ed. Carol Diament (Northvale, N.J., and London: Jason Aronson, 1989), pp. 33–41.

14. Ibid.

15. Esther Perel, "Detoxifying Our Relationships," *Lilith* 17 (Fall 1987): 15–19; see also Dan Dorfman, "We're Having Too Much Fun to Marry," *Sh'ma* (January 22, 1982): 41–44; and Melanie Shimoff, "I Am a Pencil: Where Are All the Pens?" *Sh'ma* (January 22, 1982): 44–45.

16. *Highlights of the CJF 1990 National Jewish Population Survey* (New York: Council of Jewish Federations, 1991).

17. Peter Medding, Gary A. Tobin, Sylvia Barack Fishman, and Mordechai Rimor, "Jewish Identity in Conversionary and Mixed Marriages," *American Jewish Year Book, 1991* (New York and Philadelphia: American Jewish Committee and the Jewish Publication Society of American, 1991). The Cohen Center Research showed that between 1960 and 1969, 91 percent of women and 78 percent of men married spouses who were born Jewish. Between 1980 and 1989, however, 55 percent of men and 70 percent of women married spouses who were born Jewish. Thus rates of intermarriage have increased dramatically for both men and women, with men increasing by 23 percentage points and women increasing by 21 percentage points since the 1960s. For Jewish men the percentage involved in conversionary marriages has remained constant—8 percent in the decade 1960 to 1969 and 7 percent in the decade 1980 to 1989. For Jewish women, percentages married to men who have converted to Judaism remain so low as to be almost negligible, at 1 percent in the decade 1960 to 1969 and 2 percent in the decade 1980 to 1989. The mean ages at first marriage in the cities studied were inmarriages, 25.9 for men and 23.2 for women; conversionary marriages, 27.7 for men and 25.7 for women; and mixed marriages, 27.4 for men and 26.0 for women.

18. Medding, et al. "Jewish Identity in Conversionary and Mixed Marriages."

19. Susan Weidman Schnedier, *Intermarriage: The Challenge of Living with Dif-*

ferences Between Christians and Jews (New York: Free Press, 1989), pp. 200–201.

20. Robert Gordis, *Love & Sex: A Modern Jewish Perspective* (New York: Farrar, Straus & Giroux, 1978), p. 23.

21. Barbara S. Cain, "Plight of the Gray Divorcee," *New York Times Magazine,* December 19, 1982; Sharon Johnson, "Expectations Higher: Many Long-Married Couples Are Divorcing," *New York Times.*

22. Helen Mintz Belitsky, "Falling from Grace: Divorced Jewish Women over 40 Often Fall Through the Cracks of the Community," *Atlanta Jewish Times,* Sept. 11, 1992, pp. 16–19.

23. Debra Renee Kaufman, *Rachel's Daughters: Newly Orthodox Jewish Women* (New Brunswick, N.J.: Rutgers University Press, 1991), p. 125, argues that "no-fault divorce laws ... have liberated many men from the obligation to support their wives and children."

24. Unfortunately, Jewish population studies do not reveal the date of degree completion, so we do not know what proportion of the divorced Jewish women's master's degrees were obtained before, during, or after their marriages—or for how many of them the pursuit of higher education was a salient factor in their divorces.

25. Sharon K. Houseknecht, Suzanne Vaughan, and Anne S. Macke, "Marital Disruption Among Professional Women: The Timing of Career and Family Events," *Social Problems* (Feb. 1984): 273–83.

26. Blu Greenberg, "Zero Population Growth: Feminism and Jewish Survival," *Hadassah Magazine,* October 1978, pp. 12–33, 29. Excerpted from *On Women and Judaism* (Philadelphia: Jewish Publication Society, 1979).

27. Linda Bayer, *The Blessing and the Curse* (Philadelphia, New York, and Jerusalem: Jewish Publication Society, 1988), p. 73.

28. Judith S. Wallerstein and Sandra Blakeslee, *Second Chances: Men, Women, and Children a Decade After Divorce—Who Wins, Who Loses, and Why* (New York: Ticknor & Fields, 1989), pp. 35–53, 296.

29. Sylvia Barack Fishman, "Family Ties: Serving Today's Jewish Households," in *Changing Jewish Life: Service Delivery and Planning in the 1990s,* ed. Lawrence Sternberg, Gary A. Tobin, and Sylvia Barack Fishman, pp. 57–85, 66.

30. Judith Lang, "Divorce and the Jewish Woman: A Family Agency Approach," *Journal of Jewish Communal Service,* 54, 3 (1978): 12.

31. Jay Brodbar-Nemzer, "Divorce in the Jewish Community: The Impact of Jewish Commitment," *Journal of Jewish Communal Service* 61 (Winter 1984): 150–159.

32. Ben Gallob, "Divorce Among Orthodox on Rise," *Jewish Advocate,* July 17, 1975.

33. Once a child is born a *mamzer,* that status remains with him or her throughout life. A *mamzer* can only marry another *mamzer* until the tenth generation. Thus not receiving a *get* is potentially a much greater problem than is mixed marriage. One can convert into Judaism; one cannot convert into legitimacy.

34. Pelz Weinberg, "The Jewish Single-Parent Family."

35. Sociologists Marshall Sklare and Steven M. Cohen were among the first to describe the impact of life cycle factors on patterns of Jewish affiliation. See Marshall Sklare and Joseph Greenblum, *Jewish Identity on the Suburban Fron-*

tier: A Study of Group Survival in the Open Society (New York: Basic Books, 1967); Steven M. Cohen, *American Modernity and Jewish Identity* (New York and London: Tavistock, 1983).

36. Pelz Weinberg, "The Jewish Single-Parent Family."
37. Ibid.

Chapter Three: Choosing Jewish Parenthood

1. Martha Ackelsberg, "Families and the Jewish Community: A Feminist Perspective," *Response* 14, 4 (Spring 1985): 5–19.
2. Susan Handelman, "Family: A Religiously Mandated Ideal," *Sh'ma* (March 20, 1987).
3. Zborowski and Herzog, *Life Is With People,* pp. 291–360.
4. Marie Syrkin, "Does Feminism Clash with Jewish National Need?" *Midstream* 31, 6 (June/July 1985), pp. 8–12.
5. Esther Fuchs, "The Literary Characterization of Mothers and Sexual Politics in the Hebrew Bible," *Semia* 46 (1989): pp. 151–66. Similar views are expressed by Mieke Bal, *Lethal Love: Feminist Literary Readings of Biblical Love Stories* (Bloomington & Indianapolis: Indiana University Press, 1987). Other feminist scholars of the Hebrew Bible, however, are much more sensitive to historic contexts and avoid the temptation to foist 1990s attitudes on ancient women and men. Among the best is Nechama Ashkenasy, *Eve's Journey: Feminine Images in Hebraic Literary Tradition* (Philadelphia: University of Pennsylvania Press, 1986).
6. Groeneman, "Beliefs and Values of American Jewish Women," pp. 30–31. The data were drawn from 956 questionnaires roughly divided between Jewish and non-Jewish informants. Of the women who completed the questionnaires 59 percent were ages twenty-five to forty-four, 41 percent ages forty-five to sixty-four. The study presents dramatic documentation of the transformation of values among American Jewish women under age forty-five.
7. Robin Marantz Henig, "Hers: Family Isn't Everything," *New York Times Magazine* (Nov. 3, 1991).
8. Frank L. Mott and Joyce C. Abma, "Contemporary Jewish Fertility: Does Religion Make a Difference?" *Contemporary Jewry* (forthcoming, 1993).
9. U.S. Bureau of the Census, Current Population Reports,Series P-20, No. 436, *Marital Status and Living Arrangements: March 1989* (Washington, D.C.: U.S. Government Printing Office, 1990); Current Population Reports, Series P-20 No. 436, *Fertility of Americans: June 1988* (Washington, D.C.: U.S. Government Printing Office, 1989); Current Population Reports, Series P-20 No. 428, *Educational Attainment in the United States: March 1987 and 1986* (Washington, D.C.: U.S. Government Printing Office, 1988).
10. Uziel Schmelz and Sergio DellaPergola, Israeli demographers who study trends in the international Jewish population, estimate that married American Jewish women are having about 1.5 children; if unmarried Jewish women are included, they estimate 1.3 total fertility for American Jewish women over age 20, in U. O. Schmelz and Sergio DellaPergola, "The Demographic Consequences of U.S. Population Trends," *American Jewish Year Book, 1983* (New York and Philadelphia: American Jewish Committee and Jewish Publication Society of

America, 1983), p. 154. They find marital fertility for the years 1970–76 to be 1.5 children per Jewish woman, with only a 1.3 total fertility rate for all Jewish women, regardless of marital status. However, it is very likely that Schmelz and DellaPergola's figures underestimate the completed fertility levels of American Jewish women, because they include women ages twenty and over. In contemporary American Jewish society, only tiny numbers of Jewish women marry before their mid-twenties, except in right-of-center Orthodox circles. Thus it may be valid to begin fertility estimates at age twenty among Jewish women in Israel or other more traditional societies, but among American Jewish women fertility statistics should probably begin with women not younger than age twenty-four.

11. Calvin Goldscheider, *Jewish Continuity and Change: Emerging Patterns in America* (Bloomington: Indiana University Press, 1986), pp. 92–98.

12. Calvin Goldscheider and Frances K. Goldscheider, "The Transition to Jewish Adulthood: Education, Marriage, and Fertility" (Paper for the Tenth World Congress of Jewish Studies, Jerusalem, August 1989), pp. 17–20.

13. Mott and Abma, "Contemporary Jewish Fertility."

14. Goldscheider and Goldscheider, "The Transition to Jewish Adulthood."

15. Susan Faludi, *Backlash: The Undeclared War Against American Women* (New York: Crown Publishers, 1991), pp. 27–29.

16. Melinda Beck with Vicki Quade, "Baby Blues, the Sequel," *Newsweek,* July 3, 1989, p. 62.

17. Ibid.

18. Margaret Sandelowski, "Fault Lines: Infertility and Imperiled Sisterhood," *Feminist Studies* 16, 1 (Spring 1990): 33–51.

19. Ibid.

20. Sherry H. Blumberg, "Some Jews Among Us—Akarah," *Jewish Marital Status: A Hadassah Study,* ed. Carol Diament (Northvale, N.J.: Jason Aronson, 1989), pp. 291–94. See also Michael Gold, *And Hannah Wept: Infertility, Adoption, and the Jewish Couple* (Philadelphia, New York, and Jerusalem: Jewish Publication Society, 1988).

21. Linda Bayer, *The Blessing and the Curse* (Philadelphia, New York, Jerusalem: Jewish Publication Society, 1988), pp. 126–27.

22. Ben Gallob, "Leader Flays Appeal for Larger Families," *Jewish Advocate,* September 20, 1979 (quoting recent issue of *Sh'ma*).

23. Greenberg, "Feminism and Jewish Survival," p. 28.

24. Blumberg, *Some Jews Among Us,* p. 292.

25. Ibid., pp. 292–94.

26. Ruth Mason, "And Baby Makes Two: Single Mothers by Choice," *Marital Status,* pp. 310–15.

27. Bayer, *The Blessing and the Curse.*

28. Groeneman, "Beliefs and Values of American Jewish Women."

29. Ibid., pp. 30–31.

30. Marge Piercy, *Small Changes* (New York: Fawcett Crest, 1974), p. 95.

31. Rebecca Goldstein, *The Mind-Body Problem* (New York: Dell Publishing Company, 1985), p. 70.

32. Grace Paley, "Dreamer in a Dead Language," *Later the Same Day* (New York: Farrar, Straus & Giroux, Inc., 1985), pp. 21–22.

33. The affectionate and caring Jewish father is hardly a new phenomenon in Jew-

ish life. Sholom Aleichem immortalized fathers who (like himself) were available, supportive, emphatic parents. However, a significant change has taken place in the amount of time Jewish fathers spend with their children from infancy onward, and also in the expectations Jewish fathers have for their female children.

34. Susan Ebert, "Balancing Family with a Career in the Jewish Community," *Impact,* Brandeis University Hornstein Program in Jewish Communal Service, xxi, 1 (Fall 1992): 6–7.

35. See Barbara Ehrenreich and Deirdre English, *For Her Own Good: 150 Years of the Experts Advice to Women* (New York: Doubleday/Anchor Book, 1978) for a brilliant description of shifting and often destructive advice to mothers.

36. Sonia Taitz, *Mothering Heights: Reclaiming Motherhood from the Experts* (New York: Morrow, 1992).

Chapter Four: *Working, Volunteering, and Jewish Living*

1. Vivian Gornick, *Fierce Attachments* (New York: Farrar, Straus & Giroux, Inc., 1987).

2. The "new familism" is a phrase suggested and explored at length in *Family Affairs* 5, no. 1–2 (Summer 1992). Barbara Dafoe Whitehead divides attitudes toward the family into "Traditional Familism: 1940s–1960s, Individualism: 1960s –1980s, and New Familism: 1990s," p. 3.

3. Urie Bronfenbrenner, "Discovering What Families Do," in *Rebuilding the Nest: A New Commitment to the American Family,* ed. David Blankenhorn, Steven Bayme, and Jean Bethke Elshtain (Milwaukee: Family Service America, 1990), pp. 27–38, p. 35; see also Sylvia Ann Hewlitt, *When the Bough Breaks: The Cost of Neglecting Our Children* (New York: HarperCollins Publishers, 1991).

4. Hasia Diner, "Jewish Immigrant Women in Urban America" (Paper prepared for the Mary I. Bunting Institute, Radcliffe College, 1979).

5. Menachem M. Brayer, *The Jewish Woman in Rabbinic Literature,* vol. 2 (Hoboken, N.J.: Ktav Publishing House, 1986), p. 48, points out that even the wives of powerful Hasidic leaders were praised for earning the livelihood of the household. Among those he lists are rabbis' wives who worked as drapers, sugar merchants, real estate brokers, and traveling peddlers.

6. *Pesachim* 47a; *Ketubot* 61b, see Mishnah Ketubot 5:5, 5:9.

7. *The Life of Glueckel of Hameln, Written by Herself* (New York: Thomas Yoseloff, 1962).

8. Bella Chagall, *Burning Lights* (New York: Schocken Books, 1946).

9. Chaim Grade, *My Mother's Sabbath Days* (New York: Alfred A. Knopf, 1986, originally published in Yiddish as *Der Mames Shabbosim,* 1955).

10. See I. L. Peretz, "A Woman's Wrath," *In This World and the Next,* trans. Moshe Spiegel (New York: Thomas Yoseloff, 1958), pp. 239–43.

11. For a fascinating, well-documented discussion of the entire subject of employment among Jewish women in Europe and immigrant America, see Susan A. Glenn, *Daughters of the Shtetl: Life and Labor in the Immigrant Generation* (Ithaca and London: Cornell University Press, 1990). Information on "Manufacturing and the Needle Trades" is found on pp. 18–26.

12. Ibid., p. 5.

13. *Sholem Aleykhem tsu Immigranten* (New York: Educational Alliance, 1903), pp. 36–37; cited in Glenn, *Daughters of the Shtetl,* pp. 77, 263.

14. Anzia Yezierska, *Red Ribbon on a White Horse* (1950; reprint, New York: Persea Books, 1987), pp. 38–39.

15. United States Immigrant Commission, *Immigrants in Cities,* vol. 1 (Washington, D.C., 1991), p. 139; cited in Glenn, *Daughters of the Shtetl,* pp. 68–69; and Paula Hyman, "Gender and the Jewish Immigrant Experience in the United States," *Jewish Women in Historical Perspectives,* ed. Judith K. Baskin, pp. 222–42.

16. Cited in Irving Howe with Kenneth Libo, *World of Our Fathers: The Journey of East European Jews to America and the Life They Found and Made* (New York: Simon & Schuster, 1976), p. 172.

17. S. M. Dubnow, *History of the Jews of Russia and Poland,* trans. I. Friedlaender (New York: Ktav Publishing House, Inc., 1975), pp. 65–120; and Deborah Weissman, *Bais Ya'akov—A Woman's Educational Movement in the Polish Jewish Community: A Case Study in Tradition and Modernity* (Master's thesis, New York University, 1977).

18. Hyman, "Gender and the Immigrant Jewish Experience in the United States," p. 232.

19. Ibid., p. 226.

20. June Sochen, "Some Observations on the Role of American Jewish Women as Communal Volunteers," *American Jewish History* 70, 1 (Sept. 1980): 23–34.

21. Aviva Cantor, "The Missing Ingredients—Power and Influence in the Jewish Community," *Present Tense* (Spring 1984): 8–12.

22. Doris B. Gold, "Women and Voluntarism," *Women in Sexist Society: Studies in Power and Powerlessness,* ed. Vivian Gornick and Barbara K. Moran (New York: Basic Books, 1971), pp. 384–400.

23. Aviva Cantor, "The Sheltered Workshop," *Lilith* 5 (1978): 20–21.

24. Frances E. Kobrin and Calvin Goldscheider, *The Ethnic Factor in Family Structure and Mobility* (Cambridge, Mass: Ballinger Publishing Company, 1978) pp. 18–19.

25. Charles Silberman, *A Certain People: American Jews and Their Lives Today* (New York: Summit Books, 1985), p. 123. See also Abraham D. Lavendar, "Jewish College Women: Future Leaders of the Jewish Community," *Journal of Ethnic Studies* 52 (Summer 1976).

26. Herman Wouk, *Marjorie Morningstar* (New York: Doubleday & Company, Inc., 1955; reprint, New York: Simon & Schuster, 1973), p. 229.

27. Barry R. Chiswick, "The Labor Market Status of American Jews: Patterns and Determinants," *American Jewish Year Book 1985* (New York and Philadelphia: American Jewish Committee and Jewish Publication Society, 1985), pp. 131–53.

28. Calvin Goldscheider, *Jewish Continuity and Change: Emerging Patterns in America* (Bloomington: Indiana University Press, 1986), pp. 125–34.

29. "He offers the child what are sometimes termed the 'advantages' or, in common American-Jewish parlance 'everything,' as in the expression: 'they gave their son everything.' 'Everything' means the best of everything from the necessities to the luxuries: it includes clothing, medical attention, entertainment, vaca-

tions, schools, and myriad other items." Marshall Sklare, *America's Jews* (New York: Random House, 1971), p. 88.

30. Arlene Cardoza, *Sequencing* (New York: Collier Books/Macmillan Publishing Company, 1986).

31. Faye J. Crosby, *Juggling: The Unexpected Advantages of Balancing Career and Home for Women and Their Families* (New York: Free Press, 1991).

32. Goldscheider, *Jewish Continuity and Change* pp. 125–34.

33. Linda Gordon Kuzmack and George Salomon, *Working and Mothering: A Study of 97 Jewish Career Women with Three or More Children* (New York: National Jewish Family Center of the American Jewish Committee, 1980).

34. Dana Vannoy-Hiller and William W. Philliber, *Equal Partners: Successful Women in Marriage* (Newbury Park, London, and New Delhi: Sage Publications, 1989), pp. 120–22.

35. Zborowski and Herzog, *Life Is with People,* pp. 130–39.

36. Sheila B. Kamerman, "Being Jewish and Being American: A Family Policy Perspective on the U.S. Policy Agenda and the Jewish Communal Policy Agenda" (Paper prepared for the American Jewish Committee's Task Force on Family Policy, February 1981), p. 23.

37. Groeneman, "Beliefs and Values of American Jewish Women."

38. See Ruth Sidel, *On Her Own: Growing Up in the Shadow of the American Dream* (New York: Viking, 1990).

39. Fertility decisions by career couples have been a favorite topic for the media. Among many articles, see Darrell Sifford, "Couples Agonize Over Parenthood," *Boston Globe,* April 24, 1980; Nan Robertson, "Job Vs. Baby: A Dilemma Persists," *New York Times,* Nov. 18, 1982.

40. Nadine Brozan, "New Marriage Roles Make Men Ambivalent About Fatherhood," *New York Times,* May 30, 1980, p. B5.

41. Kuzmack and Salomon, "Working and Mothering," p. 23.

42. Linzer, *The Jewish Family.*

43. Kuzmack and Salomon, *Working and Mothering,* p. 23.

44. "Single Parents Demand Services," *The Jewish Advocate,* May 3, 1984.

45. See Arlie Hochschild, *Second Shift: Working Parents and the Revolution at Home* (New York: Viking, 1989); and Roslyn K. Malamud, *Work and Marriage: The Two Profession Couple* (Ann Arbor: University of Michigan Research Press, 1984).

46. From an interview with Dr. Barbara J. Berg by Margaret Shakespeare, "The Career, the Husband, the Kids, and Everything," *Working Woman,* December 1990, pp. 94–98.

Chapter Five: Broadening Sexual and Gender Roles

1. Judith S. Antonelli, "Yeshiva Dean Talks of Sexuality and Modesty," *Boston Jewish Advocate,* February 15, 1991.

2. Isaac Bashevis Singer, "Yentl the Yeshiva Boy," in *The Collected Stories* (New York: Farrar, Straus & Giroux, 1966; reprinted in *Follow My Footprints,* 1992, ed. Fishman), pp. 141–60.

3. For example, see Robert Bly, *Iron John: A Book About Men* (Reading, Mass.: Addison-Wesley, 1990); Christopher Lasch, *Culture of Narcissism: American Life in an Age of Diminishing Expectations* (New York: Norton, 1991); and Camille Paglia, *Sexual Personae: Art & Decadence from Nefertiti to Emily Dickinson* (New Haven: Yale University Press, 1990).

4. Naomi Wolf, *The Beauty Myth: How Images of Beauty Are Used Against Women* (New York: William Morrow and Company, Inc., 1991). See especially the chapters on "Hunger," pp. 179–217, and "Violence," pp. 218–69.

5. Carol Gilligan, *In a Different Voice: Psychological Theory and Women's Development* (Cambridge, Mass.: Harvard University Press, 1982).

6. Carolyn Heilbrun, *Toward a Recognition of Androgyny* (New York: W. W. Norton, 1992); *Reinventing Womanhood* (New York: W. W. Norton, 1981).

7. Greenberg, *On Women and Judaism,* p. 119.

8. Sally Priesand, *Judaism and the New Woman* (New York: Behrman House, 1975), p. 25.

9. Tikvah Frymer-Kensky, *In the Wake of the Goddesses* (New York: Free Press, 1991).

10. See Menachem M. Brayer, *The Jewish Woman in Rabbinic Literature: A Psychohistorical Approach* (Hoboken, N.J.: Ktav Publishing House, 1986), vol. 1, pp. 23–95, 121–86; vol. 2, pp. 8–11, 58–59, 131–46. See also Tamara Frankiel, *The Voice of Sarah: Feminine Spirituality and Traditional Judaism* (San Francisco: Harper, 1990). A reasonable summary of some rabbinic attitudes can be found in John Milton's poem *Paradise Lost,* which incorporates rabbinic interpretation. See Sylvia Barack Fishman, *"Paradise Lost* as a Midrash on the Biblical Bride of God," *From Ancient Israel to Modern Judaism: Intellect in Quest of Understanding,* vol. 4 (Providence, R.I., and Atlanta, Ga.: Brown University/Scholar's Press, 1990).

11. For an excellent annotated bibliography of current interpretations, see Joan Scherer Brewer, ed., *Sex and the Modern Jewish Woman* (New York: Biblio Press, 1986). I discuss Jewish attitudes toward sexuality in the context of Jewish Literature in *Follow My Footprints,* pp. 8–13.

12. Tova Rosen, "On Tongues Being Bound and Let Loose: Women in Medieval Hebrew Literature," *Prooftexts* 8 (1988): 67–87, cites love lyrics such as the following: "The time for love making has come! / Go down, why do you tarry / To pasture in her garden? / She keeps her fresh pomegrantes out of sight, / But you, do not fear when she brings them out."

13. "Asceticism has been foreign to Judaism of every period; the Jewish religion has never in all of its 2500 year history had eunuch priests or virgin priestesses, never had a celibate clergy, never had monastic orders of either sex, never had any idea for its spiritual elite other than marriage and fatherhood. . . . However, the condemnation of homosexuality in biblical Judaism was if anything reinforced by contact with the pederasty of the Hellenistic diaspora. Not just the eccentric and opinionated Philo Judaeus, but even the ideologically colorless historian Josephus denounce male homosexuality in unsparing terms and in works meant for pagan readership. If Paul himself had homosexual tendencies, he would have suffered a severe personality conflict aggravated by his need to reject homosexuality on religious grounds. This could have motivated the as-

cetic teachings—alien to Judaism, but destined to find a reception in Christianity, that led in later centuries to exaggerated practices.... obligatory heterosexuality inflicted on homosexual subjects to disguise their psychological "I cannot" as a moral "I will not." *New York Times,* March 9, 1991. Percy, Johansson, and Dynes, "Of Paul, Asceticism, and Homosexuality."

14. Maimonides, *Mishnah Torah,* Isurei Be'ah 21:8.

15. Niddah 13a; Maimonides, *Mishnah Torah,* Isurei Be'ah 21:18; Tur Eben ha-Ezer 22.

16. *Ketubot* 61b, 62b; *Mishnah Torah,* Ishut 14:1.

17. The *Iggeret Ha-Kodesh,* literally the "holy epistle," is an anonymous thirteenth-century cabalistic work that broke ground as the first work openly to apply Jewish mystical teachings to everyday behavior. It deals extensively with sexual relations between husband and wife.

18. The *shekhinah* is one of several Hebrew names referring to the Divine presence; it is usually taken to embody the feminine aspects of Godhead.

19. For a fascinating and thorough discussion of sexuality within marriage according to Jewish law, see Rachel Biale, *Women and Jewish Law* (New York: Schocken Books, 1984), pp. 121–46.

20. For three modern, positive commentaries on the spiritual import of women's immersion in the waters of the ritual bath, see Rachel Adler, "Tumah and Taharah–Mikveh," in *The Jewish Catalog,* comp. and ed. Richard Siegel, Michael Strassfeld, and Sharon Strassfeld (Philadelphia: Jewish Publication Society, 1973); Barbara Rosman Penzer and Amy Zweiback-Levenson, "Spiritual Cleansing: A Mikvah Ritual for Brides," *Reconstructionist* (Sept. 1986): 25–29; Greenberg, "In Defense of the Daughters of Israel," *On Women and Judaism,* pp. 105–23.

21. As one example of writings that depict changing sexual mores among emancipated European Jews, Sholem Asch's trilogy, *Three Cities,* describes not only the virtuous Jewish matron Rachel-Leah but also women who had abandoned Jewish sexual norms along with Jewish life-styles and rituals. Featured among his characters are a wealthy, assimilated Russian Jewish lawyer's wife, Olga Michaelovna, who is seduced by her daughter's fiance, and Rachel-Leah's vibrant daughter Shosha, who becomes a leader in socialist activities.

22. Sydney Stahl Weinberg, *The World of Our Mothers* (Chapel Hill: University of North Carolina Press, 1988), draws on letters between mothers and daughters which vividly describe this historical period.

23. Neil M. Cowan and Ruth Schwartz Cowan, *Our Parents' Lives* (New York: Basic Books, 1989), p. 165.

24. Interview with Rose Janofsky in ibid., p. 162.

25. Herman Wouk, *Marjorie Morningstar* (New York: Pocket Books, 1955), pp. 739–41.

26. Carol Tavris and Susan Sadd, *The Redbook Report on Female Sexuality* (New York: Delacorte Press, 1977), cited in Brewer, *Sex and the Modern Jewish Woman,* p. B-45.

27. Susan Weidman Schneider, *Jewish and Female: Choices and Changes in Our Lives Today* (New York: Simon & Schuster, 1984), p. 214.

28. Reportedly Rabbi Moses Tendler acknowledged the existence of such "tefillin dates" in a 1985 symposium on the ethics of sex therapy and Jewish law. Lynn

Davidman, "Sex and Modern Jewish Woman: An Overview," in Brewer, *Sex and the Modern Jewish Woman* pp. 1–16, citing Rabbi Moses Tendler at a "Symposium on Ethics of Sex Therapy and Jewish Law," December 1985, New York, N.Y., pp. 7 n., 14. Quoted from chapter, "The Resilience of Orthodoxy," in Sara Bershtel and Allen Graubard, *Saving Remnants; Feeling Jewish in America* (New York: Free Press, 1992), p. 204.

29. Rebecca Goldstein, *The Mind-Body Problem,* pp. 87–91.

30. Alexandra J. Wall, "Jewish Organizations Mobilizing for Pro-Choice March in Capital," *Jewish Telegraphic Agency Community News Reporter,* March 27, 1992.

31. David M. Feldman, *Marital Relations, Birth Control, and Abortion in Jewish Law* (New York: Schocken Books, 1974). See also Adena K. Berkowitz, "Thinking About Women in Abortion Controversies," *S'vara: A Journal of Philosophy, Law and Judaism* 2, 2 (1991), pp. 25–28.

32. Sarah Silver Bunim, *Religious and Secular Factors of Role Strain in Orthodox Jewish Mothers* (Ph.d. dissertation, Wurzweiler School of Social Work, Yeshiva University, New York 1986), pp. 88, 132, 178.

33. "The second passage bearing directly upon the subject of therapeutic abortion occurs in rabbinic literature. The mishnah reads: 'If a woman is having difficulty in childbirth (so that her life is endangered), one cuts off the embryo, limb by limb, because her life takes precedence over its life. If most of the foetus (or the head) has emerged, it may not be hurt, for we do not set one life aside for the sake of another.' This classical passage clearly embodies the principle that the foetus is a limb of its mother. In Rashi's words, 'The life of the mother in childbirth takes precedence over that of the embryo to the very last moment of pregnancy.' " Robert Gordis, *Love & Sex: A Modern Jewish Perspective* (New York: Farrar, Straus & Giroux, 1978), p. 141.

34. Biale, *Women and Jewish Law,* discusses among others a case in Exodus in which an accidental abortion may be caused by a man's striking a pregnant woman in the course of a fight with her husband. The law rules that if the woman suffers a miscarriage, the man who struck her is fined, but if the woman loses her life, the man must pay with his. Not only is there a clear distinction between the lives of the woman and the fetus, there is also a clear distinction between the importance of the loss of a fetal life—only potentially human—and a woman's actual human life.

35. Gordis, *Love & Sex,* p. 145.

36. Carin Rubinstein, "The Joys of a 50/50 Marriage: Why Couples Who Share Money and Power Have a Better Time in Bed," *Working Mother,* April 1992, pp. 59–63.

37. Groeneman, "Beliefs and Values of American Jewish Women."

38. Ibid., pp. 30–31.

39. Judith Levine, "Thinking About Sex," *Tikkun* 3, 2 (March/April 1988): 43–45.

40. Amy Pagnozzi, "Virgins with Attitudes," *Glamour,* April 1992, pp. 235–37, 293–97.

41. Evelyn Torton Beck, ed., *Nice Jewish Girls: A Lesbian Anthology* (Trumansburg, N.Y.: Crossing Press, 1984).

42. Articles about rabbis performing or considering such ceremonies appear frequently in the Jewish press. See, for example, Dale V. Normal, "Lesbian Wed-

ding Under Consideration by Local Rabbi," *Boston Jewish Advocate,* April 3, 1992, p. 1.

43. Adina Abramowitz, "Growing Up in Yeshiva," in *Twice Blessed: On Being Lesbian, Gay, and Jewish,* ed. Christie Balka and Andy Rose (Boston: Beacon Press), pp. 21–29.

44. Marcia Freedman, *Exile in the Promised Land* (Ithaca, N.Y.: Firebrand Books, 1990).

45. Anne Lapidus Lerner, "Judaism and Feminism: The Unfinished Agenda," *Judaism,* pp. 167–73.

46. Judith Plaskow, *Standing Again at Sinai: Judaism from a Feminist Perspective* (New York: HarperCollins Publishers, 1990), pp. 197–208.

47. Ibid., pp. 208–09.

48. Jennifer Moses, "She's Changed Our Lives: A Profile of Betty Friedan," *Present Tense* 15, no. 4 (May/June 1988): pp. 26–31.

49. Debra Renee Kaufman, *Rachel's Daughters: Newly Orthodox Jewish Women* (New Brunswick, N.J.: Rutgers University Press, 1991), pp. 9–10. See also Lynn Davidman, *Tradition in a Rootless World: Women Turn to Orthodox Judaism* (Berkeley and Los Angeles: University of California Press, 1991).

50. Kaufman, *Rachel's Daughters,* p. 23.

51. Ibid., p. 90.

52. Ibid., pp. 52–70.

53. One student, for example, had a very Jewishly knowledgeable, poetic and insightful reaction to a scene in Sholem Asch's novel *Three Cities,* in which his heroine is indulging in her daily bath:

    The picture Sholem Asch paints of Rachel-Leah's bath of "lukewarm rain-water" is her true mikveh experience: "The sins of the intervening years were washed away, the sins of poverty and encroaching age; and Rachel-Leah quitted the wash basin fresh and purified, as if new-born." Noticably her purification is not tied in any way to her menstrual cycle. What she is purified *for* is her *self*, not her husband or their sexual relationship. What she is "purified" *from* is also not her husband or her menstruation but the deep undulations of her own past, the dredges wrecked upon her by class and her body's own mortal servitude. This purification is daily. Her cycle is of the sun, not lunar: daily she comes around to what Asch calls this "Sabbath hour." Almost a daily re-creation and at the end she can survey her own work and take stock of herself with a "very good." As a "newborn" she "dried her hair" (dries off the amniotic fluids), "drank tea by the milky light of the table lamp" (drinks her first mother's-milk), and passes through her own collective memory of destiny. (Raquel Kosovske, 1991).

54. Rachel Adler, "Tumah and Taharah: Ends and Beginnings," ed. Elizabeth Koltun, *The Jewish Woman: New Perspectives* (New York: Schocken, 1976), p. 71.

55. M. Wechsler, "Ritual, Purity and Jewish Women." (Unpublished paper, Harvard University, 1981), p. 24.

56. Some of these explorations are based on writings such as those by Rabbi Yaakov Emden (eighteenth century), who writes in *Shalot Yaavetz* 2, no. 15:

    Those who prefer the concubinal arrangement may certainly do so . . . for perhaps the woman wishes to be able to leave immediately without divorce proceedings in the event she is mistreated, or perhaps either party is unprepared for the heavy responsibilities of marital obligations . . . in such cases the Torah offered the option of the concubinal relationship, a relationship which is mutually initiated orally and terminated orally. . . . Marriage is not mandatory. . . . And those who claim that living together is a violation of a biblical commandment to marry, are mistaken . . . for the Torah did not mandate marriage, only that man be fruitful and multiply . . . and that precept can be fulfilled properly in a non-marital relationship.

One such modern exploration can be found in Eugene Borowitz, *Choosing a Sex Ethic: A Jewish Inquiry* (New York: Schocken Books, 1970).

57. Tavris and Sadd, *Redbook Report on Female Sexuality,* pp. 97–102.
58. Brewer, *Sex and the Modern Jewish Woman,* p. B-50.
59. David Johnson, "Justice Official Sees Weakening of Moral Fiber," *New York Times,* October 8, 1992, p. A20. Woody Allen, apparently genuinely puzzled by the assumption that his affair with lover Mia Farrow's daughter Soon-Yi was morally questionable, stated in a press interview that his actions were acceptable because "the heart wants what it wants." Conservative Attorney General William P. Barr asserts that Allen is a paradigmatic figure of the moral bankruptcy of contemporary culture: "The heart is presented as an unreasoning tyrant over which reason, and therefore morality, has no influence. . . . Try that as an instruction for your children when they ask you if a particular course of action is good or bad."
60. Susan Jacoby, "Calipers of Patriarchs," a review of Carol Tavris, *The Mismeasure of Woman* (New York: Simon & Schuster, 1992), in *New York Times Book Review,* March 29, 1992, pp. 9–10.

Chapter Six: Sanctifying Women's Lives

1. Courtesy of Bat Kol, an Orthodox feminist group, in Schneider, *Jewish and Female,* p. 133.
2. Philip Roth, *The Counterlife* (New York: Farrar, Straus & Giroux, Inc., 1986; reprint, Penguin Books, 1989), p. 323.
3. The full text of the *zeved habat* ceremony can be found in the Sephardi *De Sola Pool* prayerbook.
4. For a listing of printed materials on *shalom bat* ceremonies see Schneider, *Jewish and Female,* pp. 121–29.
5. Roselyn Bell, "Thank Heaven for Little Girls," *The Hadassah Magazine Jewish Parenting Book* (New York: Free Press, 1989), pp. 19–24.
6. Quoted in Bell, "Thank Heaven for Little Girls," p. 23.
7. A female "circumcision" refers to the mutilation of infant or adolescent female genitalia practiced in some African and Islamic societies: Such operations are in essence clitoridectomies, for the purpose of reducing female sexual desire in the adult woman, and they have been widely condemned by the medical community and by feminists around the world. The vast majority of Jewish birth ceremonies for girls do not involve any physical marking of the child, although some radical Jewish feminists have suggested that a hymenotomy may be an appropriate operation. In E. M. Broner's novel *A Weave of Women,* for example, a women's commune in Israel performs a hymenotomy on a newborn infant girl as part of her dedication ceremony, to free her from the oppressions of virginity that have historically contributed to women's status as objectified,

valued property. See E. M. Broner, *A Weave of Women* (New York: Holt, Rinehart & Winston, 1978), pp. 20–31. According to traditional Jewish law, however, the hymenotomy would be prohibited, as are all mutilations of the body with the exceptions of male circumcision and operations required for medical purposes.

8. September 25, 1991, Congregation Shaarei Tefillah, Newton Centre, Massachusetts.

9. Sarna noted that the latter name derives from the biblical matriarch Leah, who greeted the birth of her sixth son with the words, *zevadani Elohim oti zeved tov,* "God has given me a choice gift" (Genesis 30:20).

10. "O my dove, in the cranny of the rocks, hidden by the cliff, let me see your face, let me hear your voice; for your voice is sweet and your face is comely."

11. "Why were the matriarchs (Sarah, Rebecca, Rachel) barren? the midrash asks, because the Holy One blessed be He yearns for their prayers and yearns for their supplications" (Midrash Rabbah, Genesis 45:4).

12. "In this prayer, we banish all of the men, even the patriarchs, and turn not only to the standard matriarchs but also to Miriam sister of Moses, Abigail the wife of King David, and Esther the Queen of Shushan, and we ask them to join in blessing our daughter on this auspicious occasion and to cause her to grow up in health, peace, and tranquillity."

13. Prayer for the onset of labor (1878). Fanny Neuda, "Prayer on the Approach of Accouchement," *tekhinne* translated by M. Mayer and published in *Hours of Devotion* (Vienna: H. L Frank, 1878), reprinted in Henry Wenkart, *Sarah's Daughters Sing: A Sampler of Poems by Jewish Women* (Hoboken, N.J.: Ktav Publishing House, Inc., 1990), pp. 140–41.

14. Prayer said by the mother after childbirth. Courtesy of Rabbi Nathan A. Barack, Newtonville, Massachusetts, 1991.

15. Eve, on the birth of Cain, Genesis 4:1.

16. Laura Geller, "Encountering the Divine Presence" (1986), in *Four Centuries of Jewish Women's Spirituality: A Sourcebook,* ed. Ellen M. Umansky and Dianne Ashton (Boston: Beacon Press, 1992), pp. 242–47. This reader contains many evocative suggestions for rituals to sanctify women's lives.

17. Irene Fine, *Midlife: A Rite of Passage and The Wise Woman: A Celebration* (San Diego, Calif.: Women's Institute for Continuing Education, 1988).

18. Additional information on Jewish feminist prayers and ceremonies can be obtained from the following sources, among others: Penina Adelman, *Miriam's Well: Rituals for Jewish Women Around the Year* (New York: Biblio Press, 1986); Marcia Falk, *The Book of Blessings: A Feminist-Jewish Reconstruction of Prayer* (San Francisco: Harper & Row, 1989); Tikva Frymer-Krensky, *Motherprayer* (Boston: Beacon Press, 1989); Marcia Cohn Spiegel and Deborah Lipton Kremsdorf, eds., *Women Speak to God: The Poems and Prayers of Jewish Women* (San Diego, Calif.: Woman's Institute for Continuing Education, 1987). In addition, from the Jewish Women's Resource Center, 9 East 69th Street, New York, one can obtain ceremonies on birth, blessing the birth of a daughter, marriage contracts, weaning prayers, Rosh Hodesh and Tu Bishvat prayers, menstruation prayers, and others.

19. Carol Kessner, "Kaplan on Women in Jewish Life," *Reconstructionist* (July–Aug. 1981): 38–44.

20. Marshall Sklare, *Conservative Judaism: An American Religious Movement* (New York, 1972), pp. 154–55.
21. Susan Gilman, "Bat Mitzvah Ceremonies Not Just Kid Stuff," *Queens Jewish Week* (New York), May 27, 1988.
22. *Jewish Telegraphic Agency Community News Reporter,* March 27, 1992.
23. Nicky Goldman, "The Celebration of Bat Mitzvah within the Orthodox Community in the United States Today" (paper for the Hornstein Program in Jewish Communal Service, Brandeis University, Waltham, Mass., Spring 1991). The names of the informants in Goldman's study have been changed for inclusion in this book.
24. Ibid., p. 7.
25. Ibid., p. 9.
26. Ibid., pp. 14–15.
27. Ibid.
28. Ibid., pp. 6–7.
29. Ibid., p. 20.
30. Rachel Adler, "Tumah and Taharah—Mikveh," *The Jewish Catalogue,* comp. and ed. Richard Siegel, Michael Strassfeld, and Sharon Strassfeld (Philadelphia: Jewish Publication Society, 1973), pp. 167–71.
31. Penzer and Zweiback-Levenson, "Spiritual Cleansing."
32. Greta Weiner, "The Mourning Minyan," *Lilith* 7 (1980), pp. 27–28.
33. Ruth R. Seldin. "Women in the Synagogue: A Congregant's View," *Conservative Judaism* 32, 2 (Winter 1979): 80–88.

Chapter Seven: *Praying with Women's Voices*

1. Kadia Molodowsky, "Song of the Sabbath," Yiddish translated into English by Jean Valentine in *A Treasury of Yiddish Poems,* ed. Irving Howe and Eliezer Greenberg (New York: Holt, Rinehart & Winston, 1969), pp. 285–86. Molodowsky was born in Lithuania in 1894. An activist and prolific writer in the Yiddish movement, she lived and wrote in Warsaw for many years. She emigrated to New York in 1935 and died in 1975.
2. The vow of an unmarried woman is only valid if it is ratified by her father (Numbers 30:6), and some vows of married women can be revoked by their husbands (Numbers 30: 14, 17; Mishnah Nedarim 11: 1, 2). An unmarried woman who is of age, however, cannot be so treated.
3. While women, like men, are liable for a complex array of responsibilities toward parents, the law does not hold women strictly accountable because the woman's husband may interfere with her daughterly duties. A woman is like a person with two masters, says the Talmud, her parents and her husband.
4. Much of the exclusion of women from responsibility for time-bound laws is based on the assumption that women will frequently be occupied with child care, and thus unable to complete religious tasks before a given deadline. Blu Greenberg, *On Women and Judaism,* pp. 62–53, summarizes the laws and concepts that most determined a Jewish woman's role thus:

   Talmudic law spelled out every facet of law as it applied to the woman. She was exempt from those positive commandments that must be performed at specific times, such as wearing the *tzitzit* and *tefilltn,* reciting the *Shema,* and the three complete daily prayer services (Kiddushin 29a; Eruvin 96b; Berakhot 20a–b; Menahot 43a). She was exempt also from certain commandments that were not time specific (Eruvin 96b). In various communal or group events, she could be a participant-observer but had no legal status in performance of ritual. This held true for the mitzvah of *sukkah,* the celebration of *simhat bet ha-sho'evah,* the redemption of the firstborn, inclusion in the minyan for grace after meals, and reading the Torah at the communal prayer service (Sukkah 2:18, 53a; Kiddushin 34a; Megillah 47b, 23a).

5. Women are not allowed to read the Torah for the congregation, for example, because of the principle of *k'vod ha-tzibbur,* the honor of the congregation; thus, the congregation would somehow be shamed or disturbed by a woman reading, and because of the male assembly's sensibilities women are excluded from a highly significant religious activity.

6. Avraham Weiss, *Women at Prayer: A Halakhic Analysis of Women's Prayer Groups* (Hoboken, N.J.: Ktav Publishing House, 1990), pp. 43–46, documents such opinions as the comments of the Meiri (Provence, 1249–1316) who notes in Beit ha-Behirah to Berakhot 47b that the *kahal,* the congregation, excludes women. Many other sources reinforce the concept that "men carry out public responsibilities; women's role is private."

7. Weiss, *Women at Prayer,* pp. 13–22, cites Maimonides (1135–1204 C.E.), *Mishnah Torah,* Tefillah 1:1–2, 4–5. The mishnah states: Women are not obligated to recite the *Shema* or to put on *tefillin,* "but that they are "obligated to pray, to place a *mezuzah* on the doorpost, and to recite the grace after meals (Berakhot 3:3). According to Maimonides, the purpose of standardized prayer was in its essence egalitarian—to give all Jews equal facility in communicating with their creator. Maimonides reports the following sequence of events: Ezra discovered that many Jews returning to the land of Israel following the Babylonian exile (538 B.C.E.) had too little facility with the Hebrew language to express their thoughts freely and coherently in the holy tongue. In response Ezra and his contemporaries in the Great Assembly standardized the format of Jewish prayer into three daily required services (reflecting the order of sacrificial services in the temple). This standardized service was built around the prayers still most familiar to contemporary Jews, the *shemoneh esray* (eighteen benedictions, sometimes called the *amidah,* "standing prayer").

Weiss explains: Maimonides argues that according to the Bible all Jews were positively commanded to pray at some time during the day, at moments of their own choosing, as the spirit might move them: "One who was eloquent would offer up many prayers and pleas. A person who was slow of speech would pray according to his ability and whenever he pleased." Biblical law did not fix a time, and this daily prayer was required of all adult Jews, regardless of gender or status as a free person or bonded servant. A contrasting explanation of the evolution of Jewish prayer—and praying women—posits that biblical prayer is modeled not on a structured daily service of the heart but no less regular, impassioned pleas for mercy at times of personal or communal stress. According to Nachmonides (1194–1270 C.E.), the Bible itself does not require daily prayer. Nevertheless, Nachmonides rules that women should pray every morning and afternoon, because women, no less than men, deeply desire divine mercy for themselves and their families. Many subsequent rabbis and Jewish thinkers have struggled with the concept of prayer as a method for dealing with humanity's existential dilemmas. Some have followed primarily the views of Maimonides, some of Nachmonides, and some have suggested differing approaches. The *Arukh ha-Shulhan* (a halakhic code by Rabbi Jehiel Michal Epstein, Belorussia, 1829–1908) rules that women must in fact pray three times a day just as men do:

> And behold, this is certain—that according to Rashi, women are obligated to recite the *tefillah* three times a day, just as men are, since according to Rashi there is no difference between a time-oriented and a non-time-oriented rabbincal commandment. Tosafot would agree. . . . since it is a prayer of mercy, the rabbis obligated them even in regard to a commandment set by time. Consequently they are obligated to perform this mitzvah the same as any man. (*Arukh ha-Shulhan* to Orakh Hayyim 106:7).

See also Irving Haut, "Are Women Required to Pray,"in *Daughters of the King: Women and the Synagogue* (New York and Philadelphia: Jewish Publication Society, 1992), ed. Susan Grossman and Rivka Haut.

8. See Chava Weissler, "Voices from the Heart: Women's Devotional Prayers," *The Jewish Almanac*, ed. Richard Siegel and Carl Rheins (New York: Bantam Books, 1980), pp. 541–45; and Emily Taitz, "Women's Voices, Women's Prayers: The European Synagogues of the Middle Ages," and Shulamith Z. Berger, "Tehines: A Brief Survey of Women's Prayers," both in *Daughters of the King,* pp. 59–87.

9. Megilla 4a; Pesachim 108b; *Shulhan Arukh,* Orakh Hayyim 271:2, 296:8.

10. Norma Baume Joseph, "Mehitzah: Halakhic Decisions and Political Consequences," in *Daughters of the King,* pp. 117–34.

11. David Philipson, *The Reform Movement in Judaism* (1907; reprint, New York: Ktav Publishing House, 1967), pp. 163–224.

12. Priesand, *Judaism and the New Woman,* pp. 30–35.

13. Philipson, *Reform Judaism,* pp. 377, 485 n.

14. Michael A. Meyer, "American Rabbis for American Israel," in *Hebrew Union College—Jewish Institute of Religion at One Hundred Years,* ed. Samuel E. Karff (Cincinnati: Hebrew Union College Press, 1976), pp. 98–99, 1–284.

15. Meyer, "A Theological School for Reform Judaism," in *HUC-JIR at One Hundred Years,* p. 59.

16. Sklare, *Conservative Judaism,* pp. 66–76.

17. Ibid., pp. 88–89.

18. Anne Lapidus Lerner, "Equal Rights for Women in American Jewry," *The American Jewish Year Book, 1977* (New York and Philadelphia: Jewish Publication Society of America, 1977), pp. 3–38.

19. Ibid., p. 21.

20. Ibid., p. 20.

21. Ibid., pp. 22–23.

22. Seldin, "Women in the Synagogue," pp. 82–83.

23. Daniel J. Elazar and Rela Geffen Monson, "The Evolving Role of Women in the Ritual of the American Synagogue," (Philadelphia and Jerusalem: Center for Jewish Community Studies, 1978).

24. Ibid., p. 4.

25. Seldin, "Women in the Synagogue," p. 83.

26. Riv-Ellen Prell, *Prayer and Community: The Havurah in American Judaism* (Detroit: Wayne State University Press, 1989), pp. 273–315.

27. Riv-Ellen Prell, *Prayer and Community*, p. 309.

28. Jonathan D. Sarna, "The Debate over Mixed Seating in the American Syna-
    gogue," in *The American Synagogue: A Sanctuary Transformed*, ed. Jack Wer-
    theimer (New York: Cambridge University Press, 1987). pp. 363–394.

29. Esther Ticktin, "A Modest Beginning," *The Jewish Woman: New Perspectives*,
    ed. Elizabeth Koltun (New York: Schocken Books, 1976), pp. 129–35.

30. Steven Martin Cohen, "American Jewish Feminism: A Study in Conflicts and
    Compromises," *American Behavioral Scientist* (March–April 1980): 519–58.

31. For an overall survey of the religious behavior and denominational identity of
    American Jews, see Gary A. Tobin and Alvin Chenkin, "A Profile of the Amer-
    ican Jewish Community: A Comparison of Selected Cities," in *American Jewish
    Year Book*, ed. David Singer and Ruth R. Seldin (New York and Philadelphia:
    American Jewish Committee and Jewish Publication Society, 1985), pp. 154–
    78.

32. For a discussion of the issue of compartmentalization as a psychological ploy by
    Jewish feminists, see Cohen, "American Jewish Feminism."

33. Diana Bletter and Lori Grinker, *The Invisible Thread: A Portrait of Jewish
    American Women* (Philadelphia: Jewish Publication Society, 1989), pp. 167–
    68.

34. Conservative *Birchot HaShachar* transpose all blessings to positive mode.

35. Rabbi Saul Berman, Brandeis University Distinguished Leaders' Institute, June
    1991.

36. Weiss, *Women at Prayer*.

37. Ibid., p. xii.

38. Aryeh A. Frimer, "Women and Minyan," *Tradition: A Journal of Orthodox
    Thought* 23, 4 (Summer 1988): 54–77, discusses the fact that the Ran and the
    Meiri say that women can constitute the quorum when they read the Megilla of
    Esther for Purim, quoting from *Megilla* 19b,; Meiri, *Berakhot* 47b; *Sefer ha-
    Mikhtam, Berakhot* 45a. He also cites both Maimonides and the Vilna Gaon to
    the effect that women can constitute the quorum of persons who can recite the
    special communal grace after meals together. See Frimer, pp. 60–61, with ap-
    propriate notes.

39. Frimer, "Women and Minyan," pp. 64–70.

40. Eliezer Berkovits, *Jewish Women in Time and Torah* (Hoboken, N.J.: Ktav
    Publishing House, 1990), p. 3–31.

41. Gordis, *Love & Sex*, pp. 9–10. Conservative thinker Rabbi Robert Gordis, in
    his analysis of love and sex in Jewish tradition, for example, makes the aston-
    ishing statement that all the biblical matriarchs dominated their husbands; as
    evidence, he cites the example of the cooperation of Rachel and Leah. Thus,
    two women who often appear pathetic to female readers—one driven to dis-
    traction by her barrenness, the other by the open lovelessness of her marriage—
    are perceived as powerful by a male reader because they dared to work together.

42. Greenberg's views are most fully articulated in Blu Greenberg, *On Women and
    Judaism: A View from Tradition* (Philadelphia: Jewish Publication Society of
    America, 1981).

43. Ibid.

44. Nancy Wartik, "An Orthodox Feminist Still Keeping the Faith: Orthodox Jew-
    ish Feminist Blu Greenberg," *Forward*, June 7, 1991, pp. 18, 21. This particular

weekly English edition of *Forward,* the once-Yiddish daily, has an excellent and comprehensive special section, "The Jewish Woman."

45. Ibid.
46. Rifka Haut, "The Presence of Women," *Daughters of the King,* pp. 274–78.
47. Francine Klagsbrun (Conservative) carried the Torah to and from the *kotel.* Geela Raizl Robinson (Conservative) led in *P'sukei d'zimrah,* the introductory prayers. Reconstructionist Rabbi Deborah Brin led *Shacharit* (morning prayer service). The Torah was opened by Dr. Phyllis Chesler, the feminist author and psychologist, and read by Rabbi Helene Ferris (Reform), Marion Krug (Orthodox), and Shulamit Magnus, who teaches at the Reconstructionist Rabbinical College. Blu Greenberg (Orthodox) was honored with the first aliyah.
48. Haut, "The Presence of Women," pp. 2, 4.
49. Ibid., pp. 4–6.
50. Ibid.
51. Judith Green, cited in Elana G. Raider, "Rebuilding the Wall: Issues of Women, Power, and Jewish Tradition" (B.A. thesis, University of California, Santa Cruz, December 1990), pp. 30–31.
52. Ibid., pp. 31–32.
53. Ibid., p. 31.
54. Ibid., pp. 34–35.
55. Ibid.
56. Harry P. Solomon, for example, explores the inclusion of the matriarchs in the birkat ha-mazon: "Traditionally, Jewish liturgy has been almost wholly lacking in reference to our matriarchs. It is as if there were no *zekhut imoteinu* (merit of our foremothers) to match the *zekhut avoteinu* (merit of our forefathers) that we invoke both as 'advocacy on high' as a model for our behavior. . . . Of all the proposals to change the wording of our prayers, it would seem that this lack is relatively easy to correct. Thus for years, some synagogues and havurot have revised the liturgy to include references to the matriarchs. And yet, even these 'easy,' nontheological changes have not been a huge success." Moreover, including feminist elements is often not as uncomplicated as it appears on the surface, Solomon insists. Harry P. Solomon, "Including the Matriarchs: A Proposal for Birkat ha-Mazon," *Reconstructionist* (March 1988): 12–14.
57. Arlene Agus, "This Month is for You: Observing Rosh Hodesh as a Woman's Holiday," *The Jewish Woman: New Perspectives,* ed. Elizabeth Koltun (New York: Schocken Books, 1976), pp. 84–93.
58. Aviva Cantor (Zuckoff), "Jewish Women's Haggadah," *The Jewish Woman: New Perspectives* (New York: Schocken Books, 1976), pp. 94–102. See also "An Egalitarian Hagada," *Lilith,* no. 9 (Spring/Summer 1982): 9–24.
59. See article (with photo) by Nadine Brozan, "Telling the Story of the Seder in a Woman's Voice," *New York Times* (Monday, April 9, 1990).
60. Pogrebin, *Deborah, Golda and Me,* pp. 17–18.
61. Ibid.
62. Generally, only more traditional groups observe the seder ceremony punctiliously enough to retain the custom of reclining. Four out of five American Jews say they attend a Passover seder. The seder, held on the first two nights of Passover in Orthodox and Conservative households and on the first night in Reform households, is a ceremonial meal at which the story of the biblical

exodus from Egypt is traditionally read from the Haggadah—which is a melange of biblical passages, rabbinical discussions, passages from the Psalms, poetry and songs—before the meal commences. In nontraditional American Jewish households, the seder service is often shortened or dispensed with, and the seder becomes simply a festive family gathering. Three Jewish holiday periods, however, retain their popularity and widespread observance: the solemn High Holidays, Rosh Hashanah and Yom Kippur, in the fall; the festive Hanukkah, the eight-day festival of lights around the winter solstice; and, above all, Passover, the eight-day festival of freedom requiring unleavened bread, in the spring.

63. *Shulhan Arukh,* Orakh Hayyim 67. The *Shulhan Arukh* was written by Joseph Caro and first printed in Venice in 1565. With commentaries and emendations added by Rabbi Moses Isserles and later halakhic authorities, the *Shulhan Arukh* became "the final authority to which one turned for the definite *halakhah*" by the seventeen century. See *The Encyclopedia Judaica* (Jerusalem: Keter Publishing House, 1971) for succinct discussions of this and all other rabbinic source materials referred to in this chapter. A discussion of the *Shulhan Arukh* is found in volume 14, pp. 1475–77.

64. Talmud *Pesachim* 108 a and b; Rashbam, eleventh-century France, quoted by the Rosh; Reb Achi. The Talmud, its glosses, and later responsa literature form a kind of transcentury exploration of possible reasons for the exemption of women. Rabbinic literature does not simply accept the exemption for women reclining without examination. One question that troubles many rabbis has to do with the basic premise of the exemption: If subordination to a husband were the only reason for exempting women from reclining, unmarried women should be required to recline, just like men. Reb Achi postulates that marital status cannot be the chief reason for exempting women from reclining. He suggests that social status and communal customs may make a difference. Women should recline at the seder table, he states, as long as they are, by virtue of their social status, *accustomed* to reclining at other times: "Women are not accustomed to reclining; therefore, even widows and divorcees don't recline. However, it is customary for *important* women to recline." Nevertheless Rashbam insists that women as a group are exempted from reclining because such a posture might be interpreted as lack of respect for husbands, to whom women are subordinate and whom they are supposed to serve.

65. Vilna Gaon quoting Rabbi Manoach in the *Shulhan Arukh,* Orakh Hayyim 67.

66. The Vilan Gaon's approach is in fact the standard for Orthodox Jewish behavior in the *Shulhan Arukh,* which serves as the most common sourcebook for traditional Jews.

67. *Shulhan Arukh,* Orakh Hayyim 67. The *Shulhan Arukh* restates the Talmudic dictate, noting that each man "shall arrange the place he sits so that he reclines in the manner of a free person (at the Passover Seder). . . . But a woman is not required to recline, unless she is an important woman."

68. Chaim Karlinsky, "Women and the Laws of Reclining at the Seder, '"*Hadarom* 51, (Spring 1981).

69. Devorah Goldman, "Fulfillment Through Prayer," *Atlanta Jewish Times,* May 22, 1992, pp. 14–15.

70. Amy Eilberg, "Encountering a Feminine God," *Moment* (April 1989): 34–38.
71. Ibid., pp. 35–36. See also Margaret Moers Wenig, "God Is a Woman and She Is Growing Older," *Best Sermons 5*, ed. James W. Cox and Kenneth M. Cox (San Francisco: HarperCollins Publishers, 1992) pp. 116–28.
72. Claudia Camp, *Wisdom and the Feminine in Proverbs* (Sheffield: Almond Press, 1985), p. 81.
73. Goldman, "Fulfillment Through Prayer," p. 15.
74. Characteristic of those different Jewish female contexts is Bella Chagall's description of a Jewish communal bathhouse to which women took their young daughters for a weekly bathing. Chagall remembers herself and her mother sitting naked on the benches as they are scrubbed by the attendants, and she remembers her mother immersing herself in the *mikvah* at the appropriate time:

> "Ko-o-o-sher!" cries the attendant, with the voice of a prophet. . . .
> Suddenly the pool splits open and mother's head emerges. She shakes off the water as if she were coming up from the very bottom of the sea. . . . Water streams down from her hair, from her ears. But she is smiling. Contentment spreads over her whole body. She walks from the water as from a fire, clean and purified. "May it do you good, may it give you health," the attendant says, smiling too. Her long, thin arms lift the sheet up high. Mother wraps herself in it as in a pair of huge white wings, and smiles on me like a white angel.
> Dressed, all finished with my steaming, I chew my glazed apple.

Bella Chagall, *Burning Lights* (New York: Schocken Books, Inc.,1946), pp. 37–38.

Chapter Eight: Educating the New Jewish Women

1. Francine Klagsbrun, adapted from *Moment* 17, no. 4 (August 1992): 14, 17.
2. See especially Kiddushin 29b and Jerusalem Talmud Berakhot 2:7 and Eruvin 10:1.
3. Kiddushin 29; Erkhim 2b, Succah 42a; Maimonides *Mishneh Torah*, Hilkhot Talmud Torah 1:1; *Shulhan Arukh*, Orakh Hayyim, Hilkhot Shabbat 343.
4. However, when Rabbi Eliezer's opinion is put back into the context from which it derives, it may be seen in another light altogether. The talmudic discussion focuses on the biblical laws of the *sotah*, a woman who is suspected of adultery by her husband, in a case where there are no witnesses to testify to the woman's guilt or innocence. Biblical law prescribes administering a potion to the woman, which will result in grave illness if she is guilty but harmless if she is innocent. The rabbis explore the possible mitigating effects of personal piety on a woman's physiological reaction to the potion. Some propose that certain meritorious behaviors might cause even a guilty woman to survive the potion unscathed. Rabbi Eliezer worries that if women were taught the oral law and they knew that through personal piety they might be allowed to cuckold their husbands and still escape punishment, they might be tempted to do so. It is for this reason that he says teaching the oral law to one's daughters is *as if* one teaches them licentiousness.
5. Rose Shoshana Zolty, in conversation and pp. 277, 290 in *Women and the Study of Torah in Jewish Law and History* (Dissertation, Department of Education, School of Graduate Studies, University of Toronto, January 1992).

6. This story is transmitted by Rashi, an acronym of the name Rabbi Solomon ben Isaac, who lived from 1040–1105 in Troyes. The most influential and widely studied rabbinic commentator on the Bible and Talmud, Rashi elaborated on this story, giving it more credence as a result. Sondra Henry and Emily Taitz "wonder what purpose the denigration of Beruriah served for those who chose to repeat this story and believe it," in Sondra Henry and Emily Taitz, *Written Out of History* (New York: Biblio Press, 1988), pp. 54–58.

7. Judith Romney Wegner, "The Image and Status of Women in Classical Rabbinic Judaism," in *Jewish Women in Historical Perspective*, ed. Judith Baskin (Detroit: Wayne State University Press, 1991) p. 76.

8. For example, Valeria the Proselyte (1st century C.E.); the clever and intelligent Ima Shalom (end of first century); wife of the selfsame Rabbi Eliezer ben Hyrcanus who opposed the education of girls; the daughters of Elisha ben Avuya (second century C.E.); the daughter of Rabbi Hisdah and wife of Rami Bar Hama, and later the wife of Rava (third century C.E.; the daughter of Rabbi Abahu (c. 300 C.E.); the foster mother of Abaye (c. 300 C.E.); the mother of Ravina (fifth century); and the women of Schekhnitziv, Babylonia. See Zolty, pp. 179–80.

9. Zolty, pp. 211–14.

10. Female Torah Scholars among the Sephardim include: "the women of the Da Pisa and Abufarhin families [who] knew all 24 books of the Bible"; "Pomona da Modena of Ferera (end of 15th century) . . . [a woman] well versed in Talmud as any man"; "Fioretta da Modena, wife of Rabbi Solomon da Modena, mother of the physician and scholar Mordekhai da Modena and ancestress of a whole line of distinguished scholars"; "Miriam Luria [seventeenth century], daughter of David Hayim Luria of Padua"; "Benvenida Ghirondi, wife of Mordekhai Ghirondi, also of Padua [who] conducted Talmudic disputations with distinguished scholars of her time." Sixteenth- and seventeenth-century Italian women were also sometimes learned enough to serve as ritual slaughterers and scribes and printers of sacred texts. Documents exist naming women who received diplomas and women who practiced these professions in Mantua, Rome, Padua, Naples, Constantinople, and Kuru Chesme on the Bosporus. Zolty, pp. 232–35.

11. Rashi's oldest daughter, Jochebed, married Rabbi Meir ben Samuel; each of their four sons became scholars: the works of their son Isaac Samuel are remembered under the acronym Rashbam and those of Jacob as Rabbenu Tam. Jochebed's sons were part of the illustrious groups of French scholars who initiated the tosaphoth school of commentary. Rashi's daughter Miriam married Judah ben Nathan, known as the Rivan; their son Yom Tov also achieved acclaim. Jochebed and Miriam's daughters, Hannah and Alvina, are documented as enjoying prominent positions in the community and among scholars because of their talmudic learning: Hannah is reported to have educated the women in her community, and Alvina served as a kind of consultant to Rabbi Isaac ben Samuel, known as the Ri, on the ritual behaviors practiced in Rashi's household. Significantly, Alvina refers to her mother Miriam as the authority. Jochebed's son, Rabbenu Tam, also married a woman named Miriam, who not only ruled on ritual questions in her own town but seems to have informed male

rabbis of those questions and decisions as well. At the end of Rashi's life, one of his daughters became his amanuensis. See Zolty, pp. 273–74.

12. Ibid., pp. 274–75.

13. Ibid., p. 275, citing *Sefer Hasidim* paragraph 313.

14. Ibid., p. 97, citing Rabbi Joshua Falk, *Perishah* on the *Tur,* Yoreh De'ah 246:15.

15. Ibid., pp. 97–98, 135 n., quoting Italian Rabbi Samuel ben Elhana Jacob Archivolti, who is cited by Rabbi Barukh Epstein, *Torah Temimah* on Deuteronomy 11:18, early-twentieth-century Russia.

16. The Arukh ha-Shulhan (nineteenth-century Lithuania) for example, states, "We have never taught women from a book, nor have we ever heard that people actually do so. Rather, every mother teaches her daughter or daughter-in-law those well-known rules women should know" (Orakh Hayyim 236, 19). Cited in Deborah R. Weissman, "Education of Jewish Women," *Encyclopedia Judaica Year Book, 1988* (Jerusalem: Keter Publishing, 1988), pp. 29–36.

17. Zolty, *Women and the Study of Torah,* pp. 99–100, citing Assaf, *Mekorot le-Toldot ha-Hinukh be-Yisrael,* vol. 4 (Tel Aviv: Dvir, 1947): 209.

18. Shaul Stampfer, "Gender Differentiation and Education of the Jewish Woman in Nineteenth-Century Eastern Europe," *POLIN* 7 (1993): 95–122.

19. For example, the *Genizah* has documents referring to Alexandrian women who raised their children "and taught them Torah." Letters written by women found in the *Genizah* show that, while many women were illiterate (as were many Arabic females), some Jewish women were well educated and were significant figures in their communities. One letter is written in poetic Hebrew and is replete with biblical allusions. Another letter from a dying mother requests her sister to make sure that her daughter receives a good religious education, and a eulogy written by a father who recalls his daughter's assiduous study and articulateness in Torah matters when she was a girl. The *Genizah* also contains a letter from a male teacher of Judaica complaining about the interference of a female teacher and the rambunctiousness of one brother and sister who attend his classes. Documents located elsewhere show that Babylonian and North African communities provided even orphan girls with enough Hebrew literacy to follow the prayer services. (Yemenite Jewish women, on the other hand, were for centuries deliberately kept illiterate.) A Rabbi Hai of nineteenth-century Baghdad instructs fathers to provide both sons and daughters with books and teachers. The *Genizah* and other sources provide us with evidence that women not infrequently served as scribes, even in countries such as Yemen; in cases where the father was a scribe and there were no sons, it was apparently customary in some communities to pass the skill (and the attendant knowledge) on to a daughter. Zolty, p. 200–209, 215.

20. Young Italian Jewish girls in the seventeenth and eighteenth centuries are described as receiving considerable levels of Jewish education either at home or in communal Jewish schools in cities such as Montaniena, Bologna, Rome, Venice, Ferrara, and Modena; in many of these cities, the employment of women as the exclusive or co-teachers of young children of both sexes is recorded. Italian Jewish women, for example, had translations of the Bible and the prayerbook in Judeo-Italian. The poems and translations of one gifted seventeenth-century

Italian Jewish woman, Deborah Ascarelli, were viewed as "religious poetry and ... recited in the synagogue." Zolty, pp. 238–45.

21. Ibid., pp. 269–70, 323–24.

22. Ibid., pp. 269–70.

23. Harvey Minkoff and Evelyn B. Melamed, "Was the First Feminist Bible in Yiddish?" *Moment* 16, 3 (June 1991): 28–33, 52.

24. Chava Weissler, "Voices form the Heart: Women's Devotional Prayers," *The Jewish Almanac,* ed. Richard Siegel and Carl Rheins (New York: Bantam Books, 1980), pp. 541–45.

25. For an overview of Peretz's sympathetic treatment of women, see Ruth Adler, *Women of the Shtetl—Through the Eyes of Y. L. Peretz* (Cranbury, N.J.: Associated University Presses, 1980); and Fishman, *Follow My Footprints,* pp. 17–118.

26. Fishman, pp. 71–75.

27. Zolty, p. 335.

28. See Brayer, *The Jewish Woman in Rabbinic Literature,* vol. 2, pp. 79–80.

29. Prell, *Prayer and Community,* p. 277, is quite simply incorrect. Despite gender differences in subject matter taught to boys and girls in many Orthodox schools, Orthodox families provided girls with more extensive Jewish education than Conservative, Reform, and Reconstructionist families as a group.

30. Rabbi Menachem Schneerson, *Me-Sichat Shabbat Parshat Emor, Erev Lag B'Omer 5770: Al Devar Hiyyuv Neshei Yisrael Be-Hinukh Limud ha-Torah,* May 1990.

31. Vanessa Ochs, *Words on Fire: One Woman's Journey into the Sacred* (New York: Harcourt Brace Jovanovich, 1990), pp. 297–300.

32. Ibid., pp. 48–49.

33. "CLAL in Israel: Men and Women Study together at Pardes," *CLAL News and Perspectives* 5, 2 (June 1990): 4, 12.

34. Some of the women Ochs describes include: (1) Penina Peli, wife of the late, brilliant Judaica professor Rabbi Pinchas H. Peli, and "a well-known activist in circles of observant women concerned with feminist issues . . . the chairperson of the Jerusalem International Conference on Halakhah and the Jewish Women"; (2) Nechama Greisman, a Lubavitch hasidic young woman pregnant with her eighth child, who gives classes in English on the weekly Torah portion for women of all ages, a "lively, confident, pretty" woman in "a blue maternity jumper and pert wig," characterized by a love of Torah, a love of Judaism, and a love of other Jews, with all their imperfections; (3) Linda Gradstein, National Public Radio reporter and a fellow student at Pardes: (4) Gabi Lev and Ruth Wider, sisters, "actresses brought up in a religious home in Sydney, Australia, who perform innovative theater pieces"; (5) Chana Safrai, director of the Judith Lieberman Institute, which offers programs in Torah study for Israeli women, a feisty woman who looks "like the lovely ample goddess of some native tribe" and who is fascinated with, among many other subjects, Jewish feminist theology; (6) Aviva Gottlieb Zornberg, who teaches more than two hundred people a week at Bruria and the Jerusalem College for Adults, whose knowledge and teaching style were such that "from phrase to phrase, breathing seemed to stop in the room as each of us marked those particular moments when the learning touched us, almost with unbearable depth. What Aviva had

to say never seemed abstract; she never performed intellectual waltzes for their own sake. . . . Aviva's teachings resounded with relevance, her words were life enhancing"; (7) and Malke Bine, a strictly Orthodox woman called by some "Jerusalem's best-known woman Talmud teacher," a "quietly spunky woman who had no instinct for self-promotion," married to a well-known *Rosh Yeshiva* (headmaster), a woman who teaches other women to "grapple and deal with the higher ideas" but appreciates the fact that women also "like to translate it into something practical." Ochs, *Words on Fire*, pp. 289–310.

35. Ibid., pp. 268–69.
36. Judith Antonelli, "New Yeshiva Takes Women's Learning to a Higher Level," *Boston Jewish Advocate*, May 22–28, 1992.
37. See Ari L. Goldman, "Jewish Women's Scholarly Gain," *New York Times*, August 2, 1992.
38. Cynthia Ozick, "Notes Toward Finding the Right Question," *Lilith*, no. 6 (1979): 19–29; reprinted in *On Being a Jewish Feminist*, ed. Susannah Heschel (New York: Schocken Books, 1983), p. 138; Rebecca Goldstein, *The Dark Sister* (New York: Viking Penguin, 1991).
39. Esther Kreitman, *Deborah* (London: Virago Press, 1983; originally published in Yiddish as *Der Shaddim Tantz*, Warsaw, 1936), trans. Maurice Carr.

Chapter Nine: Breaking Through Jewish Ceilings

1. Vicki Cabot, "On Shabbos the Rabbis Wear Skirts," *Greater Phoenix Jewish News*, Sept. 11, 1992, pp. 10–11.
2. Brayer, *The Jewish Woman in Rabbinic Literature*, p. 16.
3. Women are also discouraged from taking a role in public life by Maimonides, *Mishnah Torah, Laws of Kingship*, chap. 1, 5; Talmud *Nidah* 30 a; Rabbi Abraham Yitzhak Hacohen Kook, *Mameray Harayah* A, 189–94. Women are permitted to take an active role in public life in certain situations in Talmud *Baba Batra* 15 a, including Tosaphot; Rabbi Aaron Halevi, *Sefer Hahinuch* 75; Rabbi Moshe Feinstein, *Igrot Moshe* Orakh Hayyim 3, 11. For an exploration of images of women in the Bible and rabbinic literature, see Fishman, "Faces of Women: An Introductory Essay," in *Follow My Footprints*. For a thorough discussion of women in leadership roles according to rabbinic prescriptions, see Zolty, *Women and the Study of Torah*, pp. 30–63, 256–58, 272–75.
4. Eliezer Berkovits, *Jewish Women in Time and Torah* (Hoboken, N.J.: Ktav Publishing House, 1990), pp. 22–23.
5. Berkovits, *Women in Time and Torah*, p. 6.
6. Pogrebin, *Deborah, Golda and Me*, pp. 44, 89–90.
7. Jacob Z. Lauterbach, Responsum on Question, "Shall Women Be Ordained as Rabbis?" 1922 CCAR, quoted in Jacob Rader Marcus, ed., *The American Jewish Woman: A Documentary History* (New York: Ktav Publishing House, Inc., and Cincinnati: American Jewish Archives, 1981), pp. 739–42:

It has been rightly said that the woman who enters a profession must make her choice between following her chosen profession or the calling of mother and home-maker. She cannot do both well at the same time. This certainly would hold true in the case of the rabbinical profession. The woman who naturally and rightly looks forward to the opportunity of meeting the right kind of man, of marrying him and of having children and home of her own, cannot give to the rabbinate that whole-hearted devotion.... She could not continue it as a married woman. For, one holding the rabbinical office must teach by precept and example, and must give an example of Jewish family and home life where all the traditional Jewish virtues are cultivated. The rabbi can do so all the better when he is married and has a home and a family of his own. The wife whom God has made as a helpmate to him can be, and in most cases is, of great assistance to him in making his home a Jewish home, a model for the congregation to follow. In this important activity of the rabbi, exercising a wholesome influence upon the congregation, the woman rabbi would be deficient. The woman in the rabbinical office could not expect the man to whom she be married to be merely a helpmate to her, assisting her in her rabbinical activities. And even if she could find such a man, willing to take a subordinate position in the family, the influence upon the families in the congregation of an arrangement in the home and in the family life of the rabbi would not be very wholesome. Not to mention the fact that if she is to be a mother she could not go on with her regular activities in the congregation.

8. *Jewish Telegraphic Agency Community News Reporter,* March 27, 1992.
9. I am grateful to Rabbi Sanford Seltzer for a conversation clarifying many of these issues.
10. Mortimer Ostow, "Women and Change in Jewish Law," *Conservative Judaism* (Fall 1974): 5–12.
11. Arthur Green, "Women and Change in Jewish Law: Responses to the Fall 1974 Symposium," *Conservative Judaism* (Spring 1975): 35–56.
12. Richard M. Yellin, "A Philosophy of Masculinity: One Interpretation," *Conservative Judaism* 32, 2 (Winter 1979): 89–94.
13. Ibid., pp. 90–91.
14. Ibid.
15. Ibid.
16. Final Report of the Commission for the Study of the Ordination of Women as Rabbis, January 30, 1979. Signed by Gerson D. Cohen, Victor Goodhill, Marion Siner Gordon, Rivkah Harris, Milton Himmelfarb, Francine Klagsbrun, Fishel A. Perlmutter, Harry M. Plotkin, Norman Redlich, Seymour Siegal, and Gordon Tucker.
17. Charles S. Liebman and Saul Shapiro, "A Survey of the Conservative Movement and Some of Its Religious Attitudes" (Survey sponsored by the Jewish Theological Seminary of America in cooperation with the United Synagogue of America, September 1979).
18. Mailings by the Conference on Halachic Process of November 5 and November 19, signed by Rabbi David Algaze, Rabbi David Feldman, Rabbi Albert Lewis, and Rabbi Hershel Portnoy.
19. Signed by Debra S. Cantor, Nina Beth Cardin, Stephanie Dickstein, Nina Bieber Feinstein, Sharon Fliss, Carol Glass, and Beth Polebaum.
20. Robert Gordis, "The Ordination of Women," in Simon Greenberg, ed., *The Ordination of Women as Rabbis: Studies and Responsa* (New York: Jewish Theological Seminary of America, 1988), pp. 47–67.
21. Interview with Beth Naditch, Brandeis student majoring in Near Eastern and Judaic Studies, who aspires to ordination from the Conservative movement's Jewish Theological Seminary, at Brandeis, Waltham, Mass., October 1991.
22. Weiss was spiritual leader of the Hebrew Institute of Riverdale and assistant professor of Judaic Studies at Stern College, when he made this suggestion,

quoted in "First woman set for Conservative ordination looks to future," *The Jewish Week, Inc.,* March 1, 1985.

23. Avraham Weiss, "Women and Sifrei Torah," *Tradition* 20, no. 2 (Summer 1982): 106–14.
24. Blu Greenberg, "Will There Be Orthodox Women Rabbis?" *Judaism,* vol. 33 (Winter 1984): pp. 23–33.
25. Jacqueline K. Levine, "The Changing Role of Women in the Jewish Community," *Response* (Summer 1972): 59–65. This is an edited text of an address to the 1972 General Assembly of CJF.
26. Amy Stone, "The Locked Cabinet, *Lilith* 1, 2 (Winter 1976–77): 17–21.
27. Barry Kosmin, "The Political Economy of Gender in Jewish Federations," *Contemporary Jewry* 10, no. 1 (Spring 1989).
28. Reena Sigman Friedman, "The Volunteer Sphere," *Lilith* 14 (Fall/Winter 1985–86): 9.
29. Edward Kagen, *A Profile of JCC Leadership* (New York, 1987).
30. Chaim I. Waxman, "The Impact of Feminism on American Jewish Communal Institutions," *Journal of Jewish Communal Service* (Fall 1980): 73–79.
31. A full exploration of the characteristics of Jewish female volunteers and leaders can be found in Sylvia Barack Fishman, "Doing It All: The 'New American Jewish Woman,' " (Los Angeles: Wilstein Institute, forthcoming).
32. Reena Sigman Friedman, "The Professional Sphere," *Lilith,* no. 14 (Fall/Winter 1985–86): 11.
33. Debby Friss, "Room at the Top?" *Hadassah Magazine,* Jan. 1987, pp. 20–23.
34. Diana Aviv and Gary Rubin, "Sexual Harassment Dubbed Hidden Jewish Agencies Scandal," *Jewish Advocate* (Boston), Oct. 25, p. 1.
35. Steven M. Cohen, Susan Dessel, Michael Pelavin, "The Changing (?) Role of Women in Jewish Communal Affairs," in Koltun, ed., *The Jewish Woman,* pp. 193–200.
36. Cantor, "The Missing Ingredients," p. 12.
37. Rifka Rosenwein, "In New Hands: How Women Have Changed the Rabbinate," *Atlanta Jewish Times,* August 14, 1992, pp. 18–21.

Chapter Ten: Balancing Jewish and Feminist Goals

1. Plaskow, *Standing Again at Sinai,* p. xvii.
2. Barbara Ehrenreich, "Cultural Baggage," *New York Times Magazine,* April 5, 1992, pp. 16–18.
3. Plaskow, *Standing Again at Sinai,* pp. 236–37.
4. Ibid.
5. For example, receiving manna in the desert, the Jews are warned to collect double portions on Friday and not to desecrate the Sabbath by collecting food. The Ten Commandments, moving from instructions about how to worship God to those that focus on how to treat other human beings, are bound together by the injunction to keep the Sabbath, which blends humanity's relationship to the Divine and humanity's responsibilities toward humankind. The first infringement of the Ten Commandments punishable by death is the man who gathers firewood on the Sabbath and is stoned to death. Isaiah's powerful plea for social moral responsibility—to "feed the hungry and house the home-

less"—is placed in the context of observing the Sabbath. To Isaiah it was inconceivable that moral order could exist without the organizing principle of the weekly Sabbaths and seasonal Jewish festivals, together with their prohibitions and appointed rituals.

6. Kim Chernin, *Reinventing Eve: Modern Woman in Search of Herself* (New York: Times Books, 1987).

7. E. M. Broner, *Weave of Women* (Bloomington: Indiana University Press, 1978; reprint, 1985).

8. Jane R. Litman, "Can a Reconstructionist Rabbi Go Too Far? *Baltimore Jewish Times,* March 27, 1988; and Jane R. Litman, "Can Judaism Respond to Feminist Criticism?" *Baltimore Jewish Times,* April 24, 1987.

9. For excellent discussions of these issues see Tikva Frymer-Kensky, *In the Wake of the Goddesses: Women, Culture and the Biblical Transformation of Pagan Myth* (New York: Free Press, 1992); and Mary Lefkowitz, "The Twilight of the Goddesses," *New Republic,* August 3, 1992, pp. 29–33.

10. See Ephraim E. Urbach, *The Sages: Their Concepts and Beliefs,*, trans. Israel Abrahams (Cambridge, Mass., and London: Harvard University Press, 1987), pp. 37–65, 97–123, 135–83, 649–90. Although strains of mysticism have surfaced at many times in Jewish history, paganism was considered anathema by religious leaders.

11. Ellen Umansky, "(Re)Imaging the Divine," *Response* 13, 1–2 (Fall–Winter 1982): 110–19.

12. Debra Cantor, "Reclaiming Religious Tradition for Women's Perspectives," lecture for the American Jewish Historical Society, October 29, 1986.

13. Umansky, "(Re)Imaging the Divine," p. 119.

14. Marcia Falk, *The Book of Blessings: A Feminist-Jewish Reconstruction of Prayer* (San Francisco: Harper San Francisco, 1993); *The Song of Songs: A New Translation and Interpretation* (San Francisco: Harper San Franciso, 1990); "Toward a Feminist Jewish Reconstruction of Monotheism," *Tikkun* 4, 4 (July/August 1989): 53–56; Lawrence A. Hoffman, "A Response to Marcia Falk," *Tikkun* 4, 4 (July/August 1989): 56–57; Rosemary Radford Reuther, *Woman Guides: Readings Toward a Feminist Theology* (Boston: Beacon Press, 1985); Carol P. Christ and Judith Plaskow, eds., *Womanspirit Rising* (New York: Harper & Row, 1979); Naomi Goldenberg, *The Changing of the Gods: Feminism and the End of Traditional Religions* (Boston: Beacon Press, 1979); Rita M. Gross, "Steps Toward Feminine Imagery of Deity in Jewish Theology," *Judaism* 30, 2 (Spring 1981): 183–93; Sharon Cohen, "Reclaiming the Hammer: Toward a Feminist Midrash," *Tikkun* 3, 2: 55–57, 93–95; Phyllis Trible, "Depatriarchalizing Biblical Interpretation," *The Jewish Woman: New Perspectives,* ed. Elizabeth Koltun (New York: Schocken Books, 1976); Arthur Waskow, "The Bible's Sleeping Beauty and her Great Granddaughters," *Tikkun* 4, 2 (March/April 1989): 39–41, 125–28.

15. For an outstanding summarizing essay on feminist insights into female allegorical figures in the Hebrew Bible, see Claudia Camp, *Wisdom and the Feminine in the Book of Proverbs* (Decatur, Ga: Almond Press, imprint of JSOT Press, 1985), especially pp. 79–147.

16. Plaskow, *Standing Again at Sinai,* pp. 116–17.

17. Jenny Bourne, "Homelands of the Mind: Jewish Feminism and Identity Politics," *Race and Class* 19, 1 (Summer 1987): 1–24.

18. Ibid., p. 7.

19. Ibid., pp. 21–22.

20. Israeli feminist Dr. Alice Shalvi reports experiences at the 1991 National Organization of Women (NOW) conference that illustrate this point. Shalvi, a professor of English who is the founder of the Israeli feminist Women's Network, has participated in many dialogue efforts. She relates that she and American Jewish feminists were distressed to learn that the only Israeli woman who was asked to speak at the NOW Conference was a Communist member of the Israeli Knesset. This, of course, would be the equivalent of asking a member of the American Communist party to be the only representative of American women. In and of itself this selection spoke volumes about anti-Jewish feeling in the American and international feminist movements. The only acceptable Israeli is a Communist—and thereby "not too Jewish," deracinated—Israeli. As the Israeli Communist woman was addressing the NOW Conference, Hanan Ashwari swept into the room with her entire entourage, interrupting the address. At the point when she entered, Shalvi reports, people—including those on the dais—clustered around Ashwari and simply acted as though the Israeli woman was not speaking. When the Israeli concluded, it was Ashwari's turn. She was supposed to speak about the condition of women in Palestinian society and in Arab countries. However, she made no pretense of addressing these issues and launched into a "vicious and skillfully manipulative attack on Israel," according to Shalvi. Using a technique some have characterized as "Oreo—a thin layer of truth sandwiched between two dark lies"—Ashwari charged that thousands of Palestinian women had lost their unborn children due to attacks by Israeli soldiers. "In fact," said Shalvi, "three Palestinian women aborted last year after being in the presence of tear gas, although it is not clear to what extent the tear gas was responsible. So how do you debate this woman? Get up and say, that's not true, *only* three women aborted? No matter what you say you look bad, and she's planted what she knows to be outright lies in people's minds." In private, Ashwari, as a Palestinian woman, sometimes speaks warmly to Israeli and Jewish women and champions the effectiveness of feminist dialogue, says Shalvi. But in public forums she and other Palestinian spokespersons often abandon the feminist stance and speak as Arabs only.

21. Plaskow, *Standing Again at Sinai,* pp. 236–37.

22. Pogrebin, *Deborah, Golda and Me,* p. 163.

23. Vivian Gornick *Fierce Attachments: A Memoir* (New York: Farrar, Straus & Giroux, 1987), pp. 44–45.

24. Elizabeth Fox-Genovese, *Feminism Without Illusions: A Critique of Individualism* (Chapel Hill: University of North Carolina Press, 1991).

INDEX